DEATH BY GOVERNMENT

R. J. Rummel

DEATH BY GOVERNMENT

R. J. Rummel

With a foreword by Irving Louis Horowitz

Transaction Publishers
New Brunswick (U.S.A.) and London (U.K.)

Second printing 1995
Copyright © 1994 by Transaction Publishers
New Brunswick, New Jersey 08903

This book is printed on acid-free paper that meets the American National
Standard for Permanence of Paper for Printed Library Materials.

Library of Congress Catalog Number: 93-21279
ISBN: 1-56000-145-3
Printed in the United States of America

Library of Congress Cataloging-in-Publication Data
Rummel, R. J. (Rudolph J.), 1932-
    Death by government/R.J. Rummel.
        p.   cm.
    Includes bibiographical references (p.   ) and index.
    ISBN 1-56000-145-3
    1. Genocide—History—20th century. 2. Violence—History—20th
century.
    HV6322.7.R861994
    364.1'51'0904—dc20   93-21279
                                                                    CIP

Contents

Figures and Tables

Figures

Tables

Foreword

It has often and properly been bemoaned, by its champions and critics alike, that the social sciences, unlike the physical sciences, do not travel. By that I presume is meant that they lack an absence of universal properties that would permit an observer in one place to readily identify the parameters of research and findings in anther place halfway around the world. Indeed, if such parochialism is endemic to the nature of the social sciences, then the very notion of science as social is itself in dispute.

However there is one great and noble exception to this complaint (I should qualify this by saying that there may be others as well — for example the work done in experimental psychology) in the realm of large-scale analysis of whole societies: Namely, the study of life and death and the forms of inflicted nasty behaviors in between. For, in the measurement of life-taking propensities of states, societies, and communities, we come upon the universal property that links all humankind.

In this small world of specialized researchers on the arbitrary foreclosure and termination of human life, national boundaries and linguistic differences among the social scientists seem magically to melt. We have social historian Alex P. Schmid in the Netherlands and his work on the politics of pain and punishment; famed psychologist Herbert C. Kelman from the United States and his studies of crimes of obedience and authority; Mika Haritos-Fatouros, also a psychologist, in Greece working on the psychology of torture; Israel W. Charny in Israel amassing worldwide studies of comparative genocides with a special emphasis on holocausts directed at the Jewish and Armenian peoples. To be sure, this is a small universe of shared information about the terrible aspects of the large universe.

These names are more illustrative than exhaustive. One might just as well mention scholars of equal rank in Canada, Japan, England, France, and Germany, also hard at work on similar and related subjects. The key is not disciplinary or national boundaries but the human subject write large — the taking of life, the maiming of life, the deformation of life — not as a morbid preoccupation but as a mechanism by which social science can join the pure and applied fields of science and medicine to heal and repair and, ultimately, to just leave alone! For those who work in this area have as a common bond a recognition that issues of life and death are critical to social research, and that the prolongation of life and the postponement of death is a common meeting ground not just for people of good will but for researchers of good research habit.

In this specialized world at which the grim side of the twentieth century is explored in depth and with a special poignancy that often defies words — but does not escape numbers — none stand taller than R.J. Rummel, political scientist at the University of Hawaii. He has brought to the study of genocide a quantitative range of figures that is truly staggering by any measurement, and the qualitative meaning of all these numbers in the study of the comparative worth of civilizations.

What Rummel has done in this book above all others is provide a conceptual map to make future studies easier. He has made the sort of hard distinctions that are data-driven between legal and outlaw states; between genocide and democide, between democratic and authoritarian systems — all anchored firmly in numbers. To be sure, numbers matter. All societies are in their nature imperfect artifacts. But those that hold as their highest value the sanctity of the person are different in their nature and essence from those who see their ultimate mission as obedience and punishment for the transgressors. This easy movement of different types of social scientists converging on the problem of life and death is fueled by the sort of data provided ad distinctions made by Rummel. Indeed, we can no longer work in this area without reference to this massive yet singular effort.

Just prior to the publication of *Death by Government* I wrote to Professor Rummel to express my appreciation for his effort, mentioning that subsequent editions of my own work in the 1970s in this area, summed up in *Taking Lives*, were not needed — thanks largely to his own extraordinary efforts. I suspect that it is a rare and exhilarating feeling to be able to paraphrase Weber and declare: What I fail to make, others will, and then have this come true in one's own lifetime. To be sure, in my own most recent effort, an essay, "Counting Bodies," it was the spirit of Rummel's work that permitted me to better understand the wellsprings of Nazism, as well as the source of Jewish survival.

Rummel's work needs no elaboration. But I would like to point to one crucial aspect that stands out above all others: the need to revise our sense of the depth of the horrors committed by communist regimes on ordinary humanity. the numbers are so grotesque at this level that we must actually revise our sense and sensibilities about the comparative study of totalitarianisms to appreciate that of the two supreme systemic horrors of the century, the communist regimes hold a measurable edge over the fascist regimes in their life-taking propensities. For, buried in the datum on totalitarian death mills as a whole is the terrible sense that communism is not "Left" and fascism is not "Right" — both are horrors — and the former, by virtue of its capacity for destroying more of its own nationals, holds an unenviable "lead" over the latter in life taking.

One might argue that the fascists had a greater sense of technological modes of destruction, but the communists utilized the natural hardships of life the better to destroy individual capacities for survival. Thus, those for whom the technology of death remains central may still prefer to think of the Nazis as worse offenders, whereas those for whom an elaborate prison system is forever enshrined as the Gulag by Solzhenitsyn will see the communists as worse offenders. But it is the wisdom of Rummel to urge us beyond such dubious honors into an appreciation of the linkages of totalitarian systems in the murderous pursuit of worthless objectives.

Professor Rummel rarely speaks about morality and virtue. His concerns are not fixated on "normative" concerns of equity and liberty, or the uneven rankings of people in societies. He is not describing the imperfections of democracies or the weakness of Western liberalism. Rather, he is by implication saying that societies in which debate and discussion do not lead to death and decimation will somehow find a means to care for themselves. In that sense, his trilogy *Lethal Politics, Democide,* and *Death by Government* represent by extension a study of the forms of democracy, the ways in which systems operate to sustain themselves without destroying opposition. This was made perfectly plain in *China's Bloody Century,* a specialized volume he wrote.

It might be that the study of positive concepts like democracy and freedom will forever remain as spongy as they seem elusive. But it may also be that we will get a better "fix" on the positive aspects of social systems once we enlist the aid of data to help us arrive at a sense of which societies can truly be called decent. Not all issues are resolved: we are not told whether centralized or decentralized societies are better or worse, whether the impulses to one or another form of societies are driven by external modes of power or internal guides of authority, whether democracy operates best in small or large states; or whether legal or ethical varieties of rule are best. But all these, while important considerations, are secondary — at least in the sense that they presuppose an environment in which life taking is suspended and life giving becomes a large norm.

We all walk a little taller by climbing on the shoulders of Rummel's work. He has helped us to redeem the highest aspirations of the founders of social science and yet remain perfectly true to the latest techniques of formal analysis. It is a pleasure to write these words as a fellow laborer in the vineyards of social research. It is no less a privilege to add that, as president of Transaction, it has been a privilege to serve as publisher of nearly all the major works of Professor Rummel. If we published nothing other than Rummel's works, the rationale for the existence of Transaction as a publisher of social science would be vouchsafed. I can think of no more fitting tribute to this singular scholar in search of collective life.

IRVING LOUIS HOROWITZ

Preface

This is my fourth book in a series on genocide and government mass murder — what I call democide. The previous works concentrated on the four regimes that have committed the most democide, specifically, the Soviet Union, nationalist China under Chiang Kai-shek, communist China, and Nazi Germany.[1] This study includes the core results of those works in addition to all other cases of democide in this century up through 1987.[2]

Given the extent and detail of these books, the reader may be surprised that the primary purpose was not to describe democide itself, but to determine its nature and scope in order to test the theory that democracies are inherently nonviolent. Democracies should have no wars between them, the least foreign violence and government-related or directed domestic violence (revolutions, coups, guerrilla war, and the like), and relatively little domestic democide. I have substantiated the war, foreign, and domestic violence parts of this theory in previous works[3] and took up the research associated with this book and its three predecessors in order to test the democide component. As will be seen, the results here clearly and decisively show that democracies commit less democide than other regimes. These results also well illustrate the principle underlying all my findings on war, collective violence, and democide: The less freedom people have, the greater the violence; the more freedom, the less the violence. I offer this proposition here as the Power Principle: power kills, and absolute power kills absolutely.

In developing the statistics for this and the previous three volumes, almost 8,200 estimates of war, domestic violence, genocide, mass murder, and other relevant data were recorded from over a thousand sources. I then did over 4,200 consolidations and calculations on these estimates and organized everything into appendix tables totaling more than 18,100 rows. These tables give the subject of an estimate, the estimated number of deaths, the period covered, the source of the data, and notes on the estimate. Also shown are my consolidations of estimates for a particular case, subject, or period and all my calculations on the estimates. The appendices for the Soviet, Chinese, and Nazi democide are in my books on them; the appendices for this book were too massive to include here (one appendix table alone amounts to over 50 pages) and are given in a supplementary volume titled *Statistics of Democide: Estimates, Sources, and Calculations on 20th Century Genocide and Mass Murder*. That volume also includes the details and results of various multivariate analyses of this democide and related data.

Then what is covered here? This book presents the primary results — in tables and figures — as well as (most important) a historical sketch of the major cases of democide — those in which 1 million or more people were killed by a regime. The first chapter is the summary and conclusion and underlines the roles of democracy and power. Chapter 2 introduces the concept of *democide*, defining and elaborating it, showing that democide subsumes *genocidal killing* as well as the concepts of *politicide* and *mass murder*, and then anticipating questions that the concept may arouse. It argues that democide is for the killing by government definitionally similar to the domestic crime of murder by individuals, and that *murderer* is an appropriate label for those regimes that commit democide. Readers satisfied with the thumbnail definition of democide as murder by government, including genocidal killing,[4] can ignore this chapter. Reading it is essential, however, for those who have a professional interest in the results or who wish to question the conclusions.

Following chapter 2 is a rough sketch of democide before the twentieth century. Although hardly any historical accounting has been done for genocide and mass murder, as for the Amerindians slaughtered by European colonists or Europeans massacred during the Thirty Years' War, a number of specific democidal events and episodes can be described with some historical accuracy, and a description of these provides perspective on twentieth-century democide. I have in mind particularly the human devastation wrought by the Mongols, the journey of death by slaves from capture through transportation to the Old and New Worlds, the incredible bloodletting of the Taiping Rebellion, and the infamous Paris executions and relatively unknown genocide of the French Revolution. The upshot of this chapter is to show that democide has been very much a part of human history and that in some cases, even without the benefit of modern killing technology and implementing bureaucracy, people were beheaded, stabbed, or sliced to death by the hundreds of thousands within a short duration. In some cities captured by the Mongols, for example, the conquerors allegedly massacred over 1 million men, women, and children.

Parts 2 to 4 present a chapter on each regime that murdered 1 million or more people in this century. These are written so as to show which regime committed what democide, how, and why. The emphasis is on the connection between a regime, its intentions, and its democide. Although each of the case studies drives toward some final accounting of the democide, the specifics of such figures and the nature and problems in the statistics are ignored. These are rather dealt with in *Statistics of Democide*, where each table of estimates, sources, and calculations in each case study is preceded by a detailed discussion of the estimates and the manner in which the totals were determined. In *Death by Government*, the historical description of a case is only meant to provide an understanding of the democide. For this reason many specific examples are given of the kind and nature of a regime's killing. I have generally avoided, however, tales of brutal torture and savage killing unless such were useful to illustrate an aspect of the democide. The chapters are ordered from the greatest of these killers to the least, as one can see from the Contents.

Part 2 presents the four *dekamegamurderers*, beginning with a chapter on the Soviet Union's nearly 61 million murdered, proceeding to chapters on communist China and Nazi Germany, and ending with a chapter on the now virtually unremembered killing by the Chinese nationalist regime. Since these four regimes were the subjects of the previous three volumes,[5] the four chapters simply summarize the democide and conclusions. I hope I will be excused for using Greek prefixes for labeling these regimes (*deka-* means ten or tens; *mega-* means million), but we need concepts for the various levels of government murder and there is no comparable English term ("murderer of tens of millions" is clumsy).

Part 3 presents, in descending order of magnitude, the *lesser megamurders* — those that have killed 1 million to less than 10 million citizens and foreigners — with a. chapter devoted to each. In some cases, as for Poland's murder of ethnic Germans and Reichdeutsch, a whole series of events spanning several countries is covered. In this case Poland's treatment of these Germans was part of a pattern of expulsion from Eastern Europe after World War II. In some cases, several successive regimes for the same country committed democide; these are therefore treated together, as for the Sihanouk, Lon Nol, Pol Pot, and Samrin regimes of Cambodia.

There were three regimes — the Czar's in Russia, North Korea's, and Mexico's from 1900 to 1920 — for which the estimates were not sufficient in number or quality to make a final determination of democide. What estimates there were total over 1 million murdered, but I treat this total as only an indictment for murder. These three are described in Part 4 as *suspected megamurders.*

In chapter 1 and in each of the case studies, I present democide totals of one sort or another. However, these figures should be treated as fundamentally nothing short of wrong, and I would be amazed if future research came up with figures within even 10 percent of mine. Regimes and their agents usually do not record all their murders, and what they do record is secret. Even when such archives are available, such as after defeat in war, and even when they are kept by the most technologically advanced of regimes with a cultural propensity for record keeping and obedience to authority, and a bureaucratic apparatus that systematically murders, the total number of victims cannot be agreed upon. Consider that, even after more than forty-five years of research by the best scholars of the Holocaust, even with complete access to all surviving documents in Nazi archives and firsthand reports of survivors and participants, the difference between the lowest and highest of the best estimates of how many Jews were killed by the Nazis is still *41 percent.*[6] The totals and figures in this book should therefore be viewed as rough approximations — as suggestive of an order of magnitude.

Such gross uncertainty creates a theoretical problem, for each democide figure — as of the Khmer Rough having killed 2 million Cambodians — must really be a numerical haze. We do not know the true total, and it may be instead 600,000 or even 3 million that they killed. Except in cases in which it is difficult to assert without qualification a specific figure (as in the chapter titles), or space and form do not allow a constant repetition of ranges, as in chapter 1, I therefore give the probable *range* of democide and then assert a "most likely" (or "probable" or "conservative") mid-estimate. Thus, I conclude in chapter 9 that the Khmer Rouge likely killed from 600,000 to 3 million of their people, probably 2 million (a mid-value, subjective probability that will be discussed shortly). For subtotals in the historical description of a case, I usually simply mention the mid-value, qualified as mentioned.

The how and why of an alleged democide range is critical and not determined casually. I have elsewhere published the methods that I use[7] to assess the democide of a regime, and should point out here that these methods are an attempt to *bracket* the unknown and precisely unknowable democide by seeking a variety of published estimates, and most important, the highest and lowest ones from pro- and antigovernment sources.[8] I then consolidate these for different aspects of a regime's democide — such as for summary executions, prison deaths, or disappearances — into low to high ranges. To get an overall range for a regime, as of that for the Khmer Rouge, I then sum all the consolidated lows to get an overall low democide, and all the consolidated highs to get an overall high.

The value of this approach lies in the great improbability that the sum of all the lowest estimates for a regime would be above the true total; or that the sum of all the highs would be below it. The fundamental methodological hypothesis here is that *the low and high sums (or the lowest low and highest high where such sums cannot be calculated) bracket the actual democide.* This of course may be wrong for some events (such as a massacre), an episode (such as land reform), or an institution (such as re-education camps), but across the

years and the many different kinds of democide committed by a
regime, the actual democide should be bracketed.

Within this possible range of democide, I always seek a prudent or
conservative mid-range estimate, which is based on my reading of the
events involved, the nature of the different estimates, and the estimates
of professionals who have long studied the country or government involved. I have sought in each case the best works in English on the relevant events so that I would not only have their estimates along with the
others, but so that their work would guide my choice of a prudent overall estimate. The details of this effort for each case are given in the relevant appendix in the related volume, *Statistics of Democide.*

Given my admission that I can only come within some range of an
actual number for democide, a range that may vary from low to high
by thousands of a percent, why then do I so precisely specify a
democide number? For example, in the chapter for communist China I
give the range of its democide as 5,999,000 to 102,671,000, most
likely 35,236,000 people killed. Why such apparent and misleading
accuracy? Why not simply make the range 5 million to 105 million,
with a mid-value of 35 million? This I would like to do (and have been
urged by colleagues to do), but for many cases the democide figures
result from calculations on or consolidations of a variety of estimates
for different kinds of democide (such as for land reform, labor camps,
and the Cultural Revolution). When all calculations or consolidations
are added together, the sum has great apparent precision. That is, the
low, high, and 35,236,000 mid-democide numbers for communist
China are sums. To give something other than these sums can create
confusion because the estimates and calculations are given in detail in
the appendices to my *China's Bloody Century.*[9]

The presentation problem is handled in the following manner.
Where specification of final democide figures is necessary, as when
the figures in a table depend upon those in an appendix, I give them
with all their seeming exactitude. Where, however, such is
unnecessary, I round off to the first or second digit and use some
adjective such as "nearly" or "around" or "about." Thus, communist
China's democide was about 35 million.

After eight years of almost daily reading and recording of the
number and instances of men, women, and children by the tens of
millions being tortured or beaten to death, hung, shot, and buried

alive, burned or starved, stabbed or chopped into pieces, and murdered in all the other ways creative and imaginative human beings can devise, I have never been so happy to conclude a project. I have not found it easy to read time and time again about the horrors innocent people have been forced to suffer. What has kept me at this was the belief, as preliminary research seemed to suggest, that there was a positive solution to all this killing and a clear course of political action and policy to end it. And the results verify this. The problem is Power. The solution is democracy. The course of action is to foster freedom.

Notes

1. Rummel 1990, 1991, and 1992.
2. I started this research in 1986, and the cutoff year for the collection of data was set as 1987. For consistency in comparing different cases and to avoid constantly having to change total figures as new democides occurred, I have stuck to the 1987 cutoff. This means that post-1987 democides by Iraq, Iran, Burundi, Serbian and Bosnian Serbs, Bosnia, Croatia, Sudan, Somalia, the Khmer Rouge guerrillas, Armenia, Azerbaijan, and others have not been included.

   I start the twentieth century with the year 1900. I realize that by our calendar the twentieth century really begins with the year 1901. However, I was uncomfortable including 1900 in the previous century.
3. See Rummel 1975–81, 1983, 1984, and 1985. While the fact that democracies don't make war on each other has been verified by others and well accepted by students of international relations, the statement that democracies have the least foreign violence has aroused controversy, and a number of studies allege they find no difference between regimes on this score. But the controversy is due to different and, in my view, inappropriate methods. I argue that the more democratic libertarian a regime, the greater the resistance to war or foreign violence. This argument should be tested in terms of the number of people killed either in total or as a proportion of the population—not, as others have done, by correlating type of regime with the number of wars it has fought. One should not be surprised, therefore, that those who correlate regime type with number of wars fought find hardly any correlation between regime type and war, since they treat all wars alike. Even the tiny democratic wars such as the American invasion of Grenada and Panama or the British Falkland Islands War are given the same weight as World War I or II for Germany or the Soviet Union. In any case, one of the side results of my study is to further substantiate that democracies have the least foreign violence; that is, that even in war, democracies suffer far fewer deaths than other regimes. See table 1.6 and figures 1.6, 1.7b, 1.7d, and 1.8.
4. According to the Genocide Convention, genocide can refer to other than killing, such as trying to destroy a group in whole or in part by taking away its children.
5. See note 1.
6. Rummel 1992, 5.
7. See Rummel 1990, appendix A; 1991, 309–316.

8. My methods have caused some misunderstanding among readers. However, that I use biased or ideological sources, as of Communist publications on American atrocities in Vietnam or official Iraqi statistics for the death toll among Kurds during the Civil War, is part of my attempt to get at the lowest or highest democide or war-dead estimates. There are therefore many items in my references that no self-respecting scholar would normally list. I include them because I use their estimates and not because I believe them to be objective or of high quality. Moreover, the omission of a particular work from the references does not mean that I have not used it. I have consulted, read, or studied for this work many times more publications than the references listed here. I include in this books' reference list only those works I have cited in a chapter or those from which I have taken the estimates listed in the appendix tables to be published in *Statistics of Democide*. The references listed in the Soviet, China, and Nazi democide books are not repeated here unless they also have been cited here or in *Statistics of Democide*.

9   Rummel 1991.

Acknowledgments

Many colleagues, students, and readers of previous drafts contributed to this effort through their ideas, comments, and suggestions, recommendation of sources, estimates, or material they passed on to me. In particular I want to thank Rouben Adalian, Belinda Aquino, Dean Babst, Yehuda Bauer, Douglas Bond, Israel Charny, William Eckhardt, Wayne Elliott, Helen Fein, Irving Louis Horowitz, Hua Shiping, B. R. Immerzeel, Benedict Kerkvliet, Milton Leitenberg, Guenter Lewy, Heath Lowry, John Norton Moore, J. C. Ramaer, Rhee Sang-Woo, Max Singer, Robert F. Turner, Spencer Weart, Christine White, and J. A. Willinge. I am especially indebted to my colleagues Manfred Henningsen and George Kent for their help and support throughout this work. I hasten to add that I alone am responsible for any errors or misconceptions that might appear here.

I also am indebted to the United States Institute of Peace for its grant to my project on comparative genocide, of which this book is a part. The views expressed here are those of the author and do not necessarily reflect the views of the Institute or its officers.

Finally and not least, my ability to complete this work and the form it took owes much to my wife, Grace — much more than she knows. Thanks, sweetheart.

1

169,198,000 Murdered
Summary and Conclusion

> *Power gradually extirpates for the mind every humane and gentle virtue.*
> —Edmund Burke, *A Vindication of Natural Society*

> *Power, like a desolating pestilence,*
> *Pollutes whate'er it touches.*
> —Shelley, *Queen Mab III*

> *Power tends to corrupt; absolute power corrupts absolutely.*
> —Lord Acton, *Letter to Bishop Creighton*

Power kills; absolute Power kills absolutely. This new Power Principle is the message emerging from my previous work on the causes of war[1] and from this book on genocide and government mass murder — what I call *democide* — in this century. The more power a government has, the more it can act arbitrarily according to the whims and desires of the elite, and the more it will make war on others and murder its foreign and domestic subjects. The more constrained the power of governments, the more power is diffused, checked, and balanced, the less it will aggress on others and commit democide. At the extremes of Power,[2] totalitarian communist governments slaughter their people by the tens of *millions*; in contrast, many democracies can barely bring themselves to execute even serial murderers.

These assertions are extreme and categorical, but so is the evidence accumulated here and elsewhere. Consider first war. Table 1.1 shows the occurrence of war between nations since 1816. Never has there been a war involving violent military action between stable democracies[3] (although they have fought, as everyone knows, nondemocracies) — most wars are between nondemocracies. Indeed, we have here a general principle that is gaining acceptance among students of international relations and war: namely, that *democracies don't or rarely make war on each other*. To this I would add that the *less* democratic two states are, the *more* likely it is that they will fight each other.

This belligerence of unrestrained Power is not an artifact of either a small number of democracies nor of our era. For one thing, the number of democratic states in 1993 is about seventy-five, or, taking into account forty-eight related territories, about one-fourth of the world's population.[4] Yet we have had no war — none — among them. Nor is there any threat of war. They create an oasis of peace.

Moreover, this is historically true of democracies as well. If one relaxes the definition of democracy to mean simply the restraint on

TABLE 1.1
Wars between Democracies and Nondemocracies, 1816–1991

Dyads [a]	Wars [b]
Democracies vs. democracies	0
Democracies vs. nondemocracies	155
Nondemocracies vs. nondemocracies	198
Total	353

a   Stable democracies. This only excludes the war between an ephemeral republican France and republican Rome in 1849.

b   Defined as any military action in which at least 1,000 persons are killed. From Small and Singer 1976, 1982; more recent estimates from the author.

Power by the participation of middle and lower classes in the determination of power holders and policy-making, then there have been many democracies throughout history. And whether considering the classical Greek democracies, the forest democracies of medieval Switzerland, or modern democracies, they did or do not fight each other (depending on how war and democracy are defined, some might prefer to say that they *rarely* fought or fight each other).[5] Moreover, once those states that had been mortal enemies, that had frequently gone to war (as have France and Germany in recent centuries), became democratic, war ceased between them.[6] Paradigmatic of this is Western Europe since 1945. The cauldron of our most disastrous wars for many centuries, in 1945 one would not find an expert so foolhardy as to predict not only forty-five years of peace, but that at the end of that time there would be a European community with central government institutions, moves toward a joint European military force by France and Germany, and zero expectation of violence between any of these formerly hostile states. Yet such has happened. All because they are all democracies.[7]

Even if all to be said about absolute and arbitrary Power was that it causes war and the attendant slaughter of the young and most capable of our species, this would be enough. But much worse, as the case studies in this book will more than attest, even without the excuse of combat, Power also massacres in cold blood those helpless people it controls — in fact, *several times more of them.* Consider table 1.2 and figure 1.1: the list and its graph of this century's *megamurderers* — those states killing in cold blood, aside from warfare, 1 million or more men, women, and children. These fifteen megamurderers have wiped out over 151 million people, almost four times the almost 38,500,000 battle dead from all this century's international and civil wars up to 1987.[8] The most absolute Powers — namely, communist USSR, China, and preceding-Mao guerrillas; Khmer Rouge Cambodia, Vietnam, and Yugoslavia, and fascist Nazi Germany — account for nearly 128 million of them, or 84 percent.

Table 1.2 also shows the annual percentage democide rate (the percent of its population that a regime murders per year) for each megamurderer; figure 1.1 graphically overlays the plot of this on the total murdered. Massive megamurderers such as the Soviet Union and communist China had huge populations with a resulting small annual

TABLE 1.2
Twentieth-Century Democide

Regimes	Years	Total	Domestic	Genocide	Annual Rate (%) [b]
		Democide (000) [a]			
Megamurderers	1900-87	151,491	116,380	33,476	.92 [d]
Dekamegamurderers	1900-87	128,168	100,842	26,690	.18 [d]
USSR	1917-87	61,911	54,769	10,000	.42
China (PRC)	1949-87	35,236	35,236	375	.12
Germany	1933-45	20,946	762	16,315	.09
China (KMT)	1928-49	10,075	10,075	nil	.07 [e]
Lesser Megamurderers	1900-87	19,178	12,237	6,184	1.63 [d]
Japan	1936-45	5,964	nil	nil	nil
China (Mao Soviets) [c]	1923-49	3,466	3,466	nil	.05 [e]
Cambodia	1975-79	2,035	2,000	541	8.16
Turkey	1909-18	1,883	1,752	1,883	.96
Vietnam	1945-87	1,678	944	nil	.10
Poland	1945-48	1,585	1,585	1,585	1.99
Pakistan	1958-87	1,503	1,503	1,500	.06
Yugoslavia (Tito)	1944-87	1,072	987	675	.12
Suspected Megamurderers	1900-87	4,145	3,301	602	.24 [d]
North Korea	1948-87	1,663	1,293	nil	.25
Mexico	1900-20	1,417	1,417	100	.45
Russia	1900-17	1,066	591	502	.02
Centi-Kilomurderers	1900-87	14,918	10,812	4,071	.26 [d]
Top 5	1900-87	4,074	2,192	1,078	.89 [d]
China (warlords)	1917-49	910	910	nil	.02
Turkey (Atatürk)	1919-23	878	703	878	2.64
United Kingdom	1900-87	816	nil	nil	nil
Portugal (dictatorship)	1926-82	741	nil	nil	nil
Indonesia	1965-87	729	579	200	.02
Lesser Murderers	1900-87	2,792	2,355	1,019	.13 [d]
WORLD TOTAL	1900-87	169,202	129,547	38,566	.09 [f]

a Includes genocide, politicide, and mass murder; excludes war dead. These are most probable mid-estimates in low to high ranges. Figures may not sum due to rounding.
b The percent of a population killed in democide per year of the regime.
c Guerrilla period.
d Average.
e The rate is the average of that for three successive periods.
f The world annual rate is calculated for the 1944 global population.

democide rate. Lesser megamurderers were far more lethal to their own populations.

Table 1.3 lists the fifteen most lethal regimes, and figure 1.2 bar graphs them. As can be seen, no other megamurderer comes even close to the lethality of the communist Khmer Rouge in Cambodia during their 1975 through 1978 rule. As will be described in chapter 9, in less than four years of governing they exterminated over 31 percent of their men, women, and children; the odds of any Cambodian surviving these four long years was only about 2.2 to 1.

Then there are the kilomurderers, or those states that have killed innocents by the tens or hundreds of thousands, such as the top five

FIGURE 1.1
Megamurderers and Their Annual Rates of Democide
(From table 1.2)

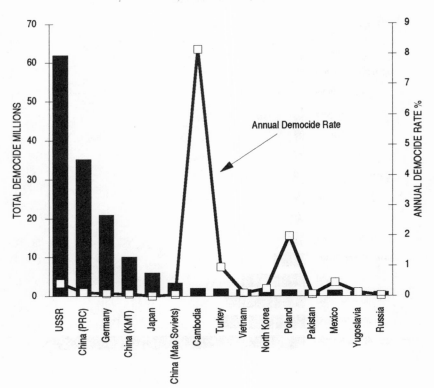

6   Death by Government

listed in table 1.2: China's Warlords (1917–49), Atatürk's Turkey (1919–23), the United Kingdom (primarily due to the 1914–19 food blockade of the Central Powers in and after World War I, and the 1940–45 indiscriminate bombing of German cities), Portugal (1926–82), and Indonesia (1965–87). Some lesser kilomurderers were communist Afghanistan, Angola, Albania, Rumania, and Ethiopia, as well as authoritarian Hungary, Burundi, Croatia (1941–44), Czechoslovakia (1945–46), Indonesia, Iraq, Russia, and Uganda. For its indiscriminate bombing of German and Japanese civilians, the United States must also be added to this list (see my *Statistics of Democide*). These and other kilomurderers add almost 15 million people killed to the democide for this century, as shown in table 1.2.

FIGURE 1.2
Democide Lethality

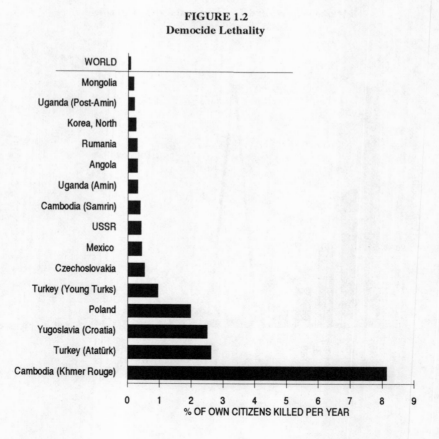

TABLE 1.3
Fifteen Most Lethal Regimes

Regime [a]	Regime			Annual Rate (%) [b]	Domestic Democide (000)	Mid-period Population (000)
	Years	Duration (years)	Type			
Cambodia (Khmer Rouge)	1975–79	3.83	C	8.16	2,000	6,399
Turkey (Atatürk)	1919–23	4.08	A	2.64	703	6,500
Yugoslavia (Croatia)	1941–45	4.17	A	2.51	655	6,250
Poland (Post-World War II)	1945–48	3.33	A	1.99	1,585	23,930
Turkey (Young Turks)	1909–18	9.17	A	.96	1,752	20,000
Czechoslovakia (Post-World War II)	1945–48	2.83	A	.54	197	12,916
Mexico	1900–1920	21.00	A	.45	1,417	15,000
USSR	1917–87	71.00	C	.42	54,769	184,750
Cambodia (Samrin)	1979–87	8.92	C	.40	230	6,478
Uganda (Amin)	1971–79	8.33	A	.31	300	11,550
Angola	1975–87	12.17	C	.30	125	3,400
Rumania (Carol/Michael)	1938–48	10.08	A	.29	484	16,271
Korea, North	1948–87	39.33	C	.25	1,293	13,140
Uganda (Post-Amin)	1979–87	8.75	A	.20	255	14,300
Mongolia	1926–87	61.17	C	.19	100	873
World	1900–1987	17.46 [c]		.24 [c]	129,909 [d]	2,325,000 [e]

Key: A = authoritarian; C = communist

a State regimes older than one year and having a population greater than 750,000.

b Percent of citizens killed through democide per year of the regime.

c Average.

d Total.

e For 1944.

Of course, saying that a state or regime is a murderer is a convenient personification of an abstraction. Regimes are in reality people with the power to command a whole society. It is these people that have committed the kilo- and megamurders of our century, and we must not hide their identity under the abstraction of "state," "regime," "government," or "communist." Table 1.4 lists the men most notoriously and singularly responsible for the megamurders of this century.

Stalin, by far, leads the list. He ordered the death of millions, knowingly set in train events leading to the death of millions of others, and as the ultimate dictator, was responsible for the death of still millions more killed by his henchman. It may come as a surprise to find Mao Tse-tung next in line as this century's greatest murderer, but this would only be because the full extent of communist killing in China under his leadership has not been widely known in the West. Hitler and Pol Pot are of course among these bloody tyrants and, as for the others, whose names may appear strange, their megamurders are

TABLE 1.4
This Century's Bloodiest Megamurderers

Dictator	Ideology	Country	Years	Murdered (000)[a]
Joseph Stalin	C	USSR	1929–53	42,672 [b]
Mao Tse-tung	C	China	1923–76	37,828 [c]
Adolf Hitler	F	Germany	1933–45	20,946
Chiang Kai-shek	M/F	China	1921–48	10,214 [d]
Vladimir Illich Lenin	C	USSR	1917–24	4,017 [e]
Tojo Hideki	M/F	Japan	1941–45	3,990 [f]
Pol Pot	C	Cambodia	1968–87	2,397 [c]
Yahya Khan	M	Pakistan	1971	1,500
Josip Broz Tito	C	Yugoslavia	1941–87	1,172 [c]

Key: C = communist; F = fascist; M/F = militarist/fascist; M = militarist

a These are the most probable estimates from a low to high range. Estimates are from or based on Rummel 1990, 1991, 1992 and *Statistics of Democide*.

b Citizens only.

c Includes his guerrilla period.

d Includes his warlord period.

e Includes one-third the democide for the NEP period 1923–28.

f Estimated as one-half the 1937–45 democide in China plus the World War II democide.

described in detail in the relevant chapters. The monstrous bloodletting of these nine men should be entered into a Hall of Infamy. Their names should forever warn us of the deadly potential of Power.

The major and better-known episodes and institutions for which these and other murderers were responsible are listed in table 1.5. Far above all is gulag — the Soviet slave-labor system created by Lenin and built up under Stalin. In some 70 years it likely chewed up almost 40 million lives, well over *twice* as many as probably died in some 400 years of the African slave trade, from capture to sale in an Arab, Oriental, or New World market.[9]

In total, during the first eighty-eight years of this century, almost 170 million men, women, and children have been shot, beaten, tortured, knifed, burned, starved, frozen, crushed, or worked to death; buried alive, drowned, hung, bombed, or killed in any other of the myriad ways governments have inflicted death on unarmed, helpless citizens and foreigners. The dead could conceivably be nearly 360 million people. It is as though our species has been devastated by a modern Black Plague. And indeed it has, but a plague of Power, not germs.

The souls of this monstrous pile of dead have created a new land, a new nation, among us. In Shakespeare's words, "This Land be calle'd The field of Golgotha, and dead men's Skulls."[10] As is clear from the megamurderers listed in table 1.2 alone, this land is multicultural and multiethnic. Its inhabitants followed all the world's religions and spoke all its languages. Its demography has yet to be precisely measured, and only two rough censuses, the most recent constituting this book, have so far been taken.[11] But this last census does allow us to rank this land of the murdered sixth in population among the nations of the living, as shown in figure 1.3.

This census and the estimates of explorers also enables us to estimate Golgotha's racial and ethnic composition, which is pictured in figure 1.4. Chinese make up 30 percent of its souls, with Russians next at 24 percent. Then there is a much lower percentage of Ukrainians (6 percent), Germans (4 percent), Poles (4 percent), and Cambodians (2 percent). The remaining 30 percent comprises a mix of Koreans, Mexicans, Pakistanis (largely ethnic Bengalis and Hindus), Turk subjects, and Vietnamese.

TABLE 1.5
Some Major Democide Episodes and Cases

Episodes / Cases	Democide (000) [a]	Years	Victims	Regime(s)
Concentration / labor camps	39,464	1917–87	anyone	USSR
Jewish Holocaust	5,291	1942–45	European Jews	Hitler's
Intentional Famine in Ukraine	5,000	1932–33	peasants	Stalin's
China Land Reform	4,500	1949–53	rich / landlords	Mao Tse-tung's
Collectivization	3,133	1928–35	peasants / landlords	Stalin's
Cambodian Hell	2,000	1975–79	Cambodian people	Pol Pot's
Cultural Revolution	1,613	1964–75	communists / officials / intellectuals	Mao Tse-tung's
German expulsion	1,583	1945–48	German Ethnics	Poland
Bengal / Hindu genocide	1,500	1971	Hindus / Bengali leaders / intellectuals	Pakistan
Armenian genocide	1,404	1915–18	Turkey's Armenians	Young Turks'
Great Terror	1,000	1936–38	communists	Stalin's
Serbian genocide	655	1941–45	Serbs / Jews / Gypsies	Croatian Ustashi
Indonesian massacre	509	1965–66	communists / sympathizers	Indonesian Army
Ugandan massacres	300	1971–79	critics / opponents / tribesmen	Idi Amin's
Boat People	250	1975–87	Vietnamese / Chinese	Vietnam
Spanish Civil War	200	1936–39	Republicans / Nationalists	Spanish Republican Gov't / Nationalist Army
Rape of Nanking	200	1937–38	Chinese	Japanese Army
"La Violencia" massacres	180	1948–58	liberals / conservatives	Colombia Liberal / Conservative Gov'ts
Tribal massacres	150	1971–72	Hutu educated / leaders	Burundi Hutu
East Timor massacres	150	1975–87	Timorese	Indonesian Army
Colonial massacres	132	1900–1918	Hereros / Hottentots / others	German kaiser's

a Most probable estimates from a low to high range. Estimates are from or based on Rummel 1990, 1991, 1992, and various tables of sources and estimates published in *Statistics of Democide*.

But still, is Golgotha dominantly Asian? European? What region did most of its dead souls come from? Figure 1.5 displays two different ways of looking at this: the percent of Golgothans from a particular region and also the percent of a region's 1987 population in Golgotha. While most, some 40 percent, are from Asia and the Middle East, the highest proportion of any region's 1987 population in Golgotha, around 22 percent, is from the territory of the former Soviet Union. In other words, Asians are the largest group while the former Soviet Union has contributed the most of its 1987 population. Note that 18 percent of Golgothans are former Europeans, including those from all of Eastern Europe except the former USSR; Europe has contributed 6 percent of its population to this land of the murdered.

FIGURE 1.3
Golgotha 1900–1987 Compared to the Populations of the Largest States in 1987

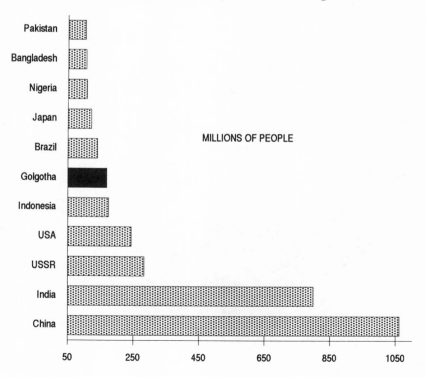

12   Death by Government

So much for Golgotha and a summary overview of its statistics. As I already have made clear, Golgotha owes its existence to Power. I can now be more specific about this. Table 1.6 summarizes the most prudent democide results and contrasts them to this century's battle dead. Figure 1.6 gives a bar chart of these totals.[12] Note immediately in the figure that the human cost of democide is far greater than that of war for authoritarian and totalitarian regimes. Democracies show a reverse pattern; however, they suffer far fewer deaths than do other regimes. In evaluating the battle dead for democracies, also keep in mind that most of these dead were the result of wars that democracies fought against authoritarian or totalitarian aggression, particularly World War I and II and the Korean and Vietnam Wars.[13]

FIGURE 1.4
Golgotha's 1900–1987 Racial/Ethnic Composition
(From *Statistics of Democide*)

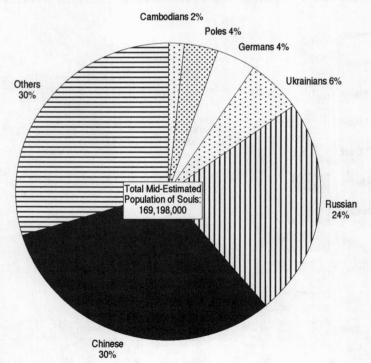

Putting the human cost of war and democide together, Power has killed over 203 million people in this century. If one were to sit at a table and have this many people come in one door, walk at three miles per hour across the room with three feet between them (assume generously that each person is also one foot thick, navel to spine), and exit an opposite door, it would take over *five years and nine months* for them all to pass, twenty-four hours a day, 365 days a year. If all these dead were laid out head to toe, assuming each to be an average of 5 feet tall, they would reach from Honolulu, Hawaii, across the vast Pacific and then the huge continental United States to Washington D.C. on the East coast, *and then back again almost twenty times.*[14]

FIGURE 1.5
Regional Origin of Golgothans (Victims of Democide, 1900–1987)
(Percentages are based on figures in *Statistics of Democide* and 1987 populations.)

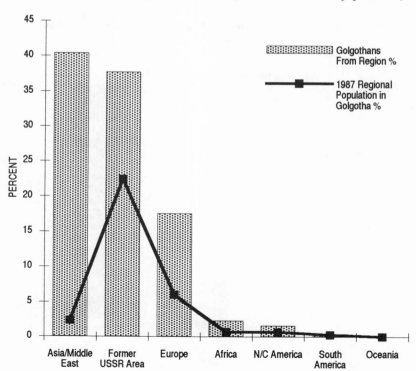

Were each of these people also to be an average of 2 feet wide, then to
bury them side-to-side and head-to-toe would take fifty-five square
miles. Even digging up every foot of all of San Marino, Monaco, and
Vatican city to bury these democide and war battle dead would not be
sufficient to inter half of them.

   Now, as shown in table 1.6 and figure 1.6, democracies themselves
are responsible for some of the democide. Almost all of this, however,
is foreign democide during war, and consists mainly of those enemy
civilians killed in indiscriminate urban bombing, as of Germany and
Japan in World War II.[15] Democide by democracies also includes the
large-scale massacres of Filipinos during the bloody U.S. colonization
of the Philippines at the beginning of this century, deaths in British
concentration camps in South Africa during the Boar War, civilian
deaths due to starvation during the British blockade of Germany in
and after World War I, the rape and murder of helpless Chinese in and

FIGURE 1.6
Deaths from Democide Compared to Deaths from International War
(From table 1.6)

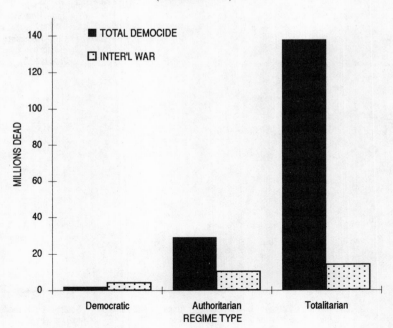

TABLE 1.6
Democide and Power

Regime [a]	Regime Power	Killed (000) [b]			Rate (%) [c]	
		Total	Domestic	Foreign	Overall	Annual
DEMOCIDE						
Democratic	least	2,028	159	1,858	0.04	0.01
Authoritarian	mid	28,676	26,092	2,584	1.06	0.21
Totalitarian	high	137,977	103,194	34,783	4.15	0.40
Communist	highest	110,286	101,929	8,357	5.35	0.52
Others [d]		518	464	54		
World		169,198	129,908	39,278	7.28 [e]	0.083 [e]

WAR	Regime Power	Total	Domestic	International	Per War [f]	% Pop. [g]
Democratic	least	4,370	5	4,365	62	0.24
Authoritarian	mid	15,298	4,774	10,523	86	0.33
Totalitarian	high	14,354	68	14,286	399	0.64
Communist	highest	9,784	68	9,715	326	0.53
World		34,021	4,848	29,174	120	1.46 [h]
World Total		203,219	134,756	68,452		8.74 [i]

a These are regimes in states, quasi-states, and nonstate groups. Classification of regimes is based on Small and Singer 1976 and Ted Robert Gurr's Polity I and II data.

b Figures for democide are the sums of the most probable mid-values in a low-high range over the period 1900–1987. Figures for war are a regime's battle dead in excess of 1,000 for 1900–1980, based on Small and Singer 1982, modified by additional data in this book. Figures may not add up due to rounding.

c. "Overall" is the average of each regime's percent of mid-period population killed through democide during the period 1900–1987. "Annual" is this average per year.

d These are groups for which a regime could not be specified, such as international terrorists and domestic guerrillas.

e The world rate is calculated for the 1944 global population.

f Average regime's battle dead per foreign war.

g Average percent of a regime's population killed in international wars.

h Percent of the world's 1944 population killed in all wars 1900–1980. The annual percentage is .018.

i Percent of the world's 1944 population killed in democide 1900–1987 and wars 1900–1980.

around Peking in 1900, the atrocities committed by Americans in Vietnam, the murder of helpless Algerians during the Algerian War by the French, and the unnatural deaths of German prisoners of war in French and U.S. POW camps after World War II.[16]

All this killing of foreigners by democracies may seem to violate the Power Principle, but really it underlines it. For, in each case the killing was carried out in a highly undemocratic fashion: in secret, behind a conscious cover of lies and deceit, and by agencies and power holders that had the wartime authority to operate autonomously. All were shielded by tight censorship of the press and control of journalists. Even the indiscriminate bombing of German cities by the British was disguised before the House of Commons and in press releases as attacks on German military targets. That the general strategic bombing policy was to attack working men's homes was kept secret still long after the war.

FIGURE 1.7a
Power Curve of Total Democide
(From table 1.6)

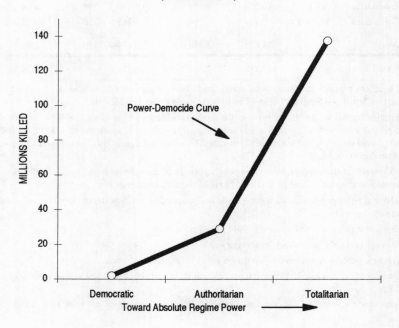

Finally, with the summary statistics on democide and war shown in table 1.6, we now can display the role of Power. Figures 1.7a-d illustrate the power curves for the total democide and battle dead (figures 1.7a-b); and for the intensity of democide and battle dead, both measured as a percent of a regime's population killed (figures 1.7a-d). In each case, *as the arbitrary power of a regime increases massively, that is, as we move from democratic through authoritarian to totalitarian regimes, the amount of killing jumps by huge multiples.*

Two more figures will exhibit the sheer lethality of Power. Figure 1.8 shows the proportion of war and democide dead accounted for by authoritarian or totalitarian power together and compares this to the democratic dead. For all this killing in this century, democide and war by democracies contributes only 1 and 2.2 percent, respectively, to the total.

FIGURE 1.7b
Power Curve of War Battle Dead
(From table 1.6)

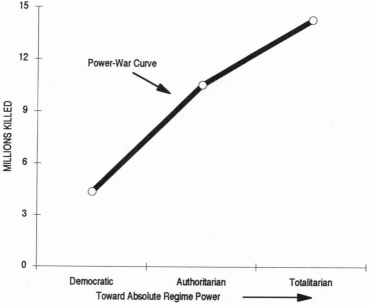

And in figure 1.9, one of the most important comparisons of democide and power in this book — the range of democide estimates for each regime — is shown. As mentioned in the Preface, I have collected almost 8,200 estimates of democide from over a thousand sources to arrive at an absolute low and high for democide committed by 218 regimes or groups. It is highly improbable that the actual democide would be below or above this range. The totals that have been displayed in previous figures have been the sum of conservatively determined mid-totals in this range, and are shown in the figure. What figure 1.9 presents for each type of regime, such as the authoritarian, is the range resulting from summing all the lows and highs for all the democide of all regimes of that type. The difference between the three resulting ranges drawn in the figure can only be understood in terms of Power. As the arbitrary power of regimes increases, the range of their democide jumps and to such a great extent

FIGURE 1.7c
Power Curve of Democide Intensity
(From table 1.6)

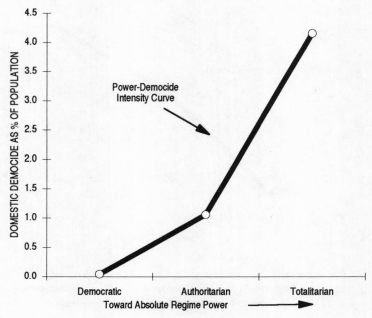

that the low democide for the authoritarian regime is *above* the democratic high, and the low democide for the totalitarian regime is *above* the authoritarian high.

So Power kills, and absolute Power kills absolutely. What then can be said of those alleged causes or factors in war, genocide, and mass murder favored by students of genocide. What about cultural-ethnic differences, outgroup conflict, misperception, frustration-aggression, relative deprivation, ideological imperatives, dehumanization, resource competition, etc.? At one time or another, for one regime or another, one or more of these factors play an important role in democide. They are essential for understanding some genocides, as of the Jews or Armenians; some politicide, as of "enemies of the people," bourgeoisie, and clergy; some massacres, as of competing religious-ethnic groups; or some atrocities, as of those committed against poor and helpless villagers by victorious soldiers. But they do not explain

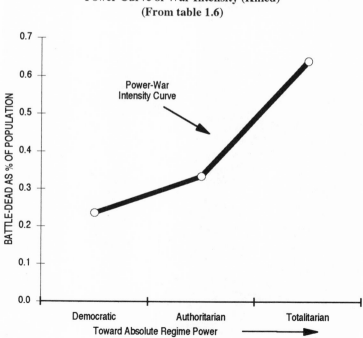

FIGURE 1.7d
Power Curve of War Intensity (Killed)
(From table 1.6)

all the killing. They only accelerate the likelihood of war or democide once some trigger event occurs and absolute or nearly absolute Power is present. That is, *Power is a necessary cause for war or democide.* When the elite have absolute power, war or democide follows a common process (which I call "the conflict helix").[17]

In any society, including the international one, relations between individuals and groups is structured by social contracts determined by previous conflicts, accommodations, and adjustments among them. These social contracts define a structure of expectations that guides and regulates the social order, including Power. And this structure is based on a particular balance of powers (understood as an equilibrium of interests, capabilities, and wills) among individuals and groups. That is, previous conflict and possibly violence determine a balance of powers between competing individuals and groups and a congruent structure of expectations (as for example, war or revolution ends in a

FIGURE 1.8
Democide Versus War Battle Dead
Democracies Versus Nondemocracies
(Figures are for total democide and total war battle dead and are based on table 1.6.)

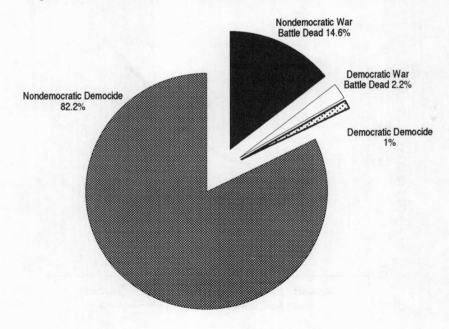

new balance of powers between nations or groups and an associated peace treaty or constitution). This structure of expectations often consists of new laws and norms defining a social order more consistent with the underlying distribution of relative power.

However, relative power never remains constant. It shifts as the interests, capabilities, and wills of the parties change. The death of a charismatic leader, the outrage of significant groups, the loss of foreign support by outgroups, the entry into war and the resulting freedom of the elite to use force under the guise of wartime necessity, and so on, can significantly alter the balance of power between groups. Where such a shift in power is in favor of the governing elite, Power can now achieve its potential. Where also the elite has built-up frustrations regarding those who have lost power, or nonetheless feels threatened by them; where it sees them as outside the moral universe,

FIGURE 1.9
Range of Democide Estimates for Regimes
(Calculated from table D.1)

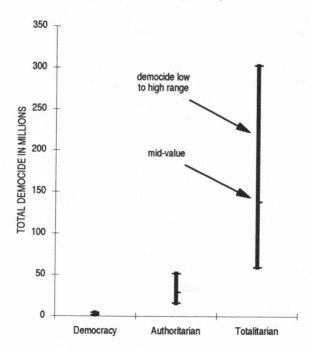

or where it has dehumanized them; where the outgroup is culturally or ethnically distinct and perceived by the elite as inferior; or where any other such factors are present, Power will achieve its murderous potential. It simply waits for an excuse, an event of some sort, an assassination, a massacre in a neighboring country, an attempted coup, a famine, or a natural disaster, to justify the beginning of murder en masse. Most democides occur under the cover of war, revolution, or guerrilla war, or in their aftermath.

The result of such violence will be a new balance of power and attendant social contract. In some cases this may end the democide, for example by eliminating the "inferior" group (as the Turks did to the Armenians). In many cases this will subdue the survivors (as happened with the Ukrainians who lived through Stalin's collectivization campaign and intentional famine). In some cases, this establishes a new balance of power so skewed toward the elite that they may throughout their reign continue to murder at will: Murder as public policy becomes part of the new social order. Consider the social orders of Hitler, Stalin, Mao, Pol Pot, and their henchmen.

As should be clear from all this, I believe that war and democide can be understood within a common framework. They are part of the same social process: a balancing of power, where Power is supreme.

It is not apparent, however, why, among states where Power is limited and accountable, war and significant democide do *not* take place. Two concepts explain this: (1) *cross pressures* and (2) the associated political *culture*. Where Power is diffused, checked, and accountable, society is riven by myriad independent groups, disparate institutions, and multiple interests. These overlap and contend; they section loyalties and divide desires and wants. Churches, unions, corporations, government bureaucracies, political parties, the media, special interest groups, and such, fight for and protect their interests. Individuals and the elite are pushed and pulled by their membership in several such groups and institutions. It is difficult for any one driving interest to form. Interests are divided, weak, ambivalent; they are cross-pressured. For the elite to sufficiently coalesce so as to commit itself to murdering its own citizens, there must be a nearly fanatical, driving interest. But even were such to be present among a few, the diversity of interests across the political elite and associated bureaucracies, the freedom of the media to dig out what is being planned or done, and the ever-present potential for leaks and fear of such leaks from disaffected elite to the media brake such tendencies.

As to the possibility of war between democracies, diversity and resulting cross-pressures operate as well. Not only is it very difficult for the elite to unify public interests and opinion sufficiently to make war, but there are usually diverse, economic, social, and political bonds between democracies that tie them together and oppose violence.

But there is more to these restraints on Power in a democracy. Cross-pressures is a *social force* that operates wherever individual and group freedom predominates. It is natural to a spontaneous social field. But human behavior is not only a matter of social forces — it also depends on the meanings, values, and norms that are present. That is, democratic *culture* is also essential. When Power is checked and accountable, when cross-pressures limit the operation of Power, a particular democratic culture develops. This culture involves debate, demonstrations, and protests as well as negotiation, compromise, and tolerance. It involves the art of conflict resolution and the acceptance of democratic procedures at all levels of society. The ballot replaces the bullet, and people and groups come to accept a loss on this or that interest as only an unfortunate outcome of the way the legitimate game is played. "Lose today, win tomorrow."

That democratic political elite would kill opponents or commit genocide for some public policy is unthinkable (although such may occur in the isolated and secret corners of government where Power can still lurk). Even public insult and dehumanization of outgroups have become a social and political evil in modern democracies. Witness the current potency of such allegations as "racism" or "sexism."

Of course, the culture of democracy operates between democracies as well. Diplomacy, negotiating a middle way, and seeking common interests are part of the operating medium among democracies. A detailed political history of the growth of the European Community would well display this. Since each democracy takes the legitimacy of the other and the other's interests for granted, conflict is only a process of nonviolent learning and adjustment. Conferences, not war, is the instrumentality for settling disputes.

In sum, then, where absolute Power exists, interests become polarized, a culture of violence develops, and war and democide follow. In this century alone, by current count, absolute — totalitarian — Power has murdered nearly 138 million people (table 1.6). Over 14 million more of the subjects of totalitarian states have died from battle in wars waged by their own regime. Where, on the other hand, Power is limited and accountable, interests are cross-pressured, and a culture of nonviolence develops, no wars have occurred and comparatively few citizens have been murdered by the governing elite — even most of those killed is questionable. About 90 percent of the citizens killed by democracies have been killed by marginally democratic Spain (during its 1936–39 civil war), India, and Peru (during its struggle against the communist Shining Path guerrillas).

This picture of Power and its human costs is new. Few are aware of the sheer democide that has been inflicted on our fellow human beings. That Hitler murdered millions of Jews is common knowledge. That he murdered overall nearly 21 million Jews, Slavs, Gypsies, homosexuals, Frenchmen, Balts, Czechs, and others, is virtually unknown. Similarly, that Stalin murdered tens of millions is becoming generally appreciated; but that Stalin, Lenin, and their successors murdered almost 62 million Soviet citizens and foreigners is little comprehended outside of the Soviet Union (where similar figures are now being widely published). Then there is Mao Tse-tung's China, Chiang Kai-shek's China, the militarist's Japan, Yahya Khan's Pakistan, Pol Pot's Cambodia, and the others listed in table 1.4, who have murdered in the millions. Even those students of genocide who have tried to tabulate such killing around the world have grossly underestimated the toll. The best, most recent accountings came up with no more than 16 million killed in genocide and politicide since World War II.[18] But this estimate does not cover even half of the some 35 million people likely murdered by just the Communist Party of China from 1949 to 1987 (table 1.2).

Moreover, even the toll of war itself is not well understood. Many estimate that World War II, for example, killed 40 to 60 million people. But the problem with such figures is that they include tens of millions killed in democide. Many wartime governments massacred civilians and foreigners, committed atrocities or genocide against them, executed them, and subjected them to reprisals. Aside from battle or military engagements, during the war the Nazis murdered around 20 million civilians and prisoners of war, the Japanese

5,890,000, the Chinese nationalists 5,907,000, the Chinese communists 250,000, the Nazi satellite Croatians 655,000, the Tito Partisans 600,000, and Stalin 13,053,000 (above the 20 million war dead and Nazi democide of Soviet Jews and Slavs). I also should mention the indiscriminate bombing of civilians by the Allies that killed hundreds of thousands, and the atomic bombing of Hiroshima and Nagasaki. Most of these dead are usually included among the war dead. But those killed in battle versus in democide form distinct conceptual and theoretical categories and should not be confused. That they have been consistently and sometimes intentionally confounded helps popularize the 60 million figure for the number of war dead in World War II, a figure that is way above the calculated estimate of 15 million killed in battle and military action. That the almost universally accepted count of genocide during this period is no more than "6 million" Jews, around 13 percent of the total wartime democide, has further muddled our research and thought.[19]

Even more, our appreciation of the incredible scale of this century's genocide, politicide, and mass murder has been stultified by lack of concepts. Democide is committed by absolute Power; its agency is government. The discipline for studying and analyzing power and government and associated genocide and mass murder is political science. But except for a few specific cases, such as the Holocaust and Armenian genocide, and a precious few more general works, one is hard put to find political science research specifically on this topic.

One university course I teach is an introduction to political science. Each semester I review several possible introductory texts (the best measure of the discipline) for the course. I often just shake my head at what I find. Juxtaposed with the democide totaled in table 1.2, the concepts and views promoted in these texts appear grossly unrealistic. They just do not fit or explain, or are even contradictory to the existence of a hell state like Pol Pot's Cambodia, a gulag state like Stalin's Soviet Union, or a genocide state like Hitler's Germany.

For instance, one textbook I recently read spends a chapter on describing the functions of government. Among these were law and order, individual security, cultural maintenance, and social welfare. Political scientists are still writing this stuff, when we have numerous examples of governments that kill hundreds of thousands and even millions of their own citizens, enslave the rest, and abolish traditional culture (it took only about a year for the Khmer Rouge to completely suppress Buddhism, which had been the heart and soul of Cambodian culture). A systems approach to politics still dominates the field. Through this lens, politics is a matter of inputs and outputs, of citizen inputs, aggregation by political parties, government determining policy, and bureaucracies implementing it. Then there is the common and fundamental justification of government that it exists to protect citizens against the anarchic jungle that would otherwise threaten their lives and property. Such archaic or sterile views show no appreciation of democide's existence and all its related horrors and suffering. They are inconsistent with a regime that stands astride society like a gang of thugs over hikers they have captured in the woods, robbing all, raping some, torturing others for fun, murdering those they don't like, and terrorizing the rest into servile obedience. This exact characterization of many past and present governments, such as Idi Amin's Uganda, hardly squares with conventional political science.

Consider also that library stacks have been written on the possible nature and consequences of nuclear war and how it might be avoided. Yet, in the life of some still living we have already experienced in the toll from democide (and related destruction and misery among the survivors) the equivalent of a nuclear war, especially at the high near-360 million end of the estimates. Yet to my knowledge, there is only one book dealing with the overall human cost of this "nuclear war" — Gil Elliot's *Twentieth Century Book of the Dead.*

What is needed is a reconceptualization of government and politics consistent with what we now know about democide and related misery. New concepts have to be invented, old ones realigned to correct — dare I write "modernize" — our perception of Power. We need to invent concepts for governments that turn their states into a border-to-border concentration camp, that purposely starve to death millions — millions! — of their citizens, and that set up quotas of those that should be killed from one village or town to another (although murder by quota was carried out by the Soviets, Chinese communists, and Vietnamese, I could not find in any introductory or general political science literature even a recognition that governments can be so incredibly inhumane). We have no concept for murder as an aim of public policy, determined by discussion among the governing elite in the highest councils, and imposed through government bureaucracy. Indeed, in virtually no index to any general book on politics and government will one find a reference to genocide, murder, killed, dead, executed, or massacre. Such is not even usually indexed in books on the Soviet Union or China. Most even omit index references to concentration or labor camps or gulag, even though they may have a paragraph or so on them.

A preeminent fact about government is that some of them murder millions in cold blood. This is where absolute Power reigns. A second fact is that some, usually the same that murder millions, also murder tens of thousands more through foreign aggression. Absolute Power again. These two facts alone must be the basis of our reconceptualization and taxonomies — not (as it is today) only whether states are developed or not, third world or not, militarily powerful or not, or large or not. Also and more important, we must consider whether Power is absolute, and whether it has engaged in genocide, politicide, and mass murder.

In any case, the empirical and theoretical conclusion is this: The way to end war and virtually eliminate democide appears to be through restricting and checking Power, i.e., through *fostering democratic freedom.*

Notes

1. Rummel 1975–81, 1983, and 1985.
2. Power capitalized stands for government power and its holders (such as Stalin), agencies (such as government departments and bureaucracies), and instruments (such as armies, concentration camps, and propaganda).
3. Since democratic Finland joined Nazi Germany in its war on the Soviet Union during World War II, Great Britain declared war on Finland. No military action apparently took place between Finland and Britain, however.
4. Were it not for India becoming authoritarian, around 40 percent of the world's population would be democratic. This is based on Freedom House's classification of states as free, partially free, or unfree, depending on their civil liberties and political rights. For its latest classification, see *Freedom Review* 24 (February 1993): 4–41.
5   For some contrary evidence from classical warfare among Greece city states, see Russett 1993, chapter 3.
6. The historian Spencer Weart has studied the history of warfare since ancient times, looking for possible examples of war between democracies. In spite of the many democracies that have existed throughout history, he has found no clear case of such a war. He is currently writing a book to present these results.

7. Even among primitive tribes, where Power is divided and limited, it seems that war is less likely. See Ember, Ember, and Russett 1991.
8. Battle dead up to 1980 is from Small and Singer's 1982 compilation of wars and battle dead. That for the remaining years is my estimate.
9. I calculate a mid-estimate of near 17,000 Africans killed in the slave trade. See *Statistics of Democide.*
10. William Shakespeare, *King Richard II*, iv, i, 144.
11. The first was by Elliot 1972.
12. Democide is appropriately compared to international war battle dead instead of to total international and domestic war battle dead. Totalitarian regimes use their absolute power to suppress any opposition before it can employ arms against it. They thus come out relatively low on domestic battle dead although still higher than democracies. What internal war does occur is usually at the inception of a regime, as in the very bloody civil war after the Bolshevik coup in Russia in 1917, or after a major war when under foreign occupation the opposition is able to arm itself and organize, as did the guerrillas that fought against Soviet reoccupation of the Baltic States after the Second World War.
13. However one evaluates the rightness or wrongness of American intervention in Vietnam, one fact has become clear from the documents, interviews, and speeches of Vietnamese officials since the end of the war: the Vietnam War was started by communist North Vietnam in order to take over South Vietnam. Since South Vietnam was recognized by a number of states, including the United States, as a sovereign state, this takeover attempt was an act of international aggression. And it was not until South Vietnam was near military collapse that the United States fully intervened with massive force. See chapter 11.
14. Back and forth, over 4,838 miles one way, near twenty times? This is so incredible that I would not believe the calculation and had to redo it several times.
15. The appropriateness of including this type of killing under democide will be discussed in chapter 2.
16. See my forthcoming book, *Statistics of Democide.*
17. See my *The Conflict Helix: Principles and Practices of Interpersonal, Social, and International Conflict and Cooperation* (New Brunswick: Transaction Publishers, 1991).
18. Harff and Gurr 1988.
19. During World War II, the Soviets committed genocide against at least nine of their distinct ethnic-linguistic subnations, including ethnic Germans, ethnic Greeks, Crimean Tatars, and Balkars. Genocides by others include those of the Germans against Slavs, Gypsies, and homosexuals; Croatians against the Serbs, Jews, and Gypsies; Serbs against Croatians and Moslems; Hungarians against their Jews; and Serbs, Poles, and Czechs against their ethnic Germans.

Part I
Background

2

The New Concept of Democide

> **Genocide:** among other things, the killing of people by a government because of their indelible group membership (race, ethnicity, religion, language).
>
> **Politicide**: the murder of any person or people by a government because of their politics or for political purposes.
>
> **Mass Murder:** the indiscriminate killing of any person or people by a government.
>
> **Democide:** The murder of any person or people by a government, including genocide, politicide, and mass murder.

Genocide is horrible, an abomination of our species, and totally unacceptable. It is an obscenity — the evil of our time that all good people must work to eradicate.

Most people recognize this evil for what it is. There is no doubt that the Nazi program to kill all Jews was genocide. Nor is there any doubt that the current Bosnian Serb massacre of Bosnian Moslems is genocide. But was it also genocide for government forces fighting a rebellion to massacre helpless villagers in the Sudan? How about the Indonesian army's purge of communists, the assassination of political opponents by the nationalist government on Formosa, the "land-reform" executions of landlords in the Soviet Union, or the rapid death of inmates in Vietnamese re-education camps? What about the absorption of one culture by another, the disease spread to natives by contact with colonists, the forced deportation of a people, or African slavery?

In international conventions and the professional literature, genocide was initially defined as the intentional destruction of people because of their race, religion, ethnicity, or other permanent group membership. The origin of the concept is the 1944 work by Raphael Lemkin on *Axis Rule in Occupied Europe*:

> New conceptions require new terms. By "genocide" we mean the destruction of a nation or of an ethnic group. This new word, coined by the author to denote an old practice in its modern development, is made from the ancient Greek word genos (race, tribe) and the Latin cide (killing), thus corresponding in its formation to such words as tyrannicide, homicide, infanticide, etc. Generally speaking, genocide does not necessarily mean the immediate destruction of a nation, except when accomplished by mass killings of all members of a nation. It is intended rather to signify a coordinated plan of different actions aiming at the destruction of essential foundations of the life of national groups, with the aim of annihilating the groups themselves. The objectives of such a plan would be disintegration of the political and social institutions, of culture, language, national feelings, religion, and the economic existence of national groups, and the destruction of the personal security, liberty, health, dignity, and even the lives of the individuals belonging to such groups. Genocide is directed against the national group as an entity, and the actions involved are directed against the individuals, not in their individual capacity, but as members of the national group.[1]

This was written at the height of the Jewish Holocaust — a clear case of a regime trying to exterminate a whole group, its intellectual contributions, its culture, and the very lives of all its people. There was an immediate need for some way to conceptualize this horror, and "genocide" did it. During the Nuremberg trials of Nazi war criminals, and in the postwar discussion and debate over how to prevent such killing in the future, "genocide" became a commonly used term. In incredibly little time, it passed from Lemkin's pages into international law. In 1946, the United Nations General Assembly recognized that "genocide is a crime under international law which the civilized world condemns, and for the commission of which principles and accomplices are punishable." Two years later the General Assembly made this resolution concrete by passing the Convention on the Prevention and Punishment of the Crime of Genocide. This international treaty, eventually signed by well over a majority of states, affirms that genocide is a punishable crime under international law, and stipulates the meaning of genocide to be

> any of the following acts committed with intent to destroy, in whole or in part, a national, ethnical, racial or religious group, as such :
>
> (a) Killing members of the group;
>
> (b) Causing serious bodily or mental harm to members of the group;
>
> (c) Deliberately inflicting on the group conditions of life calculated to bring about its physical destruction in whole or in part;
>
> (d) Imposing measures intended to prevent births within the group;
>
> (e) Forcibly transferring children of the group to another group.

Note that the Convention is consistent with Lemkin's definition and elaboration. Relevant here, however, is the fact that both define genocide as the intent to destroy in whole or part a group either by killing members of the group or *by other means*, such as by preventing births in the group or by causing serious mental harm. That is, according to both Lemkin and the Convention, genocide does *not* necessarily have to include killing.

This has been the source of much confusion. In the early years of its use, "genocide" was applied almost exclusively to the Jewish Holocaust and then, especially through the work of Armenian scholars, to the mass murder of Armenians by the Young Turk regime during World War I (as described in chapter 10). However, scholars increasingly have come to realize that restricting the killing aspect of the concept to those murdered by virtue of their indelible group membership does not completely account for the millions wiped out by the Nazis.

How then do we conceptualize the purposeful government killing of protesters and dissidents, the reprisal shooting of innocent villagers, the beating to death of peasants for hiding rice, or the indiscriminate bombing of civilians? How do we conceptualize torturing people to death in prison, working them to death in concentration camps, or letting them starve to death, when such killing is done out of revenge, for an ideology, or for reasons of state having nothing to do with the social groups to which these people belong?

Because of such questions scholars have generalized the meaning of "genocide." In some cases it has been extended to include the intentional killing of people because of their politics or for political reasons,[2] even though this aspect was explicitly excluded from the Genocide Convention. Some scholars have extended the definition of genocide to cover any mass murder by government.[3] Some have stretched the concept much further, for example by characterizing the unintentional spread of disease to indigenous populations during European colonization, including that in the American West.[4] To all these scholars, the critical aspect of "genocide" is intentional government killing.

All this is confusing. Both the nonkilling aspect of "genocide" and the need to have a concept that covers other kinds of government murder have led to the following being called genocide: the denial of ethnic Hawaiian culture by the U.S.-run public school system in Hawaii; government policies that let one race adopt the children of another race; African slavery by Whites; South African Apartheid; the murder of women by men; death squad murders in Guatemala; deaths in the Soviet gulag; and, of course, the Jewish Holocaust. The linking of such diverse acts or deaths under one label created an acute conceptual problem that begged for the invention of a new concept that covers and is *limited to* intentional government murder. Thus did both Barbara Harff[5] and I independently develop the concept of *politicide* for a government's premeditated killing of people because of their politics or for political reasons. But this new concept was still not sufficient, since it did not apply to many mass murders by government, such as the working of POWs to death by the Japanese army in World War II or the killing of Black Africans that resisted enslavement.

Already in general use is the concept of "mass murder" or "massacre." Although usage varies, both usually mean the intentional and indiscriminate murder of a large number of people by government agents, such as the shooting down of unarmed demonstrators by police, or the lobbing of grenades into prison cells by soldiers before retreating under pressure from enemy troops. The terms can also include the random execution of civilians (as in the German reprisals against partisan sabotage in Yugoslavia), working prisoners to death (as in the Soviet Kolyma mining camps), the blanket firebombing of cities (as in the British-American bombing of Hamburg in 1943), the atomic bombing of Hiroshima and Nagasaki, or atrocities committed by soldiers (as in the 1937–38 Japanese rape and pillage of Nanking during which Japanese soldiers probably killed some 200,000 people.

We also have the concept of "terror" as applied to government killing. This term usually means the extrajudicial execution, slaying, assassination, abduction or disappearance forever of targeted individuals. That is, the killing is discriminative. Its purpose may be to exterminate actual or potential opponents or for social prophylaxis — as Aleksandr Solzhenitsyn characterized Stalin's countrywide elimination of undesirables.[6] Such killing also may be for the purpose of promoting fear among a people and thus ensuring their obedience and subservience.

Then there is killing that does not easily fit under any of these labels. There is, for example, murder by quota carried out by the Soviets, Chinese communists, and North Vietnamese. For the Soviet and Vietnamese communists, government (or party) agencies would order subordinate units to kill a certain number of "enemies of the people," "rightists," or "tyrants," leaving precise application of the order to the units involved. Moreover, millions of people wasted away in labor or concentration camps not because of their social identity, their political beliefs, or who they were, but simply because they got in the way, violated some Draconian rule, did not express sufficient exuberance for the regime, innocently insulted the Leader (as by sitting on a newspaper with the picture of Stalin showing), or simply because they were a body that was needed for labor (as the Nazis would grab women innocently walking along a road in Ukraine and deport them to Germany for forced labor). And there are the hundreds of thousands of peasants that slowly died of disease, malnutrition, overwork, and hunger in Cambodia as the Khmer Rouge forced them under penalty of death to labor in the collectivized fields, expropriating virtually their whole harvest and refusing them adequate medical care.

Even when applicable, the concepts of "genocide," "politicide," "mass murder" or "massacre," and "terror" overlap and are sometimes used interchangeably. Clearly, a concept was needed that includes all intentional government killing in cold blood and that is comparable to the concept of murder for *private* killing.

The killing of one person by another is murder whether done because the victim was of a particular color, refused to repay a loan, or hurled an insult. It is murder whether the killing was a premeditated act or the result of reckless and wanton disregard for life. It doesn't matter whether the killing is done for high moral ends, altruistic reasons, or any other purpose. Killing is murder under Western and most other legal codes (unless officially authorized by government, as for judicial executions or military combat). However, as a crime, murder is limited by definition to the taking of another's life in some way. Although we use murder metaphorically, as in someone "murdering" the language, it is not considered murder in a criminal sense to hurt someone psychologically, to steal their child, or to rob them of their culture.

I thus offer, as a concept analogous to public murder, the concept of democide, or murder by government agents acting authoritatively, Its one root is the Greek *demos*, or people; the other is the same as for genocide, which is from the Latin *caedere*, to kill. Democide's necessary and sufficient meaning is the intentional government killing of an unarmed person or people. Unlike the concept of genocide, *it is restricted to intentional killing of people* and does not extend to attempts to eliminate cultures, races, or peoples by other means. Moreover, democide is not limited to the killing component of genocide, nor to politicide, mass murder, massacre, or terror. It includes them all and also what they exclude, as long as the killing is a purposive act, policy, process, or institution of government. In detail, *democide* is any action by government:

(1) designed to kill or cause the death of people
    (1.1) because of their religion, race, language, ethnicity, national

origin, class, politics, speech, actions construed as opposing the government or wrecking social policy, or by virtue of their relationship to such people;

(1.2) in order to fulfill a quota or requisition system;

(1.3) in furtherance of a system of forced labor or enslavement;

(1.4) by massacre;

(1.5) through imposition of lethal living conditions; or

(1.6) by directly targeting noncombatants during a war or violent conflict, or

(2) that causes death by virtue of an intentionally or knowingly reckless and depraved disregard for life (which constitutes *practical* intentionality), as in

(2.1) deadly prison, concentration camp, forced labor, prisoner of war, or recruit camp conditions;

(2.2) murderous medical or scientific experiments on humans;

(2.3) torture or beatings;

(2.4) encouraged or condoned murder, or rape, looting, and pillage during which people are killed;

(2.5) a famine or epidemic during which government authorities withhold aid, or knowingly act in a way to make it more deadly; or

(2.6) forced deportations and expulsions causing deaths.

This definition has the following qualifications and clarifications.

(a) "Government" includes de facto governance — as by the Communist Party of the People's Republic of China — or by a rebel or warlord army over a region and population it has conquered — as by the brief rule of Moslem Turks (East Turkistan Republic) over part of Sinkiang province (1944–46).

(b) "Action by governments" comprises official or authoritative action by government officials, including the police, military, or secret service; or nongovernmental action (e.g., by brigands, press-gangs, or secret societies) that has or is receiving government approval, aid, or acceptance.

(c) Clause 1.1 includes, for example, directly targeting noncombatants during a war or violent conflict out of hatred or revenge, or to depopulate an enemy region, or to terrorize civilians into urging surrender. Concrete examples of such instances could include indiscriminate urban bombing or shelling, or blockades that cause mass starvation.

(d)   "Relationship to such people" (clause 1.1) includes relatives, colleagues, coworkers, teachers, and students.

(e)   "Massacre" (clause 1.4) includes the mass killing of prisoners of war and of captured rebels.

(f)   "Quota" system (clause 1.3) includes randomly selecting people for execution in order to meet a quota; or arresting people according to a quota, some of whom are then executed.

(g)   "Requisition" system (clause 1.3) includes taking from peasants or farmers all their food and produce, leaving them to starve to death.

(h)   Excluded from the definition are:

(h.1)   execution for what are internationally considered capital crimes, such as murder, rape, spying, treason, and the like, so long as evidence does not exist that such allegations were invented by the government in order to execute the accused;

(h.2)   actions taken against armed civilians during mob action or riot (e.g., killing people with weapons in their hands is not democide); and

(h.3)   the death of noncombatants killed during attacks on military targets, so long as the primary target is military (e.g., during bombing of enemy logistics).

Table 2.1 gives an overview of the concept of democide in relation to the other concepts mentioned previously and placing them within the context of democidal sources of mass death.

Democide is meant to define the killing by government, just as the concept of murder defines individual killing in domestic society. Here, intentionality (premeditation) is critical, including *practical* intentionality. If a government causes deaths through a reckless and depraved indifference to human life, the deaths are as though intended. If through neglect a mother lets her baby die of malnutrition, this is murder. If we imprison a girl in our home, force her to do exhausting work throughout the day, not even minimally feed and clothe her, and watch her gradually die a little each day without helping her, then her

TABLE 2.1
Sources of Mass Death

Intentional
   War
      international /domestic

Democide
   genocide
      Nazi killing of Jews or Gypsies
      Khmer Rouge killing of Vietnamese
      Soviet killing of Volga Germans
   politicide
      Hitler's 1934 purge of the SA
      Viet Minh murder of nationalists
      Libya bombing of a civilian airliner
   mass murder/massacre
      Nazi reprisals in Yugoslavia
      Vietnamese murder by quota
      Japanese rape of Nanking
   terror
      Guatemala death squads
      Stalin's 1936–38 purge of communists
      Argentina's disappearances

Unintentional
   Famine
      by nature
         China's 1936 famine
      government created [a]
         China's 1959–62 Great Famine
   Disease
      by nature
         1918 influenza pandemic
      government created[a]
         Soviet 1918–23 typhus epidemic
   Disaster
      storm
      earthquake
      fire
      etc.

a Intentionally man-made famine or disease is included under democide and may constitute genocide, politicide, or mass murder.

inevitable death is not only our fault but our practical intention. It is murder. A parallel can be made with the Soviet government's transport of political prisoners to labor camps, during which hundreds of thousands of them died at the hands of criminals or guards, or from heat, cold, and inadequate food and water. Although not intended (indeed, this deprived the regime of their labor), the deaths were still public murder. It was democide.

Moreover, when conceptually there is not a clear domestic analog to murder, as in the indiscriminate bombing of urban areas, I have tried to follow the Geneva Conventions and Protocols.[7] Killing helpless people in time of war, or military action in breach of the Geneva agreements, is a violation of the international law they codify and is ipso facto democide. Therefore, the forced detention of prisoners of war under conditions that cause their death is democide, as is death caused by medical experimentation on them. Bombing, shelling, or bombarding civilians indiscriminately is also democide, as is the forced removal of all foodstuff in occupied areas that causes the death of the inhabitants from starvation. Similarly, food blockades that cause the indiscriminate death of civilians is democide, as was the largely British blockade of the Central Powers during and after World War I. As Article 14 to Protocol II of the Geneva Conventions affirms: "Starvation of civilians as a method of combat is prohibited."[8]

I have to again be absolutely clear on the meaning of democide since so much of the democide that I describe in subsequent chapters takes place in time of war. War-related killing by military forces that international agreements and treaties directly or by implication prohibit is democide, whether the parties to the killing are signatories to the agreements and treaties or not. Killing that is explicitly permitted is not democide. Thus, the death of civilians during the bombing of munitions plants in World War II was not democide. Nor is the death of civilians democide when, because of navigation or bombing errors or the malfunction of equipment, bombs land on a school or hospital, unless it is clear that the bombing was carried out recklessly in spite of a high risk to such civilian buildings. Nor is the death of civilians democide when these deaths have occurred in a bombed village beneath which have been built enemy bunkers. Nor is democide the death of civilians caught in a cross fire between enemy soldiers, or while willingly helping troops haul supplies or weapons.

Seldom is it easy to distinguish between democide in time of war and war deaths. War deaths comprise those who are killed in battle or from battle-related disease and famine. Deaths from democide are those victims (which may include the military, as when POWs are massacred) of wartime killing, that has been internationally prohibited — what may be called war crimes, or crimes against humanity.

What then about the U.S. firebombing of Tokyo or atomic bombing of Hiroshima and Nagasaki during World War II? I recently received a letter from a colleague who was distressed that I would count deaths from such raids as U.S. democide. I discuss this to some extent in *Statistics of Democide*, but here I might note that these attacks constituted indiscriminate civilian bombing and would thus be by Article 48 to Protocol I of the Geneva conventions unlawful. The Article reads:

> In order to ensure respect for and protection of the civilian population and civilian objects, the Parties to the conflict shall at all times distinguish between the civilian population and combatants and between civilian objects and military objectives and accordingly shall direct their operations only against military objectives.[9]

Article 51 makes the meaning of this more specific:

> Indiscriminate attacks are prohibited. Indiscriminate attacks are:
>
> (a) those which are not directed at a specific military objective;
>
> (b) those which employ a method or means of combat which cannot be directed at a specific military objective; or
>
> (c) those which employ a method or means of combat the effects of which cannot be limited as required by this Protocol; and consequently, in each such case, are of a nature to strike military objectives and civilians or civilian objects without distinction.[10]

And still more specifically:

> Among others, the following types of attacks are to be considered as indiscriminate:
>
> (a) an attack by bombardment by any methods or means which treats as a single military objective a number of clearly separated and distinct military objectives located in a city, town, village or other area containing a similar concentration of civilians or civilian objects.[11]

Pulling all this together, a death constitutes democide if it is the intentional killing of an unarmed or disarmed person by government agents acting in their authoritative capacity and pursuant to government policy or high command (as in the Nazi gassing of the Jews). It is also democide if the death was the result of such authoritative government actions carried out with reckless and wanton disregard for the lives of those affected (as putting people in concentration camps in which the forced labor and starvation rations were such as to cause the death of inmates). It is democide if government promoted or turned a blind eye to the death even though it was murder carried out "unofficially" or by private groups (as by death squads in Guatemala or El Salvador). And the death also may be democide if high government officials purposely allowed conditions to continue that were causing mass deaths and issued no public warning (as in the Ethiopian famines of the 1970s). All extrajudicial or summary executions comprise democide. Even judicial executions may be democide, as in the Soviet show trials of the late 1930s. Judicial executions for "crimes" internationally considered trivial or noncapital — as of peasants picking up grain at the edge of a collective's fields, of a worker telling an antigovernment joke, or of an engineer making a miscalculation — are also democide.

I have found that in the vast majority of events and episodes, democide is unambiguous. When under the command of higher authorities soldiers force villagers into a field and then machine-gun them, there should be no question about definition. When a group armed by the government for this purpose turns the teachers and students out of school, lines up those of a particular tribe, and shoots them, it is surely democide. When all foodstuffs are systematically removed from a region by government authorities and a food blockade put in place, the resulting deaths must be considered democide. Sad to say, *most cases of government killing in this century are that clear*. The number of deaths will be hazy for many of these cases; the perpetrators and intent will not.

Notes

1. Lemkin 1944, 79.
2. See, for example, Fein 1984, Kuper 1981, and Porter 1982.
3. See, for example, Chalk and Jonassohn 1988 and Charny 1991.
4. See Stannard 1992.
5. See Harff and Gurr 1988.
6. Solzhenitsyn 1973.
7. On these I have found the commentaries in Bothe, Partsch, and Solf 1982 particularly useful.
8. Ibid., 1982, 679.
9. Ibid., 1982, 280–81.
10. Ibid., 297.
11. Ibid.

3

Over 133,147,000 Murdered
Pre-Twentieth-Century Democide

> *Agamemnon: "My dear Menelaus, why are you so chary of taking men's lives? Did the Trojans treat you as handsomely as that when they stayed in your house? No; we are not going to leave a single one of them alive, down to the babies in their mothers' wombs — not even they must live. The whole people must be wiped out of existence, and none be left to think of them and shed a tear."*
>
> —Homer, *Iliad*

The mass murder by emperors, kings, sultans, khans, presidents, governors, generals, and other such rulers of their own citizens or of those under their protection or control is very much part of our history. In ancient times, captured cities or towns would be pillaged and their inhabitants massacred; whole lands would be turned into regions of ruins and skeletons. Even the Hebrews, according the Bible, put to the sword those they conquered. It was the Assyrians, however, whose reputation would be transmitted down the ages as one of particular savagery. They would reward their soldiers for every severed head they brought in from the field, whether enemy fighters or not. They would decapitate or club to death captured soldiers; they would slice off the ears, noses, hands and feet of nobles, throw them from high towers, flay them and their children to death, or roast them over a slow fire. Consider what one historian writes about the capture of Damascus by King Sargon of Assyria.

> Sargon had the defeated king of Damascus burned alive before his eyes. The wives and daughters of the captured king were destined for the Assyrian harems and those who were not of noble blood were condemned to slavery. Meanwhile the soldiery had been massacring the population, and brought the heads of their victims into the king's presence, where they were counted up by the scribes. Not all the male prisoners were put to death, for the boys and craftsmen were led into captivity, where they would be assigned to the hardest tasks on the royal building projects, where the swamps which cover so much of Mesopotamia must have caused an enormously high rate of mortality. The remainder of the population were uprooted and sent to the other end of the Empire.[1]

But such barbarity not only happened in classical times. After the capture of Bram in 1210, the Albigensian Crusaders, Christians all, took 100 of the captured soldiers and gouged out their eyes, cut off their noses and upper lips, and had them led by a one-eyed man to Cabaret, yet to be attacked.[2] This was done to terrorize Cabaret into immediate surrender.

Genocide, massacre, and human slaughter; pillage, rape, and torture have been much more common than war and revolution. But historians ordinarily do not dwell on such events. And even the few that do very rarely attach numbers to them. They prefer the glamour of war, of diplomacy, of the clash of nations and personalities. In revenge for an arrow from Nishapur's walls that killed Jinghiz Khan's son-in-law in 1221, when the city was finally captured, the Mongol Tolui massacred its unarmed inhabitants.[3] This ancient capital of Khorassan in Persia was then a "scene of a carnival of blood scarcely surpassed even in Mongol annals.... [S]eparate piles of heads of men, women, and children were built into pyramids; and even cats and dogs were killed in the streets."[4] An utterly fantastic 1,747,000 human beings reportedly were slaughtered, a number exceeding the contemporary population of Hawaii, Rhode Island, or New Hampshire; a number that is around a *third* of the total Jews murdered by Hitler.[5] This possibly world-record massacre is only a fugitive datum, unrecorded in most histories. It is the magnificence of Jinghiz Khan, the court intrigues, the great Mongol conquests, and their eventual threat to Europe that is drama. And while some other great massacres, such as those of the Crusaders, do get some attention, it is only as a small part of the larger doings of kings, dukes, and sultans. It is hard for Western historians to ignore, for example, the alleged 40,000 to possibly even over 70,000 men, women, and children that were butchered after the Christian Crusaders took Jerusalem in 1099.[6] Yet I know of no study that focuses on this massacre by itself; or even a chapter in a book.

Surely one may point out that such killings were then the stuff of war and thus not of interest apart from war, no more than is a particular bloody battle. But some battles have been the focus of much historical interest. Who has not read in detail about the battle of Thermopylae pass in 480 B.C, where a small Greek force held out to the last man for three days against an invading Persian army. In truth, massacres are simply not of great interest. They are horrible, despicable, loathsome acts of the state or its agents. They are outright mass murder. And, apparently say the historians, it is best not to dwell on them.[7]

Those cases of mass murder for which historians do estimate the toll are only a small number of those mentioned in the literature. Historians will note, for example, that "40 cities and towns were sacked and all inhabitants massacred in the conquest," or "the city was finally taken and all killed;" or being specifically unspecific: "The scene of desolation that must have presented itself in the northern borderland of Persia at this time is terrible. From the banks of the Oxus to Asterabad every town of any importance was reduced to ruins, and its inhabitants slaughtered [by the Mongols]."[8]

There are other cases of mass killing that are beyond belief, but for which specific numbers are unrecorded. For example, it is written that in the twelfth and thirteenth centuries the Sultan of Delhi, Kutb-d Din Aibak, slaughtered his subjects by the hundreds of thousands,[9] which at least gives us an order of magnitude. But one can only guess at the many thousands murdered by Sultan Muhammad bin Tughlak, who, according to a Moslem historian, slaughtered Hindus such that "there was constantly in front of his royal pavilion and his Civil Court a mound of dead bodies and a heap of corpses, while the sweepers and executioners were wearied out by their work of dragging" the poor souls "and putting them to death in crowds."[10] Then there was the worldwide, day-by-day democide. Without any historical notice, people must have been murdered in small groups, put in prisons and dungeons to waste sway, slaughtered by whole families in the countryside. In the full run of written human history, individual farmers or common folk running athwart officials, knights, samurai, nobles, soldiers, and the like, on the roads or in the towns, were simply decapitated, run through, or raped and killed, surely totaling in the millions over the centuries.

In any case, we can make note of the various institutions, revolutions, wars, empires, states, and social patterns through or by which people have been murdered en masse. One such is slavery. Until modern times slavery was almost universal, and in most parts of the world the slave's life was wholly dependent upon the master. But even before being sold, millions of people were killed while being pressed into legal slavery — during slave raids, transportation on slave ships, and overland convoys — or they died from associated deprivation and disease. In the sixteenth to nineteenth centuries alone the death toll among African slaves being transported to the New World may have been over 1,500,000,[11] possibly 2 million.[12] Millions more died in capture and in transit to the Orient or Middle East. And just among those kept in Africa some 4 million may have died.[13] Overall, in five centuries, Europeans, Arabs, Asians, and African slave traders possibly murdered nearly 17 million Africans; perhaps even over 65 million.[14] I am sure that this total only partly excavates such cold-blooded, government-approved or -committed bloodletting known as slavery.

But slavery was just one of many historical institutions through which people were murdered en mass. Another was the massacre. The most noted of these have been committed by armies during crusades, war, or conquest. It was not rare for armies to butcher tens of thousands of unarmed men, women, and children in captured towns and the neighboring countryside. In this the Mongol armies have had no peers. I mentioned the 1,747,000 people possibly killed in

Nishapur. In 1219 Jinghiz Kahn's army captured Bokhara and allegedly murdered 30,000; another 30,000 were murdered in captured Samarkand.[15] In 1221 a Mongol army seized Merv and reportedly took 13 days to slaughter 1,300,000 inhabitants[16] Historians also record that in 1220 the Mongols killed 50,000 in Kazvin after it was captured,[17] 70,000 in Nessa, and a similar number in Sebzevar.[18]

It is written that in 1221, the Mongol Tului slew 700,000 to 1,300,000 people in Meru Chahjan, one of the four main cities of Khorassan in the Northern borderland of Persia. Upon capture the inhabitants were made to evacuate the city, a four-day task. Then they were distributed among the Mongols and massacred. It took 13 days to count corpses. Among those who hid from the massacre, 5,000 were killed by Mongol detachments when they later emerged.[19]

Also, the entire population of Rayy, a city with 3,000 mosques, was slaughtered.[20] Herat was later captured, but only some 12,000 soldiers and their dependents were killed. However, after the inhabitants later rebelled, Jinghiz Khan angrily sent his general Noyan against them. The city was recaptured and it took a whole week to burn it down and murder its estimated 1,600,000 people. Many thousands escaped, but Noyan later sought and killed over 2,000 of them.[21] Then in 1226–33 there was the nearly total extermination — truly a genocide — of the Tanguts and their kingdom of Hsi-Hsia in China (in the province of Kansu). The Tanguts would not supply horses or auxiliaries for Jinghiz Khan's war against Khwarizmian. This was insolence that could not be tolerated. After winning the war he then turned with vengeance on the Tanguts. But as the campaign began he was thrown from his horse and seriously injured. Even then he would not stop the campaign, pledging that even "if it means my death I will exterminate them!"[22] At his command and with sheer slaughter as its ultimate goal, the Tanguts were defeated in one battle after another and pursued. According to a Mongol bard, "To escape the Mongol sword, the inhabitants in vain hid in the mountains ... or, if that were not possible, in caves. Scarcely one or two in a hundred succeeded. The Fields were covered with human bones."[23] Upon finally defeating the Tangut chief and driving him into the mountains, the bard continues, Jinghiz Khan

> seized from him his tents, his treasure-laden camels, all his people, till all this was scattered as so much ash. Tanguts of an age to bear arms he had

slaughtered, the lords being first to die.... [As to the rest, he left these orders for his soldiers:] As many Tanguts as you can take are yours to do as you please with.[24]

When in 1233 the last Tangut capital, Ning-hsia, fell to the Mongols, as willed by the dying Jinghiz before his death, all defenders were killed to the last generation. "The Conqueror of the world had for his funeral rites the massacre of an entire people."[25]

The Mongols subsequently invaded what is Iraq and in 1258 the Mongol Khulagu captured Baghdad, sacked and burned the city, including most mosques, and reportedly annihilated 800,000 of its people.[26] For good reason, as all this horrible killing of helpless people shows, have the Mongols become justly known for their bloody conquests and disregard of life. As the historian of the Mongols J. J. Saunders points out, there was

> something indescribably revolting in the cold savagery with which the Mongols carried out their massacres. The inhabitants of a doomed town were obliged to assemble in a plain outside the walls, and each Mongol trooper, armed with battle-axe, was told to kill so many people, ten, twenty or fifty. As proof that orders had been properly obeyed, the killers were sometimes required to cut off an ear from each victim, collect the ears in sacks, and bring them to their officers to be counted. A few days after the massacre, troops were sent back into the ruined city to search for any poor wretches who might be hiding in holes or cellars; these were dragged out and slain.[27]

Such horrible mass murder was part of their strategy. They wanted to so terrorize those in their path of conquest that cities and nations would immediately surrender when the first armed Mongols were seen in the distance. Better to bow and acknowledge a new lord than chance fighting, losing, and everyone dying.

Even well over a century after Jinghiz Khan's death, the Mongols still were engaged in conquest, spreading destruction and death from one part of Asia to another. Tamerlane (or Timur Lenk), a Turk who proclaimed himself restorer of the Mongol Empire,

> razed Isfarā'in to the ground in A.D. 1381; built 2,000 prisoners into a living mound and then bricked them over at Sabsawār in 1383; piled 5,000 human heads into minarets at Zirih in the same year; cast his Luri

prisoners alive over precipices in 1386; massacred 70,000 people and piled the heads of the slain into minarets at Isfahan in 1387; ... buried alive 4,000 Christian soldiers of the garrison of Sivas after their capitulation in 1400; and built twenty towers of skulls in Syria in 1400 and 1401.[28]

As best I can figure from such accounts, and recognizing that at best they all are the roughest approximations, the Mongol khans and their successors and pretenders possibly slaughtered around 30 million Persian, Arab, Hindu, Russian, Chinese, European, and other men, women, and children.[29] As incredible as this huge estimate seems, that it gives some indication of the sheer human cost of Mongol conquest can be inferred just from Khubilai Khan's rule over China. According to a Chinese writer, "in gaining and maintaining his throne [he] slaughtered more than 18,470,000 Chinese."[30] Given the contemporary Mongol census of almost 58,834,711 people,[31] from 1252, when Khubilai was granted full power over the Eastern Mongol Empire, through his conquest of all of China in 1279 and to his death in 1294 — for two generations — he killed something like 1 out of every 137 Chinese *each year*. Even if the figures are highly exaggerated, which is probable, and he annually killed 1 out of 1,000, the inhumane barbarity would be no less.

While the Mongol Khans may have established a historical record for individual massacres, surely various Chinese Emperors were in the same league. Observe the bacchanalia of blood by Chang Hsien-chung when, near the end of the Ming Dynasty in 1644, he conquered Szechwan province and in Chengtu declared himself emperor of the Great Western Kingdom. The Chinese chronicles say that when the scholars rejected his imperial claim he immediately had them all massacred. Then

> he set about destroying all the merchants, then all the women and all the officials. Finally he ordered his own soldiers to kill each other. He ordered the feet of the officers' wives to be cut off and made a mound of-them, and at the top of the mound he placed the feet of his favorite concubines. For some reason he was obsessed with ears and feet, and since it was too much trouble to bring the bodies of the villagers who lived in remote outlying districts to Chengtu, he ordered his private guards to bring him their ears and feet, and he carefully counted them. When the massacre was over, he ordered that there should be placed in a prominent position in Chengtu an inscription carved in stone, reading:

> Heaven brings forth innumerable things to help man.
> Man has nothing with which to recompense Heaven.
> Kill. Kill. Kill. Kill. Kill. Kill. Kill.[32]

Even the great emperor who unified China and gave it his name, Qin (pronounced Chin) Shihuang, buried alive 346 scholars in order to discourage opposition.[33] Burying people alive seems to have been a favorite murder weapon of Chinese rulers and emperors. For example, when the ruler of the Wei kingdom (Zaozao) conquered Xuzhou, "he buried alive several dozens thousands civilians."[34]

As one Chinese dynasty was taken over from another, there was a tremendous loss of life from war, mass murder, and associated hardship, famine, and disease. This can be seen from the resulting steep declines in population — really demographic catastrophes proportionally akin to that which took place in Cambodia in 1975–79 with the takeover by the bloody Khmer Rouge. Consider that

> in the eight years that the Han Dynasty was being replaced by the Qin Dynasty [221–207 B.C.], the population of China decreased from 20 million to 10 million.
> …
> In the Dong (Eastern) Han Dynasty [206 B.C.–220 A.D.], the population of China was 50 million. After the transition of power to the Three Kingdom period [222–589], the population decreased to 7 million.
> …
> In the Sui Dynasty [581–618], the population of China was 50 million. After the transfer of power to the Tang Dynasty [618–907], only one third was left.
> …
> At the peak of the Song Dynasty [960–1279] the population was about 100 million. But in the beginning of the Qing Dynasty in 1655, the population was 14,033,900. During the 20-year period from 1626 to 1655, the population decreased from 51,655,459 to 14,033,900.[35]

Some sense of the pure slaughter underlying these population collapses can be had from more recent massacres. For example, in just the one year 1681, for just the Triad Rebellion, in merely the one province of Kwangtung, with the rebellious defeated, "some 700,000 people [were] executed." Eventually the province was almost depopulated.[36]

The sanctity of life did not increase with time. During the last century, over some fifteen years, the Teiping Rebellion cost possibly "tens of millions" of lives,[37] maybe even as many as 40 million.[38] Some 600 cities were "ruined."[39] Because the rebellion began in the province of Kwangsi, imperial forces allowed no rebels speaking the local dialect to surrender. All were slaughtered.[40] Indeed, massacre on both sides of the conflict during this and the almost concurrent Nein Rebellion was general. For one county in the province of Anhwei, for example, local scholars lamented that out of a population of 300,000 Chinese, "By the time the rebels were cleared only a little over 6,000 survived. This is a catastrophe unique for the locality since the beginning of the human race."[41] Overall, 70 percent of the province's population were killed or died.[42]

When the Taiping rebels captured Nanking in 1853, they killed all the Tartars garrisoning the city. But this was not enough. They also murdered all Tartar family members. In total, about 25,000 people may have been wiped out.[43] When imperial troops recaptured Nanking the following year, they in turn allegedly exterminated about 100,000 rebels, and in just three days.[44]

Imperial troops followed the same quick and bloody policy in Canton and along the Pearl River: After they recaptured this area from the rebels, they are said to have beheaded 700 to 800 inhabitants a day, whether rebel collaborator or not, ultimately killing another 100,000 people. Just in the province of Kwangtung, it is written that 1 million were executed.[45] This is more than the total number of Americans killed in all the civil and international wars the United States has fought in its whole history, including the War of Independence.

But there is more. There also was the nearly concurrent Moslem uprisings with their attendant slaughter. For the province of Yunnan, 5 million out of 8 million may have died. When the last Muslim stronghold fell to imperial forces, 20,000 men, women, and children were "put to the sword."[46] In Shensi province the population fell from 700,000 or 800,000 Moslems to between 20,000 and 30,000 in ten years. Even most of the 50,000 to 60,000 Moslems that fled to Kansu province perished. All told, still a much larger number of Chinese were massacred by Moslem rebels or otherwise died.[47]

The number of Chinese and their subjects so murdered down through the centuries must be in the tens of millions, even excluding the Mongol carnage. Putting together estimates of population declines and massacres, I guess that roughly 34 million Chinese and their subjects were killed in cold blood. It is not inconceivable that this historical democide might have even exceeded 90 million dead.[48]

In massacre and generalized killing, other nations have made their own very bloody contributions to our history. When the Ottoman Mohammed II laid siege to and finally took Constantinople in 1452, he massacred thousands.[49] Sixteen-century Sultan Selum (The Grim), father of Süleyman, whose campaign diary will be quoted below, killed his father, two brothers, many nephews, sixty-two other relatives, and seven grand viziers during his eight-year rule. It is said that he inaugurated this bloody reign by slaughtering 40,000 Turkish Shi'ites.[50]

In destroying whole populations and in the pursuit and accomplishment of mass murder, Europeans were no better. In 1527 the army of Tirolese condottiere Frunsberg and Charles, Duke of Bourbin, captured and sacked Rome. Historians record that at a minimum 2,000 corpses were thrown into the Tiber river and 9,800 dead buried;[51] many more were killed. During the Thirty Years' War, the Count of Tilly and Count zu Pappenheim may have massacred as many as 30,000 inhabitants of Magdeburg when the city fell to them after a six-month siege.[52] Magdeburg was only one of numerous massacres of this very destructive war.

But probably a greater number of common folk died when towns and farms in the path of invading or marauding armies were pillaged and families killed. Moreover, many died from famine and disease caused by passing armies. The German Empire alone may have lost more than 7,500,000 people in the Thirty Years' War,[53] most doubtless perishing from such causes. The population of Bohemia was reduced from around 4 million to possibly no more than 800,000.[54] Putting a number of such figures together, I estimate that in this war alone from 2 million to over 11 million people were probably murdered[55] — that aside from combat and nondemocidal famine and disease.[56]

And the Crusades of the Middle Ages should not be ignored. In the aforementioned 1099 sack of Jerusalem, in addition to the 40,000 to over 70,000 Moslems that may have been butchered, the Crusaders herded surviving Jews into a synagogue and burned them alive.[57] Interestingly, in light of the Mongol and Chinese hecatombs, this massacre of unarmed Moslems and Jews "has long been reckoned among the greatest crimes of history."[58] In 1209, the Albigensian Crusaders also slaughtered some 15,000 to 60,000 inhabitants of Béziers, after which the city was plundered and burned.[59] And in 1236, when the Jews of Anjou and Poitou refused to be forcibly baptized, the Crusaders reportedly trampled 3,000 of them to death with their horses.[60]

That such killing is done by armies during war, crusades, or conquest should not mitigate the responsibility of governments. Often the heads of governments have led their armies. Generals have sometimes been rewarded for their bloody deeds, and in any case, not punished. Governments have generally accepted the fruits of their military victories, not excluding the riches of wealthy cities that were sacked, no matter the human cost in innocent lives. That such killing was traditional or customary, served a military purpose (removing an enemy population from the rear; creating terror and fear among populations in the line of advance), gave incentive to the troops (rape and booty in the offing), or enriched the state, should not lessen in our eyes the monstrous immorality of this killing.

Besides the siege-take-and-massacre of war or conquest, there is generalized murder in or after rebellions or revolutions. Here the responsibility of government is more direct. We have already seen much of this in the Teiping and Moslem rebellions in China. History is full of other examples, such as the 1876 Bulgarian rebellion against the Ottoman Empire that was brutally suppressed by the Sultan: about 60 villages were destroyed, and 12,000 to 15,000 massacred. In one reported incident, a church was set ablaze to burn alive the 1,200 people who had gathered inside for protection.[61] From 1567 to 1573, the Duke of Alba (representative to the Low Countries of Philip II, King of Spain) tortured to death and otherwise killed 18,000 Protestants to maintain order, or so it is said.[62]

One of the best-publicized historical democides is that of the Great Terror of 1793–94 in revolutionary France. The Revolutionary Tribunal and its equivalent in the provinces may have executed up to 20,000 of the nobility, political opponents, and alleged traitors.[63] And. although often reported as a civil war, in fact a full-scale genocide was carried out in the Vendée in which possibly 117,000 inhabitants were indiscriminately murdered.[64]

ilar kind of massacre is that of scapegoats for major human
The presence of Jews in Christian Europe has always
provided an easy explanation for catastrophes like the plague. "Why
are people getting sick and dying en masse? Because the Jews are
poisoning the water." Jews everywhere were thus attacked during the
Black Death of 1347–52 that killed around 25 million Europeans.
Jews were massacred wholesale. For example, in Mainz, Germany,
6,000 were recorded killed; in Erfurt, 3,000 died. "By the end of the
plague, few Jews were left in Germany or the Low Countries."[65]

As already shown, mass murder is not confined to legitimate governments and their agents. Rebellious groups or nations sometimes
succeed in forming a temporary government and, as did the Teiping
rebels, use their power to slaughter civilians and massacre suspected
opponents. Although hardly significant in its scope, to an American one
of the more interesting of these is the Mountain Meadows Massacre by
the Mormons. To escape persecution by Gentiles, the Mormons fled
west to the Utah Territory and succeeded in turning it into a de facto,
independently governed theocracy. Seeking revenge for past wrongs
done them by Gentiles, and in a declared state of war against the federal
government, church leaders assembled Indian "confederates" to set up
an ambush at Mountain Meadows of a passing wagon train of twenty to
twenty-five prosperous immigrant families. During the resulting battle,
Mormon militia appeared, ostensibly to save the train from the Indians.
But after disarming the defenders by a ruse, they slaughtered 121 men,
women, and children. (Some escaped to tell the tale.)[66]

Then there are the colonial "peace-keeping" massacres of tribes or
primitive groups engaged in raiding or limited tribal warfare. One
example is an 1849 expedition sent out against certain native tribes of
the coast of Borneo. Under the direction of Sir James Brooke, British
Rajah of Sarawak, the expedition annihilated a force of Dyaks
allegedly returning from a piratical excursion against coastal tribes.
About 1,500 to 2,000 of them were killed by cannon shot, musket, and
grapeshot. This was simply wanton massacre of a native tribe engaged
in traditional, limited native warfare.[67]

Sometimes natives or offending groups were simply killed. An
extraordinary case of this was the Dutch orchestration of the massacre
of the Chinese in Jakarta (then Batavia). The Dutch first had the
Chinese confined

inside the walls of Batavia, stripping them of the smallest kitchen knife and putting them under a dusk-to-dawn curfew. The Dutch then distributed arms to what they themselves called "the low-class masses" and gave these "mobs" a free hand to massacre the helpless Chinese. The rapine inside Batavia was allowed to go on from the 9th to the 22nd of October, 1740. While the "mobs" were despatching Chinese lives inside Batavia, [Dutch East India Company] troops killed those who had fled from the city before the curfew and roamed in Batavia's environs.

At the end of the *"Grand Guignol"* inside Batavia, most sources agree, 10,000 city-Chinese lost their lives, but little is said about the many more who must have perished outside the city's walls. Of the 80,000-odd Chinese in Batavia's environs prior to the extermination only around 3,000 survived.

...

Finally, it is notable that the Dutch declared an open season on the Chinese all over Java. Governor General Valckenier mentioned that in June 1741 the Council of the Indies voted for a "general massacre of the Chinese over the whole of Java." Thus, 6 months after the first slaughter, a rerun took place in Semarang (Central Java). Likewise, "in other parts of Java the violence continued ... the Chinese of Soerabaia and Grisee [East Java] were also massacred."[68]

Not to be overlooked is the democide that is associated with the clash of civilizations, and in particularly the European conquest of the Americas. There is no ambiguity about the outright massacres that occurred, such as the Puritan killing of 500–600 Pequot Indians at Mystic Fort in 1637[69] and the French annihilation of perhaps 1,000 Nanchez Indians in the lower Mississippi after defeating them in 1731.[70] As everyone knows, such also occurred with postconquest expansions of national frontiers, as in the United States. Although cowboy and Indian movies leave the impression that Indians were massacred by the tens of thousands, actual body counts show that the numbers were really much smaller. To consider one notorious massacre, in 1864 citizen and military troops enlisted from the Colorado territory and led by Colonel John Chivington surrounded and surprised Cheyenne at Sand Creek in the Colorado Territory. Two-thirds of them women and children, the Indians tried to surrender and parley, but all were killed without mercy, their bodies scalped and mutilated. In total, from 70 to 600 were massacred, the latter the upper estimate of the Colonel; 130 killed seems closer to the truth. It was argued that this massacre did not reflect government policy, and it was the subject of army and congressional investigations. But other than Chivington resigning his commission, no one was punished.[71] Just to note the other most well known massacres by cavalry: at Washita, 103 Cheyenne were killed in 1868; in 1870, at Piegan Village, 173 Indians were killed; and at Wounded Knee in 1890, it was possibly 146 Sioux.[72] Also often cited is the Bear River Massacre of 1863 in which 250 Shoshoni were wiped out. This began as a battle between Indians and soldiers but degenerated into a slaughter of helpless and wounded Indians.[73]

While these were the largest American massacres, there undoubt-edly were numerous small ones. Moreover, many Indians were killed by vigilantes while local government looked the other way, or were murdered individually by settlers. Taking all the army-Indian battles and massacres into account, probably no more than some 3,000 Indi-ans were killed in the years 1789 to 1898. Settlers and vigilantes likely killed a thousand more. Since many of these Indians were killed in pitched battles, it seems very unlikely that the number of Indians mas-sacred outright by cavalry and settlers in the American West could have been more than 4,000, and was probably a good number less.[74] But this is not the whole story. Many Indians also died from barbarous mistreatment or conditions purposely forced upon them.

For example, there was the fate of the Californian Yuki Indians. Originally having a population of around 3,500, in a little more than thirty years its numbers fell to about 400 through "kidnapping, epidemics, starvation, vigilante justice, and state-sanctioned mass killing."[75] Moreover, there was the so-called Trail of Tears deaths. In the 1835 treaty of New Echota with the U.S. government, Cherokee leaders of a minority faction, and without the approval of the majority, agreed to the nation's moving out of Georgia to west of the Mississippi River. Although many prominent Americans publicly opposed such a deportation, in 1838 President Van Buren ordered the army to enforce the treaty. At gun point the Cherokees were thus made to trek west to Oklahoma in the winter of 1838–39. The resulting exposure and disease killed off nearly 25 percent of the tribe, or about 4,000 people.[76] While the Federal Government's responsibility is mitigated by the treaty, the cruelty of the enforcement amounts to indirect massacre. It was democide. Perhaps overall, considering these and other cases and including massacres, by 1900 some 10,000 to 25,000 Indians may have been killed.[77]

But these estimates are only a fraction of the overall democide among Indian inhabitants of all the Americas. Before the conquest of the New World, the Indian population may have numbered from 8 million to 110 million,[78] perhaps even 145 million.[79] A moderate population estimate consistent with the latest research is of 55 million Indians.[80] Almost totally as a result of several waves of disease carried to the Americas by the conquering and colonizing Europeans, the Indian population dropped steeply by tens of millions, even possibly by as much as 95 percent.[81] In Mexico alone, the Indian population may have fallen by 23 million to under 2 million.[82] Including those Indians who were killed in warfare and democide, perhaps 60 million to 80 million Indians of Central and South America and the Caribbean died as "a result of the European invasion."[83]

Judging what proportion of this mammoth toll constituted democide by the invading armies and colonists is hardly better than picking a number out of the air. No doubt there was much indiscriminate and outright murder. No doubt conditions were forcibly imposed on whole tribes and led to their rapid near extinction. No doubt large numbers of Indians died from inhumane treatment, especially under forced labor. And no doubt in some cases disease may have been knowingly spread.[84] But even Professor David Stannard, author of *American Holocaust*,[85] who clearly blames Europeans for many of these deaths, is unwilling to give even a rough approximation of the "genocide."[86] I found one overall estimate of 15 million Indians killed in what appears to be democide, but this figure is given without citation or elaboration.[87] In any case, judging by the bloody history of this period of colonization throughout the Americas, a democide of 2 million would seem a rough minimum and 15 million a maximum. Even if these figures are remotely true, this subjugation of the Americas is still one of the bloodier of the centuries-long, democides in world history.

Natives elsewhere were similarly mistreated and murdered. The Australian aborigine, for example, were massacred by soldiers and killed indiscriminately by settlers, often with actual or tacit government approval. In Tasmania alone, by 1832 as many as 700 out of an original population of 1,000 may have been killed.[88] In all of

Australia, the aboriginal population in 1788 was about 300,000, divided into about 500 tribes, each with a distinct dialect and culture. In the resulting frontier conflict with settlers during the eighteenth and nineteenth centuries, possible 20,000 or more aborigines were killed.[89]

The manner in which some of this killing was conducted is clear from the Burke Town correspondent's report in the Port Denison *Times* of 4 June 1868:

> I much regret to state that the blacks have become very troublesome about here lately. Within ten miles of this place they speared and cut steaks from the rumps of several horses. As soon as it was known, the Native Police, under Sub-Inspector Uhr, went out, and, I am informed, succeeded in shooting upwards of thirty blacks. No sooner was this done than a report came in that Mr. Cameroon had been murdered at Liddle and Hetzer's station.... Mr. Uhr went off immediately in that direction, and his success I hear was complete.... Everybody in the district is delighted with the wholesale slaughter dealt out by the native police, and thank Mr. Uhr for his energy in ridding the district of *fifty-nine* (59) myalls.[90]

Such killing of natives verges on genocide, and doubtless this was the intention of some settlers. In the 1868 massacre, the complicity of the Australian government is an open question. But the role of government in some other recorded genocidal massacres is clear. For example, I have already mentioned some acts of genocide, or attempts to liquidate in whole or in part, racial, religious, ethnic, or cultural groups, such as Sultan Tughlak's systematic slaughter of Hindus. It is recorded that in the twelfth or thirteenth century Sultan Firoz Shaw invaded Bengal and offered a reward for every Hindu head, subsequently paying for 180,000 of them. For another sultan — Sultan Ahmad Shah — whenever the number of Hindus killed in his territory *in one day* totaled 20,000, he celebrated with a three-day feast.[91]

Although not competing in numbers with those massacred in Asia and the Americas, Europeans had their share of such genocidal massacres. An illustrative case is the St. Bartholomew's Day Massacre. On 24 August 1572, either King Charles IX or his court unleashed a slaughter of French Calvinists that spread from Paris to the whole country. In this famous massacre, a contemporary Protestant estimated that 300,000 were killed; later estimates reduced this to 100,000, then 36,000.[92]

A more recent example of genocidal massacres took place in the Ottoman Empire. It was composed of diverse nations, which were often treated with great cruelty by the ruling Turks. The Turks' massacre of Bulgarians in 1876 has already been mentioned, but this was but one of many of their massacres of national groups. In 1822, they allegedly killed 50,000 Greeks, largely in Scio (Chios); 10,000 Nestorians and Armenians in Kurdistan in 1850; and 11,000 Maronites and Syrians in Lebanon and Damascus in 1860.[93] In 1894, Sultan Abdul Hamid, ruler of the Ottoman Empire, treated a refusal of Armenian mountaineers in the Sossoun district to pay a protection tribute to Kurdish chiefs as a rebellion and launched a nationwide campaign of terror against all Armenians. The Sultan is reported to have said that "the way to get rid of the Armenian question is to get rid of the Armenians."[94] This solution to the "Armenian Question" amounted to a partial genocide, and a warm-up for the near total genocide of the Armenians during World War I described in chapter 10. From 1894 to 1896 the Sultan carried out a systematic campaign of murder. Armenians would be burned alive in their own churches, shot or cut down in the streets as they fled Turkish mobs or troops, or dumped into harbors to drown. These were the lucky ones. Many were tortured, raped, or otherwise brutalized before being killed. Probably between 100,000 to over 300,000 Armenians were massacred.[95] When these killings are added to those by various Ottoman sultans through the centuries, the sultan regimes at the very least must have exterminated some 2 million Armenians, Bulgars, Serbs, Greeks, Turks, and other subjects.

Such massacres and genocides as those of the Mongols and Ottomans are episodic and usually discrete in time or place. But there are other types of government killing that are routine or ritualistic and, except for the more dramatic events, may simply involve a few people killed in cold blood here, a few there. Across the land and years these few accumulate to a colossal slaughter. Such was the Catholic Church's treatment of heretics, who were hunted and when allegedly found, tortured, burned at the stake, or left to die of privation and disease in dungeons. During the thirteenth-century Albigensian Crusade in France, for example, historians count 140 heretics burned to death at Minerva, 400 in Lavaur, 60 in Cassè, 183 in Montwimer, 210–15 at Montségur, and 80 in Barleiges.;[96] in the Roman arena at Verona, Italy, 200 heretics were burned at the stake.[97]

The Spanish Inquisition established in 1480 by King Ferdinand and Queen Isabella, and that was led from 1483 to 1498 by the Dominican monk de Torquemada, may have burned to death as many as 10,220 heretics in total; 125,000 possibly died from torture and privation in prison.[98] A secretary of the inquisition says that no more than 4,000 were burned to death altogether. But this number of heretics may have been so killed in Seville alone.[99] Perhaps a more realistic figure is that of the General Secretary of the Inquisition, who estimated that 8,800 people were killed by fire from 1480 to 1488, and from 1480 to 1808 the victims may have totaled 31,912.[100] During the most intensive years of the inquisition, about 500 people per year also may have been burned to death in the New World.[101] Note that many of these poor people were not simply killed. They died by a means

> which was carefully selected as among the most poignant that man can suffer. They were usually burnt alive. They were burnt alive not unfrequently by a slow fire. They were burnt alive after their constancy had been tried by the most excruciating agonies that minds fertile in torture could devise.[102]

The Catholic Church's attempt to so purge heretics had its counterpart in the Protestant Reformation's campaign against witches. Witches were believed to have sold their soul to the devil for magical powers. While the Salem witch trials of Massachusetts in 1692 give the impression that early Americans were particularly prone to this superstition, it was really in Europe, particularly in Germany and France, that the torture and killing of alleged witches was most prevalent. Under Calvin's government of Geneva in 1545, for example, thirty-four women were recorded burned or quartered for witchcraft. In the late years of the sixteenth century, witch hunts reached their peak. In some German cities, historians estimate that as many as 900 "witches" in a year were killed, often after agonizing torture to force out confessions; in some villages hardly a woman was left alive. In total, throughout Christendom more than 30,000 "witches" may have been killed;[103] Taking into account the routine nature of these killings, the final figure may be around 100,000.[104] It might even reach 500,000.[105]

Whether of heretics or witches, this was a religiously induced and ritualistic form of government killing. Witches were presumably allied with Satan; heretics presumably had defied or defiled God. Sacrifice is another religion-based form of killing that is government practiced or approved. As an appeasement of or offering to a deity, sacrifice has often been extravagant in the number of lives it has demanded. Just consider the Grand Custom in Dahomey: When a ruler died, hundreds, sometimes even thousands, of prisoners would be slain. In one of these ceremonies in 1727, as many as 4,000 were reported killed.[106] In addition, Dahomey had an Annual Custom during which 500 prisoners were sacrificed.[107] But these sacrifices were small stuff compared to those of the Aztecs in 1487: To inaugurate a new temple, prisoners were murdered by the thousands. The victims formed long lines along the main roads into the city while waiting to mount the central temple's steps to be forcibly laid on an alter. Then their breasts were cut open and their hearts torn out by one of the four sacrificers at work. A figure of 80,400 thus sacrificed in four days has been handed down, but Nigel Davies, the author of a foremost work, *Human Sacrifice*, rightly questions this number (by my calculations, if each sacrificer took just one minute to complete his bloody task, it would take nearly 14 days working 24 hours a day to kill this number) and even believes that 20,000 seems high.[108] The Aztecs conducted sacrifices as a matter of course and often accumulated the skulls of their victims on racks outside their cities. One conquistador wrote of a rack outside of Tenochtitlan with about 136,000 skulls. If the collection of skulls started in 1428, this was an average addition of 1,500 skulls per year.[109]

The Inca of Peru also made human sacrifices, but on a much smaller scale. These were usually associated with the accession or death of a king or some other high personage. Sacrifice might be made if such a person was severely ill. In the case of a ruler dying, his servants, court officials, favorites, and concubines would be killed. As many as 4,000 paid this price upon the death of the Inca Huayna Capac, for example.[110]

Government-administered or -permitted sacrifice is a vast historical dimension of the slaughtered innocents. Unlike the few recorded cases, as for the Aztecs and Dahomey, the number of unknown people decapitated, punctured, burned, sliced, stoned, beaten, or suffocated to death against their will to appease or glorify some deity, or celebrate or inaugurate some occasion or building, is uncounted, but must add up over the world and centuries to millions, if not tens of millions of dead. Even when cities or nations were faced with defeat in war, human sacrifices were made to appease the gods. Thus Carthage, besieged by the Roman army in 146 B.C., killed 200 sons of noble families as an offering to Baal.[111] The Scandinavians would try to stop a plague by burying children alive; the Incas would kill children four to six years old to prevent the emperor from getting sick, or to make him well were he to get sick. Across many cultures, adults or children would be interred under new buildings, city gates, or bridges.[112] In 1565, Rajah Narayana of Assam, India, celebrated a new temple by sacrificing 140 men, whose heads he offered on copper plates to Kali.[113] Hindu rites often involved sacrifice. For instance, a male child would be killed every Friday evening in the temple of Shiva at Tanjor.[114]

It is hard to find a tribe, kingdom, or ancient civilization that did not practice sacrifice of some sort. In my home state of Hawaii, well before colonization by the United States, people would be killed if the Hawaiian king got sick, and more would continue to be slain, sometimes twenty at a time, until he got well. If he died, then his household would be killed to keep him company in the next world. In building a royal canoe, a man would be killed at the base of the tree from which the wood was cut; another when it was finished; others at the launching ceremony.[115]

One kind of sacrifice must not go unmentioned, although it is virtually ignored in the literature. This is the sacrifice of colonial subjects through forced labor to satisfy private greed or state power. The work gangs of the twentieth-century gulags in the Soviet Union and communist China are not an invention of our era. In some form or another they have always existed, as has forced labor to discharge fraudulent debts or contracts; or by contract with the head of a tribe. All the European colonial powers seemed to have extorted labor from their subjects in Africa, Asia, and the New World through such devices. For the Spanish, German, and Portuguese subjects, this was particularly deadly. In some cases the average colonial plantation or estate laborer probably did not survive for more than a couple of years. It was sometimes easier or cheaper to "replenish the stock" than to provide health-maintaining food, clothing, medical care, and living quarters. I suspect that at a rock-bottom minimum, 10 million colonial forced laborers must have died thusly.[116] The true toll may have been several times this number.

This does not even weigh the human cost of the state's conventional forced labor — that of subjects compelled to man galleys, sail ships (as by the operation of press-gangs in British ports), carry supplies and weapons in time of war or rebellion, build pyramids, construct fortifications, or build roads, bridges, dams, canals, and the like. Indeed, the use of such forced labor, or corvée, has been traditional in Asia, even up to recent decades. Sometimes this labor served in lieu of taxes, where the subject was decreed to owe to the king or emperor or state a month or more of labor per year. While perhaps justifiable in theory, the practice often meant that overseers would execute the laborer that was too often late for work, slow on the job, sickly, or critical of the work. This treatment of their forced laborers — the whole Cambodian population — by the Khmer Rouge of our time, as described in chapter 9, mirrors that of many if not most regimes throughout history.

Yet another type of government killing whose victims may total millions is infanticide. In many cultures, government permitted, if not encouraged, the killing of handicapped or female infants or otherwise unwanted children. In the Greece of 200 B.C., for example, the murder of female infants was so common that among 6,000 families living in Delphi no more than 1 percent had two daughters.[117] Among 79 families, nearly as many had one child as two. Among all there were only 28 daughters to 118 sons.[118] Unwanted children

> were thrown into rivers, dung heaps, and cesspools. Wild animals were everywhere. Feeding upon children was part of their sustenance, as Euripides noted in his play *Ion*, "A prey for birds, food for wild beasts, too."
> ...
> Cities became deserted and the land became barren. Family life was disappearing.[119]

Indeed, the law demanded that imperfect children be killed; someone even wrote a text on *How to Recognize a Newborn That Is Worth Rearing*.[120]

But classical Greece was not unusual. In eighty-four societies spanning the Renaissance to our time, "defective" children have been killed in one-third of them.[121] In India, for example, because of Hindu beliefs and the rigid caste system, young girls were murdered as a matter of course. When demographic statistics were first collected in the nineteenth century, it was discovered that in "some villages, no girl babies were found at all; in a total of thirty others, there were 343 boys to 54 girls.... [I]n Bombay, the number of girls alive in 1834 was 603."[122] Instances of infanticide such as those occurring in India are usually singular events; they do not happen en masse. But the accumulation of such officially sanctioned or demanded murders comprises, in effect, serial massacre. Since such practices were so pervasive in some cultures, I suspect that the death toll from infanticide must exceed that from mass sacrifice and perhaps even outright mass murder.[123]

The death toll may be similarly high for official state executions for social or political reasons or, in our contemporary perspective, for trivial infractions, such as stealing bread or criticizing the royal garden. Consider that in London in the last eleven years of Henry the VIII's reign, there were some 560 executions per year — over one a day.[124] This was terribly excessive, even for the age. In contrast, note that the number executed by the Paris central criminal court from 1389 to 1392 was only 25 per year; the number of public executions in Brussels over the nearly two-century span between 1404 and 1600 was only slightly more than 5 per year.[125] On the other hand, King Henry VIII was probably outdone by many kings, emperors, and other rulers throughout the centuries. Historical statistics do not allow even a wild guess at an overall minimum number executed throughout the world for trivial or political offenses or as part of government terror. But note that a very low estimate of 1,000 executed per year would add up to 5 million killed in fifty centuries. Make this a possibly more realistic 10,000 such executions around the world per year and the pre-twentieth-century toll since Christ would be 19 million people killed by the state for trivial offenses.

Then there are the untold millions that have died in prison or other forms of detention from simple mistreatment, neglect, malnutrition, exposure, and preventable disease, as in the Soviet gulag. The inhumanity of France's penal colony called Devil's Island (in French Guiana) is well known. Less well known was the sometimes barbarous nature of the transportation of convicts to Australia by Britain —

sometimes a horrible voyage of as much as eight months. For one such fleet of convicts

> 267 died aboard and three vessels alone landed sick convicts of whom 124 died almost immediately. The dead were thrown naked into Sydney harbor. An army officer aboard, Cap Hill, pointed out that the masters of the transport ships, unlike slave captains, had no financial interest in landing their human cargo in healthy condition: "The slave traffic is merciful compared to what I have seen in this fleet." Evidence given to Parliament in 1812 showed that those transported included boys and girls of 12 and men and women over 80.[126]

Throughout history there has been the particularly lethal treatment of prisoners of war. If their lives were spared they were often sent to work as slaves in mines, on galley ships, in swamps, or at other labor that killed them off rapidly. The Mongols used their prisoners in the front ranks when attacking fortified cities and towns, and forced them to fill in moats or prepare catapults close to the dangerous walls. If not turned into slaves, prisoners of war were often simply killed, captured garrisons massacred. Thus the Crusaders killed 2,500 Moslem prisoners before Acra.[127] And the Turkic conqueror Tamerlane, whom we met previously in the context of his massacres of civilians and pyramids of severed heads, slaughtered 100,000 prisoners outside of Delhi. When Tamerlane

> advanced on Delhi after winning many victories and capturing a hundred thousand prisoners, it occurred to him that he had only to threaten to kill all his prisoners and the rulers of the city would capitulate. Unfortunately the ruse failed, and [Tamerlane] found himself in a position which he found distasteful, especially since most of the prisoners had already been given as slaves to his *amirs*, his officers, and the scholars who were in his retinue. He issued orders that all the prisoners [100,000 of them!] were to be strangled within an hour. A contemporary chronicler speaks of the repugnance felt by a scholar, who would not have voluntarily slain even a sheep, when he saw his fifteen slaves being strangled.[128]

Sixteenth-century Sultan Süleyman (The Magnificent), who extended the Ottoman Empire to its maximum power, left proof that his murder of thousands of prisoners was no more significant than the weather. Consider just one day in his words from his campaign diary:

"The emperor, seated on a golden throne, receives the homage of the viziers and the beys; massacre of 2,000 prisoners; the rain falls in torrents."[129]

Even in Europe, the slaughtering of captured garrisons has not been unusual even up to modern times. During the Thirty Years' War, for example, Count of Tilly captured Neubrandenburg in 1631 and allegedly killed a garrison of 3,000; the same year, Gustavus, King of Sweden, captured a garrison of 2,000 at Frankfurt an der Oder and killed all its members.[130] Death might come slowly, as prisoners were tortured and mutilated for amusement or to terrorize opposing armies and nations. Even among those Christian states that prided themselves on their humanity, prisoners of war were treated abominably. During the American Civil War, for example, Northern soldiers being held in the Southern prison of Andersonville over a six-month period in 1864 died at an annual rate of 79 percent. In total, 10,000 perished. Northern prisons were only a little better: For the whole war, their death rate for Southern prisoners of war was approximately 23 percent — about the same death rate as in the Soviet gulag.[131] Overall, 19,060 Southerners died. For both North and South, many of these deaths could have been avoided had proper food, clothing, and medical care been provided.

Finally, there is the killing that takes place on a ruler's whim. A pointed finger or slight nod, and some noble, attendant, concubine, or commoner is immediately grabbed and done away with. Two examples should suffice to clarify this type of government murder. During the British colonization of India, a "party given by the Mogul governor of Surat, the very first British settlement, was rudely interrupted when the host fell into a sudden rage and ordered all the dancing girls to be decapitated on the spot, to the stupefaction of his English guests."[132]

Shaka, the king of the African Zulus, was a similarly impulsive murderer. Those in attendance to him or in conference with him never knew when he might point them out for immediate death. No reason was ever given. One of the first white men to visit Shaka observed that

on the first day of our visit we had seen no less than ten men carried off to death. On a mere sign from Shaka, viz: the pointing of his finger, the victim would be seized by his nearest neighbors; his neck would be twisted, and his head and body beaten with sticks, the nobs of some of these being as large as a man's fist. On each succeeding day, too, numbers of others were killed; their bodies would then be carried to an adjoining hill and there impaled. We visited this spot on the fourth day. It was truly a Golgotha, swarming with hundreds of vultures.[133]

Of all this pre-twentieth-century killing — massacres, infanticide, executions, genocides, sacrifices, burnings, deaths by mistreatment, and the like — that to which we can put numbers adds up to a grand total of from nearly 89 million to slightly over 260 million men, women, and children. An appropriate mid-democide estimate might be around 133 million killed. The more exact total given by a variety of calculations is shown in table 3.1 along with the more extraordinarily bloody or interesting cases I have sketched above. To get some idea as to how far this total may be off, observe that if governments massacred people in previous centuries in the same proportion to world population as in our century, then as shown in the table's hypothetical total (calculated from the twentieth-century democide rate derived in subsequent chapters and the world's population for each century since 30 B.C.),[134] almost a fantastic 626 million people would have been killed, even possibly over 1,138 million — over a *billion* people. As should be clear, an estimated pre-twentieth-century democide of nearly 133 million cannot even approximate the actual number murdered by governments or their surrogates, and probably reflects only a small fraction of those so wiped out during the thousands of years of written history.

Whatever the true statistics, there is no need to know the actual number killed to see that government has been truly a cold-blooded mass murderer, a global plague of man's own making. While diseases may have killed more people in a shorter time (perhaps 25 million died from the Black Plague in Europe from 1348 to 1349),[135] government-committed, encouraged, or permitted murder has been a continuing year-by-year scourge up to and through the twentieth century.

Not even considered thus far is the human cost of war — another way governments act as an agent of death. For the years 1740 to 1897 there were reportedly 230 international and revolutionary wars; according to one count, these wars killed 20,154,000 people.[136] If with more tolerance for gross estimation we accept the calculations

TABLE 3.1
Selected Pre-Twentieth-Century Democide[a]

Case	Years [b]	Democide (000) [c]
In China	221 B.C.–19 C. A.D.	33,519 [d]
By Mongols	14 C–15 C	29,927
Slavery of Africans	1451–1870	17,267
Of American Indians	16 C–19 C	13,778
Thirty Years' War	1618–1648	5,750
In India	13 C–19 C	4,511 [e]
In Iran	5 C–19 C	2,000 [d,e]
In Ottoman Empire	12 C–19 C	2,000 [e]
In Japan	1570–19 C	1,500 [e]
In Russia	10 C–19 C	1,007 [e]
Christian Crusades	1095–1272	1,000
By Aztecs	Centuries	1,000 [f]
Spanish Inquisition	16 C–18 C	350
French Revolution	1793–94	263
Albigensian Crusade	1208–1249	200
Witch Hunts	15 C–17 C	100
Total for All Cases	pre–20 C	133,147
Hypothetical Total	30 C B.C.–19 C A.D.	625,716 [g]
International War-Related Dead	30 C B.C.–19C A.D.	40,457 [h]
Plague Dead (Black Death)	541 A.D.–1912	102,070 [i]

a From *Statistics of Democide*

b Unless otherwise noted, years and centuries are A.D.

c Unless otherwise noted, these are a best guess estimated in a low to high range

d Excludes democide in China by Mongols

e An absolute low

f A very speculative absolute low

g From *Statistics of Democide*. Calculated from the twentieth-century democide rate and the population for each century since 30 B.C.

h From *Statistics of Democide*. Total undoubtedly inflated by democide.

i A minimum. Includes plague dead in circa 541–542 A.D.; 1346–1771 in Europe; 1771 in Moscow; 1894 in Hong Kong; and 1898–1912 in India. From Duplaix 1988 (677–678).

that have been made of those killed in all international wars since 30 B.C., we get the 40,457,000 dead shown in table 3.1.[137] This is less than a third of the overall democide that we have been able to estimate. There should be little doubt that while pre-twentieth-century war has been of great historical interest and drama, governments have killed many times more people in cold blood than they have in the heat of battle. As noted in chapter 2, this is even true of our century. In any case, governments — particularly nondemocratic governments — clearly should come with a warning label: "This power may be a danger to your life and limb."

The question for this book is not whether such killing has continued into the twentieth century, which no informed reader could deny, but rather what form this killing has taken and what has been its toll. In answering this I want to be as precise as possible about the numbers. The better data available for our century should help to answer the what and particularly the why of such awful destruction of human life.

Notes

1. Contenau 1954, 148.
2. Oldenbourg 1961, 136.
3. Saunders 1971, 60–61.
4. Ibid., 61.
5 This toll for the massacre at Nishapur is reported by Durant 1950, 339; Saunders 1971, 241n. 6; Howorth 1965, 88; and Petrushevsky 1968, 485. Only Petrushevsky claims it an improbable figure. A massacre this large does seem numerically impossible, but consider this: The inhabitants of a captured city would often be divided among the Mongol soldiers for killing, possibly as many as several dozen or more to a man. Moreover, Mongol armies could be as large as 100,000 men or more, and the massacres might go on for weeks. Nonetheless, any such figures must be understood as simply suggestive of a possible order of magnitude.
6. Oldenbourg 1966, 140; Durant 1950, 591–92.
7. See *Statistics of Democide* for historical instances of massacres, mass murder, genocide, and other forms of democide mentioned in the literature and to which I could attach numbers.
8. Howorth 1965, 92.
9. Durant 1954, 463.
10. Ibid., 461.
11. Manning 1992, 119.
12. Johnson 1991a, 321.
13. Manning 1992, 119.
14. From *Statistics of Democide.*

15. Howorth 1965, 79; Durant 1950, 339.
16. Durant 1950, 339.
17. Howorth 1965, 82.
18. Ibid., 86.
19. Ibid., 87.
20. Durant 1950, 339.
21. Howorth 1965, 91. Without citation, Durant 1950 claims that 60,000 were killed (p. 339).
22. Grousset 1966, 278.
23. Ibid., 280.
24. Ibid.
25. Ibid., 286–87. "The elimination cannot, however, have been quite total, since a considerable number of Tangut subjects were allotted to the Lady Yesüi" (ibid., 287).
26. Howorth 1965, 200; Durant 1950, 340.
27. Saunders 1971, 65.
28. Toynbee 1947, 347.
29. From *Statistics of Democide*.
30. Howorth 1965, 381n.1.
31. Ibid., 1965, 381.
32. Payne 1973, 64.
33. Cox 1989, 1.
34. Guantao 1984.
35. Ibid.
36. Purcell 1963, 166.
37. Chesneaux 1973, 39.
38. Michael and Taylor 1975, 183.
39. Purcell 1963, 168.
40. Ho 1959, 237.
41. Ibid., 239.
42. Chesneaux 1973, 40.
43. Pelissier 1967, 109.
44. Ibid., 157.
45. Purcell 1963, 167.
46. T'ien 1981, 1.
47. Ho 1959, 247.
48. See *Statistics of Democide*.
49. Durant 1957, 183.
50. Severy 1987, 566.
51. Durant 1953, 632.
52. Wright 1965, 244n. 67; Durant and Ariel 1961, 563.
53. Wedgwood 1961, 496.
54. Wright 1965, 244n. 67.
55. See *Statistics of Democide*.
56. Recall that I define as democide a famine and disease that is intentionally manmade with reckless abandon for human life, such as by an army purposely laying waste to the countryside.
57. Durant 1950, 591–92. Oldenbourg 1966 puts the overall number at nearly 40,000 killed (p. 140).

58. Oldenbourg 1966, 137.
59. De Sismondi 1826, 37.
60. Durant 1950, 393.
61. Walker 1980, 107.
62. Paris 1961, 4; *Encyclopædia Britannica* 1973, 1:504.
63. Burns and Ralph 1955, 2:95; Sydenham 1965, chap. 8.
64. Ladouce 1988, 686, 690.
65. Duplaix 1988, 681.
66. Wise 1976, 35, 177, 240; Brooks 1950.
67. Chamerovzow 1850.
68. Kemasang 1982, 68. Quotes within the quote are from Twan Djie Liem.
69. Chalk and Jonassohn 1990, 190–91.
70. Ibid., 179–80.
71. Hoig 1961; Russell 1973, 45.
72. Russell 1973, 45–46.
73. Madsen 1985, 199–200.
74. Russell 1973, 43, 61–62.
75. Chalk and Jonassohn 1990, 199.
76. *Encyclopædia Britannica* 1973, 5:451; Charny 1982, 11.
77. From *Statistics of Democide.*
78. *Encyclopædia Britannica* 1973, 12:54.
79. Stannard 1992, 342n. 23; from a paper by Henry F. Dobyns reassessing his published lower figures.
80. See, for example, Ubelaker 1992 and White 1993.
81. Whitmore 1992, 2. This high is from Henry F. Dobyns.
82. Lancaster 1990, *Expectations of Life,* 437.
83. Stannard 1992, 95; 1992a, 431.
84. For a "well-documented" case of an attempt by the British to purposely spread disease to the Indians in order to exterminate them, see Chalk and Jonassohn 1990, 177.
85. Stannard 1992.
86. Personal communication.
87. Wertham 1962, 140.
88. Ryan 1981, 174.
89. Broome 1982, 11, 51.
90. Reynolds 1972, 22.
91. Durant 1954, 461.
92. Kelley 1974, 199–200; Paris 1961, 4; Soman 1974, vii-viii gives a figure of 2,000 killed, but this probably was only for Paris. According to Durant and Ariel 1961, 352, the estimates vary from 5,000 to 30,000.
93. Greene 1895, 96.
94. Boyajian 1972, 83.
95. Lang 1981, 8–10; Boyajian 1972, 83; Libaridian 1987, 229n. 11; Hovannisian 1986, 25.
96. Oldenbourg 1961, 141, 149, 361, 394.
97. Davies 1981, 244.
98. Paris 1961, 4. *Encyclopædia Britannica* 1973, 12:272, claims that Torquemada had only 2,000 heretics burned to death.
99. Durant 1957, 216.

100.   Ibid., 215.
101.   Davies 1981, 249.
102.   Lecky 1925, 41–42.
103.   Burns and Ralph 1955, 2:602–604.
104.   Hirsch and Smith 1991, 402.
105.   Heinsohn and Steiger 1985, 144.
106.   Davies 1981, 146. Davies believes this figure an exaggeration.
107.   Ibid., 150.
108.   Ibid., 217–18.
109.   Ibid., 218–19.
110.   Ibid., 261–62.
111.   Ibid.
112.   Ibid., 21.
113.   Ibid., 76.
114.   Ibid.
115.   Ibid., 191–92.
116.   From *Statistics of Democide.*
117.   Breiner 1990, 49–50.
118.   Ibid., 50–51.
119.   Ibid.
120.   Ibid., 50.
121.   Ibid., 8.
122.   Davies 1981, 78.
123.   In many cultures, infanticide was the custom and government simply observed it. Should this then be treated as democide? I already have treated as democide the murder of POWs, the massacre of the inhabitants of a captured city, the killing of slaves, and the sacrifice of unwilling subjects, even though in many places and times these have also been customary. The issue is whether the definition of democide is wholly descriptive or in part, at least, moral. I mean it here to be descriptive, in that when the described conditions exist (government intentionality, the killing of disarmed subjects, etc.), then democide has occurred. This is not a statement of the morality of the act at the time in the eyes of that culture or perpetrator. Indeed, many cultures may have deemed this democide highly moral, as for sacrifice. It is to say, however, that since I believe democide in any of its aspects to be a crime against humanity, were such past acts, such as systematic government-aided and -abetted sacrifice, to be committed today, I would consider them immoral crimes demanding restrictive and punitive action by the international community.
124.   Bowers 1984, 135.
125.   Pinheiro 1991, 182.
126.   Johnson 1991a, 250.
127.   Durant 1950, 599.
128.   Payne 1973, 66. See also Durant 1954, 463.
129.   Severy 1987, 573.
130.   Durant and Ariel 1961, 563.
131.   Rummel 1990, table 1B, line 113.
132.   Davies 1981, 94.
133.   Walter 1969, 134.
134.   See *Statistics of Democide.*

135.   Durant 1957, 64.
136.   Eckhardt and Köhler 1980, 368.
137.   Eckhardt 1991, 7.

Part II

128,168,000 Victims
The Dekamegamurderers

4

61,911,000 Murdered
The Soviet Gulag State

When we are reproached with cruelty, we wonder how people can forget the most elementary Marxism.

—Lenin

"How long will you keep killing people?" asked Lady Astor of Stalin in 1931.
Replied Stalin, "The process would continue as long as was necessary" to establish a communist society.

Probably almost 62 million people, nearly 54,800,000 of them citizens, have been murdered by the Communist Party — the government — of the Soviet Union.

Old and young, healthy and sick, men and women, even infants and the infirm, were killed in cold blood. They were not combatants in civil war or rebellions; they were not criminals. Indeed, nearly all were guilty of ... nothing.

Some were from the wrong class — bourgeoisie, landowners, aristocrats, kulaks. Some were from the wrong nation or race — Ukrainians, Black Sea Greeks, Kalmyks, Volga Germans. Some were from the wrong political faction — Trotskyites, Mensheviks, Social Revolutionaries. Some were just their sons and daughters, wives and husbands, or mothers and fathers. And some were in lands occupied by the Red Army — Balts, Germans, Poles, Hungarians, Rumanians. Then some were simply in the way of social progress, like the mass of peasants or religious believers. And some were eliminated because of their potential opposition, such as writers, teachers, churchmen; or the military high command; or even high and low Communist Party members themselves.

In fact, we have witnessed in the Soviet Union a true egalitarian social cleansing and flushing: no group or class escaped, for everyone and anyone could have had counterrevolutionary ancestors, class lineage, or counterrevolutionary ideas or thoughts, or be susceptible to them. And thus, almost anyone was arrested, interrogated, tortured, and after a forced confession of a plot to blow up the Kremlin, or some such, shot or sentenced to the dry guillotine — slow death by exposure, malnutrition, and overwork in a forced labor camp.

Part of this mass killing was genocide, as in the wholesale murder of hundreds of thousands of Don Cossacks in 1919,[1] the intentional starvation to death of about 5 million Ukrainian peasants in 1932–33,[2] or the deportation to mass death of 50,000 to 60,000 Estonians in 1949.[3] Part was mass murder, as of the wholesale extermination of perhaps 6,500,000 "kulaks" (in effect, the better-off peasants and those resisting collectivization) from 1930 to 1937,[4] the execution of perhaps a million Party members in the Great Terror of 1937–38,[5] and the massacre of all Trotskyites in forced labor camps.[6]

And part of the killing was so random and idiosyncratic that journalists and social scientists have no concept for it, as in hundreds of thousands of people being executed according to preset government quotas. Says Vladimir Petrov (who in 1954 defected while still a spy-chief in Australia and whose credibility and subsequent revelations were verified by a Royal — Australian — Commission on Espionage),[7] about his work during the years 1936 to 1938:

I handled hundreds of signals to all parts of the Soviet Union which were couched in the following form:

"To N.K.V.D., Frunze. You are charged with the task of exterminating 10,000 enemies of the people. Report results by signal. — Yezhov."

And in due course the reply would come back:

"In reply to yours of such-and-such date, the following enemies of the Soviet people have been shot."[8]

From time to time, in one period or another, quotas also were generally assigned for the numbers to be arrested throughout the length and breadth of the Soviet territory. Solzhenitsyn makes these quotas basic to the Great Terror of 1936 to 1938:

> The real law underlying the arrests of those years was the assignment of quotas, the norms set, the planned allocations. Every city, every district, every military unit was assigned a specific quota of arrests to be carried out by a stipulated time. From then on everything else depended on the ingenuity of the Security operations personnel.[9]

But murder and arrest quotas did not work well.[10] Where to find the "enemies of the people" they were to shoot was a particularly acute problem for the local NKVD, which had been diligent in uncovering "plots." They had to resort to shooting those arrested for the most minor civil crimes, those previously arrested and released, and even mothers and wives who appeared at NKVD headquarters for information about their arrested loved ones.

We lack a concept for murder by quotas because we — including the journalist, historian, and political scientist — have never before confronted the fact that a government can and has killed its own people for apparently no reason. For the same reason, neither do we understand the execution of starving peasants who fish in a stream without Party permission (trying to steal state property), or for the pinning of a ten-year sentence on the first one to stop clapping after Stalin's name has been mentioned at a public meeting.[11] Nor for the execution of a fourteen-year-old because his father was purged; nor for the Red Army's not only permission for but encouragement of mass rape and murder of civilians in virtually every country it newly occupied during World War II.

In sum, the Soviets committed a democide of almost 62 million people, over 7 million of them foreigners. This staggering total is beyond belief. But, as shown elsewhere,[12] it is only the prudent, most probable tally in a range from a highly unlikely low figure of around 28,000,000 (almost 4,300,000 foreigners); and an equally unlikely high of nearly 126,900,000 (including about 12,100,000 foreigners).

Table 4.1 gives a breakdown of the most probable central estimates of the number of people killed by the various agents of murder for each period of Soviet history. The Soviet death toll from international and civil wars and rebellions is also shown for comparison. Figure 4.1 displays the relative contribution of the democide agents (components) to the overall total of nearly 62 million; figure 4.2 overlays the total democide per period by the annual democide rate.

It is impossible to comprehend this democide. Focusing on the most probable estimate of almost 62 million murdered, it is over four times the battle dead (15 million) for all nations in the Second World War.[13] Indeed, it exceeds the total number of deaths (nearly 34 million) from all this century's international, civil, guerrilla, and liberation wars, including the Russian civil war.[14]

Now consider just the low democide estimate of 24,063,000 citizens murdered. This is an absolute, rock-bottom low. It is calculated by summing all the most conservative, lowest estimates for all kinds, sources, and periods of democide for the period 1917 to 1987,[15] and it is highly improbable that all these hundreds of very low estimates are correct. The low of 24,063,000 killed is more than 20 million below the forty-two-year average (1918–59) low estimate among experts or knowledgeable Soviets;[16] more important, it is more than 15 million below the forty-two-year average of those low estimates based on census data.[17] Yet this lower limit of 24,063,000 citizens murdered is itself much greater than the 15 million battle dead of the Second World War — the largest, most lethal war of all time.

This absolute minimum is already so overwhelming that one's horror, shock, or disbelief could hardly be increased were the number five times higher, as is the high estimate. Nor can any moral or practical conclusion that one would draw from this low be altered in the slightest by focusing on the more probable, middle estimate of almost 54,800,000 citizens killed.

Whether the actual democide is this low, or higher, four points should be made. First, suicides are excluded. But given the pervasive fear, the number of terror-related suicides would without doubt add significantly to the democide total were they to be included. Second,

TABLE 4.1
Overview of Soviet Democide [a]

Period	From	Democide (000)			Components (000)				
		Total	Citizens	Rate %[b]	Terror	Deport.	Camps[c]	Famine[d]	Wars[e]
Civil War	1917	3,284	3,284	0.43	750	?	34	2,500	1,410
NEP	1923	2,200	2,200	0.25	?	?	232		?
Collectivization	1929	11,440	11,440	1.04	1,733	1,400	3,306	5,000	0.20
Great Terror	1936	4,345	4,345	0.89	1,000	65	3,280		1.20
Pre-WWII	1939	5,104	4,438	1.02	1,932	283	2,889		256
World War II	1941	13,053	10,000	1.21	1,257	1,036	10,761		19,625
Post-War ...	1946	15,613	12,448	0.88	1,376	1,557	12,348	333	90
Post-Stalin	1954	6,872	6,613	0.08	250	8	6,613		22
Total [f]	1917	61,911	54,769	0.45	>8,298	>4,349	39,464	7,833	>21,403

a Most probable central values in a low-high range. All figures from Rummel 1990, table 1.1.
b Annualized rates for mid-period populations. The total is the weighted average. For citizens only.
c Camp totals include transit deaths
d Famine totals are only for those included as democide.
e Wars and rebellions; includes Nazi-caused famine. Shown for comparison only.
f Numbers may not add up to the total democide for each period due to rounding.

in many cases the relatives of those murdered were also killed by virtue of their relationship, and the democide figures take these into account. But these figures do not measure the misery among those loved ones left alive — the mothers and fathers, the husbands or wives, or the children of those killed. No accounting is made of those who died of heartbreak, who gave up on life and succumbed to disease or privation, or whose remaining years were full of anguish and bitterness. Finally is the fact that tens of millions of people were intentionally, knowingly killed on a continental scale.

Of course, this accounting begs the most probing questions. What actually happened? When? Why? How are we to understand this democide? I have tried to answer specifically these questions in the book-length study of Soviet democide of which this chapter is a summary, but the key to it all can be outlined here: Marxism plus Power.

FIGURE 4.1
Democide Components and Soviet War / Rebellion Killed, 1917–87
(From Table 4.1)

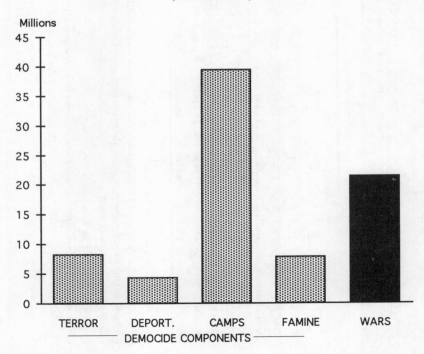

In November 1917, Lenin led his small Bolshevik party in a very risky but ultimately successful coup against the provisional democratic socialist government of Aleksandr Kerensky. This was not just a seizure of power and change of leadership but a revolutionary transformation in the very nature and worldview of governance. It was the creation of a unique reason-of-state and the institution of an utterly cold-blooded social engineering view of the state's power over its people. This unparalleled, brand-new Bolshevik government married a fully self-contained secular philosophy of nature and the Good to an initially shaky, but an eventually absolute, ahistorical political force —

FIGURE 4.2
Soviet Democide and Annual Rate by Period
(From Table 4.1)

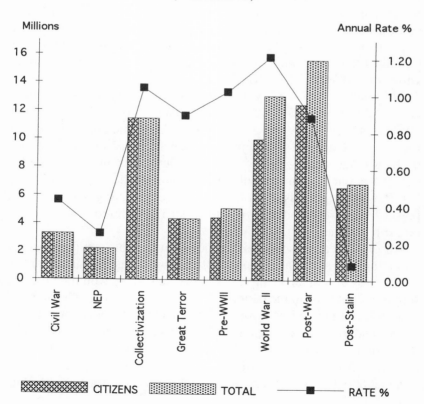

a melding of an idea and power. It was then and until its collapse in the late 1980s, *utopia empowered*.[18]

The philosophy had a universal perspective: it was a theory about reality (dialectical materialism), about man in society (historical materialism); about the best society (communism); about implementing public policy (a socialist dictatorship of the proletariat); and about political tactics (revolution, vanguard, party, etc.). And its praxis was to be absolute in scope, absolute in power, and absolute in technique. Quoting Lenin: "The scientific concept of dictatorship means nothing else but this: power without limit, resting directly upon force, restrained by no laws, absolutely unrestricted by rules."[19]

The theoretical part of this communist ideology was first developed in the works of the nineteenth-century philosopher and political economist Karl Marx and his followers. Lenin, both a philosopher and a political revolutionary, added a political program and tactics. Lenin's peculiar brand of communism became known as bolshevism before and for decades after he successfully seized power in Russia. In our time, the ideology is called Marxism, or, more specifically, Marxism-Leninism to denote the revisions introduced by Lenin. Henceforth, I will simply refer to it as Marxism.

Marxism is thoroughly uncompromising. It knows the truth absolutely; it knows Good (communism) and Evil (capitalism, feudalism); it knows the way (a socialist dictatorship of the proletariat). Once this ideology seized the authority and naked power of the Russian state — its army, police, courts, prisons — it moved to put its Marxist program into effect. And thus, the history of the Soviet Union was simply this: a protracted, total engineering application of power to demolish and then rebuild all social institutions — to create on earth the Marxist utopia.

Absolute ideas plus the absolute power of the state could mean only one thing: the state and its monopoly of force was the instrument of "progress," of utopian change. Thus, the Red Army would be used to suppress resistance to the taking of private property (being a source of evil); a secret police force would be created to uncover enemies of the people and to eliminate opponents. Law would become an instrument of terror and revolutionary change; court trials, if held, would be predetermined as the clergy of Marxism saw necessary. And permitted as a matter of course were governmental lies, deceit, robbery, beating, torture, and the murder of almost 62 million people, all of which was instrumental to the communist future.

Most important, in this ideology of Power, the living were to be sacrificed for the unborn. The living were objects, like mortar and bricks, lumber and nails, to be used, manipulated, piled on each other, to create the new social structure. Personal interests and desires, pain or pleasure, were of little moment — insignificant in the light of the new world to be created.[20] After all, how could one let, say, Ivan's desire to till the land of his father, Mikhail's desire to purchase better shoes, or Aleksandr's desire to store food to preserve his family through the winter stand in the way of the greater good of future generations? This ideological imperative can be seen in Lenin's attitude toward the famine of 1891–92 on the Volga. As Russians, regardless of class and ideology, tried to help the victims, Lenin opposed such aid, arguing that famine would radicalize the masses. Said Lenin, "Psychologically, this talk of feeding the starving is nothing but an expression of the saccharine-sweet sentimentality so characteristic of our intelligentsia."[21]

Ideology and absolute power are the critical variables in Soviet democide. They explain how individual communists could beat, torture, and murder by the hundreds, and sleep well at night. Grim tasks, to be sure, but after all, they were working for the greater good. They explain how Soviet rulers, particularly Lenin and Stalin, could knowingly command the death of hundreds of thousands.

However, in human affairs, especially at the level of societies and nations, no ideology, religion, or policies are pure and simple. The practical articulation and implementation of Marxism has been swayed or refracted, hindered or aggravated, aided or abetted, by Russian tradition and racism, by Russian imperialism and chauvinism.

Moreover, communists have not been immune to the lust for power for its own sake. Surely, the clichés of power — power aggrandizes itself, power can only be limited by power, and absolute power corrupts absolutely — apply no less to Marxists than to other rulers. But throughout this history, Marxism was mediating, channeling, directing: communism was the Good, the state (read ruler) must have and use absolute power to create this better world; any one or any thing that actually or potentially hindered this power or future had to be eliminated.

Notes

1. "The suppression of the Don Cossack revolt ... of 1919 took the form of genocide. One historian has estimated that approximately 70 percent ... were physically eliminated" (Heller and Nekrich 1986, 87). Around 1900, the Don region had a population of about 1,000,000 Cossacks (ibid., 78).
2. Conquest 1986, 306. "It certainly appears that a charge of genocide lies against the Soviet Union for its actions in the Ukraine. Such, at least, was the view of Professor Rafael Lemkin who drafted the [Genocide] Convention" (ibid., 272). The "Ukrainian famine was a deliberate act of genocide of roughly the same order of magnitude as the Jewish Holocaust of the Second World War, both in the number of its victims and in the human suffering it produced" (Mace 1986, 11).
3. "The swath cut by deportation was so wide that the issue of genocide ought to be considered.... Most Estonian deportees never returned, having largely perished. In the case of 'kulaks', all members of a population group, identified through past socio-economic status, were deported, regardless of their individual present behavior. There was no legal way to leave the condemned social group. In the case of children, the guilt was hereditary. If destroying a social group entirely, with no consideration of personal behavior, is genocide, then the March 1949 deportation would seem to qualify" (Taagepera 1980, 394).
4. Conquest 1986, 306. "The genocide against the peasants ... was unique not only for its monstrous scale; it was directed against an indigenous population by a government of the same nationality, and in time of peace" (Heller and Nekrich 1986, 236). The Soviets finally appeared to admit to this genocide in the late 1980s. In the *Moscow News*, a Moscow-published, English-language newspaper, it was written: "In what amounted to genocide, between five and ten million people died during the forced collectivization of farming in the early thirties" (Ambartsumov 1988).
5. Hingley 1974, 284; Medvedev 1979, 102.
6. Medvedev 1979, 117.
7. Petrov and Petrov 1956, 9–10.
8. Ibid., 73–74. One such telegram to Sverdlovsk ordered that 15,000 "enemies of the people" be shot (74).
9. Solzhenitsyn 1973, 1971.
10. "NKVD cadres themselves were terrorized into 'production' frenzies by surprise visits from NKVD headquarters officials. In an unannounced visit to the Rostov NKVD office, Genrikh Lyushkov, a high-ranking state security officer, charged the gathered officials with laxness in pursuing enemies and immediately fingered three of their own number as enemies; the intimidated district chief quickly prepared the charges and had his own accused men shot" (Dziak, 1988, 68). The NKVD was the People's Commissariat for Internal Affairs, the predecessor to the KGB.
11. Solzhenitsyn 1973, 69–70.
12. Rummel 1990, app. 1.1.
13. Small and Singer 1982, 91.
14. For wars 1900–1980. From table 1.6.
15. The estimates and sources are given in the various appendices in Rummel 1990.
16. See Rummel 1990, 18, line 76.

17. See Ibid., line 88.
18. This is a paraphrase of the title of Heller and Nekrich's 1986 history of the Soviet Union, *Utopia in Power.*
19. Leggett 1981, 186.
20. See Heller 1988.
21. Conquest 1986, 234.

5

35,236,000 Murdered
The Communist Chinese Anthill

> *Apart from their other characteristics, China's 600
> million people have two remarkable peculiarities;
> they are, first of all, poor, and secondly blank. That
> may seem like a bad thing, but it is really a good
> thing. Poor people want change, want to do things,
> want revolution. A clean sheet of paper has no
> blotches, and so the newest and most beautiful words
> can be written on it, the newest and most beautiful
> pictures can be painted on it.*
>
> —Mao Tse-tung

Those who were shocked by the June 1989 Beijing massacre and repression of prodemocracy demonstrators should not have been. Such cruelty and mass killing are a way of life in China. Indeed, no other people in this century except Soviet citizens have suffered so much mass killing in cold blood as have the Chinese.

They have been murdered by rebels conniving with their own Empress, and then with the defeat in war of the dynasty, by soldiers and citizens of many other lands. They have been killed by mini-despots — warlords — who ruled one part of China or another. They have been slaughtered because they happened to live where nationalists, warlords, communists, or foreign troops fought each other. They have been executed because they had the wrong beliefs or attitudes in the wrong place at the wrong time. They have been shot because they criticized or opposed their rulers. They have been butchered because they resisted rape, were raped, or tried to prevent rape. They have been wiped out because they had food or wealth that soldiers or officials wanted. They have been assassinated because they were leaders, a threat, or potential antagonists. They have been blotted out in the process of building a new society. And they have died simply because they were in the way.

These poor souls have experienced every manner of death for every conceivable reason: genocide, politicide, mass murder, massacre, and individually directed assassination; burning alive, burying alive, starvation, drowning, infecting with germs, shooting, stabbing. This for personal power, out of feelings of superiority, because of lust or greed, to terrorize others into surrendering, to keep subjects in line, out of nationalist ideals, or to achieve utopia.

China began the century with a weak and corrupt dynasty on the verge of collapse and beset by European imperialism. Fifty years later China had become truly independent and sovereign, but also was in the grip of an alien, totalitarian ideology that allowed little room for personal rights or individual freedom. Democracy, an ideal that motivated many of those that worked to bring down the dynasty and create a republic in the early years of this century, seemed even less possible in the 1950s and 1960s then it had before.

Between the extremes of a very traditional, authoritarian dynasty and arbitrary, totalitarian rule, the Chinese people have in one region or another gone through multiple governance. After the dynasty fell in 1911, China was governed by an ineffective and disunited republican government. When General Yüan Shih-k'ai, the one unifying leader of this government, died in 1916, China was largely divided by warlords, who governed their separate regions as though they were sovereign and independent countries. Many were absolute dictators, fighting hundreds of wars to gain more power or to protect their territory.

In the midst of this political anarchy rose two forces. One was that for national unity, self-determination, directed democracy, and socialism or modernization; the other was for revolutionary communism. The first force was led by Sun Yat-sen and the party he founded, the Kuomintang. At first, this party combined both the communists and those noncommunists who were seeking to create a modern, national state into one drive to defeat the warlords and unify China.

But these incompatible forces soon fell out. Subservient to Moscow, the communists sought to dominate the Kuomintang and prematurely organize revolution in the streets. Chiang Kai-shek, the acknowledged leader of the Kuomintang and republican forces after Sun Yat-sen's death, turned on the communists in a bloody coup in 1927, massacring thousands of them. From that time on, there would be negotiations, truces, and common fronts, but the fundamental risk to Chinese life and limb was determined for the next twenty-two years: It was a life and death, three-cornered struggle between the centrifugal forces of the warlord dictators and the exclusively integrating, but opposing, forces of the totalitarian communists and authoritarian nationalists (as Chiang Kai-shek's Kuomintang Party and government became known). As though this deadly struggle was not enough, Japanese forces entered the fray in 1937 to subordinate China to its own concept of a unified Asia — under Japanese guidance, of course. While ostensibly this intervention and the consequent Sino-Japanese War forced the nationalists and communists into a common front, each maneuvered for strategic advantage. Soon Japanese soldiers would be able to enjoy a picnic while watching them kill each other.

The defeat of Japan in 1945 by the United States presaged, after some hesitation and truce, the final struggle between the nationalists and communists for total victory. Warlordism had been virtually extinguished in the previous years; now only the two antagonistic forces remained. This massive and bloody civil war, involving millions of troops, militia, and peasant laborers; rebellions, massacres and terror; destructive inflation and ruin, ended with the total victory of the communists on Mainland China by the end of 1949.

In all these military struggles from 1900 to 1949, with soldiers of one or another of the hundreds of armies crisscrossing the land, in total probably almost 9 million soldiers and civilians were killed. This is a death toll virtually the same as that for all nations involved in all the battles of World War I.

But our interest here is not in the war dead but in the innocents and helpless who were slaughtered during, between, or after these wars. They were killed because they happened to live in the wrong place, or because they were victims of the repression and terror of those armies or governments that occupied their land. Of those killed by warlords little need be said. Although some warlords were considerate of their subjects, ruling benevolently, generally they were tyrants brooking little opposition. Repression was often massive, and massacres were not infrequent; opposition usually meant death. The figures on those killed by the warlords are the roughest of all. Putting available information together and making some conservative guesses, I estimate that some 910,000 people likely were murdered by the warlords or their soldiers, perhaps even a third more than this.[1]

It is a commentary on China's modern history that this number — nearly a million killed, incredible in itself, much more than the battle dead in all American wars since 1775 — will look small when compared to the millions killed by the nationalists (see chapter 7), the communists, and the Japanese. Before letting this estimate get lost among these much larger figures, I should reemphasize it here: the warlord toll alone ranks these Chinese dead among the major victims of democide in this century — greater in number than the contemporary democide in Idi Amin's Uganda (300,000 killed),[2] Burundi (150,000 killed),[3] and Indonesia (729,000 killed, including in East Timor),[4] to mention the more recently prominent.

In many ways, as we will see, the nationalists were no different than the warlords. They murdered opponents, assassinated critics, and employed terror as a device of rule. Moreover, nationalist soldiers, like many warlord soldiers, were considered scum, lower than vermin. They were beaten, mistreated, often poorly fed and ill paid; and if wounded or sick they were left to fend for themselves, often to die slow and miserable deaths. In turn, soldiers often treated civilians no better. Looting, rape, and arbitrary murder were risks that helpless civilians faced from passing soldiers or from those occupying or reoccupying their villages and towns.

As also we will see, from the earliest years to their final defeat on the mainland, the nationalists likely killed between almost 6,000,000 and nearly 18,500,000 helpless people, probably around 10 million of them. This incredible number is over a million greater than all the aforementioned some 9 million war dead in all the hundreds of wars and rebellions in China from the beginning of the century to the nationalist final defeat. It ranks the nationalists as the fourth greatest megamurderers of this century, behind the Soviets, Chinese communists, and German Nazis. This democide is even more impressive when it is realized that the nationalists never controlled all of China — perhaps no more than 50 to 60 percent of the population at its greatest.

Before passing on to the communists, we should not ignore Japanese democide in China, which will be briefly discussed in chapter 8. Japanese indiscriminate killing of Chinese became widely known and almost universally condemned as criminal in the late 1930s. World opinion was especially horrified over what became known as "The Rape of Nanking," but this was not an isolated case. From one village, town, or city to another, the Japanese often killed the inhabitants, executed suspected former nationalist soldiers, beat to death or buried alive those disobeying their orders or showing insufficient respect, and mistreating many others. Much if this killing was done in cold blood and thoughtlessly — as one would swat a fly. An example of this that most sticks in my mind is of one Japanese officer's use of Chinese prisoners for "kill practice" by his inexperienced soldiers.[5]

Moreover, the Japanese terror-bombed Chinese cities and towns, killing civilians at random (that this was done by the Anglo-American Allies during World War II hardly excuses it — official U.S. protests to Japan at the time condemned such "barbarism"). And they widely employed germ warfare. Over some major cities, for example, the Japanese released flies infected with deadly plague germs, causing epidemics.

Overall and quite aside from those killed in battle, the Japanese probably murdered close to 4 million Chinese during the war; even possibly as many as almost 6,300,000. Some readers who were prisoners of the Japanese during the war or who remember the Tokyo War Crimes Tribunal revelations after the war will hardly be surprised by these numbers. What is shocking is that the nationalists likely murdered some 2 million more during the war, and that this toll, or something like it, is virtually unknown. Apparently, the nationalists got away with megamurder; responsible Japanese were tried as war criminals.

As for the communists, from their very formation as a Party on the Soviet model (with the help of Soviet advisors), the Chinese communists used the same kind of repression and terror employed by the Chinese nationalists. They executed so called counterrevolutionaries, nationalist sympathizers, and other political opponents. The Communist Party itself and its army were systematically purged and rectified several times, one purge alone in 1942 involving 10,000 executions.[6] But, unlike the warlords and nationalists, the communists also murdered as part of, or as a spillover from, trying to "reform" or radically change the countryside and its power structure. They were ideologically driven.

Landlords, rich peasants, the gentry, and the bourgeoisie were the enemies, to be exterminated or won over; but in any case, their land and riches were to be distributed among the poor peasants. In the beginning, the emphasis was largely on rent reduction and some power redistribution; but during the Sino-Japanese War and especially the civil war, radical land reform — the seizure of all "excess" land and its redistribution, the rough equalization of wealth, and the punishment, often execution, of "bad" landlords, "bullies" and former officials — became general operating procedure. In this the communists developed and honed the procedures they would apply throughout the whole country once victorious.

Up to 1 October 1949, when Mao Tse-tung officially proclaimed the People's Republic of China (PRC), the communists, acting as the de facto government of the regions they controlled, killed from almost 1,800,000 to almost 11,700,000 people, most likely close to 3,500,000. This is about one-third the democide of the nationalists. Of course, the communists usually controlled a much smaller population. But they also treated their soldiers much better, the process of conscription was not a death trap, and officials and officers were far less corrupt and undisciplined. Thus, the population was less subject to arbitrary killing; and what killing did take place was often part of a program or campaign mapped out in advance. Even in newly conquered areas, when peasants spontaneously would take matters into their own hands, round up some hated local bullies or former officials and beat them to death, it generally was within the communist scheme. Otherwise, the party's Central Committee would have made reference to communist goals while instructing cadre to prevent such "antisocial action."

Once control over all of China had been won and consolidated, and the proper party machinery and instruments of control put generally in place, the communists launched numerous movements to systematically destroy the traditional Chinese social and political system and replace it with a totally socialist, top-to-bottom "dictatorship of the proletariat." In the beginning their model was Stalin's Soviet Union; Soviet advisors even helping to construct their own gulag. Their principles derived from Marxism-Leninism, as interpreted by Mao Tse-tung. Their goals were to thoroughly transform China into a communist society. In this the communists were consistent with their beginnings, but they now had a whole country to work with, without the need to give tactical or strategic consideration to another force — the nationalists or Japanese — seeking and capable of destroying them.

Beginning in 1950, carefully and nationally organized movements were spawned in rapid succession: Land Reform, Suppressing Anticommunist Guerrillas, New Marriage System, Religious Reform, Democratic Reform, Suppressing Counterrevolutionaries, Anti-Rightist Struggle, Suppressing the "Five Black Categories," etc. Each of these was a step toward the final communization of China; each was bloody — self-consciously bloody. Witness what Mao himself had to say in a speech to party cadre in 1958:

> What's so unusual about Emperor Shih Huang of the Chin Dynasty? He had buried alive 460 scholars only, but we have buried alive 46,000 scholars. In the course of our repression of counter-revolutionary elements, haven't we put to death a number of the counter-revolutionary scholars? I had an argument with the democratic personages. They say we are behaving worse than Emperor Shih Huang of the Chin Dynasty. That's definitely not correct. We are 100 times ahead of Emperor Shih of the Chin Dynasty in repression of counter-revolutionary scholars.[7]

Only when these movements, and especially the final, total collectivization of the peasants and "Great Leap Forward," destroyed the agricultural system, causing the world's greatest recorded famine — 27 million starved to death[8] — did the communists begin to draw back from or slacken their drive. Shortly after this famine, in the mid-1960s, an intraparty civil war erupted between Mao Tse-tung and his followers, who wanted to continue the mass-based revolution, and a more moderate, pragmatically oriented faction. The resulting "cultural revolution" probably cost over 1,600,000 lives.[9] Mao won, but only temporarily. With his death soon after, the pragmatists and "capitalist roaders" regained power and launched China into a more open, economically experimental direction, even, on a more liberal path — until the Tianamen Square demonstrations and subsequent massacres of 1989.

Finally in control of a unified China, the goal the nationalists could never achieve; finally able to put into effect for the whole nation their principles and plans, honed through twenty-one years of experimentation in their enclaves during the nationalist years; finally able to discard any tactical considerations about public opinion, peasant support, or encouraging volunteers for the militia and army; the communists could create their utopia. In this they utterly failed, as did the communists in the Soviet Union and Eastern Europe. But the people paid the price for these greatest of social experiments.

Indeed, from October 1949 to 1987, the Chinese Communist Party (CCP) probably killed more than 35,200,000 of its own subjects. These were "landlords" and "rich" peasants, "counterrevolutionaries" and "bandits," "leftists," "rightists," and "capitalist roaders," "bourgeoisie," scientists, intellectuals, and scholars, Kuomintang "agents" and Western "spies," "wrong" and "bad" elements, and often loved ones, relatives, and friends. Even babies. If this seems exaggerated, consider the report of the Minister of Public Security, Hsieh Fu-chih, in which he cites the case of production brigade leaders in one rural county who murdered in one day, in ten brigades, all those with "bad" personal or family backgrounds, including "landlords, rich peasants, counterrevolutionaries, bad elements, and rightists and their children, including babies."[10]

All such human beings were sacrificed for the most massive, total social engineering projects ever forced on any society in modern history, including the Soviet Union. For total communist power, over half a billion peasants were sacrificed, and the independent landlord, "rich" peasant, and gentry were destroyed. It was for the forced, temporary redistribution of land to the peasants to buy their acquiescence to the party. It was for the subsequent nationalization and seizure of this land for communes, a military-like "factoryization" of the peasant and farming. It was for the achievement of total power over the family — even its mating and sexual practices. It was for the full control and nationalization of all private contracts and businesses. It was for the eradication of any possible opposition to party doctrine and policies by intellectuals and scholars. It was for the proletarianization of scholarship and science and all highly skilled occupations. It was for the elimination of any "wrong thoughts" through regular struggle ("brainwashing") sessions in every neighborhood, group, and organization. And it was for the purging of any dissidents or opponents of the current party line, whatever the top party members at the time should pronounce it to be. In short, as for the Soviet Union, the sacrifice was for total control over all behavior and thought in the achievement of Marxist utopia.

For the reader who lives in a democratic system in which individual lives are precious (where even the execution of a vicious murderer of a hundred people may be forbidden by law, or allowed only after years of appeals and minute inspection for fairness of the murderer's trial) and who is ignorant of the massive killing caused by the Soviet Union, that the Chinese communist government should murder some 35,200,000 of its own citizens for social or political reasons is incredible, unbelievable, sheer anticommunist propaganda. Yet this figure may be a gross undercount. Based on the estimates of various experts, sinologists, interviewees, refugees, and even communist officials themselves,[11] the death toll could be much higher, maybe as high as almost 102 million people. Of course, the count also could be much lower, but taking into account the lowest published estimates, no lower than about 6 million. For the most probable estimate and its components over different periods, see table 5.1.[12]

Now, even this rock-bottom estimate of around 6 million killed would be an absolutely incredible toll for those who have lived all their lives in democracies without experiencing any of the mass killing machines that have passed for governments in this century. Yes, the Nazi's murdered around 5,300,000 Jews,[13] but that was an aberration. Hitler was mad. But the Chinese communists, Mao Tse-tung and especially Zhou Enlai, murdering at least this many people?

While the exact figures can never be known and any estimate will be disputable, what is undeniable is that the Chinese communists did kill millions in their nearly forty-year reign over China, not to mention the additional millions they killed before "liberation." To deny this is to be blind to the diverse sources of evidence, to even what the communist media have admitted and the statements of high party members themselves.

When a much-respected, top party man like Zhou Enlai is quoted by Edgar Snow, a sympathetic writer, as admitting to 830,000 "enemies of the people" being destroyed in only a little over three years, he should be heard.[14] And, of course, so should the supreme ruler of China, Mao Tse-tung, when he admits to killing tens of thousands of scholars,[15] or to executing at least 800,000 landlords in the early 1950s alone.[16] Then there are statements by various communist officials, one admitting, for example, to the execution of 180,000 to 190,000 people — 14 out of every thousand — in merely six months in just the province of Kwangsi.[17] The heads of four of six administrative regions reported that they executed 1,176,000 people in only one year.[18] Some other officials admitted to killing 2 million.[19] Lest it seem that all official estimates are of this "low" magnitude, consider the percentages given in the official report of Deng Zihui, vice-chairman of the Central South Administrative and Military District: they imply that 9 million peasants were executed during only two years.[20] A former high official gave a figure of 15 million Chinese losing their lives from all party movements over three years.[21] While such official and unofficial estimates by those in a position to know something of the killing are not consistent, clearly

TABLE 5.1
PRC Democide, 1949–87 [a]

Period	Years	Democide (000)	Death Rates (%) Period	Annual	Deaths from War/Rev. (000)
Totalitarianization	1949–53	8,427	1.48	0.35	2,785
Collectivization	1954–58	7,474	1.21	0.24	25
Retrenchment	1959–63	10,729	1.63	0.33	26
Cultural Revolution	1964–75	7,731	0.96	0.08	563
Liberalization	1976–87	874	0.09	0.01	42
Total	1949–87	35,236	4.49	0.12	3,440

a Periods may not add up to totals due to rounding. Data is from Rummel 1991, Appendix II.1.

they agree on one bloody fact: masses upon masses of people were purposely killed.

This democide has continued in recent years, as evidenced by the executions of those involved in or supporting prodemocracy demonstrations in the late spring of 1989. But this democide is at a much reduced level from previous years, especially when compared to that which took place during the PRC's first three decades. To see this, consider figure 5.1, which bar graphs the democide by the periods given in table 5.1, and overlays the bars with the annual democide rate (a similar plot for the Soviet Union was shown in figure 4.2 of chapter 4). Figure 5.2 divides the democide into its components. Clearly, most people were killed by the deadly labor camps (as was also the case for the Soviet Union). Figure 5.3 compares the democide per period to the number of deaths in famine, war, and revolution.

As for the Soviet democide, these deaths are impossible to digest. It is hard to imagine 1,000 killed, not to mention 1 million. Perhaps a way of better comprehending this is in terms of the rough risk of a citizen's being killed by the Communist Party of China. Since 1949, conservatively, forty-five out of every thousand people have been killed, or almost *one out of every twenty men, women, and children.*

Why all this Chinese democide? For the same reason it occurred in the Soviet Union: as the working out of Marxism, whether of Marxism-Leninism or Marxism-Leninism-Stalinism in the USSR, or Marxism-Leninism-Maoism in the PRC. In each case, Power was nearly absolute, the central tenets of Marxism the bible, high communist officials its priests, the Communist Party its church, and the achievement of the Marxist heaven — communism — the ultimate goal. In each country, the same classes — bourgeoisie, priests, landlords, the rich, and officers and officials of the previous regime — were sinful, enemies of the Good. Capitalists or their offspring were especially evil. The verdict for such class membership was often death.

Moreover, belief in Marxism was so fanatical among communists in both systems, they were so sure that they knew the absolute truth, that they would brook no opposition, antagonism, or displeasure by intellectuals or the masses. Typical of Marxist parties, rigid, doctrinaire intolerance was considered a virtue. Opposition, or to be labeled a "counterrevolutionary" by either party, could be a death warrant.

Reminiscent of medieval, European religious wars, even disagreement among top party members could end in internecine warfare, as in the "Great Terror" in which perhaps 1 million party members were executed in the Soviet Union from 1936 to 1938,[22] and the "Cultural Revolution" in China in which nearly 1,600,000 people were slaughtered (excluding battle dead).[23] In both cases this butchery was launched by the "Great Leader," in both cases they succeeded in eliminating their opponents, and in both cases their class line and their cultivated demigod-images did not last long after their deaths.

As Marxists, parties in both the USSR and the PRC embarked on a fantastic reconstruction of their societies: both tried to collectivize all

FIGURE 5.1
PRC Democide and Annual Rate by Period
(Data from Table 5.1)

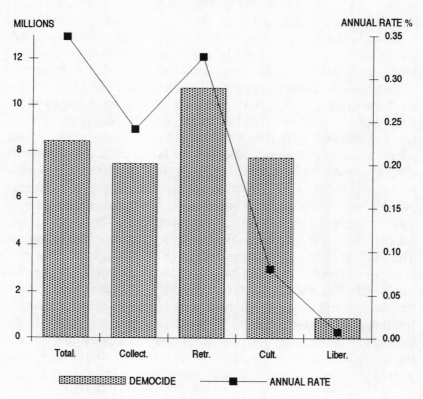

the peasants (including nomads) and nationalize all farmland, killing millions in the process. The resulting massive famines set unprecedented records: that in China left, at a conservative count, 27 million people dead, the world record for a famine;[24] that in the Soviet Union starved 7 million to death (5 million Ukrainians intentionally so),[25] second only to China in this century. The consequence for social welfare and health was equally disastrous. Malnutrition, hunger, and impoverishment were endemic before and after these famines. For both systems, the following gallows humor of two Chinese refugees summed the situation up.

FIGURE 5.2
PRC Democide by Source
(Data from Rummel 1991)

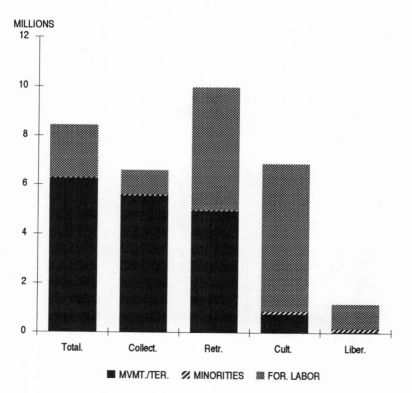

MILLIONS

■ MVMT./TER.   ▨ MINORITIES   ▨ FOR. LABOR

Total.   Collect.   Retr.   Cult.   Liber.

"I used to wonder," said one, "why they made us all so thin. If we had been fat their police could have seen us better."

"True," said the other, "but then they couldn't get so many of us into one prison cell."[26]

Both parties exercised total state socialism, the Marxist-Leninist transition stage to final communism. The party tried to control all, even life within the family. Work and even killing was organized by quotas (in the PRC's "Anti-Rightist" movement, all schools below the university level "were assigned quotas — between 5 and 10 percent of their staffs — to be delivered to the state as 'rightists.'")[27] The rhythm of life was geared to five-year plans, and all major decisions about life

FIGURE 5.3
PRC Democide, Famine, and War/Revolution Deaths by Period
(Data from Rummel 1991)

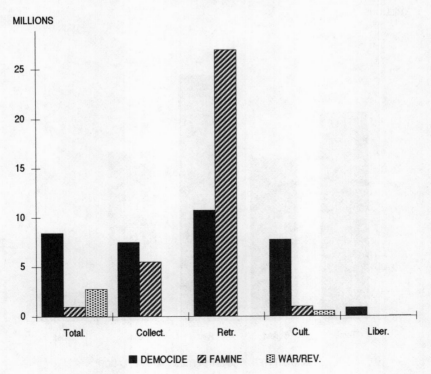

— where one might live, work, or go to school, and what one might do for a job or career — were made by central planners and the top party officials in general, and interpreted at the individual level by local communist cadre. The scope of such decisions invaded the most personal and intimate aspects of human life — even, in China, as to how many children one could have and when; or whether husbands and wives would live thousands of miles apart (labor office officials routinely assigned people to jobs for the convenience of the party, about 8 million workers being forced to live apart from their spouses at one time).[28]

Neither party obeyed any law. To paraphrase a Western belief, no communist was beneath the law. Written law, courts, judges, and the whole paraphernalia of a functioning legal system served both parties as expedient political tools to construct a communist society, liquidate bad classes, and punish opposition. As Mao said to Edgar Snow, "We don't really know what is meant by law, because we have never paid any attention to it!"[29]

Both parties resorted to a slave (forced labor) system. For some decades, in each country at least 10 million prisoners at any one time were housed in thousands of lethal forced-labor camps. The reason for such incarceration was often class membership or opposition to the regime, or even idiosyncratic (in the Soviet Union, ten years for wrapping fish in a newspaper showing a picture of Stalin; in China, fifteen years for absentmindedly scratching one's back with Mao's little red book),[30] or none at all. Regardless of the excuse, prisoners were exploited, worked, and treated as no slave master would treat his slaves (who were valuable personal property). To the Marxists of both parties, these forced laborers were only expendable, easily replaceable worker ants in the making of utopia. Millions were worked to death in both systems or allowed to succumb to exposure, disease, malnutrition, or hunger. For both countries, more thus died in these hell holes than were shot or otherwise murdered by the party outside of them: probably around 15,700,000 in China,[31] almost 39,500,000 in the Soviet Union.[32] These numbers do not even include all those collectivized, ill-fed and ill-clothed peasants who would be worked to death in the fields. Just consider the report of the *Honan Peasant's Daily*, a provincial newspaper, that during two 1959 summer weeks alone, 29,000 died from overwork and malnutrition while in the fields.

Other papers revealed that 7,000 similarly died in Kiangsi, 8,000 in Kiansu, and 13,000 in Chekiang.[33] This, from communist newspapers.

For both parties, the cadres guilty of murdering hundreds and even thousands of people slept well at night, their consciences undisturbed, for they had the ultimate Marxist justification for their actions: They were creating a better world of greater abundance in which hunger, poverty, exploitation, inequality, and war would be only awful memories; they were removing the social refuse and sewage; they were applying social prophylaxis. After all, "to make an omelet, one must break eggs."

The outrageous irony of all this is that for both systems (as now also revealed for the former Marxist systems of Poland, East Germany, Czechoslovakia, Hungary, Bulgaria, Rumania, and Albania), with all these people murdered; all this loss of freedom, individuality, and dignity; all this totalitarian social engineering; the survivors were still worse off, not better.[34] This, in spite of the previous nationalist and warlord repression and terror, nationalist corruption and incompetence, and wars, rebellions, and democide.

More millions died of hunger in famines than ever before; even in the off-famine years, more were continually hungry and malnourished — the caloric intake alone did not catch up to and pass the low level of the late 1920s and early 1930s until about 1978, or about 30 years after the Communist victory.[35] Even the Chinese press admitted that per capita food available from 1956 to 1976 did not increase; that in large areas of the Northwest "the production level and living standard of the masses to the present are lower than those of pre-liberation [before 1949] days or the time of the War of Resistance against Japan [1937–45]."[36] Indeed, Li Xiannian, the deputy chairman of the party, "reportedly" estimated in 1949 that 100 million "were still living in serious want."[37] But even this huge number may be too conservative by half. The *Chinese Journal of Agricultural Economics* gave results of a survey showing that in the period 1977 to 1979, no fewer than 200 million people were still living well below the level of minimal subsistence.[38] Understandably, many had turned to begging, which was licensed by the party. One newspaper (*Guang Ming Daily*) revealed that from 1966 to 1977, about 30,000 peasants in one county of Henan province (one of every seven in the county) "were forced each winter and spring to apply for permits to go begging elsewhere."[39]

More were imprisoned. Tens of millions more were deported to labor on marginal and inhospitable lands as "free" laborers, or to be slaves in forced labor camps. And for all, the overall quality of life was much less. In both the Soviet Union and China (and Eastern Europe), peasants and urbanites alike remembered their lives before the revolution as happier ones.

While political executions and imprisonment, corruption, hunger, begging, and exploitation had existed before, communism in the Soviet Union and China spread and magnified these social evils such that they afflicted almost every family lacking high party members, and even deeply corrupted the party itself. At the end of her book on interviews with Chinese refugees, Suzanne Labin sums it up thusly:

> The real atmosphere of China under communism was provided by the same few words which came again and again like a litany in the memories of all of them, simple words which evoked the same nightmare: terror, rationing, compulsory political lectures, public confessions, shortage, twenty-four catties of rice, requisitions, queues, arrests, no medicaments, forced labour, brain-washing, moral bombardments, punishment, hunger, fear...."[40]

Of course, these were the recollections of refugees. But this experience was apparently shared widely in China. As Fox Butterfield lamented:

> Almost every Chinese I got to know during my twenty months in Peking had a tale of political persecution.... From their stories it seems as if a whole generation of Chinese ... had known nothing but arbitrary accusations, violent swings in the political line, unjustified arrests, torture, and imprisonment. Few Chinese I knew felt free from the fear of physical or psychological abuse and a pervasive sense of injustice.[41]

On this sacrifice of over 35,200,000 souls for a better society, consider the words of Lao Baixing, a communist cadre who had lectured the anthropologist Steven Mosher, then doing research on peasant life in his village, on the positive accomplishments of the revolution. They had become good friends, and Mosher developed a fine appreciation for Lao Baixing's intelligence, insight, and knowledge. During one of Mosher's last nights in the village, Lao Baixing visited him to say good-bye. As they drank together, the cadre began to reminisce about his life as a tenant farmer before the revolution and "[l]ayers of deception were tumbling away as he spoke." After talking about how his family life before the revolution was not "that bad" (except during the Sino-Japanese War), he went on to say:

> Times were *good*. People had *money*. You could buy *anything*. Goods have never been abundant since then. There are always shortages. Before, if you had money you could buy anything. Now a lot of things go through the back door, and only those with foreign currency [from relatives overseas] or officials can afford it. The people in power now have many more special privileges than before the liberation. They can purchase fish or high-quality rice that the masses can't even if they have the money.
>
> Another thing that they say about the old times is how the village heads oppressed the masses. You know, our village leaders then, the village gentry, were not bad men. Even if one or two were bad men, they had little power. The brigade cadres now have much more power to control people than the old village leaders. Now they can fine you, or struggle you, or assign you to a difficult task. Now you even have to have their permission on a travel permit to leave the county or spend the night outside the brigade. They decide everything for their own benefit, even though they say that it is for the people.
>
> [After chatting awhile longer and on his way out, Lao Baixing hesitated by the gate and said] There is one thing more you should know. That first night, when I came and talked to you about the liberation. I was instructed to come.[42]

Of course, he forgets or did not know that times were not good for many, that landlords and nationalist officials did murder many peasants, that many lived a life of bare existence, and that many peasants died from the wars, rebellions, and soldiers that crisscrossed the land. But he is right in spirit: never before had the impoverishment and hunger and fear been so widespread. Only now, in the late 1980s and early 1990s, with economic liberalization, are the Chinese people finally emerging from this profound physical and mental impoverishment.

Notes

1. Rummel 1991, table 1.A, line 121.
2. From *Statistics of Democide.*
3. Ibid., line 254.
4. Ibid., line 1241.
5. Wilson 1982, 80.
6. Labin 1960, 35.
7. Li 1979, 12.
8. Coale 1984, 70; Kane 1988, 84–85; Yi 1989, 153.
9. Rummel 1991, app. II.1.
10. Rice 1972, 460.
11. These estimates and sources are given throughout the various appendices in Rummel 1991.
12. These figures are from the estimates and sources detailed in Rummel 1991, app. II.1.
13. See Rummel 1992, table A, line 1204.
14. Garside 1981, 307.
15. Li 1979, 12.
16. Quigley 1962, 142.
17. Tennien 1952, 195.
18. Domes 1973, 51.
19. Quigley 1962, 142.
20. Yi 1989.
21. Labin 1960, 49.
22. Rummel 1990, 122, line 93.
23. Rummel 1991, table II.A, line 294a.
24. Ibid., line 592.
25. Rummel 1990, 102, lines 138 and 228.
26. Labin 1960, 369.
27. Thurston 1987, 68.
28. Butterfield 1982, 332.
29. Li 1979, 12.
30. Garside 1981, 213.
31. Rummel 1991, table II.A, line 539.
32. Rummel 1990, 17, line 20. This includes transit deaths.
33. Chu 1963, 74.
34. For a statistical and comparative analysis of communist accomplishments in China and the Soviet Union, among other communist countries, see Eberstadt 1988. His findings for the Soviet Union were well verified after the Soviet collapse.
35. Eberstadt 1988, 145.
36. London and Lee 1983, 6.
37. Ibid.
38. Ibid.
39. Ibid.
40. Labin 1960, 369.
41. Butterfield 1982, 347.
42. Mosher 1983, 308–9.

6

20,946,000 Murdered
The Nazi Genocide State

If I should find a Ukrainian who is worthy to sit with me at the table I must let him be shot.

—Reichskommissar Erich Koch

Regardless of the massive democide by the Soviets or communist Chinese, the only government mass murder that the world remembers and our school books describe is the Nazi genocide of the Jews in which "6 million" were slaughtered. But even this count ignores the vast number of other people the Nazis exterminated. Overall, by genocide, the killing of hostages, reprisal raids, forced labor, "euthanasia," starvation, exposure, medical experiments, terror bombing, and in the concentration and death camps, the Nazis murdered from about 15,000,000 to over 31,600,000 people, most likely closer to 21 million men, women, handicapped, aged, sick, prisoners of war, forced laborers, camp inmates, critics, homosexuals, Jews, Slavs, Serbs, Czechs, Italians, Poles, Frenchmen, Ukrainians,

112 Death by Government

TABLE 6.1
Selected Nazi Democide and European War Dead

Type of Death	Number Killed [a]
Democide	20,946,000
Genocide	16,315,000
Homosexuals	220,000
Gypsies	258,000
Jews	5,291,000
Slavs (Eastern)	10,547,000
Institutional Killing [b]	11,283,000
Forced Euthanasia	172,500
Forced Labor	1,861,000
Prisoners of War	3,100,000
Concentration/Death Camps	6,063,000
Democide in Occupied Europe	19,315,000
Denmark	700
Norway	1,500
Luxembourg	2,000
Bulgaria	7,000
Belgium	51,000
Italy	64,000
Rumania	70,000
Austria	133,000
Greece	140,000
Netherlands	176,000
Czechoslovakia	214,000
Baltic States	255,000
France	256,000
Hungary	406,000
Yugoslavia	625,000
Poland	5,400,000
USSR	12,250,000
World War II European War Dead [c]	28,736,000
Germany [d]	5,200,000
Other Europe [e]	23,536,000

a All democide figures are the prudent mid-figures from Rummel 1992 (appendix table A). The subclassifications of democide are incomplete and overlap and therefore will not sum to the total democide.

b Includes the killing of Jews, Gypsies, etc.

c. Exclusive of democide.

d From Rummel 1992, appendix table A

e Excludes all non-European nations. From Wright 1965 (1542–43).

and so on. Among them were 1 million children under eighteen years of age.[1]

Table 6.1 subdivides this democide in various ways and compares it to the war dead for Germany and other European nations.

These people were murdered for three basic reasons: One was for hindering or actually or potentially opposing the Nazi regime, its aggression against other countries, or the occupation of the country by Nazi forces. Such was the reason for Hitler's assassination by the hundreds of the top members of the Nazi SA (Storm Troop)[2] in June to July 1934, which under Ernst Röem was becoming a strong competitor to the SS (Defense Corps).[3] It was also the reason for the execution of perhaps 5,000 Germans after the attempted assassination of Hitler in 1944, and for the execution, disappearance, or slow death by concentration camp of critics, pacifists, conscientious objectors, campus rebels, dissidents, and others throughout the thirteen-year history of the regime in Germany. Almost 290,000 Germans probably were thus killed, not counting Jews, some homosexuals, and those forcefully "euthanized." If these latter are included, at least some 500,000 Germans were murdered, probably about 760,000. As shown in table 6.2, this was nearly one out of every hundred Germans. If we

TABLE 6.2
Nazi Democide Rates

Category	Democide Rates (%) [a]		Odds of Dying [d]
	Overall	Annual	
Germany	1.08	0.08	1 in 93
Occupied Europe	6.50	1.08	1 in 15
Overall	5.46	0.91	1 in 18
Nine Chronic Diseases [b]	2.56 [c]		1 in 39

a Democide rates are from Rummel 1992 (appendix table A). Overall rate is calculated as (democide/population) X 100. Annual rate is: (overall rate)/(6 years). For Germany the division is by 12.42 years.

b Diseases are stroke, heart disease, diabetes, chronic obstructive lung disease, lung cancer, breast cancer, cervical cancer, colorectal cancer, and liver disease.

c Rate is 426 per 100,000 for the United States in 1986, multiplied by 6 for comparability to above overall rates that are for six years.

d Based on the overall rate.

include the 5,200,000 German civilians and military killed in Hitler's aggression against other countries, then the chances of an average German surviving the regime was slightly better than eleven to one — awfully low odds for a life.

As high as this cost was for the Germans, it was generally far higher for other countries invaded and occupied by the Nazis, particularly in Eastern Europe. Not only were critics and opponents eliminated as a matter of course, but any serious potential opposition was prevented by simply exterminating the top leaders, intellectuals, and professionals. Aside from Jews, the Germans murdered nearly 2,400,000 Poles, 3,000,000 Ukrainians, 1,600 Russians, and 1,400 Byelorussians, many of these the best and the brightest men and women. Including Jews, nearly one out of every six Poles or Soviet citizens under Nazi rule was killed by them in cold blood.

Aside from actual or potential critics and opponents, throughout occupied Europe the Nazis used terror and reprisal to maintain control and to prevent attacks on Germans. The clandestine killing of a German soldier could mean the roundup and execution of all the men in a nearby village, the village's total destruction, and the deportation of all the women and children to a concentration camp. Dozens and even hundreds of hostages would be shot in retaliation for sabotage. In some occupied areas in which the Nazis had to contend with well-organized and active guerrilla units, they applied a simple rule: 100 nearby civilians would be massacred for every German soldier killed; 50 for every one wounded. Often this was a minimum that might be doubled or tripled. Vast numbers of innocent peasants and townsfolk were thus killed, possibly as many as 8,000 in Kragujevac,[4] 1,755 in Kraljevo,[5] and 80,000 in Jajinci,[6] to name just in a few places in Yugoslavia alone. Most executions were small, but the number executed added up over time, as can be seen from the following record in an official German war diary:

16 December 1942: "In Belgrade, 8 arrests, 60 Mihailovich [the guerrilla Chetnik leader] supporters shot."

27 December: "In Belgrade, 11 arrests, 250 Mihailovich supporters shot as retaliation."[7] A German placard from Belgrade announces 50 hostages shot in retaliation for the dynamiting of a bridge during this December.

25 May 1943: 150 hostages shot in Kraljevo

October: 150 hostages shot in Belgrade.[8]

50 hostages shot in Belgrade in August 1943.[9]

150 Serbs shot at Cacak in October.[10]

And so on. In Greece, as another example, the Nazis may have burned and destroyed as many as 1,600 villages having populations between 500 and 1,000,[11] no doubt massacring many of the inhabitants beforehand. Overall, hundreds of thousands were slaughtered in Yugoslavia, Czechoslovakia, Greece, and France. Millions were slaughtered in Poland and the Soviet Union.

But above all, people were machine-gunned in batches, shot in the head at the edge of trenches, burned alive while crowded into churches, gassed in vans or fake shower rooms, starved or frozen to death, worked to death in camps, or simply beaten or tortured to death because of their race, religion, handicap, or sexual preference.

Consider the account of an Einsatzgruppe (a mobile SS killing squad) at labor, as declared under oath by Hermann Friedrich Graebe, a director and chief engineer of a branch of the Josef Jung Construction Company of Solingen. While visiting the firm's projects at Dubno in the Ukraine, he heard about the mass killing taking place at a construction site. Going there to see for himself, he witnessed the following.

> I saw great mounds of earth about 30 meters long and 2 high. Several trucks were parked nearby. Armed Ukrainian militia were making people get out, under the surveillance of SS soldiers. The same militia men were responsible for guard duty and driving the trucks. The people in the trucks wore the regulation yellow pieces of cloth that identified them as Jews on the front and back of their clothing.
> ...
> The people from the trucks — men, women, and children — were forced to undress under the supervision of an SS soldier with a whip in his hand. They were obliged to put their effects in certain spots: shoes, clothing, and underwear separately.... Without weeping or crying out, these people undressed and stood together in family groups, embracing each other and saying good-bye while waiting for a sign from the SS soldier, who stood on the edge of the ditch, a whip in his hand, too. During the fifteen minutes I stayed there, I did not hear a single complaint or a plea for mercy. I watched a family of about eight: a man and woman about fifty

years old, surrounded by their children of about one, eight, and ten, and two big girls about twenty and twenty-four. An old lady, her hair completely white, held the baby in her arms, rocking it, and singing it a song. The infant was crying aloud with delight. The parents watched the group with tears in their eyes. The father held the ten-year old boy by the hand, speaking softly to him: the child struggled to hold back his tears. Then the father pointed a finger to the sky and, stroking the child's head, seemed to be explaining something. At this moment, the SS near the ditch called something to his comrade. The latter counted off some twenty people and ordered them behind the mound. The family of which I have just spoken was in the group. I still remember the young girl, slender and dark, who, passing near me, pointed at herself, saying "twenty-three." I walked around the mound and faced a frightful common grave. Tightly packed corpses were heaped so close together that only the heads showed. Most were wounded in the head and the blood flowed over their shoulders. Some still moved. Others raised their hands and turned their heads to show they were still alive. The ditch was two-thirds full. I estimate that it held a thousand bodies. I turned my eyes toward the man who had carried out the execution. He was an SS man; he was seated, legs swinging, on the narrow edge of the ditch; an automatic rifle rested on his knees and he was smoking a cigarette. The people, completely naked, climbed down a few steps cut in the clay wall and stopped at the spot indicated by the SS man. Facing the dead and wounded, they spoke softly to them. Then I heard a series of rifle shots. I looked in the ditch and saw their bodes contorting, their heads, already inert, sinking on the corpses beneath. The blood flowed from the nape of their necks. I was astonished not to be ordered away, but I noticed two or three uniformed post men nearby. A new batch of victims approached the place. They climbed down into the ditch, lined up in front of the previous victims, and were shot.

On the way back, while rounding the mound, I saw another full truck which had just arrived. This truck contained only the sick and crippled. Women already naked were undressing an old woman with an emaciated body; her legs frightfully thin. She was held up by two people and seemed paralyzed. The naked people went behind the mound.
...

The next morning, returning to the construction, I saw some thirty naked bodies lying thirty to fifty yards from the ditch. Some were still alive; they stared into space with a set look, seeming not to feel the coolness of the morning air, nor to see the workers standing all around. A young girl of about twenty spoke to me, asking me to bring her clothes and to help her escape. At that moment we heard the sound of a car approaching at top speed; I saw that it was an SS detachment. I went back to my work. Ten minutes later rifle shots sounded from the ditch. The Jews who were still alive had been ordered to throw the bodies in the ditch; then they had to lie down themselves to receive a bullet in the back of the neck.[12]

Such mobile killing squads eventually murdered over 1 million people guilty of nothing more than their religion; another some 350,000 were probably killed by the army, antipartisan units, higher SS and police, in Ghettos, or while fleeing.[13] This does not even take into account the trainloads of mainly Jews, but also sometimes of Gypsies and other "undesirables," murdered in Nazi death camps.

The primary such death camp was Auschwitz in Poland. After arrival by train, the Jews and others were passed one-by-one before camp doctors who would choose on the spot those fit enough to work — in seconds one's fate was determined. The doctor's thumb motioning to the right meant work and life, at least for awhile, even for those destined for medical experiments; to the left meant death in hours. Unaware of their fate, those sent left first had their luggage taken away and then were separated into groups of men and women. They were led to the extermination camp (Auschwitz II, or Birkenau), sometimes while being entertained by a symphony orchestra of prisoners.

When they reached the halls in front of the gas chamber they saw signs reading "Wash and Disinfection Room". Inside they were made to strip, being told that they would all have to take showers. Their valuables and clothes were collected, for which they got receipts. Presumably as a health measure, women had their hair cut off. Finally, under the stern orders of guards, all were crowded into the "shower room." Those that became suspicious and hesitated were driven inside with whips and rods. The doors were closed and locked. Once trapped inside, most victims could see that death was minutes away. The false shower facilities did not work, and from outside the lights were all turned off.

The powerful poison gas (Zyklon B, or hydrogen cyanide) was brought to the gas chamber by a Red Cross vehicle, and an SS man wearing a gas mask carried the gas containers to the building, lifted a glass shutter over a latticed entrance, and emptied the contents into the chamber. Nearby, the political chief of the camp started his stopwatch.

As the first pellets sublimated on the floor of the chamber, the law of the jungle took over. To escape from the rapidly rising gas, the stronger knocked down the weaker, stepping on the prostate victims in order to prolong their life by reaching the gas-free layers of air. The agony lasted for about two minutes; then the shrieking subsided, the dying men slumping over. Within four minutes everybody in the gas chamber was dead. The gas was now allowed to escape, and after about a half-hour the doors were opened. The bodies were found in tower-like heaps, some in sitting or half-sitting position under the doors. The corpses were pink in color, with green spots. Some had foam on their lips; others bled through the nose.[14]

In some camps with much smaller gas chambers and where carbon monoxide was used, such as at Belzec, so many victims might be forced into the chamber that there was no room to move. Once the gassing started, they might take up to three hours to die. One visitor to the site who put his ear to the wall to hear what was going on as the Jews died observed, "Just like a synagogue."[15] As one witness observed, when finally all inside were dead and the doors opened, "the bodies were thrown out blue, wet with sweat and urine, the legs covered with excrement and menstrual blood."[16]

So many gassed per day, so many cremated per hour — it was a stopwatch system, at the center of the best in human technology, knowledge, and efficiency, and carried out by what was considered in the 1930s to be one of the most civilized, educated, and developed nations in the world. In Auschwitz alone around 1,250,000 innocents, mainly Jews, may have perished on the human-to-ashes conveyer belt.[17] Possibly 2 million people were similarly massacred in other death camps like Maidanek, Treblinka, and Skarzisko Kamienno — more likely closer to 1,500,000.[18]

As all this makes clear, the Nazi leaders were absolute racists; they believed utterly in the superiority of their Aryan race. They had no doubt that they were the pinnacle of racial evolution, that eugenically they were the best. Lest this seem an exaggeration, consider the text on Eastern Europeans that was distributed to the SS from the SS main office.

The sub-human, this apparently fully equal creation of nature, when seen from the biological viewpoint, with hands, feet and a sort of brain, with eyes and a mouth, nevertheless is quite a different, a dreadful creature, is only an imitation of man with man-resembling features, but inferior to any animal as regards intellect and soul. In its interior, this being is a cruel chaos of wild, unrestricted passions, with a nameless will to destruction, with a most primitive lust, and of unmasked depravity.

For not everything is alike that has a human face.[19]

So science proved, they thought. And therefore no inferior group could be allowed to pollute their racial strain.

Inferior races were like diseased organs that had to be surgically removed for the health of the body. One Nazi doctor, looking at the smoking crematoria at Auschwitz, was asked how he could reconcile the slaughter with his Hippocratic oath. In the Nazi world, his answer was justification enough for the pain and death inflicted on millions: "When you find a diseased appendix, you must remove it."[20]

Nothing could allow the master race to be weakened. Therefore, the Jews and Gypsies must be exterminated. So must also the homosexuals and handicapped. So must also the Slavs, not only because of their biological inferiority but also to make room for the superior race to expand and grow. But then the Nazi program ran into the problem of numbers. Exterminating millions of Jews and Gypsies had been hard enough, but the Slavs numbered in the tens of millions. So they envisioned a two-part approach: reduce the number of Slavs through execution, starvation, and disease, and after the war, which the Nazis would of course win, deport the remaining 30 or 40 million to Siberia.

These genocides likely cost the lives of about 16,300,000 people: nearly 5,300,000 Jews, 260,000 Gypsies, 10,500,000 Slavs, and 220,000 homosexuals as well as another 170,000 handicapped Germans. Through repression, terrorism, reprisals, and other cold-blooded killing done to impose and maintain their rule throughout Europe, the Nazis murdered millions more Frenchmen, Dutch, Serbs, Slovens, Czechs, and others. In total, almost 21 million human beings.

Annually, as shown in table 6.2, the Nazis killed six to seven people out of every hundred in occupied Europe. The odds of a European surviving under Nazi occupation was about fifteen to one. As table 6.2 shows, this is less than *half* the odds of an American surviving nine of the worst diseases, specifically stroke, heart disease, diabetes, chronic obstructive lung disease, lung cancer, breast cancer, cervical cancer, colorectal cancer and liver disease.[21]

Moreover, even though the Nazis hardly matched the democide of the Soviets and communist Chinese, as shown in table 6.3, they killed proportionally more. Figure 6.2 illustrates this well: The annual odds of dying under Nazi occupation were almost two-and-a-half times that of Soviet citizens being killed by their government since 1917; over nine times that for Chinese living in communist China after 1949. In competition for who could murder proportionally the greatest number of human beings, the Japanese militarists come closest. The annual odds of surviving their occupation of China, Korea, Indonesia, Burma, Indo-China, and elsewhere in Asia were 101 to one. Given the years and population available to this gang of megamurderers, the Nazis have been the deadliest killers among them, the Japanese militarists next so.

TABLE 6.3
Comparison of Nazi Democide to That of Other Regimes [a]

| Government | Population | Period | Democide [a] | | Odds of Dying [f] |
			Killed	Rate [e]	
Soviet Union	cit./for. [b]	1917–87	61,911	.45	1 in 222
Communist China	citizens	1949–87	35,236	.12	1 in 833
Nazi Europe	**Europe [c]**	**1939–45**	**20,946**	**1.08**	**1 in 93**
Nationalist China	citizens	1929–49	10.075	.07	1 in 1,428
Japanese Militarists	Asia [d]	1937–45	5,964	.28	1 in 101
Nazi Germany	**citizens**	**1933–45**	**762**	**0.08**	**1 in 1,235**

a Figures are from tables 6.1 and 6.2 for Nazis; from Rummel 1990 for the Soviets; from Rummel 1991 for the Chinese; and from chapter 8 for the Japanese militarists. Governments are rank ordered by their democide.

b Citizens and foreigners

c Occupied Europe, excluding Germany

d Occupied Asia, excluding Japan

e Percentage annual rate. Soviet rate for citizens only.

f In any year. Calculated using the annual democide rate: 1 in (100/(% annual rate)).

FIGURE 6.1
Nazi Democide Compared to That of Others
(Data comes from table 6.3.)

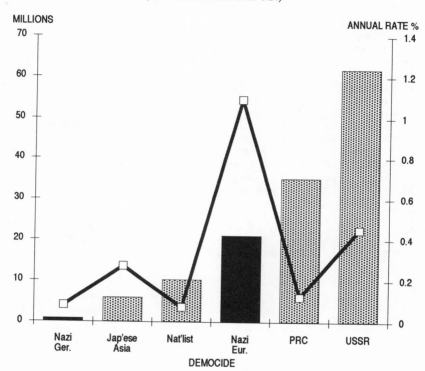

Notes

1.   Feig 1990, 174.
2.   This was a private, quasi-military organization of storm troopers, Sturmabteilung, that Hitler began to organize as his private army in 1921, long before he came to power.
3.   The Schutzstaffel.
4.   Seton-Watson 1961, 120–21.
5.   Browning 1990, 70.
6.   Martin 1978, 48.
7.   Ibid., 47.

8. Ibid., 47–48.
9. Ibid., 70.
10. Ibid., 78.
11. Macksey 1975, 158.
12. Poliakov 1971, 125–26.
13. Hilberg 1961, 767.
14. Hilberg 1961, 627.
15. Ibid.
16. Ibid., 628.
17. This is a substantial revision of the 4,500,000 figure I used in Rummel 1992, for which I relied on Kogon 1960, 251, and which figure was in the range of deaths given by others. However, more recent research has strongly suggested that such estimates were much inflated and that the true toll for all victims may be between 1,100,000 and 1,500,000. A new plaque put up at Auschwitz now reads "May this place, in which the Hitlerites murdered some one and a half million men, women and children—mainly Jews from various countries of Europe—for ever be a cry of despair and a warning to mankind. Auschwitz-Birkenau 1940–1945."
18. Kogon 1960, 250. The larger figure includes ghetto deaths; the smaller may not.
19. Kamenetsky 1961, 38–39.
20. Ibid., 226.
21. As reported in a study by the National Centers for Disease Control, 427 Americans out of every 100,000 died from these nine diseases in 1986 (*Honolulu Star-Bulletin*, 28 November 1990, p. 1).

7

10,214,000 Murdered
The Depraved Nationalist Regime

In one place outside of Kweiyang where the draftees passed through, there were so many abandoned bodies that even the air became unbearable to breathe. The odor was so odious that one had to hold one's nose constantly if one wished to avoid vomiting.

—Chiang Meng-lin,
President of the Chinese Red Cross

Chapter 5 on the Chinese communists gave some background for understanding nationalist democide. Once Chiang Kai-shek had largely defeated the warlords in 1927 and moved toward a nationalist government of China, he turned on communist allies, purging them from his party and major cities. From then to his final defeat in 1949, there would be negotiations, truces, and common fronts with the communists. But for the common Chinese the killing never really stopped — not by the communists and not by the nationalists.

123

Throughout this period, the nationalist government was authoritarian and militaristic, really fascist in outlook and style. Chiang Kai-shek saw as ideal a government organized and governing along military lines. In this he was like the Japanese militarists of his time, which might be expected of someone who had been educated in a Japanese military academy.

The nationalists were not very different from their chief adversaries, the communists. In fact, in their absolute one-party rule (by the Kuomintang), their intolerance of dissent, and their willingness to use and expend human beings like so many wooden chop sticks, the nationalists were indistinguishable from the communists. It was not for lack of effort that during their rule of Mainland China the nationalists were never able to impose a communist-style, hierarchical structure of power. They murdered opponents, assassinated critics, and employed terror as a device of rule. A wave of massacres during the 1927 to 1928 period, for example, was described as follows by the newspaper *China Forum*,

> The Terror extended to every village, town, city and industrial district. The gates of towns and cities were closed and soldiers turned loose on the population. The soldiers looted, raped, left the streets littered with corpses and the wells clogged with the bodies of outraged girls and women.[1]

Such nationalist terror continued through the early 1930s, the Sino-Japanese War years, and into the civil war period. Indeed, executions, assassinations, mass murder, and disappearances were if anything even more widespread during this final period, reaching their peak activity as the nationalists fled in defeat. In one prison, for example, as the nationalist troops evacuated and communist troops moved in, 200 to 300 political prisoners were shot and burned. The missionary who reported this massacre points out that "this must have been done with the full consent of Chiang Kai-shek, for they were important people and he had not left yet."[2]

The deadliness of nationalist repression was most clear to all on Formosa (Taiwan). China ceded Formosa to Japan after losing the 1895 Sino-Japanese War. At the end of the (Second) Sino-Japanese war in 1945, the nationalists occupied Formosa and set up an administration on the island (which had not been legally returned to

China, so that the nationalists were in fact stewards of the island's wealth and population). All the nationalist evils experienced on the mainland, such as corruption, suppression of dissent, heavy taxes, and assassinations, were soon inflicted on the Formosans, particularly under nationalist General Chen Yi. The pillage was compounded by open looting of the island's wealth and arrogant treatment of, and discrimination against, Formosans.

The nationalists acted as conquerors, and Formosans soon began to feel that life under the Japanese had been much better. They began to demonstrate, organize, and petition for better treatment and representation. Finally, in February 1947, after a demonstration had been fired on by police and mainland Chinese attacked by Formosans, General Chen promised reforms. But this was a mask behind which he ordered that reinforcements be dispatched from the mainland. The next month, the nationalists launched a bloody campaign of repression all over the island, murdering perhaps 10,000 people,[3] possibly even 40,000,[4] including some of the Formosan's foremost leaders. Executions continued for several months and were resumed again as Chiang Kai-shek began to prepare his retreat to Formosa in 1948.

But nationalist killing went beyond purges and repression. It was also strategic and ideological. After the purge of communists in 1927, the nationalists sought out communists or communist sympathizers for execution wherever they might be. Whenever they defeated the communists in a particular region and occupied or reoccupied it, they killed anyone they felt had cooperated with the communists or had been tainted by them.

When, during the nationalist's fifth "bandit extermination" campaign in 1933 to 1934, the communists made their historic and famous, year-long retreat — Long March — across twelve provinces to a more secure region in north Shensi, the nationalists executed many of those that were left behind. Such was done, for example, in the model Red county of Xingguo where "probably" 2,000 of the remaining Ninth Red Army and party people were killed.[5] In Ning-tu, members of 8,334 households (perhaps some 41,670 people) were murdered; over 12,000 men in the former communist capital of Juichin were killed.[6] But these deaths may have been a small fraction of the total. Says Ho Ping-ti in his study of China's population during this period,

Nationalist reprisals were also severe in other old Red bases. Huang-an county in Hupei, with a pre-1934 population of some 160,000, had but 66,000 in 1953. For six years after the Communist retreat the eighty-li stretch between Hsin-hsien and Lo-t'ien in Hupei remained entirely leveled by the Nationalists and turned into a no-man's-land.... [J]ournalists testified to the general under population of the southern and central Kiangsi area. As has been shown, the 1953 population of Kiangsi was given as 31.4 per cent less than that of 1850.[7]

According to Edgar Snow, "the Kuomintang itself admits that about 1 million people were killed or starved to death in the process of recovering Soviet Kiangsi."[8]

In many other areas, including those along the route of the Long March, the nationalists ordered that as a matter of necessity the civilian population be exterminated. All this was in line with one of Chiang Kai-shek's speeches, wherein he remarked that in long-held communist areas "it was impossible to tell a Red-bandit from a good citizen."[9] In the Oyüwan Soviet (in eastern Hupeh province) alone, by the end of the campaign the population had been decreased by about 600,000.[10]

The Sino-Japanese war and its aftermath provided the nationalists with special opportunities for democide. For example, there were the former Chinese puppet soldiers who fought for the Chinese government set up by the Japanese in occupied territory. Usually they were poor peasants impressed into service and lacking any conception of events beyond their simple lives. After the Japanese surrender, many melted into the mass of postwar refugees or joined the communist army, 75,000 eventually doing so.[11] But many made the mistake of returning home after the war. The nationalists shot many of them.

Much other nationalist killing took place in the countryside as they took over from the Japanese at the end of the war, or reoccupied territory captured from the communists during the civil war (as during the extermination campaigns against the communists in the prewar years). In the train of nationalist soldiers came the former landlords, officials, and the like. Soon becoming local officials, such as bailiffs or district heads, they then either killed those peasants they feared or had grudges against, or gave their names to the secret police or army for execution.

Of course, an active search for communist sympathizers was made; those found, reported, or suspected were often shot or buried alive. In Honan's Anyang County, for example, the county government claims that 400 men, women, and children were killed or buried alive after the area was captured by nationalist forces. Says correspondent Jack Belden: "I have every reason to believe [these figures] are not exaggerated. In one village, while I was there, twenty-four bodies, including women and children, were exhumed from a common pit where they had been buried alive and then been partially uncovered and eaten by dogs."[12]

In another village of 130 people and twenty-eight families, members of twenty-four families had been buried alive or shot. In another group of eighteen villages, the army killed forty-six former communist cadre and militiamen, shooting seven, burying alive thirty-five, and forcing the remainder to hang themselves.[13]

In northern Kiangsu, those that had been active or held some position in one of the communist organizations before the nationalists took over were arrested and required to surrender their weapons. Since most had no weapons, a tael of gold was demanded as a fine, allegedly to arm the self-defense militia. The gold really went into the pockets of officials. If the prisoners had no weapon or gold, they were killed if the official was in that kind of a mood.[14]

A former peasant, who joined the communist army after experiencing a landlord's reprisal when the nationalists returned, described to Jack Belden what happened:

"He shot my wife, my brother and my baby."

I just stared at him.

"He buried alive four members of my family. My son, my uncle, my nephew and one married daughter who had come home on a visit. One boy — he has six years — got away. They bayoneted him, but the knife slid along his forehead and he didn't die."
...

He stopped speaking, his throat hard and his eyes looking straight ahead. I was silent for a minute, then asked.

"Why was this killing? Was there a connection between you?"

"There was a connection. There was a famine in the village in 1943. We had no food to eat as many others. In the winter he lent me grain. When the fall came I could not pay it back. I had eight mow [one and one-third acres] of land and he took four. He was the bodyguard of the district Japanese puppet leader. He had a pistol and there was nothing I could do. I was without politics, but when the [communists] 8th Route Army came and asked our grievances, I told them. They said the poor should not lose their means of living for such reasons and we ought to struggle against the landlords. So I helped lead the struggle. I paid him the debt I owed him, but not the interest, and took back my four mow of land. For this he hated me. Then the Kuomintang came and I knew it was not safe for me and I took to the hills. He was angry to find I had gone. So he killed all of my family members.[15]

As small as all these numbers are, they add up. According to one communist source, in just one subdistrict the total killed by returning nationalists was nearly 10,000 people.[16] Considering that this went on in one way or another in an area encompassing over 100 million peasants, the human toll must have been huge. I estimate it at almost 1,200,000,[17] but even twice this mortality would not be surprising.

One particular source of nationalist democide was the nationalist soldier. He was considered scum, lower than vermin. He was beaten, mistreated, often fed poorly and ill paid. Nationalist officers squeezed their soldiers' rations, leaving many of them to endure nutritional deficiencies and to barely survive on the verge of starvation. The soldiers often wore the same uniforms throughout winter; they generally had no soap or bathing facilities in their army camps; kitchens may have been located near latrines; drinking water was seldom boiled; and they ate out of the same pot. Sanitary and medical practices were very primitive, if present at all. Disease was widespread, of course, with malaria being most prevalent. Some soldiers could not go even a short distance; many died along the side of the road from disease or starvation. Those too sick or weak were sometimes dumped on stretchers along the road to die. Wrote one reporter: "where troops have passed, dead soldiers can be found by the roadside one after another."[18] During the redeployment of one supposedly good outfit that still could fight, 30 percent of the soldiers died while marching 500 miles.[19] This despicable treatment of soldiers was nearly democidal in itself, but what is most salient here is that these miserable soldiers could hardly treat civilians with much more sympathy.

Where nationalist Chinese armies were garrisoned or passed, villages and peasants in the field might suffer looting, burning, rape, and murder, often abetted if not condoned by their officers. After all, it was the soldier's "compensation." Consider that in Hupeh province in May 1943, "Chinese troops ordered whole towns evacuated on grounds of military necessity — and then plundered them for everything of value. Persons too old to move and who remained in the towns were killed as traitors."[20] During the war, peasants often had as much to fear from their own soldiers as they did from the Japanese. Sometimes they simply revolted or turned on the soldiers to exact revenge.

A vastly greater democide involved the military's treatment of its conscripts during the Sino-Japanese War and the following civil war. Conscription generally descended like an act of a malevolent God on poor and defenseless men. Peasants in the field, workers going to their job in the morning, or men caught on a road could be jumped on by troops, manacled together, and marched off to a camp tens, if not hundreds, of miles away. In one case, a platoon of soldiers led by their company commander seized a man dressed in civilian clothes on the road. He turned out to be the battalion commander. Outranked by his prisoner and terrified by his mistake, the company commander immediately murdered his prisoner, but he too was later shot.[21]

Competing with roving units of soldiers, civilian press-gangs also seized passersby and sold them to the army. In Chengtu during one early recruitment drive,

a black-market recruit, a trussed-and-bound victim of the press gangs, was sold for ... the purchase price of five sacks of white rice or three pigs.

In one Szechwan district the village headman stationed himself at a crossroads with armed soldiers and seized a fifty-year-old man and his grandson. The boy was leading the grandfather to the hospital, but it made no difference; off they went to the recruit camp.[22]

Resistance meant death or mutilation. Those who could not keep up as they trudged toward a camp might be shot. Those who tried to escape usually were shot. Those who disobeyed orders often were shot. Moreover, on the way to camp conscripts were poorly fed, if at all. Some starved to death on the way. And there was no medical help if they became sick. In short, they were treated even worse than soldiers already on active duty. Foreigners would often report seeing these sad lines of ragtag conscripts chained together, shuffling along with their heads down under armed escort like so many chain-gang prisoners.

"Frequently, only half of the draftees would ever reach base camp."[23] Often only 10 percent of the conscripts would arrive alive.[24] Chiang Meng-lin, a famous educator and then president of the Chinese Red Cross, reported meeting a group of draftees in a reception center at Kweiyang. They said that of the 700 of them that started out for camp all but seventeen died on the way.[25]

Those that survived found camp conditions little better and the mortality hardly less. Of 40,000 conscripts arriving at a camp near Chengtu during one conscription drive, no more than 8,000 remained alive by the end of the drive.[26] When the news about the Nazi concentration camps at Belsen and Buchenwald broke, doctors working in one Chinese army camp could hardly be horrified: the description of the Nazi camps was little different from that of the ones they were working in, they said.[27]

The treatment of these conscripts was a national scandal. Some of Chiang Kai-shek's U.S. and influential Chinese advisors objected strenuously. In a memorandum to Chiang, General Albert Wedemeyer, commander of U.S. forces in China from late 1944 and chief of staff to Chiang Kai-shek, wrote: "Conscription comes to the Chinese peasant like famine or flood, only more regularly — every year twice — and claims more victims. Famine, flood, and drought compare with conscription like chicken pox with plague."[28] Further confirming what the doctors in one camp had to say above, Wedemeyer reported that the "hospitals" these conscripts were sent to in the camps were similar to Buchenwald.[29]

How many died during conscription? Of the 14 million the nationalists record as being conscripted during the Sino-Japanese War, Professor Ch'i Hsi-Sheng points out that about 11 million either deserted or "perished."[30] Mentioning the same number of conscripts, Theodore White and Annalee Jacoby come up with 7 million dead or missing.[31] Chiang Meng-lin, who as mentioned above was the president of the Red Cross, calculated the number of conscript deaths before induction as "no less than 14 million"[32] Believing that this figure "is probably meant" to be 1,400,000, Sinologist Lloyd Eastman puts the number of deaths at "well in excess of one-million."[33] For demographer Ho Ping-ti, it "would be surprising" if the number of deaths was less than the official number of battle killed and wounded — 3,081,293 men.[34] It seems to me that something near this number would be a most prudent estimate of this incredible democide. Even then it is close to the total military battle dead for Germany in all of World War II, and twice the number for Japan; only the Soviet Union lost in battle more soldiers than the number of these poor Chinese conscripts who died at the hands of press-gangs or their own soldiers.[35]

And this calculation does not even include those killed in or dying from the conscription drives during the subsequent civil war. As the manpower shortage grew, due to the demands of the civil war, recruits were enlisted in increasingly "harsh" conscription drives.[36] And in the words of Suzanne Pepper, an expert on this period, "there was no evidence to suggest much improvement during the civil war years."[37] Nor is there evidence that the risk to life and limb of poor peasants, or the profit of press-gangs, was much less than during the war against Japan. As one Chinese correspondent summed it up in December 1946:

> as soon as the news arrived, the people felt it to be a great disaster but the *hsiang* [administrative village], *pao* [six to fifteen chia], and *chia* [six to fifteen families] chiefs ran about happily. Good fortune had arrived for them once again since they would now have an opportunity to rake in a few more dollars.[38]

This civil war conscription may have cost more than 1,100,000 additional lives.[39]

The nationalists' cold-blooded treatment of their own people is best exemplified by their savage use of the Yellow River during and after the Sino-Japanese War. As the Japanese moved west toward the strategic railroad junction of Chengchow in 1938, there to link up with other Japanese forces for an advance on Hankow, the nationalists dynamited the Yellow River dikes in two places. The river, the largest in North China, flooded across Honan's plains and raced into the province of Anhwei, carving out a new course before surging into the ocean south of the Shantung Peninsula, ignoring its former outlet to the north. Three provinces and forty-four counties were inundated;[40] between 4,000 and 5,000 villages and eleven large towns were flooded.[41]

This monstrous flood was unleashed after long deliberation and was timed to create the maximum inundation by taking advantage of the spring runoff. The aim was to obstruct north-south transportation routes for the Japanese and to halt their offensive in the region. But the cost in Chinese lives from the resulting manmade flood was horrendous. After the war, the Institute of Social Sciences of the Academy Sinica and the China National Rehabilitation and Relief Agency carried out a joint study on the damage caused by this disaster. They concluded that 20.1 percent of the population — 3,911,354 people — in the provinces of Honan, Anhwei, and Kiangsu were displaced, and that these provinces lost 90 to 100 percent of their summer and 50 to 90 percent of their winter crops. And 893,303 people died.[42]

Understandably, the public was outraged by these deaths, and the nationalists felt it necessary to lie: the Japanese did it, they claimed.[43]

Hardly chastised by this public shock, the nationalists engineered another catastrophic Yellow River flood during the civil war. In order to divide communist armies in North China by a barrier of water, and thus release nationalist troops for an attack on Yenan (the communist capital), the nationalists repaired the dikes that they had dynamited during the war. Unfortunately, in the years since, some 400,000 peasants had settled on and tilled about 800,000 acres of the old river bed;[44] new towns and villages had grown up there. Warned of the nationalists' intent, peasants tried to build dikes around their towns and villages. But they and the laboring peasants were bombed and strafed by Chiang's air force. Reported the United Nations Relief and Rehabilitation Administration in March 1947:

> The final closure operations had been rushed under strong Nationalist military pressure and in disregard of agreements previously made with UNRRA and Border Region representatives.... Plans which UNRRA, CNRRA and Border Region personnel had made to alleviate the adverse economic effects of the river diversion ... had not been carried out. Dike

work was made difficult by frequent Nationalist air attacks upon the dike workers.[45]

Even ships of the United Nations Relief and Rehabilitation Administration carrying dike repair and relief materials were bombed.[46]

The resulting flood, surging down the old channel and flooding the neighboring low lands, inundated nearly 500 villages and made over 100,000 people homeless.[47] More hundreds of thousands were threatened by gradually rising waters. This was the time of the wheat harvest, and no doubt much of it was destroyed, with consequent famine and disease. Perhaps some 6,000 people died from the consequent disruption and associated disease.[48]

Nationalist-made floods were one mortal risk; another was nationalist-aggravated famines. Consider the terrible famine in Honan province from 1942 to 1943. The immediate cause was a drought, but the famine was greatly intensified by nationalist policies, corruption, and extortion of grain from the peasants. In fact, the nationalists "pressed the starving people ruthlessly for taxes."[49] While thus depriving the peasants of the means to buy food, the nationalists also forcibly requisitioned what little food the peasants had, even down to seed grains. They even grabbed entire harvests.[50] As nationalists transported or smuggled food out of the region, much of it to be sold by local officials and officers, peasants died of starvation.

> The army officers and local officials who collected the grain regarded their right to tax as a supplement to their salary, a franchise to loot.
> ...
> Even American relief authorities, operating with American money, were forced to beg army officers for the rights to buy private hoards for distribution back to the very peasantry from whom the grain had been extorted.[51]

Neighboring provinces had sufficient grain, but Shensi could not be forced to give up its reserve in favor of Honan without upsetting a "delicate balance of power," and the area commander in Hupeh would not allow grain to be moved into Honan.[52]

"The result was wholesale famine in the winter of 1942–43, with many seeking subsistence by eating bark, roots, and animal fodder.

Cannibalism was reported."[53] By the time it was over, 2 million to 3 million starved to death or died of related diseases. Afterward, many of those surviving were rounded up for forced labor for the army, to build roads, or to dig an antitank ditch over 480 kilometers long. Nearly 1 million had to build dikes along the Yellow River. They received no pay; often they had to find their own food.[54] One can only guess at how many of these survivors also died.

In 1943 to 1944 there was a drought-caused, nationalist-aggravated famine in Kwangtung. While people were starving there, nationalist officials and army officers smuggled out rice they extorted from the peasants. Much of this rice was sold to the Japanese for high personal profit. Over 1,500,000 people died.[55] This became a major national scandal and cost the nationalists much support. It helped destroy what was left of the nationalists' moral case against the communists.

While attributing proportional responsibility in these Honan and Kwantung famines is very subjective, making the nationalists responsible for half of those who starved to death, or 1,750,000 to 2,500,000 Chinese, seems only just, as well as reasonable.[56]

In sum, from the earliest years to their final defeat on the mainland, the nationalists likely killed from less than 6 million to more than 18,500,000 helpless people, probably around 10,200,000. Table 7.1 gives the relevant, most probable figures for the three most important periods during the nationalist years, and for comparison the figures for the communists in the areas they controlled and the (nondemocidal) famine deaths and war/rebellion Chinese dead. As can be seen, during these years the nationalists murdered over a million more than the number that died either from famine or from all the wars and rebellions, including the Sino-Japanese War. Figure 7.1 compares the nationalist and communist totals to that overall; table 7.2 gives the democide rates for the nationalists and communists.

These data rank the nationalists as the fourth greatest demociders of this century, behind the Soviets, Chinese communists, and Nazis. This democide is even more impressive when it is realized that the nationalists never controlled all of China, perhaps 50 to 60 percent of the population at most.

How do we understand all this nationalist killing? Some of it was ideological, as with the communists. The nationalists believed in unifying and modernizing China, in improving the lot of the poor

TABLE 7.1
China's Democide, Famine, War, and Rebellion Dead, 1928-1949 [a]

| Period | Year | Democide (000) | | | | Other Dead (000) | | | Total Dead (000) |
		Total [b]	Communist	Nationalist	Japanese	Famine [c]	War/Rebellion [d]		
Nationalist Reign	1928-1937	2,724	850	1,524		6,500	406		9,629
Sino-Japanese War	1937-1945	10,216	250	5,907	3,949	2,250	7,140		19,605
Civil War	1945-1949	4,968	2,323	2,645		25	1,201		6,194
Total	1928-1949	17,907	3,423	10,075	3,949	8,775	8,747		35,428

a All figures are from Rummel 1991 (table 1.A). These are the most probable values in a low-high range of estimates. Columns may not sum to totals due to rounding.

b Totals may include other sources of democide than those shown, such as warlords.

c Non-democidal famine

d Only Chinese war-dead.

peasant, and in making China free of foreign influence and control. But such generalities hide a fundamentally fascist and militarist view of governance. The people were to be led, the government was to oversee all, power was to be hierarchical, one great party — the Kuomintang — would define the necessary policies, and the great government and party leader Chiang Kai-shek would provide the shining light. The nationalists were intolerant of opposition and criticism. They alone knew the true road to a better China, and those who stood in the way or aided their domestic enemies must be eliminated. Special among these were the communists and their leftists sympathizers, who were not only in ideological error but posed a dangerous threat to the regime. They were the expressed enemy, and all had to be exterminated.

But ideology only explains part of the nationalist democide. Sheer lust for power on the part of nationalist officials and officers, greed, corruption, fear of retribution (as from peasants who had grievances), and simple wanton disregard for human life were all part of a thoroughly perverted political system that bred lethal power jockeying, deadly status conflict, money grubbing at the expense of human lives, corruption as hundreds of thousands died of hunger, and lethal incompetence.

The system was also fundamentally out of control. Not even Chiang Kai-shek could fully command it, as could be seen from the millions that died from conscription, even though he tried to correct the system and executed some of those in charge. In effect, the nationalists

TABLE 7.2
Period and Annual Democide Rates (%) [a]

Period	Years	All China		Communists		Nationalists	
		Period	Annual	Period	Annual	Period	Annual
Nationalist Reign	1928–37	0.56	0.07	2.43	0.29	0.63	0.07
Sino-Japanese War	1937–45	2.04	0.25	0.43	0.05	2.29	0.28
Civil War	1945–49	0.97	0.24	1.33	0.33	0.79	0.19

a All figures are from Rummel 1991 (table 1.A). China's democide rate includes sources of democide other than those of the nationalists and communists.

conquered the warlords by absorbing many of them into the system, but they in turn created an administration of local and petty lords. Fear revenge from a peasant from whose family you stole land? Point him out to the local commander as antinationalist and he will vanish. Want the wife of a local merchant? A little gold for the local official will make the husband disappear forever. Want to make some extra money? Help round up some peasants on the road by force, tie them up, and sell the lot to the local commander as army "recruits."

This system fostered mass murder. Add an ideological overlay to it, such as the need to exterminate a dangerous domestic enemy, such as the communists, or the desire to survive against a foreign enemy, like the Japanese, and a truly incredible democide is the result — slightly over 10,200,000 people, *more than the total population of Greece, or Belgium, or Cambodia.*

FIGURE 7.1
Nationalist versus Communist Democide
(From table 7.1)

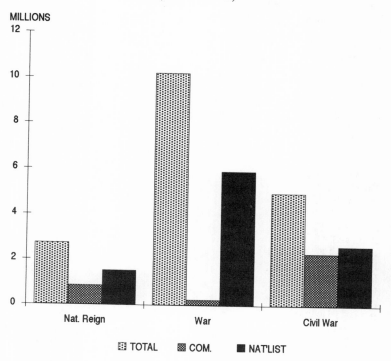

Notes

1. Quigley 1962, 73.
2. Stockwell 1953, 56.
3. Michael and Taylor 1975, 448.
4. Harff and Gurr 1988, 364.
5. Salisbury 1985, 203.
6. Ho 1959, 250.
7. Ibid.
8. Snow 1937, 186. See also Pelissier 1967, 333.
9. Snow 1937, 313–14.
10. Ibid., 314.
11. Botjer 1979, 240.
12. Belden 1949, 224.
13. Ibid., 224–25.
14. Pepper 1978, 300.
15. Belden 1949, 260–61.
16. Pepper 1978, 303.
17. Rummel 1991, app. 7.1
18. Eastman 1980, 123.
19. White and Jacoby 1946, 135.
20. Eastman 1980a, 298–99.
21. White and Jacoby 1946, 274.
22. Ibid.
23. Ch'i 1982, 162.
24. Archer 1972, 117.
25. Chiang 1969, 223.
26. White and Jacoby 1946, 275.
27. Ibid.
28. Sheridan 1975, 261.
29. Ibid., 262.
30. Ch'i 1982, 162.
31. White and Jacoby 1946, 132.
32. Chiang 1969, 225.
33. Eastman 1980, 120.
34. Ho 1959, 250–51.
35. Wright 1965, 1542.
36. Pelissier 1967, 485.
37. Pepper 1978, 166.
38. Ibid., 163.
39. Rummel 1991, app. 7.1
40. Ho 1959, 235.
41. Eastman 1980, 93.
42. Ho 1959, 235.
43. Clubb 1978, 224.
44. Belden 1949, 355.
45. Ibid., 356n. 2.
46. Ibid., 355.

47. Ibid., 356.
48. Rummel 1991, app. 7.1.
49. Sheridan 1975, 262.
50. Eastman 1980, 181.
51. White and Jacoby 1946, 175.
52. Ibid., 173.
53. Eastman 1980, 181.
54. Ibid.
55. Peck 1967, 21.
56. Rummel 1991, app. 5.1.

Part III

19,178,000 Victims
The Lesser Megamurderers

8

5,964,000 Murdered
Japan's Savage Military

The evidence shows that most of these massacres were ordered by commissioned officers, that some of them were ordered by high-ranking generals and admirals, that in many cases commissioned officers were actually present during their commission, observing, directing or actually doing the killing.

—Judgment of the Tokyo War Crimes Trials

In pursuit of an utterly racist policy during World War II, the Germans murdered millions of unarmed civilians in cold blood; obeying merciless ideological imperatives, the Soviets also massacred millions of helpless people. Like the others, the Japanese slaughtered millions during World War II, but not strictly because of racism or ideology. Rather, Japanese armies and secret police killed defenseless people seemingly as a matter of tactics, expedience, convenience, revenge, recreation, and an utterly amoral disregard for human life and

143

suffering. The Japanese believed themselves superior to other Asians and by policy severally punished resistance in occupied countries. The military rulers of Japan were also ardent national socialists, in the sense of believing in total national control over the country's economy and resources and centralized direction of the people's welfare. Said one military officer in 1936, "We desire a community in which all people are able to work to the fullest degree, accepting twenty per cent of the results of their labor as their private income and turning the rest over to the government as national income."[1] Also fervent nationalists, the military believed in the inherent superiority of Japan and its destiny as ruler of Asia.

But unlike Germany and the Soviet Union, there was not a general policy to exterminate certain races or categories of people, like professionals, former government officials, bourgeoisie, priests, landlords, etc. Rather, people were killed as an example to others who might oppose Japanese occupation. They were killed to erase a population supporting anti-Japanese guerrillas, to eliminate witnesses or a distraction (like a crying baby) to a looting or rape in process, to punish enemy soldiers who had surrendered for their cowardice, to avenge forgetting to bow to a Japanese soldier, to squeeze out the maximum labor from Asian and POW laborers at the minimum costs, to liquidate forced laborers too sick or broken for further toil, to experiment with bacteriological and chemical weapons, to train soldiers in killing, to practice rifle marksmanship or the use of the bayonet, or to revenge an attack on a soldier ... or they were killed just for the fun of it.

This is not to say that the highest Japanese authorities are absolved of responsibility for such killing. The Tokyo War Crimes Trials found them directly responsible for the democide — they knew what their troops were doing. As stated by Judge Hsiang regarding China, for example, "Knowledge of these continuing atrocities by Japanese soldiers in China was brought home to the Japanese High Command and to the Japanese government in Tokyo. Notwithstanding frequent notification and protest, the atrocities continued. This was the Japanese pattern for warfare."[2]

Such was especially the case with the atrocities committed in Nanking after occupation by the Japanese army in December 1937. Nanking was filled with hundreds of thousands of refugees, perhaps boosting its population to a million,[3] and as the then capitol of China it also had a high concentration of foreign diplomats, missionaries, and news correspondents. Japanese butcheries and barbarities thus became immediately known to the world and labeled as the Rape of Nanking. There is no need here to go into all the detail. Suffice it to say that looting, burning, torture, and rape were open and rampant. Some streets were littered with bodies. Chinese men who looked like they might have been soldiers were taken away to be machine-gunned in batches, and many foreigners told of coming upon Japanese soldiers in the act of rape. Protests against the rape of a daughter or wife often meant death, the rape victim herself often being shot or bayoneted afterward.

The final Nanking death toll would never be known, but the number of victims counted and buried within four months by "Tsung-shan-tang Teams" amounted to 112,266; those buried by the Red Swastika society numbered 43,071.[4] Estimates of the total killed vary widely. Doubtless unaware of the burial statistics, Arthur Zich gives a figure of 40,000 dead;[5] Dick Wilson claims that 100,000 dead was the official nationalist figure;[6] the chief prosecutor of the District Court of Nanking testified after the war to 260,000 dead.[7] Based on Chinese sources, a Japanese writer estimated the toll as 300,000,[8] apparently now also the official Chinese figure.[9] Perhaps a prudent estimate is of 200,000 murdered.

How are we to understand what happened in Nanking? Said Matsumoto Shigei, a correspondent in Shanghai, to some Western friends:

> It is the army. You can't know what they are like. You didn't meet those poor peasants who have been brutalized after years in the army. They are permitted to do this. It is worse than that; they are encouraged. It is their reward for taking a town; the officers promise them three days to do what they like, when a town is captured. They always do.... It is because Nanking is so important that you Americans hear about it this time, but it has always been true. It is a universal shame.[10]

And to be sure, in each of the other large cities that fell to the Japanese, including Peking, Shanghai, Hankow, and Canton, "Rape, pillage, and murder were the order of the day."[11] Indeed, according to Judge Hsiang's statement at the Tokyo Trials, the conduct of the Japanese soldiers at Nanking was no isolated instance. It was typical. Of the numerous incidents of this character, the judicial agencies of China have officially reported more than 95,000 separate cases perpetrated during the period from 1937 to 1945 and in every province in occupied China.[12]

If from no other source, the stories of returning Japanese soldiers made clear the extensiveness of such massacres and atrocities. Indeed, the military became concerned that these stories might provoke public criticism at home, and it ordered commanders in the field to instruct the soldiers to keep quiet about them upon reaching Japan. Classified top secret and transmitted to Japanese army commanders in China, these orders specified some of the objectionable stories soldiers were telling, such as:

One company commander unofficially gave instructions for raping as follows: "In order that we will not have problems, either pay them money or kill them in some obscure place after you have finished."

If the army men who participated in the war were investigated individually, they would probably all be guilty of murder, robbery or rape.

At ... we captured a family of four. We played with the daughter as we would with a harlot. But as the parents insisted that the daughter be returned to them we killed them. We played with the daughter as before until the unit's departure and then killed her.

The prisoners taken from the Chinese Army were sometimes lined up in one line and killed to test the efficiency of the machine gun.[13]

In China alone, possibly nearly 2,600,000 unarmed Chinese civilians were thus murdered.[14]

But China was only one country occupied by Japan. When Japan expanded the war into the Pacific and elsewhere in Asia after her attack on Pearl Harbor, the Japanese military also expanded the democide. In the Philippines, "the Japanese had carried out a broad, calculated plan of atrocities on orders from Tokyo. The purpose of the mass-scale terror was to cow the newly occupied islands into submission."[15]

Captured Japanese diaries make clear what this meant. Wrote one soldier in his diary: "Taking advantage of darkness, we went out to kill the natives [Filipinos]. It was hard for me to kill them because they seemed to be good people. The frightful cries of the women and children were horrible. I myself ... killed several persons."[16] Wrote another, after watching his comrades torture Filipino prisoners: "It is pitiful, and I couldn't watch. They also shot them and speared them to death with bamboo lances."[17] From the diary of a Japanese warrant officer: "We are ordered to kill all the males we find.... Our aim is to kill or wound all the men and collect information. Women who attempt to escape are to be killed. All in all, our aim is extinction of personnel."[18] And from still another diary: "Because 90 percent of the Filipinos are not pro-Japanese, Army Headquarters issued orders on the 10th to punish them. In various sectors we have killed several thousands (including young and old, men and women, and Chinese). Their homes have been burned and valuables confiscated."[19]

How cold, calculated, and official some of this killing was is clear from a Manila Navy Defense Force and Southwestern Area Fleet Operation order discovered in Japanese files after the war.

> When killing Filipinos, assemble them together in one place as far as possible, thereby saving ammunition and labour.

> Disposal of the dead bodies will be troublesome, so either assemble them in houses scheduled to be burned or blown up or push them into the river.[20]

After the war, U.S. military units tried to document such massacres and atrocities in the Philippines. From the evidence they collected, the U.S. war department estimated that 89,818 to 91,184 Filipino civilians had been murdered.[21] This was nearly seven out of every thousand Filipinos — a rate close to the nearly nine out of a thousand Soviets killed during Stalin's Great Terror of the late 1930s.[22]

Other occupied territories suffered no less. At Pontianak, Dutch East Indies, in January 1944, 1,340 Dutch, Indonesian, and Chinese were executed for allegedly conspiring against the Japanese, only 63 having been given some sort of trial.[23] Also in the East Indies between 1943 and 1944, 1,000 were executed at Mandor,[24] 240 at Sunggei Durian, and 100 at Katapang.[25] At Mantanani, Borneo, the Japanese machine-gunned Sulaks, including women, and subsequently killed the wounded; following this, twenty-five women and four children were massacred.[26] On the Dinawan Islands, 66 were killed out of a population of 120.[27] In Dabon, Malaya, 30,000 Chinese were executed by the Japanese secret police.[28] In French Indochina in March 1945, 600 people were massacred by the Japanese 37th Division.[29] At Singapore during two days in February, 5,000 Chinese were massacred; in the following two months, many thousands more were executed in Johore province.[30] In Liaoning province, Manchuria, 3,000 "civilians were forced to serve as coolies in constructing military defense works and were then slaughtered to guard the secrecy."[31] Also in Manchuria, 3,000 human guinea pigs were experimented to death in order to develop biological weapons of war.[32] And so on.

In total, as shown in table 8.1, those civilians massacred or dying from atrocities in China, the Philippines, French Indochina, the Dutch

TABLE 8.1
Japanese Democide in World War II
(000)

Component	Democide (000)		Total [c]
	In China [a]	Elsewhere [b]	(000)
POWs/internees	400	139	539
Forced laborers	142	868	1,010
Massacres/atrocities	2,850	758	3,608
Bombing/CB warfare	558	?	> 558
Democidal famine	?	250	> 250
Total [c]	> 3,949	> 2,015	> 5,964
Democide Rate (%)	1.2 [d]		1.01 [e]
Annual Demo. Rate (%)	0.13 [d]		0.28 [e]

a From Rummel 1991 (appendix 6.A); for July 1937 to August 1945.

b From *Statistics of Democide*; for July 1937 to August 1945

c Figures may not add up exactly due to rounding

d For China's population under Japanese control, and ignoring POW and bombing/CB warfare deaths. Taking these and the whole population into account gives a % rate of .88, annualized at .10.

e Based on a Japanese imperial population of 376 million, at its largest. Rate for December 1941 to August 1945. For China (proportionately calculated) pre-December 1941 democide is excluded.

East Indies, Singapore, Malaya, Burma, and on the many occupied Pacific Islands, may have totaled over 4 million men, women, and children; surely no less than some 1,644,000.[33]

This staggering number does not even include those dying from forced labor.

> Several of Western survivors testified that the Japanese treatment of the Asian slave workers was far worse than the treatment accorded European and American prisoners. Indonesian coolies who suffered from cholera, for example, were often forced into common pit graves and buried alive. Other coolies were regularly beaten and humiliated; women among them were insulted and violated.... [O]ne Japanese doctor viciously beat the coolies he examined for cholera, whether they had the disease or not (it made no sense that he struck them). The Western prisoners looked on in shock at this inhuman behavior, but a Japanese physician explained lightly to the Europeans that "coolies are subhuman and not worthy of consideration."[34]

The Japanese required labor to help man the factories in Japan; and in occupied areas, it was needed to build roads and railroads, to construct fortifications, and to be general beasts of burden for the army. Sometimes the conscripts were shipped over great distances by sea for this purpose. The conditions aboard the ships carrying these forced laborers were uniformly abysmal: the "coolies were forced below decks, kept short on water and rations, provided with virtually no sanitary facilities, and beaten mercilessly."[35] If these ships were sunk by Allied submarines or aircraft, the helpless coolies could hardly expect to be released from their barred holds; and if they did manage to escape their sinking ship, they might be machined gunned in the water or left to drown.

Many forced laborers were thus shipped, along with POWs, to Thailand (then Siam) and Burma to hack out of solid tropical forest the notorious 250-mile Burma-Thailand railroad that the Japanese were constructing to link Bangkok and Rangoon. Many slaved along the river Kwai Noi, the setting for the fictional 1957 British movie *Bridge on the River Kwai*. This dramatized some of the misery and atrocities perpetuated against POWs forced to work on the railroad but ignored the even worse hardships and conditions of the Asian laborers. While out of 46,000 to nearly 50,000 POWs some 16,000 died in eighteen months,[36] a 32 to 35 percent mortality, as many as 100,000 of the 120,000 to 150,000 Asian forced laborers may have died,[37] or 83 percent. Each mile of the railroad may have cost as many as 64 POW and 400 Asian lives. Japanese authorities were clearly responsible for most of these deaths. Indeed, captured "Japanese field orders repeatedly emphasized that prisoners thought to be of no use were to be killed."[38]

These deaths were not just an aberration due to unusually inhospitable conditions of a tropical rain forest or especially savage commanders. Many forced laborers shipped to Japan also died, in fact possibly 60,000 Koreans out of 670,000 and 10,272 Chinese (including those dying along the way) out of 41,862;[39] one report is of 418 deaths in one unit of 981 Chinese workers.[40] Elsewhere, other Asian forced laborers suffered even more. In one estimate, out of over 500,000 Indonesian (Dutch East Indies) forced laborers taken from their homes, only a "small fraction" returned after the war.[41] For the whole Japanese empire during the war, how many forced labors were executed or died from maltreatment or killing conditions, is only an informed guess. Perhaps 1 million dead would be closest to the truth. One estimate is that over half of the "Asian press-gangs perished."[42]

As clear from the toll on the Burma-Thailand railroad, prisoners of war were killed or died in large numbers as well. During the infamous 1941 Bataan Death March, 17,200 U.S. and Filipino captives died.[43] Captured or surrendered prisoners of war were often murdered en masse or used for deadly labor. This was especially true for Chinese POWs.

The Japanese government did not recognize that a state of war existed with China. It was an "incident." Nor did it ratify the 1929 Geneva Convention governing the treatment of prisoners of war (the navy vice-minister, among others, argued that it would cause one-sided obligations, since Japanese soldiers would die before being taken prisoner, and would thus mean that the POWs would be treated better than the Japanese military treat their own soldiers).[44] Neither was there a bureau set up in the Japanese government for the care of Chinese POWs. In Premier (1941–44) and Minister of War (1940–44) Tojo's view, it "was not necessary during the China Incident."[45]

This policy meant in general that no camps were set up for Chinese prisoners of war. Rather, many were shot outright, often after being tortured. The Japanese army often fought "slaughter battles," officially reporting the number of Chinese soldiers killed and rifles captured afterwards. Revealingly, it might report something like 14,000 to 15,000 dead counted on the field, but with only 600 or 700 rifles captured.[46] Obviously, since the Chinese army would hardly have been allowed to go over the field of battle to recover rifles, the difference must be largely due to surrendered or captured Chinese being killed.

Some lucky Chinese POWs were given a chance to join the Chinese puppet forces under Japanese command, but in the main survivors were worked to death as beasts of burden, or used by the Japanese army for practice. A favorite was for soldiers to hone their bayonet skills against tied up POWs. Sometimes the POWs would be used for rifle practice, lined up like so many cardboard targets along a pit, with aim points pinned on their chest.

Overall, according to the prosecution at the Tokyo War Crimes Trial, as many as 1 million Chinese POWs may have been murdered.[47] But given that one respected sinologist now estimates that no more than 500,000 Chinese soldiers were captured,[48] a more prudent estimate may be the 400,000 killed that is shown in table 8.1.

American, British, and other Western POWs were better treated than Asians. Still, they were subject to frequent beatings, disciplinary torture, poor and insufficient food, exposure, and lack of medical care. Moreover, they were often transported on unmarked Japanese ships, with no notice being given the Allies about their presence. If a ship was torpedoed, like the coolies they might die in locked holds or be killed in the water. Consider the Japanese *Junior Maru* that was torpedoed off Sumatra while carrying 2,300 POWs and 5,000 Asian coolies. Based on affidavits from people aboard the ship, testimony given at the Tokyo Trial reported that "after the ship had been torpedoed, the prisoners of war and coolies were machine-gunned in the water. Others who tried to board rafts had their hands chopped off and their skulls smashed in."[49]

But even if their ships were not sunk, POWs might not survive the ocean trip. Of the 1,650 shipped to Japan aboard the *Oryoku Maru* in December 1944, a "conservative estimate" is that about 450 arrived alive; and even among these survivors, some 200 died within two months of arrival.[50]

Of all Japanese democide, the best statistics are on Western POWs. Out of 25,600 captured Americans, 10,650 died;[51] the British lost 12,433 out of 50,016 (not counting colonial forces);[52] for both countries together, the death rate was nearly 31 percent. Considering that these POWs were incarcerated for several years, the death rate is not up to Soviet gulag standards under Stalin, but it certainly surpasses by far the Western POW death rate in Nazi camps of 4 percent.[53] Among all Western Allied forces, as shown in table 8.1, about 139,000 POWs and internees probably died in Japanese captivity.

Besides massacres, atrocities, forced labor, and POW deaths, any Japanese democide count should include those civilians killed in Japan's indiscriminate bombing of cities and towns and especially in its germ warfare against civilians. In hundreds of incidents in China the Japanese spread typhoid, paratyphoid, cholera, dysentery, plague, and anthrax germs from the air (as by containers of infected fleas), on the ground, in wells, by releasing infected prisoners, or by contaminating food supplies.[54] The combination of conventional terror bombing and germ warfare in China possibly killed almost 560,000 Chinese civilians.

When all these democide figures are summed, a total of nearly 3 million to almost 10,600,000 people probably was murdered, most likely close to 6 million, as shown in table 8.1. Given the size of the Japanese World War II empire at its maximum and the democide for the period December 1941 to the end of the war, this is a toll of almost one per hundred subjects, or an annual rate of almost three per thousand. This is a high risk of dying, possibly in a very agonizing and prolonged manner. Still, if there is such a thing as a competition in inhumanity, the Japanese record is not quite up to Soviet standards, where from 1917 to 1987 the annual democide rate was between four and five per thousand.[55] But it does exceed that of the Chinese communists, whose annual democide rate from 1949 to 1987 has been a little over one per thousand.[56]

Figure 8.1 shows the components of Japanese democide. Even if the mid-estimate were to be too high and the low in fact the true number, some 3 million killed is a crime against humanity of the first magnitude. In reflection of this, Allied war crimes commissions throughout the Far East condemned 920 Japanese to death and 3,000 others to prison terms, not counting the top twenty-five top leaders tried in the Tokyo War Crimes Trials.

The immediate explanation of these atrocities and other Japanese democide lies with a morally bankrupt political and military strategy, military expediency, and military custom and national culture. The strategy was to terrorize the Chinese, Filipinos, and others into submission by mass killing. Moreover, civilian lives, no matter the number, were subordinate to whatever local tactics were expedient at the moment ("to clear a guerrilla zone, kill all the civilians"; "to chastise the city's population for an anti-Japanese poster, kill a hundred"). And to satisfy military needs, as well as the soldier's libido, civilians were as so many draft animals, expendable whores, or stuffed targets.

One example recorded in a Japanese soldier's diary well illustrates what this involved. With regard to Chinese prisoners lined up along a

FIGURE 8.1
Components of Japanese Democide in World War II
(From table 8.1)

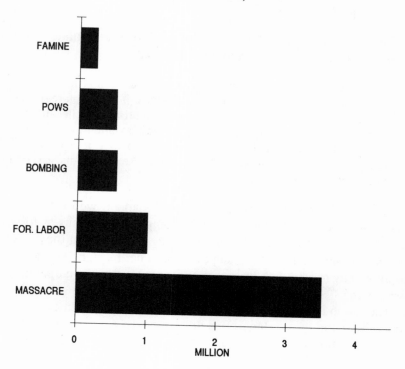

pit in Shanxi province, China, a Japanese officer told his men: "You have never killed anyone, so today we shall have some killing practice. You must not consider the Chinese as a human being, but only as something of rather less value than a dog or cat. Be brave!"[57] When none volunteered to do the killing, he lost his temper and directly ordered his men by name to move forward and kill the Chinese with their bayonets. With the officer's curses in their ears, they obeyed.

Some particular aspects of Japanese culture at the time also facilitated democide. What these aspects might be was pointed out by David James, a Japanese area scholar and former Japanese POW.

> Japanese atrocities have their genesis in the hakko-ichi-u of the Nippon Shoki: the oneness of the Japanese national family — the unity of Tenno, State and People. No matter what a Japanese may do to a foreigner he acts as one of the national family. For that simple reason, one Japanese will refrain from interfering with the action of another Japanese even when he knows that it is immoral — even absolutely contrary to his own moralism.[58]

Japanese culture also helps explain the Japanese attitude towards prisoners of war. Said Tojo before the Tribunal,

> the Japanese idea about prisoners is different from that in Europe and America. In Japan it is regarded as a disgrace [to be captured]. Under Japanese criminal law, anyone who becomes a prisoner while still able to resist has committed a criminal offense, the maximum punishment for which is the death penalty. In Europe and America, it is different. A person who is taken prisoner is honored because he had discharged his duties, but in Japan, it is very different.[59]

Captain Francis P. Scott, an American chaplain who interviewed many of the convicted Japanese POW camp commandants as to why they treated their prisoners in the way they did, said that they "had a belief that any enemy of the emperor could not be right, so the more brutally they treated their prisoners, the more loyal to the emperor they were being."[60]

There also may be some truth to the argument that at least regarding the lives of foreigners, Japanese soldiers obeyed a situational ethic — what was moral depended on what was necessary, desirable, or expedient in a particular situation — rather than following an internalized, absolute ethic as many do in the West.[61] The Western ethic provides moral rules and an associated feeling of guilt for their disobedience, even in a strange and foreign land. With his situational ethics, the Japanese soldier placed in foreign surroundings loses his moral compass. Too much can be made of this, however, for it should be noted that after the Boxer rebellion was crushed in 1900, the French, British, German, and U.S. soldiers sacked Beijing and environs, looting, raping, and killing. In atrocities at that time, there was apparently little distinction between the "guilt-directed" actions of Western soldiers and the "situationally directed" Japanese contingent also involved.[62]

But aside from such arguable factors, surely military custom and training did play a role in the Japanese democide. The brutal, dehumanizing treatment of Japanese soldiers by their superiors must have disposed them to treat others, especially foreigners, in a like if not even more brutal manner. Soldiers were routinely slapped and beaten by their superiors; whole units could be subject to this punishment, if not dangerous punitive marches or exercises, for the behavior of one of their men; just a moan from a soldier being beaten could provoke much greater punishment for him and his unit. Moreover, officers lacked even the barest essentials of a liberal education.

Said General Akira Muto, senior staff officer at the Rape of Nanking and the Rape of Manila,[63] in response to the question as to how he could explain such behavior: "There is no army in the world or government in the world that will instruct its people to shoot or kill children or the civilian population." In answer to whether his conscience was troubled by being at both Nanking and Manila, he said. "Yes. After the atrocities in Nanking and Manila ... I felt that something was lacking in the Japanese military education." About being shamed over the behavior of the Japanese army, he said: "I felt it was a shame." He noted that after World War I, when Japanese troops were sent into Siberia, "such tendencies toward atrocity came into the limelight, thereby proving that the quality and character of the Japanese was slowly deteriorating."[64]

Whatever the cause or explanation, it should be clear that once Japanese soldiers had absolute power over helpless Chinese,

Indonesians, Koreans, and others, they murdered them by the millions
— millions of people guilty of only being in the wrong place at the
wrong time.

Notes

1.   Byas 1942, 36.
2.   Pritchard and Zaide 1981, 3,888.
3.   Ibid., 187.
4.   Ibid., 4:537.
5.   Zich 1977, 23.
6.   Wilson 1982, 82.
7.   Pritchard and Zaide 1981, 4,537.
8.   Wilson 1982, 81.
9.   Dower 1986, 326n. 26.
10. Wilson 1982, 78.
11. Brackman 1987, 187.
12. Pritchard and Zaide 1981, 3,867–3,888. See also Brackman 1987, 40, 158; and
     Pelissier 1967, 379.
13. Pritchard and Zaide 1981, 49,618–49,619.
14. All this chapter's total or subtotal estimates of Chinese killed are from Rummel
     1991, chapter 6. All other estimates are from *Statistics of Democide*. Where
     overall subtotals or totals are given, the Chinese part of that is from the 1991
     source; the remaining is from *Statistics of Democide*.
15. Brackman 1987, 244.
16. Ibid., 251.
17. Ibid.
18. Pritchard and Zaide 1981, 12,567–12,568.
19. Ibid., 12,575.
20. Ibid., 12,567.
21. Ibid., 40,384–40,385.
22. Rummel 1990, table 1.1.
23. Pritchard and Zaide 1981, 40,092.
24. Ibid., 13,515.
25. Ibid.
26. Ibid., 40,294.
27. Ibid., 40,295.
28. Ibid., 5,649.
29. Ibid., 40,090.
30. Ibid., 40,087.
31. Ibid., 454.
32. Williams and Wallace 1989, 35.
33. These figures are summed from *Statistics of Democide,* and Rummel 1991, table
     6.A, lines 59 and 85, and 75% of line 29.
34. Brackman 1987, 256–57.
35. Ibid., 260.
36. Zich 1977, 151; Pritchard and Zaide 1981, 40,008.

37. Pritchard and Zaide 1981, 40,008.
38. Johnson 1983, 428.
39. Dower 1986, 47.
40. Pritchard and Zaide 1981, 4,628.
41. Dower 1986, 327n. 39.
42. Brackman 1987, 253.
43. Piccigallo 1979, 66.
44. Pritchard and Zaide 1981, 27,178–27,180.
45. Brackman 1987, 266.
46. Byas 1942, 144–45.
47. Pritchard and Zaide 1981, 3,244.
48. Eastman 1980, 204n. 93.
49. Pritchard and Zaide 1981, 13,564.
50. Ibid., 12,724.
51. Kerr 1985, 339.
52. Pritchard and Zaide 1981, 14,904.
53. Johnson 1983, 428.
54. This is documented in Williams and Wallace 1989, 68.
55. Rummel 1990, table 1.1.
56. Rummel 1991.
57. Wilson 1982, 80.
58. James 1951, 176.
59. Brackman 1987, 267.
60. Ibid., 251.
61. Eastman 1980a, 301.
62. See O'Connor 1973, chap. 16.
63. As American forces fought for Manila, the capital of the Philippines, against 16,000 Japanese naval and 4,000 army troops during February–March 1945, the Japanese troops went wild in an orgy of raping and killing civilians. Overall, close to 100,000 Filipinos died in the battle or were murdered (Steinberg 1979, 136).
64. Brackman 1987, 267–68.

9

2,035,000 Murdered
The Hell State
Cambodia Under the Khmer Rouge

*Later a new interrogator, one I had not seen before,
walked down the row of trees holding a long, sharp
knife. I could not make out their words, but he spoke
to the pregnant woman and she answered. What
happened next makes me nauseous to think about. I
can only describe it in the briefest of terms: He cut
the clothes off her body, slit her stomach, and took
the baby out. I turned away but there was no escaping the sound of her agony, the screams that slowly
subsided into whimpers and after far too long lapsed
into the merciful silence of death. The killer walked
calmly past me holding the fetus by its neck. When he
got to the prison, just within my range of vision, he
tied a string around the fetus and hung it from the
eaves with the others, which were dried and black
and shrunken.*

—Haing Ngor, *A Cambodian Odyssey*

In proportion to its population, Cambodia underwent a human catastrophe unparalleled in this century. Out of a 1970 population of probably nearly 7,100,000[1] Cambodia probably lost almost 4 million people to war, rebellion, manmade famine, genocide, politicide, and mass murder. From democide alone, almost all concentrated in the years 1970 to 1980, successive governments and guerrilla groups murdered almost 3,300,000 men, women, and children (including 35,000 foreigners). Most of these, probably close to 2,400,000, were murdered by the communist Khmer Rouge.

In other areas of the world, democide has not significantly affected population totals, for they are too large. The margin of error alone exceeds the magnitude of the democide. But for Cambodia the relatively small population clearly shows the demographic cataclysm. Figure 9.1 graphically illustrates this. The population for 1970 that

FIGURE 9.1
Estimated Versus Predicted Cambodian Population
(Mid-polynomial population fits from *Statistics of Democide*.)

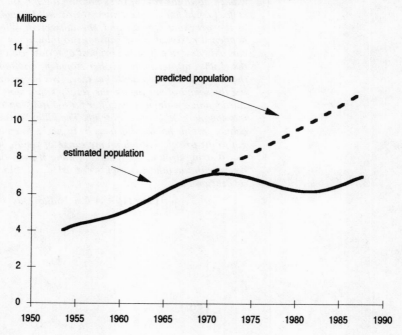

should have grown to about 11,650,000 by 1987 turned out to be only near 7 million, even lower than it was in 1970.[2]

There are three periods to this catastrophe, and each involves war and democide. The first begins with General Lon Nol's coup against his head of government, Prince Sihanouk, in March 1970. The coup precipitated an all-out guerrilla war against Sihanouk by the Khmer Rouge, a war that eventually would involve the United States and North and South Vietnam. This period ended with the Khmer Rouge takeover of the capital of Phnom Penh in April 1975 and the complete surrender of Lon Nol's government and troops. Over the next four years (the second period), the Khmer Rouge leadership tried to consolidate power and establish a totally self-reliant, independent, and communist society. It not only refused to bow to Vietnam's power and recognize her brotherhood as a fellow communist nation, but openly provoked her to war.

In December 1978, Vietnam launched an all-out offensive against the Khmer Rouge, easily defeating them and taking over the capital the next month. The Vietnamese established a puppet government headed by Heng Samrin, a former high officer of the Khmer Rouge who had fled to Vietnam to avoid being purged. This third period saw the alleviation of the harshest policies of the Khmer Rouge, the establishment of more conventional communist practices, and a guerrilla war fought principally by the Khmer Rouge and two other groups against the Samrin regime. These periods and their effect on the population are shown in figure 9.2.[3] Most of the demographic catastrophe is due to democide, as shown in figure 9.3.

The Lon Nol period that began with a coup in 1970 was a violent shift of gears from the preceding government and political philosophy. It determined the shape of the political and military struggle to follow, and ultimately prepared the way for the Khmer Rouge victory four years later. My discussion of the Lon Nol period, therefore, must begin with these prior years and the policies, rebellion, and democide that marked them.

After its independence from France in 1953, Cambodia had been led in one form or another by popular Prince Norodom Sihanouk. Crowned King in 1941 by the French when he was eighteen years old, he later manipulated the French into granting Cambodia full independence in 1953. In 1955, he abdicated the throne, became premier, and had his "royal crusade" approved by a national referendum. He then ran the country with a light authoritarian hand, stressing the racial descent of the majority ethnic Khmers from the ancient kingdom at Angkor and instilling pride in their being Cambodians. He had little patience for rebellion, however.

In order to build a sugar refinery at Kompong Kol, near Samlaut, government officials expropriated land in 1966 without just compensation. This fueled local tensions, which had already been aroused by the use of troops in the region to aggressively collect taxes. When troops were deployed for this purpose in Battambang in early 1967, villagers attacked a detachment and killed two soldiers. This was the spark that was needed; villagers throughout the region rose up in protest against the government.

FIGURE 9.2
Estimated Effects of Regime on the Cambodian Population
(Mid-polynomial fits from *Statistics of Democide*)

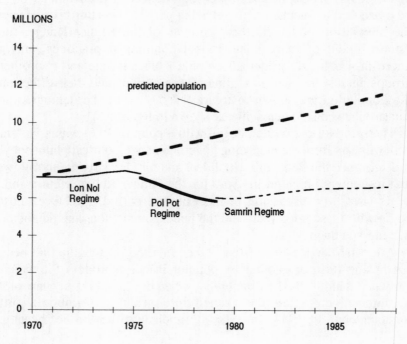

Sihanouk was on an extended trip to France at the time, but the government responded vigorously, no doubt with his approval. Paratroopers and the national police were sent into the region to quell the unrest. They were merciless. Said one critic later, "The pacification of the disturbed region was undertaken with the rude vigor peculiar to a soldiery who had been promised a monetary reward for each severed head they might forward to military headquarters in Phnom Penh."[4]

By June, over 4,000 villagers in Battambang province had fled to escape pacification.[5] That month Sihanouk announced that the trouble had ended, but this was only a prelude to more brutal suppression. Villages were bombed and strafed; others, including Beng Khtum, Thvak, and Russey Preas, were leveled; some the army first surrounded before massacring all their inhabitants. Much of this was carried out under the orders of Lon Nol. To assure him that his orders were being obeyed, his troops sent severed heads of their victims to

FIGURE 9.3
Sources of Unnatural Cambodian Deaths
(From table 9.1)

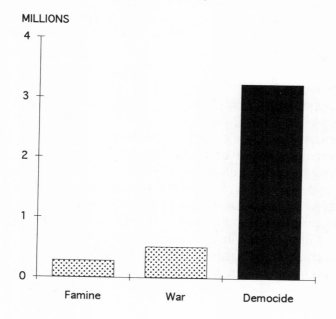

him at Phnom Penh. In at least one ghastly case trucks filled with heads, only heads, were dispatched from Battambang.[6]

By early 1968, many more provinces had become involved, particularly Kampot, Kompong Speu, and Kompong Chhnang.[7] There were new riots in Samlaut; more troops were sent to troubled regions; more villagers were clubbed to death, including resettled Vietnamese and other ethnic minorities; more lost their heads; some fifty villages were burned. Across the country, many fled to the forests, including thousands of students and teachers.[8] Aside from the death toll, some 4,000 people were arrested, and perhaps at least another 5,000 fled.[9] It was not until 1970 that this unrest was finally crushed.

Other rebellions also occurred during the late 1960s. In particular, the highland Khmers in the tribal areas of Ratanakiri and Mondolkiri rose up against what they claimed was racial domination by the government, and in protest against the settlement in their area of refugees and retired soldiers.[10]

These rebellions were not organized by communists, although the government blamed the communists and foreign agents. There were communist guerrillas at work, however, and they doubtless participated in and used the rebellions to their advantage. In any case, to Sihanouk these troubles provided an excuse to launch a vigorous hunt for suspected communists. In Kompong Cham, for example, a friend of one communist was arrested, but when he provided no help in the search for the communist and tried to escape, he was beheaded and disemboweled.[11] Provincial officials elsewhere were apparently ordered to help kill peasants guilty only of living in communist-infected areas. One witness reports that in Prey Totoeng, palm fronds were used to saw off the heads of two young children who allegedly were couriers for the guerrillas. Also, Sihanouk reportedly ordered that forty school teachers he suspected of subversive activity be thrown from the cliff at Bokor.[12] Some may have taken days to die.[13] Moreover, a former communist courier in the late 1960s claims that troops in Kompong Cham arrested and executed over a hundred suspected subversives, mainly students from the province capital; he also claimed that at O Korum fifteen women, villagers, and intellectuals were executed.[14] And prisoners from Samlaut or Dambar, the home areas of the Khmer Rouge, had their stomachs cut open before being tied to trees and left to die in agony. Captured rebel villages were destroyed, their inhabitants killed.[15]

TABLE 9.1
Cambodian Dead, 1967–87 [a]

Source of Deaths	From	To	Number Dead
War/Rebellion [b]	Mar 1970	1987	514
Famine/Disease [c]	Mar 1970	1987	280
Democide [d]	Mar 1970	1987	3,186
Democide by Regimes	Mar 1970	1987	2,292
Sihanouk [e]	1967	Mar 1970	12 [h]
Lon Nol	Mar 1970	Apr 1975	15
Khmer Rouge	Apr 1970	Jan 1979	2,035
domestic	Apr 1970	Jan 1979	2,000
foreign [e]	Apr 1970	Jan 1979	35 [h]
Samrin	Jan 1979	1987	230
Democide by Guerrillas	Mar 1970	1987	372
Khmer Rouge [e]	1967	Mar 1970	1 [h]
	Apr 1970	Apr 1975	211
[e]	Jan 1979	1987	150 [h]
Other groups [e]	Jan 1979	1987	10 [h]
Democide by foreigners [f]			522
South Vietnam [e]	Mar 1970	1973	1 [h]
North Vietnam [g]	Mar 1970	1987	461
United States	Mar 1970	Aug 1973	60
Khmer Rouge Total	Mar 1970	1987	2,397 [i]
Overall Dead	Mar 1970	1987	3,979 [i]

a All figures are from table 9A.1 in *Statistics of Democide* and are mid-values in a low-high range. Values may not add exactly due to rounding.

b Figure for war dead, excluding democide.

c Nondemocidal only. Includes death from malnutrition.

d Includes democidal famine/disease and military action (e.g., bombing).

e Estimated democide is the low.

f In Cambodia.

g Vietnam after 1975.

h This is a low estimate.

i Includes 35,000 foreign dead.

The causes of the rebellions and communist insurrection, and the barbarous manner in which they were suppressed further radicalized the peasants, created candidates for the communists, and intensified a left-right struggle among the elite. Not coincidentally, the Khmer Rouge, at first just one sect among diverse communist groups, undertook its violent struggle for power at the height of the rebellion in 1968. In the next year its members may have numbered about 2,400; the Khmer Rouge says it had 4,000 organized soldiers.[16] Sihanouk's army numbered 35,000.[17] By 1970, according to the CIA, Khmer Rouge guerrillas may have numbered 10,000. Yet, if a Vietnamese estimate is to be believed, the party membership was only 800 during this period.[18]

Even rough estimates of the overall toll from the unrest and guerrilla war are not easily available, but Sihanouk himself once mentioned that he saw a figure of 10,000 dead.[19] Probably not included are the 1,500 Khmer Rouge that Sihanouk claimed were executed during 1967–68.[20] Given the extent of the unrest, and the savagery with which it was put down and the communist guerrillas pursued, I estimate a democide toll of at least 12,000 from 1967 to Sihanouk's deposition in 1970. Although this number murdered is high by any standards, and exceeds by far the number of Cambodians killed in World War II and the First Indochina War (1946–54),[21] it is virtually insignificant in comparison to the deaths caused by war, rebellion, and democide in later years. The most probable figures outlining this catastrophe are shown in table 9.1, along with democide totals for subsequent regimes.

During the 1960s, Cambodia's geographic position was most unfortunate. On the western border, and on the western half of the northern border, was an unstable, Western-oriented Thailand; on the eastern half of the northern border was Laos, riven by a communist-led civil war; and on the northeastern border was North Vietnam, engaged in a war against South Vietnam, which lies along Cambodia's southeastern border. To maintain the independence of Cambodia from all the powers involved, Sihanouk at first tried to balance between communist and Western interests, accepting aid from both. But in 1965 he cut ties with the United States, arguing that the dignity of Cambodia had been infringed. He then began to tilt toward the communist bloc, developing particularly warm relations with China, while still officially maintaining a neutralist position. Nonetheless, during his rule, the North Vietnamese were able to develop a crucial supply, infiltration, and reinforcement network of bases and roads — the Ho Chi Minh Trail — from North Vietnam, through northeastern and eastern Cambodia and into South Vietnam. Until Sihanouk was deposed, Hanoi based about 40,000 troops in Cambodia,[22] mainly near this pipeline. But Sihanouk also gave tacit approval to its heavy bombing by the United States.

As Cambodia became increasingly drawn into the Vietnam War, as Sihanouk appeared to lean more and more to the left, as domestic communists became more threatening and leftist influence in the government apparently stronger, the Prince faced increasing opposition from the right. Even his enormous popularity seemed threatened. Public dissatisfaction grew as the economy continued the decline it had begun in 1966, inflation increased, and the government tried to squeeze more revenue out of the population. Nonetheless, to most peasants the Prince remained a god-king. It was the middle class and the intellectual and professional elite that were becoming disaffected. Especially fueling dissatisfaction was government incompetence and wide-scale corruption that reached into the highest levels of government and the military. Many of the elite wanted Sihanouk to lean toward, if not side with, the West, and to concentrate more on economic development. Particularly, they wanted the government and military cleansed of corruption and incompetents. But of greatest moment was the dissatisfaction of the top military itself, which saw Sihanouk as cozening up to communists abroad, allowing Cambodian sovereignty to be wantonly violated by the North Vietnamese, and insufficiently vigorous in fighting domestic communists.

This came to a head in March 1970 while Prince Sihanouk was abroad. With the military taking up strong points around Phnom Penh, Premier and Army Chief General Lon Nol, backed by Acting Prime Minister Sirik Matak, forcibly took over the government. The coup was confirmed by the National Assembly, which, under military guard, voted unanimously to depose the prince. Hardly commensurate with his ever-present sense of dignity, Sihanouk, who was in Moscow at the time, was informed by the Soviets about his being dumped. Incensed, he flew to Beijing as scheduled, but there held negotiations with the Khmer Rouge about joining forces to overthrow the new regime. Out of this emerged the fateful National United Front that would include both the Khmer Rouge and supporters of Sihanouk.

This United Front may have been the major element in the final victory of the Khmer Rouge five years later. Of course, the United Front gave the Khmer Rouge a legitimacy it had not had before. But more important, some of the reverence in which so many common folk held Sihanouk must have been transferred to the Khmer Rouge, thus encouraging support for the group and consequent recruitment. This popularity, combined with their attractive rhetoric about liberating Cambodia from oppressors and imperialists, enabled the Khmer Rouge to field about 15,000 troops in late 1970 and to have 60,000 more Cambodians in guerrilla and regional units.[23] By the middle of 1971, the Cambodian main force units had grown to eighteen battalions,[24] and their total strength to 125,000;[25] U.S. intelligence estimated that the Khmer Rouge and the North Vietnamese controlled 2 to 3 million people[26] and two-thirds of the land.[27] By late 1972, the communists had further expanded to around 200,000 regular and guerrilla troops (slightly smaller than the Lon Nol army), and held sway over at least half the population.[28] This popular phase lasted until 1973, when the Khmer Rouge began to impose collectivization and the harsh rules to be discussed later (in some places collectivization even began as early as 1971).[29] Then the peasants turned against the Khmer Rouge, many fleeing their occupation zones.[30]

In the postcoup government, Lon Nol became prime minister, commander-in-chief, and head of state of the Khmer Republic. Perhaps the most relevant characterization of him is that he commanded the vicious suppression of the Samlaut rebellion in 1967–68, and as a colonel in 1952 he led antiguerrilla operations in the Battambang Autonomous Region. According to one participant, his forces "would move into villages, kill the men and women who had not already fled, and then engage in individual tests of strength which consisted of grasping infants by the legs and pulling them apart."[31]

Lon Nol had nebulous plans to restore Cambodia's ancient glory and tried to prove that such lighter-skinned people as the Chinese and Vietnamese were inferior to the Khmer race. He sought the advice of astrologers[32] and was a poor general and administrator; during his five-year rule, incompetence and corruption flourished. One example is the wide-scale creation of "phantom soldiers" — names on the military payroll that existed only so that commanders could pocket their pay. The U.S. Agency for International Development estimated that 20 to 40 percent of all military pay was thus stolen.[33] The only way to get anything done by the regime seemed to require bribery (called "bonjour"). All this contributed to Lon Nol's final defeat.

But in April 1970 Lon Nol's takeover held promise. It looked like he might limit corruption, put the communists in their place, and with U.S. help kick the North Vietnamese out of the country. But the common folk were not cheered — they loved Sihanouk, and his deposition caused widespread and massive demonstrations. These were usually unarmed protests, but nonetheless Lon Nol's troops in Chambak and many other places fired upon the demonstrators, sometimes even with machine guns.[34] In Kompong Cham some 40,000 Khmer and Cham peasants and mountaineers demonstrated for the prince, looted houses not showing his portrait, and burned the courthouse. Two government representatives sent to calm them were killed. The mob then seized whatever vehicles it could, including busses, and headed for Phnom Penh. On the outskirts of the capital the army fired on the protesters, killing many.[35] At Koki they were attacked by artillery.[36] Near Skoun, another convoy headed toward the capital was strafed by the air force, and forty were killed. Another sixty were killed when troops fired on demonstrators at Kompong Cham.[37] There, "an angry mob seized one of Lon Nol's brothers ... killed him, cut his liver out and forced a restaurant owner to fry the liver and feed the slices to the crowd."[38]

The Lon Nol coup was pro-American and dedicated to defeating the communist insurgency and ejecting all Vietnamese from the country. But it was also dedicated to Khmer rebirth and to glorification of the ethnic Khmer. Foreign religions were suspect, particularly Catholicism with its allegiance to the Pope. And minorities — and in particular the ethnic Vietnamese — were victimized by the new regime., In several cases it committed outright genocide against Catholics and Vietnamese. For example, in the month after seizing power, government troops in the town of Prasaut killed eighty-nine Vietnamese in cold blood.[39] On the isthmus of Chrui Changwar (or Chruoy Chang War), 515[40] to 800[41] ethnic Vietnamese from a

Catholic settlement were rounded up, had their hands tied behind their backs, were taken out on the Mekong River, shot, and dumped dead or still alive into the water.[42] In Takeo, journalists arrived shortly after another massacre of 100 Vietnamese, including possibly 30 children.[43] Visiting a school yard where much of the killing had been done, they found that

> it looked like an abattoir, with flies buzzing through the classroom and over the pools of coagulating blood. Dozens of wounded Vietnamese lay on the ground, gasping and writhing in the sun, watched by young Cambodian soldiers who lounged against the walls with spent cartridge cases around their feet. The soldiers had come the night before: "They shot and shot and shot," wept one teen-age boy. One man, lying on his back in his own blood, had stuffed his clothes into his gaping stomach. There was a hospital only one hundred yards away, but no help had been given.[44]

In the month after the coup, U.S. and South Vietnamese forces invaded Cambodia in order to destroy North Vietnam's logistical network and bases supporting its war against South Vietnam. Two months later, the United States withdrew, but the South Vietnamese stayed in the country for two more years and more than avenged Lon Nol's massacre of Vietnamese.[45] While this "incursion" had notable short-run success, it also drove the Vietnamese out of their border sanctuaries and deeper into Cambodia. Whether this was a cause or not is in hot dispute, but in any case Hanoi and the Vietcong also began to attack any government forces they met, invaded other parts of the country, and waged an anti-Lon Nol propaganda campaign. They appealed to the peasants by wearing badges supporting Sihanouk and promising to restore him to power, and they played tapes of Sihanouk calling on the people to rebel against the Lon Nol government. It worked. The Vietnamese were often met with joy as liberators, and some provincial administrations defected to them. Those held responsible for the coup, particularly civil servants, schoolteachers, and students, were executed.[46]

In alliance with the Khmer Rouge, who now had a secondary military role, the Vietnamese launched major operations against the Cambodian army, achieving much success. In a matter of months, Vietnamese and Khmer Rouge forces commanded half of Cambodia.[47] The Lon Nol regime was barely able to withstand this onslaught from foreign and domestic communists. Indeed, by the end of 1972, its survival was doubtful. In January 1973, ostensibly at the request of Lon Nol,[48] the United States launched a massive bombing campaign to interdict and destroy communist forces from the air. This was an undeclared strategic alteration in U.S. war operations in order to force a cease-fire and a negotiation among all Cambodian parties toward some kind of coalition government.[49]

In addition to bombing supply routes and North Vietnamese bases along the Cambodian border, the United States carried out high-level carpet bombing of communist concentrations and "enemy" villages deep in Cambodia, as well as tactical defensive and offensive support of Cambodian army units on the ground. Hidden from the American people at the time, this was by any standards an enormous operation. Until 15 August 1973, when Congress brought a halt to the bombing and all direct military involvement in Indochina, 257,465 tons of bombs were dropped,[50] or half again more than the 160,000 tons of bombs dropped on Japan during the whole Second World War.[51]

In Washington, the bombing may have been justified as a necessary act of war to defend the country against a communist takeover. And it may have been necessary to secure the western flank of South Vietnam, thus ensuring its defense after the planned U.S. military withdrawal. Nonetheless, the implementation of the bombing was, for helpless civilians on the ground, gravely flawed. Bombing maps were out of date, insufficiently scaled, and sometimes even incorrect. Intelligence was grossly inadequate and the choice of targets cavalier. The often casual requests by the Cambodian military for air strikes usually were not carefully evaluated. And almost half the bombing was on the more heavily populated areas.[52] Moreover, the box within which the B-52s dropped their bombs was about two miles long by half-a-mile wide.[53] Since villages were often closer than these dimensions,[54] they would often be hit by bombs inadvertently, wiping out homes, farm animals, and peasants. William Harben, the chief of the political section at the U.S. embassy in Phnom Penh, said of this bombing that "I began to get reports of wholesale carnage.... One night a mass of peasants from a village near Saang went out on a funeral procession. They walked straight into a 'box.' Hundreds were slaughtered."[55] Perhaps not atypical is the story of the village of Banteay Chrey, in northern Kompong Cham province, in which no communist troops had been garrisoned, although apparently they had visited it. A peasant refugee from the village reported that in 1973

> the Vietnamese stopped coming [to the village]; in the same year, the village had to endure three months of intense bombardment by American B-52 planes. Bombs fell on Banteay Chrey three to six times per day, killing over one thousand people, or nearly a third of the village population, in the three months.
> ...
> [After that] there were few people left to be seen around the village, and it was quiet.[56]

In sum, regardless of whether intentions were good or not, there was a reckless and wanton disregard of the consequences of this bombing campaign on noncombatants. This was democide. Peaceful villages by the hundreds were purposely or recklessly destroyed from the air. Among Cambodian refugees interviewed by Westerners, a common tale was of the horror of U.S. bombing and the loss of loved ones.

Of course, there are no accurate figures for the number of Vietnamese soldiers, communist guerrillas, and civilians killed in this bombing. Estimates range from 30,000[57] to a Khmer Rouge estimate of 1 million dead.[58] A former minister in the Lon Nol government claimed that at least 600,000 had been killed.[59] Based on such figures, I suggest that probably around 400,000 died. Some were doubtlessly killed during well-focused attacks on Vietnamese-Khmer Rouge forces or bases. Obviously, estimating the proportion of dead resulting from democide (attacks with careless disregard for the noncombatants beneath the bombs) is guesswork. After some study of the campaign, I suggest that, conservatively, about 10 to 25 percent of the dead may have comprised democide, that is a range of 3,000 to 200,000 dead, most likely 60,000. This toll is listed in table 9.1.

There was another human cost of this bombing. Peasants subjected to the bombing were outraged. It generated fierce hatred for the government that had brought such a horror upon them, and for the United States. This anger was well exploited by communist recruiters and propagandists. But, in particular, the bombing gave the Pol Pot faction the political leverage it needed to consolidate its power among the contending communist groups.[60] And it gave them time. Without the bombing, the communists would probably have won in 1973, when the Khmer Rouge still were much divided among themselves and the Pol Pot group openly resisted.[61] Indeed, there was actually fighting between Khmer Rouge militias.[62]

The North and South Vietnamese committed their own democide in the country, and each is responsible for thousands, if not tens of thousands, of deaths among helpless Cambodian civilians, as shown in table 9.1.

But the greatest democide during these years was committed by the Khmer Rouge. Although they at first fought alongside Vietnamese forces, they had no love for them. Sometimes they even betrayed or fired on them. In Kompong Thom province, for example, in September 1970 the Khmer Rouge fired on Vietnamese forces from behind, even as they were attacking a government unit.[63] Prefiguring their disregard for human life during their rule to come, the Khmer Rouge purged their ranks of those who were insufficiently dedicated or had the wrong background, those who had been trained in Hanoi or been Khmer Vietminh, or those who held "incorrect" doctrines.[64] Virtually all of these were killed in suicidal missions assigned them or murdered by 1973.[65] The Khmer Rouge even massacred whole families that had done nothing more than shelter Vietnamese when they occupied a village or town.[66]

Most deadly was their general treatment of urbanites and peasants living in their controlled areas, particularly beginning in 1973. As they would do when they assumed full power, the Khmer Rouge rapidly emptied cities, dispersing the people into the countryside and forcing them to assume the lives of peasants — a life which was becoming increasingly horrible. In occupied areas, religious practice, including the Buddhism so central to the Cambodian way of life, was forbidden. So was any religion — among those executed for exercising their religion were five priests.[67] Money was eliminated, as were free speech and free travel, even between villages; old songs were forbidden. Farming was completely collectivized;[68] eating was communal; peasants worked according to schedules and rules set up by the Khmer Rouge cadre, each of whom had absolute command over the life or death of each peasant. In some places one worked virtually every day from morning to well after dark; and death in the field, village, or town could come from violation of the smallest rule.

At Baray township in Kompong Thom, for example, the Khmer Rouge killed a number of people for minor infractions.[69] Said one soldier who had been stationed in this region, the Khmer Rouge were

> led by very severe men.... Their discipline was terrible; there were many executions.... Buddha statues were destroyed and pagodas secularized ... youths forced to work very hard, especially when the villages had been reorganized and rebuilt; the Organization [Khmer Rouge] had not allowed the construction of individual houses; there were camps for women, children, young women and young men; meals were eaten communally and rations consisted only of rice soup without meat ... Children were forbidden to respect their parents, monks to pray, husbands to live with their wives.[70]

Predictably, hunger soon appeared. Villagers stole food and were executed as a result.[71] As one former communist soldier observed, "people were eating banana leaves, sugar-palm roots, coconuts, and finally weeds. Then there was nothing left at all. In the end the people rebelled, killing cadres in all villages."[72] Recalled a peasant from the Eastern Zone, "rice was stored in collective warehouses, and food ran short. Eventually people ate only rice gruel, with salt, water and banana stalks. We had to get permission to raise our own poultry, under pain of imprisonment."[73]

Anyone sixteen or over was forced to serve in the Khmer Rouge army; in some areas, refusing conscription could mean death.[74] Related an ethnic Chinese woman living in Koh Kong province, "In 1974 they recruited every youth 16 years old or more into the army.... Some who didn't go were killed."[75]

Stalinist purges and executions among the Khmer Rouge grew, as did the cost of crossing the leadership and local cadre. About half the party's membership in 1970 was quietly exterminated.[76] Reported the aforementioned ethnic Chinese woman living in Koh Kong province,

> [Khmer Rouge] armed forces from Kompong Seila arrived in Koh Kong.... Prachha was arrested and taken away. They said he was going to study, but actually they killed him. Everybody in Koh Kong was afraid, because their leader had been taken away. Prasith disappeared about the same time.... It got harder and harder. The Khmer Rouge began killing people; people who did anything wrong were taken away and shot.[77]

All this was in old occupied areas. For those newly conquered, the horror was even greater. When the Khmer Rouge took over the former royal capital of Oudong, they forced its population to immediately evacuate into the jungle. In the process, they killed all school teachers and government officials and leveled the town. Witnessed one peasant from a nearby village,

> Forty thousand people were sent in all directions. The Khmer Rouge burnt houses everywhere. Uniformed Lon Nol soldiers were executed along the way.... People were split up into groups of fifty, two hundred, or three hundred and escorted by groups of Khmer Rouge. Of those sent on to Region 31, and further — to Pursat and Battambang in some cases — only one in five survived to return five years later.[78]

In short, the Khmer Rouge instituted a system of terror. This caused many under their control to flee to South Vietnam or to Lon Nol-held areas, particularly Phnom Penh. Such flight eventually caused the Khmer Rouge to lessen the harshness of their rule, and in 1974 they again allowed private eating.[79] Once in full power, however, with nowhere in the country for the people to flee nor Lon Nol forces for the Khmer Rouge to fear, they reintroduced total revolution, and with greater harshness. More on this later. But the upshot here is that the toll in lives from this forcibly imposed life, and the number murdered by the Khmer Rouge, must be at least in the tens of thousands, and when the 2,500,000 to 3,000,000 people they controlled[80] is taken into account, as well as the number that they probably killed when they were in power, the toll quite possibly could be 200,000 or more (see table 9.1). This democide by the Khmer Rouge, a human disaster for any country, carried out even before they finally took over the government of Cambodia, usually is ignored when the costs of Khmer Rouge rule are estimated.[81] But surely it should be included in red ink on the Khmer Rouge ledger, as it has been here.

Many Cambodians also died from the war — as military families caught in the cross-fire (families often traveled to the front with their soldiers), or as other noncombatants caught up in battle. As the war raged, it involved a fluid, often deadly, ill-defined front between five conflicting forces: the Cambodian army, the Khmer Rouge and other Khmer communist guerrillas and troops, the Vietcong, the North and South Vietnamese armies, and the U.S. army and air force. This was a war in which a peasant could live under three different masters in the same day, or die in the struggles among them.

On the government side, perhaps 150,000 soldiers died in battle.[82] During much of the war, Lon Nol's forces numbered no more than 200,000 personnel,[83] although this number was constantly renewed as soldiers defected, disappeared, or were killed. But the number of civilians that died from the war is even greater. One popular estimate is 600,000 dead.[84] But this appears to include both democide and war deaths. Removing the latter, probably some 200,000 civilians were killed indirectly and from the battles, shelling, and bombing.

In total, nearly 180,000 to almost 1,400,000 Cambodians died from war or democide during the Lon Nol years, probably about 700,000. Most likely, some 290,000 of these were murdered by the Khmer Rouge or by U.S. bombs. Considering that the population was slightly over 7 million at the time of the Lon Nol coup, this killing had a measurable impact on the population, which can be seen in the Lon Nol population curve shown in figure 9.2. Note that it visibly departs from what would have been normal population growth and almost flattens out; indeed, by the end of the Lon Nol regime in April 1975, the population deficit thus created was likely more than 800,000 Cambodians.[85]

In 1973, Khmer Rouge forces were on the outskirts of Phnom Penh, but the conjunction of heavy U.S. bombing, poor Khmer Rouge battlefield tactics, and lack of ammunition, as well as a firm defense by Lon Nol's troops, saved the city. Moreover, about this time North Vietnamese troops began to shun battle and retire from their occupied areas, moving the bulk of their deployed forces back toward the Cambodian-South Vietnamese border or into South Vietnam itself. By mid-1973 there were only some 3,000 troops and 2,000 political cadres deployed outside the sanctuary area along the border.[86] Perhaps this redeployment was due to North Vietnam's having signed the Paris Peace Agreement with the United States in January 1973 that in effect ended direct U.S. involvement in the Vietnam War. The North Vietnamese may have been concerned about provoking renewed U.S. engagement in the area, particularly in support of Lon Nol. Moreover, and perhaps more important, they may have been shifting their military axis for the final death blow against South Vietnam, mistakenly leaving their "fraternal" indigenous ally, the Khmer Rouge, to seize power.

In 1973, the Khmer Rouge broke away from Hanoi and took over the war effort, initiated their radical revolution in occupied areas, and fully engaged government troops. While using North Vietnamese logistics, the Khmer Rouge were basically on their own. They gradually reduced the area of government control to a finger of territory extending northwest from Phnom Penh. The capital itself soon came under direct attack, much of which was outright democide.

Once within range they demonstrated their attitude toward the people of Phnom Penh by showering rockets and artillery shells over the heads of the defenders into the city. Day after day, night after night the missiles fell haphazardly into the streets, smashing a group of children here, a family there, a rickshaw driver pedaling home after work, houses and schools. The principal line of fire was directly into an area in which thousands of refugees squatted, and so it was the most wretched of the city who suffered worst from this, as from every other, desolation of the war. On one day in February 1974 alone, Khmer Rouge gunners killed 139 people and blew to smithereens the houses and shacks that gave meager shelter to some ten thousand people. More than one thousand people died in this one series of attacks before Lon Nol's troops were finally able to push the guns and rocket launchers out of range of the town.[87]

In April of 1975 the capital could no longer be defended. The heart of the regime had been eaten away by corruption, dependence on U.S. aid (nearly a million dollars a day for over five years),[88] the black market, hunger and malnutrition, an almost complete loss of fighting morale, and the virtual collapse of the traditional Cambodian social structure. Lon Nol and some other high officials fled to the United States, while many others remained, even though some of them were on the Khmer Rouge death list. With the folded U.S. flag under his arm, the American ambassador exited in an American helicopter. The Cambodian army declared a cease-fire and laid down its arms. And a rag-tag bunch of solemn, black pajama-clad teenagers with red scarves and Mao caps, carrying arms of all descriptions, walked or were trucked from different directions into Phnom Penh. They were part of an army of 68,000 soldiers. They had achieved victory for a party that had only 14,000 members.[89]

At first, the people hardly knew what to make of this victorious army. The war was over, the killing had stopped, and the people showed their relief and happiness. The Khmer Rouge were cheered, and there were public and private celebrations. Many intellectuals and middle-class Cambodians were disgusted with the corruption they had seen about them and were willing to try anything that might bring change, even communism. But even before they could settle down and enjoy the peace — even as, metaphorically, the champagne was still being drunk — the Khmer Rouge ordered everyone out of the city at gunpoint. In this and all newly occupied cities and towns, the order to evacuate was implacable. Everyone. All 2 million[90] to almost 3 million[91] in the capital, and in the days following perhaps 200,000 in Battambang, 130,000 in Svay Rieng, 60,000 in Kompong Chhnang, 60,000 in Kompong Speu, 50,000 in Siem Reap, and so on.[92] Four million[93] to nearly 4,240,000[94] overall; whether sick, infirm, or aged; whether being operated on or in labor with child. The order was implacable: "Go! Go! You must leave!"

And they did. Families left in any way they could: the wealthy or middle class in cars; some on heavily loaded motor scooters or bicycles; the poor on their feet. Some ill or infirm hobbled along; some thrown from hospitals crawled along on hands and knees. Reported a British journalist who from the French embassy watched the slowly moving mass of evacuees, the Khmer Rouge were

> tipping out patients [from the hospitals] like garbage into the streets.... Bandaged men and women hobble by the embassy. Wives push wounded soldier husbands on hospital beds on wheels, some with serum drips still attached. In five years of war, this is the greatest caravan of human misery I have seen.[95]

Failure to evacuate meant death. Failure of any in the mass of humanity that clogged the roads out of a city and in the neighboring countryside to obey Khmer Rouge orders meant death. Failure to give the Khmer Rouge what they wanted, whether car, motor scooter, bicycle, watch, whatever, meant death.

Which direction the people exited the city depended on which side of it they were on when they received the evacuation order. Those that were refugees were often told to return to their home village; but for the mass, and particularly the urbanites, where they went after evacuation and what village they were eventually settled in depended on the whim of the Khmer Rouge troops along the way. Some food was provided, and here and there shelter was occasionally available, but even for those to whom "aid" was given, the trip was hell. People were jumbled together, trudging along for days or weeks, usually with whatever clothes or covering they could grab and provisions taken at the last moment. Many had minimal supplies, since they had believed the Khmer Rouge, who had said that the evacuation would only be for a few days. The very young and old, those already sick or injured or infirm, that is, those most susceptible to the elements, sickness, and hunger, soon died on the roads or trails. One of these trudging millions, a medical doctor named Vann Hay, said that every 200 meters he saw a dead child.[96]

Including those killed outright, the toll from this utterly outrageous and unbelievable policy is in dispute. Whether 40,000 to 80,000 evacuees died, as one scholar not unsympathetic to the Khmer Rouge at that time claims,[97] or 280,000 to 400,000, as the CIA estimates,[98] the sheer horror of this urban expulsion is undeniable. As word about it reached the outside world via the few foreigners remaining in the capital at the time, many were incredulous while others were shocked. It should be noted again, however, that the Khmer Rouge had similarly ejected people from urban areas under their control during the war. They were only faithful to their own doctrine.

Explanations or justifications for this evacuation range from a fear that Americans would retaliate for the defeat of their ally by bombing the capital (then why were other cities and towns evacuated?); an expectation that the urban food supply would not support both the natives and the newcomers (then why the incredible rush, with the inevitable loss of lives?), to a strategic decision that the small number of Khmer Rouge troops could not secure the city against Lon Nol holdouts and opposing guerrillas (again, then why the other evacuations?). Whatever the partial validity of these explanations, the evacuation was dominantly a matter of ideology. The Khmer Rouge saw the city as the home of foreign ideas and of capitalists and their supportive bourgeois intellectuals. The city was thoroughly corrupt and had to be cleansed. Those who had been corrupted by the city — its professionals, businessmen, public officials, teachers, writers, and workers — must be either eliminated or re-educated and purified. And the best way to remake the corrupted minds that were allowed to survive was by common toil in the fields alongside pure peasants. Consider the slogans broadcast over Radio Phnom Penh and given at meetings at the time: "What is infected must be cut out," "What is rotten must be removed," "What is too long must be shortened and made the right length;" "It isn't enough to cut down a bad plant, it must be uprooted."[99] This inhuman expulsion was first and foremost an opening salvo in the Khmer Rouge campaign to utterly rebuild Cambodian culture and society; to construct pure communism forthwith.

As the evacuees reached their home villages or were assigned one, there was usually no relief from the horrors already suffered; they were just different in kind. Here one must be careful. Under Khmer Rouge rule Cambodia was not one totalitarian society ruled by one set of doctrines or rules except at the most abstract and general level. That is, everywhere peasants were to be collectivized (95 to 97 percent of the population eventually were to live on collective farms),[100] and everywhere, new (the evacuees) and old peasants (nonevacuees) were expected to work solely for Angkor (the Organization, a commonly used euphemism among the cadre for the Khmer Rouge). But, as to how such abstractions were to be applied, under what rules, and with what punishment for violations, varied from one district to another and from one region to another.

Much of the reason for this variation was that the Khmer Rouge themselves were not unified except around some very general communist prescriptions, such as that collectivization is good, private business is evil. The leadership was divided in power and doctrine, and more or less insecure. This was especially true among the Khmer Rouge governors of the different zones into which the country was divided, who operated more or less as warlords, and among their district and village heads. Moreover, in most places life was better in the second or third year of the regime than it was in the first or last year; in some places the reverse was true. Therefore, in one village, region, or year, peasants could be fairly well fed; in another they could be dying from hunger and malnutrition. In one village a mistimed tear or chuckle could mean death; in the next it could mean interrogation and torture ("Admit it. You hate Angkor; you worked for the CIA"); in another a warning, reprimand; and yet in another, nothing.

Nonetheless, Pol Pot and his cohorts managed to hold the initiative, establish control throughout the country, and create a surprising uniformity. Variation from one part of the country to another involved living conditions, not rights. Under the Khmer Rouge, no Cambodian was free. There were no political, civil, or human rights. Cambodians could not freely travel, not even from village to village; there was no freedom of speech. Religion, traditionally Buddhism, was not allowed. Freedom of organization did not exist. While freedom to pick one's husband or wife and cohabit varied from place to place, sexual freedom was severely controlled. There were no appeals, no courts, no judges, no law. No one has ever reported a trial during this period.[101]

There were no practicing lawyers, doctors, teachers, engineers, scientists, or the like. These professions were deemed unnecessary or presumed to contain simple truths any peasant could pick up through experience. Those who had been such professionals under the old regime were either killed or had to work in the fields like everyone else, depending on the local cadre and region. That this would create human dilemmas of the most excruciating kind is obvious. Just consider the doctor Haing Ngor, whose wife suffered life-threatening complications during childbirth. To help her deliver the baby meant his death (under the rules men were forbidden to deliver their wives' babies); to use his medical skills to save her would in effect tell the cadre that he was a doctor and meant his death, and possibly that of his wife and newborn; to do nothing might mean their death anyway. But still the wife might pull through. He did nothing (and perhaps he could do nothing anyway — he had no appropriate medical instruments) and his wife and baby died, leaving a gaping wound in his heart that has never healed.[102]

In other words, the Cambodia of the Khmer Rouge was a nation-sized concentration camp in which all suffered the torments of hell. It was divided into compounds with keepers, each applying the heat, brimstone, and pitchforks to his inmates largely as he saw fit. There were no rights, but everywhere in this hell inmates had two duties: instant and unquestioning obedience to every command of the Khmer Rouge cadre; and work. The result was terror, fatigue, hunger, disease, and death.

Some uniform conditions framing and defining this hell have already been mentioned. There are others, and for completeness they are put together in table 9.2, but, in sum, the people

slept in barracks, ate in canteens, gave up their young children, and worked. All else was banned: markets, money, schools, books, religion, prayer, idle hours of conversation and laughter, music. The people worked every day with rare days off for "political education." The work day began about six in the morning and could last until eight or ten in the evening. The work day, like the amount of food and quality of shelter, varied dramatically, but the common condition for the city people that first year was fatigue mixed with fear.[103]

While these conditions collectively encompass this hell and communicate some of the horror, they fail to give a feel for its true terror and pain. After all, these conditions could define the absolute slavery of previous centuries, except that slaves were owned, and thus normally taken care of; under Pol Pot the people were public property, and thus suffered the neglect, misuse, and waste of any public property. But what is peculiar to the Khmer Rouge hell was the intentionally imposed suffering. To convey this through the life of one village I will quote extensively from the story of Thoun Cheng, a refugee interviewed by Chanthou Boua and Ben Kiernan at a Lao refugee camp,[104] and whose account of the U.S. bombing of his village I have already given. In April 1975, Khmer Rouge troops came to his village of Banteay Chrey in Kompong Cham province.

It was not long before they began imposing a very harsh life-style on the villagers. Everybody was now obliged to work in the fields or dig reservoirs from 3 or 4 a.m. until 10 p.m. The only breaks were from noon until 1 p.m. and from 5 to 6 p.m. (This compared to an average 8-hour day worked by the ... farmers in preceding years.) One day in 10 was a rest day, as well as three days each year at the Khmer New Year festival. Land became communal.

Also from 1975, money was abolished and big houses were either demolished and the materials used for smaller ones, or used for administration or to house troops. The banana trees ... were all uprooted on the orders of the Khmer Rouge and rice planted in their place. Production was high, although some land was left fallow and rations usually just consisted of rice porridge with very little meat. After the harvest each year, trucks would come at night to take away the village's rice stores to an unknown destination.

In 1975, the Khmer Rouge also began executing rich people (although they spared the elderly owner of 800 hectares), college students and former government officials, soldiers and police. Cheng says he saw the bodies of many such people not far from the village. Hundreds of people

TABLE 9.2
Living Conditions under the Khmer Rouge

Civil/Political
    no freedom to travel abroad or from village to village
    no freedom to choose employment
    no freedom of speech
    no freedom of organization
    no freedom of religion (no religion allowed)
    no courts, judges, or appeals
    no codified law or rules
Social/Cultural
    no public or private worker rights
    no independent work or living (all in collectives)
    no skilled private or public medical care
    no foreign medicines
    no mail or telegrams
    no radio, television, or movies
    no international telephones or cables
    no newspapers, journals, or magazines
    no books or libraries
    no general schooling
    no holidays or religious festivals
Economic
    no money (all money eliminated)
    no banks
    no wages or salaries
    no markets
    no businesses
    no restaurants or stores
Personal
    no independent eating (all cooked and ate collectively)
    no personal food
    no regional gastronomic specialties (all ate the same)
    no private plots to grow food
    no personal names (one had to give up his old name)
    no independent family life
    no sexual freedom
    no music
    no freedom from work after the age of five
    no personally owned buses, cars, scooters, or bicycles
    no personal clothes, pots, pans, watches, or anything
    no freedom to cry or laugh
    no private conversation

also died of starvation and disease in the year after April 1975 Cheng says. (After the war ended [in 1975] there was no resumption of medical supplies).

...

During 1976–77 most of the Khmer Rouge leaders in the village changed six times. More than 50 Khmer Rouge were executed in these purges.

Then, from January 1977, all children over about eight years of age, including people of Cheng's age (20), were separated from their parents, whom they were no longer allowed to see although they remained in the same village. They were divided into groups consisting of young men, young women and young children, each group nominally 300-strong. Their food, mostly rice and salt, was pooled and served communally (sometimes there was samlor, or Khmer-style soup).

...

Also in early 1977, "collective marriages," involving hundreds of mostly unwilling couples, took place for the first time. All personal property was confiscated. A new round of executions, more wide-ranging than that of 1975 and involving anyone who could not or would not carry out work directions, began. Food rations were cut significantly, leading to many more deaths from starvation, as were clothing allowances (three sets of clothes per person per year was now the rule). Groups of more than two people were forbidden to assemble.

In such villages and many regions of the country, anyone who had been a top military man, official, bureaucrat, businessman, or high monk were executed upon discovery — as was their whole family — sometimes after extended torture. For example, the Khmer Rouge came to believe that the villagers of Kauk Lon really were former Lon Nol officers, customs officials and police agents. Troops forced all of them — about 360 men, women, and *children* — to march into a nearby forest. As they walked among the trees, they were ambushed by waiting machine gunners, who cut them all down.[105]

Then there was the massacre at Mongkol Borei....

A communist commander named Prom ordered a squad of fifteen young soldiers to punish some former government officials "because they worked for Lon Nol." Led by an officer called Taan, who was in his early thirties, the soldiers rounded up ten civil servants together with their wives and children, about sixty people in all. They bound the hands of each behind the back, forced them aboard a truck and at about 5 P.M. drove them some

3 kilometers out of town to a banana plantation adjoining Banteay Neang village.

Weeping, sobbing, begging for their lives, the prisoners were pushed into a clearing among the banana trees, then formed into a ragged line, the terrified mothers and children clustering around each head of the family. With military orderliness, the communists thrust each official forward one at a time and forced him to kneel between two soldiers armed with bayonet-tipped AK-47 rifles. The soldiers then stabbed the victim simultaneously, one through the chest and the other through the back. Family by family, the communists pressed the slaughter, moving methodically down the line. As each man lay dying, his anguished, horror-struck wife and children were dragged up to his body. The women, forced to kneel, also received the simultaneous bayonet thrusts. The children and babies, last to die, were stabbed where they stood.[106]

A Thai military analyst observed that this methodical purge even got down to cousins of cousins of former soldiers.[107]

Similar slaughter often awaited those having had any relations with the West or Vietnam (even in some cases the Soviet Union), or having opposed the Khmer Rouge. As to these and other executions and deaths, the depth of the horror varied across the country. Perhaps in half of Cambodia, maybe a third,[108] many who had been Lon Nol soldiers or lower officers, doctors, teachers, government bureaucrats, officials, or intellectuals, lived in constant terror of being uncovered, for it could mean torture and would mean execution. Even those discovered with Western possessions, such as books, or who spoke French or English, could be executed. Even those who had an education beyond the seventh grade or, in some areas, those who wore glasses.[109]

The scale of these executions can be gauged from the admission of Chong Bol, who claimed that as a political commissar at the end of 1975 he had personally participated in the execution of 5,000 people.[110] Think about this for a moment. If this murderer had been a citizen of most other countries and had admitted to killing even half this many people in cold blood, he would be recorded as history's most monstrous murderer. However, as an officer of a government — like many Nazi SS, or Soviet death camp or Chinese commissars, who also personally exterminated thousands — his actions will be labeled instead as acts of the Khmer Rouge, Nazis, Soviets, or communist

186 Death by Government

Chinese. The individual killer will be forgotten. Such heinous crimes are thus depersonalized and their horror lost among general abstractions.

Then there was the killing of people for laziness,[111] complaining, wrong attitudes, or unsatisfactory work. I will give only one example of this, but as a teacher, it is for me the most hideous of all the accounts I have read. This is the Buddhist monk Hem Samluat's description of an execution he witnessed in the village of Do Nauy.

> It was ... of Tan Samay, a high school teacher from Battambang. He was accused of being incapable of teaching properly. The only thing the children were being taught at the village was how to cultivate the soil. Maybe Tan Samay was trying to teach them other things, too, and that was his downfall. His pupils hanged him. A noose was passed around his neck; then the rope was passed over the branch of a tree. Half a dozen children between eight and ten years old held the loose end of the rope, pulling it sharply three or four times, dropping it in between. All the while they were shouting, "Unfit teacher! Unfit teacher!" until Tan Samay was dead. The worst was that the children took obvious pleasure in killing.[112]

Of course, love between people could not be allowed — it interfered with work. Not only was sex between the unmarried absolutely forbidden, but in some places boys and girls were threatened with execution for as little as holding hands.[113]

Normal family life, including love and sorrow, was impossible in some villages. Children were taken away from their parents to live and work in labor brigades. If they died of fatigue or disease, which many did, their parents would eventually be informed. At this point what emotion the parents showed could mean life or death. If they wept or displayed extreme unhappiness, this showed bourgeois sentimentality. After all, their children had sacrificed themselves for the revolution and the parents should be proud, not unhappy. Similarly, a wife expressing grief over an executed husband — an enemy of the revolution — was explicitly criticizing the Khmer Rouge. This unforgivable act of sentimentality and individuality could mean death.

The tale of Bunheang Ung vividly illustrates the danger of normal feelings. In December 1977 his work group was sent to work in Phum Maesor Prachan hamlet. Coincidentally, his aunt of which he was very fond, lived there and he had not seen her for some time.

When he met her suddenly one day he impulsively took her hand. "I forgot, you see," Bun later explained. "I missed her, and I was pleased to see her." Immediately a Khmer Rouge cadre shouted at him. Bun dropped his aunt's hand and jumped away, but the crime had been committed. A meeting of Bun's [work] group was immediately called to deal with this serious breach of the rules. Bun was several criticized for his failure to develop a revolutionary morality. His action proved that he had failed to change his mode of thinking and failed to renounce the corrupt morality of the old regime. It was a most serious charge. Bun apologized. His group leader advised him to change his ways, or he would be punished most severely. Bun had no need to ask what that punishment would be.... [114]

Even calling one's wife by some term of endearment was forbidden. Haing Ngor had been overheard doing this by spies who also reported that he had eaten food he picked rather than bringing it in for communal eating. Interrogated about these sins, he was told, "The *chhlop* [spies] say that you call your wife 'sweet.' We have no 'sweethearts' here. That is forbidden." He then was taken to a prison where he was severally tortured, had a finger cut off and an ankle sliced with a hatchet. He barely survived.[115]

Not only was normal family life impossible, but everywhere the very heart of peasant life was destroyed. Hinayana Buddhism had been a state religion, and the priesthood of monks with their saffron robes a central part of Cambodian culture. Some 90 percent of Cambodians believed in some form of Buddhism, and many had received a rudimentary education from the monks. Indeed, it was customary for young people to become monks for part of their lives. So central and locally powerful an institution could not be allowed to be independent, so the Khmer Rouge set out with vigor to destroy it. Monks were defrocked; many were simply executed. All the top hierarchy and most of the others were killed — one estimate is that out of 40,000 to 60,000 monks only 800 to 1,000 survived to carry on their religion.[116] We do know that of 2,680 monks in eight monasteries, only 70 were alive in 1979.[117] As for the Buddhist temples that populated the landscape of Cambodia, virtually all, 95 percent, were destroyed;[118] the few remaining were turned into warehouses or used for some other demeaning purpose. Incredibly, in the very short span of a year or so, the Cambodian people had the center of their culture, its spiritual incarnation, and its institutions wiped out.

188 Death by Government

This was genocide, and it was pervasive. In most if not all of the country at one time or another, simply being of Chinese, Vietnamese, Thai, or Lao ancestry was sufficient for execution. Even Cambodian minorities, such as the Moslem Cham, were sought out and killed as part of a "centrally organized genocidal campaign."[119] Whole Cham villages were leveled.[120] For example, in the district of Kompong Xiem five Cham hamlets were demolished and their population of 20,000 reportedly massacred; in the district of Koong Neas only four Cham apparently survived out of a population of 20,000 inhabitants.[121] The Cham Grand Mufti was thrown into boiling water and then hit on the head with an iron bar; the First Mufti was beaten to death and thrown into a ditch; the Second Mufti was tortured and disemboweled; and the chairman of the Islamic Association of Kampuchea died of starvation in prison.[122] In total, nearly half — about 125,000 — of all the Cham in the country were murdered.

As to the other minorities, the Khmer Rouge killed about 200,000 ethnic Chinese — almost half the ethnic Chinese population in Cambodia. For ethnic Chinese in this part of the world, it was a disaster unparalleled in modern times. Also killed were 3,000 Protestants and 5,000 Catholics; around 150,000 ethnic Vietnamese (over half); and 12,000 ethnic Thai (out of 20,000).[123] One Cambodian peasant, Heng Chan, whose wife had been of Vietnamese descent, had not only his wife murdered by the Khmer Rouge, but also five sons, three daughters, three grandchildren, and sixteen other of his wife's relatives.[124] In this genocide, the Khmer Rouge probably murdered 541,000 Chinese, Chams, Vietnamese, and other minorities — about 7 percent of the Cambodian people.

As though this were not enough, many who were guilty of only having lived in a city, or of nothing whatsoever, were worked to the point of life-endangering exhaustion and fed barely enough to keep them alive while further weakening their bodies through extreme malnutrition (the average number of calories provided per day was 800 to 1,200, while for light labor the minimum average required is 1,800),[125] and were provided no protection against the dangers of exposure and disease (even Pol Pot admitted in 1976 that 80 percent of the peasants had malaria).[126] In many places people died like fish in a heavily polluted stream.

Of the approximately 1,000 people inhabiting the New Village of Ta Orng, about 100 adults and the same number of children died in the month of June [1975]. The New Village of Sambok Ork contained 540 people when organized in late April. In the months of July and August two to five people died daily, according to the philosophy professor Phal Oudam, who was drafted to file biweekly reports of deaths to *Angka Loeu* [Khmer Rouge]. Out of roughly 800 inhabitants in Phum Svay Sar, north of Kompong Thom, about 150 died in the summer. Of 300 residents in Tha Yenh, southwest of Battambang, 40 percent were unable to walk, and 67 had died by October.[127]

The horror is that people are not fish, but thinking, feeling, loving human beings.

Of course, the Khmer Rouge cadre was largely exempt from the exhausting work, exposure, and starvation. But they too were not spared the fear of death. They also could be killed for infractions of minor rules. Even more important, as the Pol Pot group maneuvered to consolidate its rule, the struggle for power at the top and the paranoia of top leaders increased. Not only was there the usual despot's fear of an opponent's knife in the night, but the fear that the revolution itself would be killed was growing. Sabotage and CIA, KGB, and Hanoi operatives were seen behind all production failures and project delays. Purge of high and low Khmer Rouge followed purge. The cells of the major security facility in Phnom Penh, Tuol Sleng (or S21), were filling up with cadre and officials, who were tortured until they fingered collaborators among Khmer Rouge higher-ups and then executed. Confessions were the aim and even interrogators who were so crude as to kill their victims before they confessed would themselves be arrested. The confession of one such interrogator gives insight into the suffering of the tortured.

> I questioned this bitch who came back from France; my activity was that I set fire to her ass until it became a burned-out mess, then beat her to the point that she was so turned around I couldn't get any answer out of her; the enemy then croaked, ending her answers.... [128]

The sheer pile of confessions forced from tortured lips ("Yes, I was a spy for the Vietnamese," "Yes, I plotted to assassinate Pol Pot") must have further stimulated paranoia at the top. How many such confessions there must have been is suggested by the recorded number of prisoners admitted to Tuol Sleng: 2,250 in 1976; 6,330 in 1977; and 5,765 for the first half of 1978.[129] And many more were admitted than these. Often, hundreds would be executed daily. For example, during October 1977, Tuol Sleng executed 418 one day, 179 the next day, and 148 people the day after that; on another day in May 1978, the number was 582.[130] Overall, some 20,000 people died or were executed in this security "office,"[131] many of them cadre. No more than fourteen people may have survived imprisonment there.[132] And this was only one such torture/execution chamber, although the primary one in the country.

Finally, in 1978 Pol Pot tried to purge the whole Eastern Zone bordering Vietnam — governor, lower officials, cadre, village heads, and innocent peasants alike. This instigated a rebellion in the region and considerable fighting took place. As the center regained control over parts of the region, all local officials and cadre were executed (some 1,000 of them had already been purged in previous years).[133] and the local people were either killed on the spot or deported to other regions to be killed later. Of these, 40,000 reportedly were concentrated in the province of Pursat and subsequently exterminated in three stages.[134] The overall toll in this one purge was at least 100,000 people.[135]

Other rebellions occurred that cost "many thousands" of lives,[136] such as in the Chikreng district, but they were all suppressed. And there were numerous coup attempts: four in 1976–77, according to Ieng Sary, the foreign minister;[137] perhaps nine or more over the life of the regime (giving substance to the regime's paranoia).[138] The attempted coups resulted in the death or disappearance of many of the highest party members, including the ministers of the interior, economy and finance, agriculture, public works, information, communications, trade, and industry and rubber plantations, and the first and second vice-president of the State Presidium.[139] There were even outright armed rebellions by troops, such as those which occurred in both the north and northwest between February and August 1977. They were suppressed, and whole units of rebels were executed.[140]

Aside from their fear of domestic enemies, the Khmer Rouge leadership hated the Vietnamese and felt no fraternal loyalty to Hanoi.

They saw the Vietnamese as racially inferior and as imperial occupiers of old Cambodian land, especially Kampuchea Krom, the southern Vietnamese delta. They saw Vietnam as the foremost danger to the Cambodian revolution and the Khmer Rouge regime; even more so than the "imperialist" capitalist United States. Even before their victory, they had tried to eliminate from their ranks Khmer Rouge trained in Hanoi, and had carried out a pogrom against ethnic Vietnamese. It was not long after their defeat of Lon Nol that they began to attack Vietnamese territory across the border. In many of these incursions they fought pitched battles with Vietnamese units, attacked and burned Vietnamese villages, and murdered their populations. One evening in September 1977, for example, a Khmer Rouge brigade crossed into Vietnam's Tay Ninh province and attacked the villages in Tan Lap and Ben Cau districts, massacring nearly 300 civilians.[141] Such cross-border massacres eventually caused an estimated 30,000 Vietnamese civilian deaths.[142] Since much of this sorry story of Cambodia involves mortality figures in the hundreds of thousands and millions, this number of lost souls may seem small, but if it were given by itself for the democide of most other regimes, it would be huge. More Vietnamese civilians were killed in Khmer Rouge massacres than the total battle deaths (27,704) of the U.S. army in the whole Korean War, and slightly fewer than the U.S. army deaths (30,899) in the Vietnam War.[143]

These Khmer Rouge attacks on Vietnam were really part of a war on Vietnam that began in March 1977.[144] At first, the Vietnamese responded vigorously, but then they seemed to take the high road, trying to accommodate Khmer Rouge border complaints and to find a basis for cooperative relations. This may have been to buy time for war preparations, however. In December 1979, as the purge of the bordering eastern region was still underway, Hanoi launched a full-scale invasion of Cambodia. Her 60,000[145] to 200,000 [146] troops with heavy weapons, gun ships, and tanks, easily rolled over the fewer and lightly armed Khmer Rouge defenders, and in the next month occupied Phnom Phen. As Vietnamese troops approached one village after another, the peasants often rebelled against the local Khmer Rouge cadre and troops, killing them with their own weapons — farm implements, sometimes even their own hands. Surviving Khmer Rouge, along with perhaps 100,000 people they forced to move with them (vengefully killing many on the way),[147] retreated to a mountainous region along the Thai border. From there and from refugee camps they soon controlled in Thailand, the Khmer Rouge carried out a guerrilla war against the Vietnamese and their puppet Samrin regime.

The human cost to Cambodia of the Khmer Rouge years is incalculable. Statistics can measure only indirectly the misery these fanatics produced during their rule and that will be its legacy for generations. Consider what suffering and social costs underlay the following: of 450 doctors practicing in Cambodia before 1975, the Vietnamese-installed Samrin regime claims there were only 50 left in the country in 1979.[148] The 20,000 teachers at the beginning of the 1970s were reduced to 5,000. An overwhelming majority of children six to fourteen years of age lack any basic education. Illiteracy climbed to 40 percent.[149] As Magstadt points out,

> The cold figures, however much they may overestimate (or underestimate) the actual number of casualties, obscure the larger sense in which every man, woman, and child in Cambodia was a victim of the [Khmer Rouge's] political obsessions. Families were torn asunder, children were orphaned, communities were shattered, property was expropriated — in short, the lives of all were wrecked in the name of a better life *for* all.[150]

This understood, the democide total can only reflect, not precisely measure, this horror. But estimating this toll is no less important, for despite this imperfection, it does give us a benchmark for comparison with other regimes, countries, and times.

Except for admissions and executions at Tuol Sleng, whatever other records the Khmer Rouge kept are not available. The only basis for any count is refugee reports of executions and deaths, which scholars have analyzed in detail,[151] and pre-and post-Khmer Rouge population censuses and predictions. And there are many more-or-less informed estimates in the literature. Some of the more scholarly or better calculated figures range from 600,000[152] through 1,500,000[153] and to 3,101,000.[154] The Samrin regime did a house-to-house census in 1982–83 and claims this showed that 3,315,000 died under the Khmer Rouge.[155] Based on these estimates, over 131 other estimates and calculations of the dead and the population loss and deficit for these years, and on my own deficit calculations, I am confident that the domestic democide lies between 600,000 and 3 million dead. A most prudent estimate is 2 million, which is close to a most likely population deficit of about 1,800,000 for these years (taking into account a probable 352,000 refugees that fled the country).[156] This deficit is shown in figure 9.2. Table 9.1 lists the democide for the Khmer Rouge regime among the other agents of democide, and figure 9.4 graphs this. As can be seen, as murderers of Cambodians, the Khmer Rouge led by Pol Pot are in a class by themselves.

Of course, their toll is nothing like the tens of millions killed by the truly big megamurderers — the Soviet Union, communist China, and Nazi Germany — which together account for over 100 million dead. But if we calculate the democide *rate*, we can see the true depth of their international crime. This is done in table 9.3 for the Pol Pot and

FIGURE 9.4
Cambodian Democide by Perpetrator

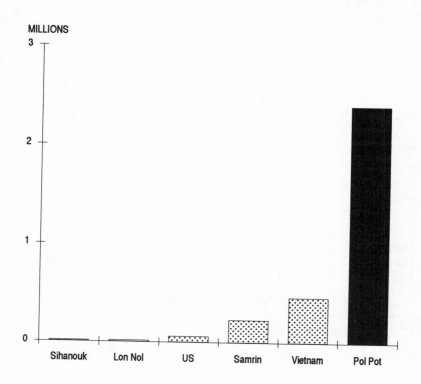

other regimes; the comparisons can be best seen in figure 9.5. This incredible regime probably wiped out in cold blood nearly one-third of all Cambodians. For each year of its short reign it killed one person out of every dozen. A Cambodian alive in 1975 had a 69 percent probability of surviving this deadly regime. These are odds of about two to one — incredibly low when one is gambling with human life.

Even Hitler might be shamed by the poor performance of his killers compared to Pol Pot's. The gap is so large that even were the true Khmer Rouge democide one-eighth that calculated here, the percent of the population murdered annually would still exceed that of the Nazis.

How do we explain this incredible killing by the Khmer Rouge? Surely the dictates of power played a role. That is, the Khmer Rouge were seriously divided, feared each other, and doubted their control over the country. Moreover, they believed that Vietnam, the United States, and the Soviet Union were seeding the country with agents and maneuvering to destroy the regime. This insecurity and paranoia led to many of the purges and executions of those who might be a danger to the regime, such as former high Lon Nol officials or officers and top Khmer Rouge members.

TABLE 9.3
Cambodian Democide Rates Compared to That of Others [a]

Government	Years	% Democide Rate [b]	
		Overall	Annual
Cambodia			
Sihanouk	1953–70	.17	.01
Lon Nol	1970–75	.21	.04
Pol Pot	**1975–79**	**31.25**	**8.16**
Samrin	1979–87	3.55	.40
USSR	1917–87	29.64	.45
China (PRC)	1949–87	4.49	.12
Nazi Germany	1933–45	5.46	.91

a Regimes only. Cambodian figures from *Statistics of Democide*. Figures for the other governments are from the respective chapters in this book.

b. Mid-rates in a low-high range. The overall rate is the percent of the population killed; the annual rate is the percent of the population killed per year. Soviet rate is for citizens only. Nazi Germany is for all of Europe, including Germany.

Moreover, the Khmer Rouge were racists not much different from the Nazis. They believed in the racial superiority of the dark-skinned Khmer over the Vietnamese, Chinese, Moslem Cham, and others. This racism underlay the genocide they committed against these minorities, and played a role in their vicious incursions into Vietnam and their massacre of its citizens. Many Khmer shared this racism, at least toward the Vietnamese, against whom they "seethed with deep hatred," say the Khmer Rouge.[157] Khmers generally referred to Vietnamese as "Yuon," a deeply debasing term perhaps akin to the American use of "chink," "gook," or "Jap."

The Khmer Rouge were trained in guerrilla warfare for years before coming to power. Day after day they had lived under the most primitive conditions, suffering hunger, disease, and exposure as well as the terror of combat, shelling, and, in the early years, U.S. bombing.

FIGURE 9.5
Cambodian Democide Rates Compared to That of Others
(Data from table 9.3)

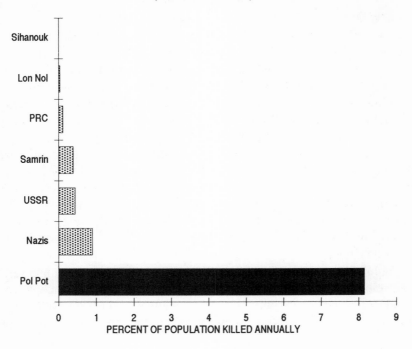

Death was all around them, and perhaps less than half of them survived. Suddenly one day they were in charge of a whole country. Add to this that most of the soldiers were shockingly young, in fact children carrying guns. Their school had been that of combat and death; killing meant nothing to them. Said one officer at a political meeting, "In the new Kampuchea, one million is all we need to continue the revolution. We don't need the rest. We prefer to kill ten friends rather than keep one enemy alive."[158] Indeed, the Khmer Rouge purposely trained many child recruits to be cruel and unemotional about causing pain and death by having them practice on monkeys, dogs, cats, and other animals. As soldiers or cadres, these killing machines could execute a starving peasant for just eating a banana collected in the forest — as we would swat a fly. As many Cambodians noted, these children followed orders like trained dogs.[159]

But the basic reason for most of this democide was ideological. The Khmer Rouge were fanatical communists and, as they told Prince Sihanouk when they had him under house arrest, "They wanted to establish the most advanced and purest form of communism in the world."[160] In its details, their Marxism was a new variant, combining in a volatile mix the Maoism of the destructive Great Leap Forward and Cultural Revolution, the Stalinism of the Soviet collectivization period in the early 1930s and subsequent Great Terror, and the obsessive and deadly nationalism of the Young Turks before and during the First World War.[161] The Khmer Rouge were willing to kill millions of Cambodians, even until no more than a million remained, to achieve three things in a few short years. One was a totally reconstructed Cambodia, completely collectivized, with no class enemies left; no imperialists or anything foreign; no feudalists or those holding power in the past, such as the monks; no capitalists. All others would work and eat communally; all would have all their needs fulfilled by the "Organization." The family structure would be unneeded, children would be taken away from their parents at a very young age and brought up by the Organization. All would be equal; all would be happy.

Second, they wanted to create immediately an independent and self-sufficient Cambodia. For the Khmer Rouge, the key concept was "independence-sovereignty."[162] Any dependence on other nations for anything — whether food, newsprint, or machinery — was to be eliminated forthwith. This was a basic, constantly reiterated fixation. To achieve this, the peasant and worker (although only a few workers, in communist terms, were left) were forced to labor morning, noon, and night, seven days a week, with some time off for exhortative and propaganda meetings. They labored to create the agricultural produce, infrastructure (roads, dams, irrigation works), and industrial base to assure this independence. All those over six years of age were required to work.[163] Those who could not work were useless mouths.

> A few days after the fall of Phnom Penh a communist soldier strode up to a blind beggar sleeping on the ground by the temple at Prek Phnov, about 9 kilometers north of the capital. Giving no warning, the soldier thrust his bayonet into the stomach of the beggar, killing him. As the black-clad executioner walked away, an onlooker, braver than most, asked him, "Why did you kill that man?"
>
> The soldier answered, "He could never work in the fields. He was useless to society. It is better for him to die."[164]

The achievement of self-reliance and communization had to be done forthwith, even if a whole generation had to be sacrificed. The communist Chinese, who themselves had caused tens of millions to starve to death from collectivization and the Great Leap Forward,[165] but who were the only foreign friends the Khmer Rouge had, tried to dissuade these impatient idealists from such a pace. Do it slowly, Chou En-lai suggested on his death bed. But the Khmer Rouge believed that they could do what every other communist nation had failed to do: create communism in seven days and seven nights. The formal program the party adopted in January 1976 envisioned creating a "wealthy, modern country by 1990."[166]

They also wanted to recover the ancient glory and lands of the Khmer Kingdom. Part of this glory, they felt, lay in the pure soul of the Khmer that existed then, a soul that had been corrupted by modern life and Western influence. Emptying the cities, forcing the millions of urbanites to work like oxen in the fields, to learn the simple peasant life, would help achieve this purification. During the evacuation of Phnom Penh, a political official explained to the French priest Ponchaud: "The city is bad, for there is money in the city. People can be reformed, but not cities. By sweating to clear the land, sowing and harvesting crops, men will learn the real value of things. Man has to know that he is born from a grain of rice!"[167] As Radio Phnom Penh declared in 1976,

> The young are learning their knowledge from the workers and peasants, who are the sources of all knowledge. Besides, no knowledge can be higher, more worthwhile, or more useful than that which has to do with production, agriculture, industry, and the experiments and techniques of production. And this knowledge is possessed by the peasants and laborers alone.[168]

And then there were the ancient lands, particularly those covered by what was then part of South Vietnam. The Khmer Rouge aimed to recover this land, and they thought they could do it. They apparently believed, as crazy as it may seem, that they could defeat Vietnam in warfare. When war did occur, they set a quota of thirty Vietnamese to be killed by each soldier.[169] And they thought that they were doing even better: on 10 May 1978, Radio Phnom Penh announced, "So far, we have attained our target: 30 Vietnamese killed for every fallen Kampuchean.... So we could sacrifice two million Kampucheans in order to exterminate the 50 million Vietnamese — and we shall still be 6 million."[170] What is the loss of 2 million (not to mention the killing of 50 million Vietnamese)? Enough people will remain to carry out the revolution and repopulate the new Cambodia.

Perhaps what made the Khmer Rouge particularly fanatical and obsessive about their Marxism was a cultural trait.

> The Khmer thinks by accretions or juxtapositions, but adheres strictly to the rules of his own internal logic. In the past, before beginning to act, every committee or council spent long hours and sometimes days drawing up statutes from which nothing was omitted, and constructing schemes, each more impracticable than the last. A simple idea, intuitively perceived, was pushed to the limits of its internal logic and often to the point of absurdity, without any regard for realities or any forethought for practical consequences. In fact, good intentions were enough, and when the scheme or statute was finally produced, the difficulties that had led to its formulation were themselves resolved or no longer relevant.
> ...
> The Chinese revolutionary principles embodied in the writings of Mao Tse-tung have been taken over and pushed as far as they will logically go, and Marxist praxis undertakes to apply them. "The revolution draws its

strength from the peasant masses." "Wars are won by encircling the towns by the countryside." Carried to extremes, this theory leads to the abolition of towns.[171]

In any case, people have to interpret the world around them through some worldview in order to act within it. This may be through gods and demons, spirits and ghosts, good and evil, Newtonian forces and fields of energy, or communists and capitalists. It should be clear that the Khmer Rouge worldview was and still is the deadliest poison to humankind of recent times.

No wonder then that Cambodians inside and outside Cambodia initially swallowed their feelings about the Vietnamese to welcome Vietnam's takeover and occupation. The new Cambodian regime established by the Vietnamese had at its head Heng Samrin, a former high-Khmer Rouge officer in the eastern region who barely escaped to Vietnam to avoid being purged in 1978. In the early 1980s, Cambodia was a satellite of Vietnam. Each government ministry had a Vietnamese "advisor" who approved or "suggested" policy. Moreover, Vietnam kept about 180,000 to 200,000 of its troops in the country,[172] a substantial number of which were used in offensive antiguerrilla operations.

Cambodia was in very sad condition when Samrin took over power. Most people were starving; many others were on the edge of starvation. The agricultural system had been brought near collapse by the Khmer Rouge's radical collectivization policies and its abysmal treatment of the peasants. With their defeat, and with considerable variation across the country, the Khmer Rouge had taken

with them or destroyed many of the essentials of rice production ... as much seed rice, seed corn, and seed tuber as they could ... as many carts, draft animals (in this case destruction meant being slaughtered and eaten or preserved for future consumption), and transportable agricultural tools (plows, digging implements, and hoes) as they could. Some villages and some entire areas were almost completely stripped. They also often took with them the most skilled and experienced sectors of the agricultural work force: the peasant-base people and the local administrative cadre who had made the ... agricultural production system work to the extent that it did.
...
It seems that in the first four months of 1979 about 1/3 to 1/2 of the pre-invasion stock of draft animals and carts and 1/2 to 2/3 of the stock of seed rice, corn and tubers were lost from the main agricultural producing areas.[173]

Not surprisingly, it looked like more than 3 million Cambodians might starve to death in 1979–80 .

Moreover, hundreds of thousands of Cambodians had fled the country and now filled newly built camps along the Thai border. Many others tried to escape on the ocean and contributed by the thousands to the boat people from Vietnam dying at sea. These refugees and the Samrin regime opened the eyes of the world community to the hell and democide of the Khmer Rouge. The United Nations, the United States, and many other nations went to considerable lengths to help the refugees and provide the new Cambodian regime with aid and technical assistance. Many refugees were thus saved from starvation and disease. Many died.

Three points should be made about the international aid given to the Samrin regime. First, the food situation in Cambodia was surprisingly, not as serious as the regime had let on and international aid givers thought, although there was some localized famine.[174] By September 1979, in some villages 10 to 20 percent of the population had died and many others were near starvation.[175] In this and the following two years, at least 500,000 may have starved to death.[176] In such a small country, this is a first-rate disaster. But it was not the 2 to 3 million deaths anticipated. At first, aid officials were surprised that famine was not widespread and clearly evident, but personal trips soon persuaded them otherwise.[177] Cambodia is a very fertile country, and once the people were free to scavenge in the forests and along the rivers, using their initiative to grow secondary crops, many who would have starved in a less bountiful country managed to survive. Moreover, in September 1979 the regime started its national famine relief program and, though too little too late, it did help save lives.

Second, while much of the food aid given Cambodia was distributed, in one way or another, the regime, particularly its new bureaucracy, often blocked needed technical help, such as badly needed medical aid.[178]

Third, while sections of the country were starving, tons of Cambodian rice were being trucked to Vietnam, along with needed "factory machinery, rubber cloth, furniture, spare parts and water pumps."[179]

The international community brought food and supplies to Cambodia, but it left much of the Khmer Rouge system in place. Social and economic centralization, and, collectivization of farming, continued under Samrin; there was continuing forced labor. That the people nonetheless survived is because the new system was considerably less rigid and demanding than had been the old one under the Khmer Rouge.

Given that Samrin and many of his high officials had been Khmer Rouge, it is understandable that control of thought and expression continued, and that purges, arbitrary arrests, torture (from which "a significant number of prisoners appear to have died"),[180] and executions were still commonplace. To be sure, the killing was nothing like what it had been under Pol Pot. It simply fell in line with that of other communist regimes, like China in the 1980s or Vietnam. Within a month or two of taking over, for example, the Samrin regime tried to evacuate from the market towns those who had returned to them after the defeat of the Khmer Rouge. Rather than doing this in days, however, the evacuation was planned to take place over months. While this was the final straw for many Cambodians, who then tried to flee to Thailand,[181] and while even after several years the human rights situation under the regime remained dismal,[182] what saved Samrin from much international criticism was the vast improvement over what had been going on before.

The civil war never really ended until about 1987. As mentioned, the Khmer Rouge resumed guerrilla warfare in 1979 (with possibly as many as 30,000 troops),[183] although perhaps for cosmetic reasons, Pol Pot was no longer the ostensible head. They extended their control from a strip of territory along the Thai border and a number of refugee camps to a considerable portion of the country. Judging by what went on in these camps behind the backs of observers, and the reports of escapees, the Khmer Rouge's murderous ways had not changed. Aside from the executions in the camps, for example, they forced "teenagers, pregnant women, and other civilians against their will to carry supplies into a war zone where they are exposed to mines, shelling and disease."[184] Two other guerrilla groups, one aligned with Prince Sihanouk, were also in the field, committing their own political killings and torture.[185]

The death toll under the Samrin regime is large by any standards. The CIA "conservatively" estimates that during July to December of the year the Khmer Rouge were kicked out, ten people died from war, famine, and disease for every one born. Overall, as mentioned, perhaps 500,000 people died of famine, caused equally by the Samrin regime and Vietnam. Overall, as broken down in table 9.1, the democide of the Vietnamese, the Samrin regime, the Khmer Rouge during their retreat and guerrilla period, and that of the other guerrilla groups, probably amounts to between 365,000 and slightly more than 1,300,000 Cambodians, most likely 850,000. Most of these deaths occurred in the first few years of the new regime. (How the Samrin and Vietnamese democides and democide rates compare to those of others involved in Cambodia can be seen in tables 9.1 and 9.2, and in figures 9.3 and 9.4). The resulting continued drop in population during this early period is graphically illustrated in figure 9.1, and more specifically in figure 9.2. It was not for several years that the population began to grow significantly.

Our English vocabulary, as rich as it is, simply has no word for the kind of state that was created by the Khmer Rouge in 1945. Nor do we political scientists have a concept or theory for it. These communists turned Cambodia into a gulag of nearly 7 million people, each a prisoner and a slave. Death often was the punishment for the violation of any one of numerous rules. But to label the Cambodia of this period a gulag state misses the sheer pain and suffering Cambodians experienced. As bad as the gulags of the Soviet Union and communist China were, in general their inmates did not suffer the torments inflicted by the Khmer Rouge.[186] The closest I can come to describing the conditions and suffering of the Cambodian people under the Khmer Rouge is "hell state."

A dungeon horrible, on all sides round,
As one great furnace flam'd; yet from those flames
No light, but rather darkness visible
Serv'd only to discover sights of woe,
Regions of sorrow, doleful shades, where peace
And rest can never dwell, hope never comes
That comes to all, but torture without end.

—John Milton, *Paradise Lost* I.61–67

Notes

1. This is a most probable mid-estimate from population analyses to be published in *Statistics of Democide.*
2. The predicted population is a most probable mid-prediction from population analyses to be published in the forthcoming *Statistics of Democide.*
3. Each of the periods was estimated separately, thus producing the slight discontinuity in the population estimates between the Lon Nol and Khmer Rouge regimes, and the latter and Samrin regimes. These are the most probable estimates and are from *Statistics of Democide.*
4. Etcheson 1984, 70.
5. Kiernan 1982, 166.
6. Ibid., 173.
7. Ibid., 167.
8. Del Vecchio 1990, 11.
9. Kiernan 1982, 166.
10. Ibid., 167.
11. Kiernan 1985, 276.
12. Ibid.
13. Ponchaud 1977, 140.
14. Kiernan 1985, 293n. 175.
15. Ponchaud 1977, 140.
16. Kiernan 1985, 284.
17. Etcheson 1984, 84.
18. Kiernan 1985, 284.
19. Kiernan 1982, 166.
20. Ibid.
21. Ibid.
22. Ngor 1987, 48.
23. Kiernan 1985, 321–22.
24. Kiernan 1982a, 262.
25. Kiernan 1985, 322.
26. Kiernan 1982a, 262.
27. Shawcross 1986, 249.
28. Kiernan 1985, 345. See also Kiernan 1982a, 311n. 118.
29. Shawcross 1986, 252
30. See Kiernan 1985, 379.
31. Told in Vickery 1982a, 96.
32. Ngor 1987, 61.
33. Shawcross 1986, 228.
34. Ngor 1987, 41.
35. Etcheson 1984, 106.
36. Ponchaud 1977, 166.
37. Ibid.
38. Ngor 1987, 42.
39. Becker 1986, 140.
40. Ponchaud 1977, 133.
41. Shawcross 1986, 132; Becker 1986, 140.

42. Ponchaud 1977, 133.
43. Sobel 1979, 7.
44. Shawcross 1986, 132–33.
45. Kiernan 1985, 307; Ponchaud 1977, 170.
46. Ponchaud 1977, 166.
47. Ngor 1987, 48.
48. Ponchaud 1977, 170.
49. Ibid.
50. Etcheson 1984, 101; Shawcross 1986, 297.
51. Shawcross 1986, 297.
52. Hildebrand and Porter 1976, 74. For a graphic display of this, see Shawcross 1986, 266–67, who gives a series of monthly maps of Cambodia showing in black the B-52 target areas and then one overlay of all of them. See also Kiernan 1985, 352 and Etcheson 1984, 100.
53. Shawcross 1986, 23.
54. Ibid., 272.
55. Ibid.
56. Kiernan 1982a, 281. See also Kiernan and Boua 1982, 331.
57. Etcheson 1984, 148.
58. Kramer 1977, 48.
59. Song 1977, A–8.
60. Kiernan 1982a, 282.
61. Kiernan 1985, 391.
62. Ibid., 357.
63. Kiernan 1982, 267.
64. Becker 1986, 151, 157
65. Stuart-Fox 1985, 29.
66. Kiernan 1985, 330.
67. Ponchaud 1977, 133–34.
68. Becker 1986, 164–66.
69. Becker 1986, 150.
70. Kiernan 1985, 371.
71. Ibid. , 370
72. Ibid.
73. Ibid.
74. Stuart-Fox 1985, 30.
75. Kiernan 1985, 380.
76. Ibid., 392.
77. Ibid., 380.
78. Ibid., 384.
79. Ibid., 379.
80. Kiljunen 1985, 55.
81. Kenneth Quinn, a Department of State specialist on Cambodia, analyzed Khmer Rouge policy and behavior during this period. His findings show that the Khmer Rouge changed little once they got into power. See Barron and Paul 1977, 59. Quinn's analysis is widely cited in the literature. See, for example, Kiernan 1982a, 278; 1985, 379 and Shawcross 1986, 321.
82. Small and Singer 1982, 231.
83. Barron and Paul 1977, 205.

84. Kiljunen 1985, 49n. 1; *Kampuchea: A Demographic Catastrophe* 1980, 2; Jackson 1989, 3n. 1
85. The calculations for this and other deficits to be given below are presented in *Statistics of Democide.*
86. Kiernan 1985, 358.
87. Shawcross 1986, 320.
88. Kiernan 1985, 413.
89. Becker 1986, 179.
90. Kiernan 1985, 416; Vickery 1989, 46.
91. According to the Khmer Rouge, as quoted in Ponchaud 1977, 20.
92. *Political Killings by Governments: An Amnesty International Report* 1983, 38–39.
93. *Kampuchea: A Demographic Catastrophe* 1980, 9.
94. This is a Khmer Rouge estimate (Hugo 1987, 245).
95. Barron and Paul 1977, 19–20.
96. *Political Killings by Governments: An Amnesty International Report* 1983, 38. In an interview ("Cambodia: The Face of Evil," 1977, 11), John Barron claims the doctor said "every 200 yards."
97. Vickery 1982, 50.
98. *Kampuchea: A Demographic Catastrophe* 1980, 9.
99. Ponchaud 1977, 50.
100. Kiljunen 1985, 50.
101. *Human Rights Violations in Democratic Kampuchea: A Report Prepared by the United Kingdom Government* 1978, 7.
102. Ngor 1987, 328–33. This is the Cambodian doctor who starred in the American movie on this Cambodian period, *The Killing Fields.* His account of his wife's death is one of the most moving in the literature on Cambodia under the Khmer Rouge. The true horror of this democide comes form the realization that this is but one such story of millions that survivors can tell.
103. Becker 1986, 180–81.
104. Kiernan and Boua 1982, 332–33.
105. Barron and Paul 1977, 79.
106. Ibid., 82–83.
107. *Time* 2 October 1978. p. 45.
108. Vickery 1983, 131.
109. *Political Killings by Governments: An Amnesty International Report* 1983, 40. Of course not everyone who wore glasses was killed. For many refugees who claimed this to be the case, "glasses" was simply metaphorical for the Khmer Rouge killing of teachers, students, and intellectuals. But in some places those who wore glasses actually were killed apparently for no other reason.
110. *Human Rights Violations in Democratic Kampuchea: A Report Prepared by the United Kingdom Government* 1978, 6.
111. Ibid., 7.
112. Barron and Paul 1977, 148–49.
113. Ibid., 135–36.
114. Stuart-Fox 1985, 93–94.
115. Ngor 1987, 216–25.
116. Hawk 1982, 20.
117. Kiernan 1990, 39.

118. *Kampuchea in the Seventies: Report of a Finnish Enquiry Commission* 1982, 42.
119. Kiernan 1988, 11, italics omitted.
120. Kiernan 1982a, 231.
121. *Political Killings by Governments: An Amnesty International Report* 1983, 42.
122. Kiernan 1988, 16.
123. Kiernan 1990, 39.
124. Hawk 1982, 20.
125. *Kampuchea: A Demographic Catastrophe* 1980, 4.
126. Zasloff and Brown 1979, 40.
127. Barron and Paul 1977, 141.
128. Puddington 1987, 20.
129. Stuart-Fox 1985, 165.
130. *Kampuchea: Political Imprisonment and Torture* 1987, 17.
131. Puddington 1987, 18; Stuart-Fox 1985, 165; Wain 1981; *Kampuchea: After the Worst: A Report on Current Violations of Human Rights* 1985, 3.
132. Wain 1981.
133. Stuart-Fox 1985, 123.
134. Kiernan 1982a, 278.
135. *Political Killings by Governments: An Amnesty International Report* 1983, 41; Kiernan 1990, 39.
136. Vickery 1983, 126.
137. Kiernan 1982a, 287.
138. Ibid., 227.
139. Ibid.
140. Stuart-Fox 1985, 119.
141. Kiernan 1983, 172.
142. Vickery 1989, 48.
143. *The World Almanac and Book of Facts* 1986, 333. Total American deaths in the Vietnam War were 58,021, including 47,321 battle deaths.
144. Kiernan 1985, 420.
145. Becker 1986, 319, claims that Vietnam used 60,000 troops against 28,000 Khmer Rouge.
146. *Kampuchea in the Seventies: Report of a Finnish Enquiry Commission* 1982, 69; Kiljunen 1985, 51, says 120,000 entered Cambodia.
147. Ngor 1987, 353.
148. Shawcross 1985, 210.
149. *Kampuchea in the Seventies: Report of a Finnish Enquiry Commission* 1982, 40.
150. Magstadt 1982, 48.
151. See, for example, Kiernan and Boua 1982 and Vickery 1983.
152. Thayer 1981, 95.
153. Kiernan 1985, v; 1990, 38.
154. Gough 1986, 66.
155. Ibid., 65.
156. See *Statistics of Democide*, forthcoming, for a discussion of the calculations. The deficit is itself the most probable value within a likely low-high range and is based on over one hundred population estimates. One should not be troubled therefore by the final estimate of the dead being slightly higher than the deficit.
157. From the *Khmer Rouge Black Book*, quoted in Kiernan 1982a, 231.

158. Yathay 1987, 148.
159. Becker 1986, 266.
160. Shawcross 1986, 391.
161. See chapter 10.
162. Ngor 1987, 197.
163. Luard 1978, 7.
164. Barron and Paul 1977, 76.
165. See chapter 5.
166. Becker 1986, 197.
167. Ponchaud 1977, 21–22
168. Ibid., 122.
169. Stuart-Fox 1985, 125.
170. Kiernan 1982a, 232.
171. Ponchaud 1977, 143.
172. Etcheson 1984, 196–97.
173. Heder 1980, 38–39.
174. Becker 1986, 440.
175. Heder 1980, 44.
176. Etcheson 1984, 148.
177. See Shawcross 1985, 212–13.
178. Ibid., 210.
179. Heder 1980, 31.
180. *Kampuchea: After the Worst: A Report on Current Violations of Human Rights* 1985, 10. See also *Kampuchea: Political Imprisonment and Torture* 1987, 41.
181. Heder 1980, 23–24.
182. See *Kampuchea: Political Imprisonment and Torture* 1987, 1.
183. Patten 1980, 36; Etcheson 1984, 197.
184. *Khmer Rouge Abuses Along the Thai-Cambodian Border* 1989, 23, 37.
185. *Kampuchea: Political Imprisonment and Torture* 1982, 2, 9, 72–73; *Kampuchea: After the Worst: A Report on Current Violations of Human Rights* 1985, 205–26, 215, 227.
186. Compare, say, Alexander Solzhenitsyn's 1963 *One Day in the Life of Ivan Denisovich*, the story of one day in the life of a gulag prisoner, to the biographies of survivors of the Khmer Rouge years, such as Ngor 1987 or Yathay 1987. The Soviet Kolyma mining camps were particularly miserable and deadly, and perhaps exceeded the horrors for most under the Khmer Rouge, but in the gulag system they were exceptional. See Conquest 1978.

10

1,883,000 Murdered
Turkey's Genocidal Purges

> It has been previously communicated that the government by the order of the Assembly (Jemiet) has decided to exterminate entirely all the Armenians living in Turkey. Those who oppose this order can no longer function as part of the government. Without regard to women, children and invalids, however tragic may be the means of transportation, an end must be put to their existence.

—Telegram from Minister of the Interior, Talaat[1]

The infamy of executing this century's first full-scale ethnic cleansing belongs to Turkey's Young Turk government during World War I. In their highest councils, Turkish leaders decided to exterminate every Armenian in the country, whether a front-line soldier or pregnant woman, famous professor or high bishop, important businessman or ardent patriot. All 2 million of them.

Armenians had been subject to genocidal massacres before, although nothing so systematic or ambitious. Throughout the previous century, Moslem Turks commonly committed such massacres, often with the connivance of the Ottoman government. The largest of these was under Sultan Abdul Hamid during the years 1894 to 1896, when the Turks killed from 100,000 to over 300,000 Armenians.[2] This shocked the Christian Powers (Great Britain roundly condemned this slaughter). They intervened to safeguard the Armenians and forced the Sultan to agree to reforms giving Armenians greater self-government in areas they dominated and more equality with Moslems elsewhere.[3] Turkey's rulers would not forget this and subsequent foreign intervention on behalf of this Christian minority.

At the turn of the century the sprawling Ottoman Empire was a multicultural, multiracial society, with substantial numbers of Greeks, Bulgarians, Armenians, and Jews, and a much smaller number of Syrians, Maronites, and Chaldeans. Nonetheless, there was a special animosity between Moslem Turks and Christian Armenians. Culturally, religiously, linguistically, and historically, they were different nations. When there was a breakdown of law and order or a disaster of some sort, Moslem mobs often turned on the nearest Armenians.

In 1908, Abdul Hamid's government was overthrown by the apparently liberal-oriented and reform-minded "Committee for Union and Progress," the so-called Young Turks. They made the Sultan accept a universally representative parliament and full religious and civil liberties — in form a liberal constitutional democracy. People in the streets were joyous and hugged each other, but they soon found reason to regret their celebration.

The European Powers viewed the Ottoman Empire as the "sick man of Europe." For decades the Empire had been breaking apart at the margins, and the Young Turk revolution only signaled its further internal weakening. More dismemberment followed: Austria-Hungary annexed Bosnia-Herzegovina, Crete proclaimed union with Greece, Bulgaria declared its independence, and Italy asserted control over Tripoli and much of Libya. These further political disasters provoked the Sultan's fanatical supporters to launch a countercoup in 1909 against the Young Turks, but they only succeeded in getting Abdul Hamid deposed and exiled. A sorry result of this turmoil was a large-scale massacre of Armenians in the Cilicia region, particularly in

Adana and its environs. Moslem mobs and Turkish soldiers, with possibly the connivance of local officials, killed around 30,000 Armenians[4] — no small number.

In spite of their liberal pretensions and initial reforms, the Young Turk "Committee of Union and Progress" that controlled the government soon became despotic. With the excuse of the countercoup, it declared a state of siege and suspended constitutional rights. It then turned against domestic opponents, moved to centralize its control, and began to suppress minorities that were seeking more autonomy. Abroad, it recklessly provoked the European Powers, who were seeking the further collapse of the Ottoman Empire, particularly Austria, Italy, and Bulgaria, and fought the Italo-Turkish War. The populace's discontent with the Young Turks grew, as did domestic chaos, and the government became more violent in its repression and terror. For example, by 11 July 1911, it had assassinated three opposition writers, one of which was killed openly on a street.[5]

Finally, in June 1912, military officers revolted, forcing the Young Turks out. This cleared the way for a new government called the "Great Cabinet" and made up largely of old dignitaries. It lasted until the outbreak of the First Balkan War in October 1912.

In spite of the domestic political confusion, the Turks fought well, repulsed a Bulgarian attack on Constantinople — now Istanbul — and fought the Bulgarian forces to a stalemate along the defensive Chatalja line. The parties soon declared an armistice, enabling the European Powers to try for a territorial settlement. By January 1913, the Turkish government appeared ready to adopt the settlement they recommended. However, this, plus the increased internal chaos and general dissatisfaction with Turkish war losses, provoked revolution.

Colonel Enver Pasha (Bey) (the hero of the 1909 Young Turk revolution), Talaat Pasha (Bey), and 200 other supporters seized the Sublime Porte, killed the liberal war minister, and grabbed power for the Young Turk Committee. Enver soon became war minister, Talaat minister of the interior, and their close ally, Djemal Pasha, minister of the navy, forming a triumvirate that would rule Turkey cruelly and autocratically for the next six years. With the government again in its hands, the Young Turks denounced the armistice and in February renewed the war with Bulgaria. They only succeeded in losing several battles and having to give up all of Turkey's remaining European territory (except for the Gallipoli and small Chatalja peninsulas). The disastrous losses in the Balkan War and the years of political turmoil incited a new call for national unity and modernization.

Many Turkish intellectuals and politicians saw the old Ottoman multicultural society and traditions as severe handicaps, and some believed it a blessing that they had lost their European territories with their different national groups. Now the country could truly become Turk. This growing sentiment of isolationism and ethnic purity sat well with the Young Turk rulers. They were supernationalists and racial purists. They wanted to create a new and glorious Turkey, as in ancient times — a Turkey of heroic warriors, of proud Turks — a Turkey that was homogenous and wholly Turkish.

To a minority of Young Turks led by Talaat Pasha, the First World War provided the golden opportunity to achieve these aims, particularly in the capture of North African territory and Turk-inhabited parts of Russia. Just before the war, Turkey had signed a defensive alliance with Germany. With the war's outbreak, Germany appeared to be winning easy victories and was pressing Turkey to enter the war, while the Allied forces (the Triple Entente of Britain, France, and Russia) seemed not to care. In October 1914, Germany unilaterally decided the question. Without consultation, the German commander-in-chief of the Turkish navy deployed it to bombard Russian Black Sea harbors and ships. Understandably, Russia then threatened war on Turkey. The Young Turk war faction, fully aware of the consequences, decided to take no action against the German admiral who had instigated the crisis. Russia declared war on Turkey in November 1914, followed a day later by Britain and France.

For Turkey, this war turned out to be yet another series of disasters. With the Third Army led by Enver Pasha himself, for example, Turkey invaded Russian Caucasia (much against the advice of the German military mission) and, at the battle of Sarikamish, suffered a calamitous defeat in winter snow. Enver lost about 80,000 men, many of them simply succumbing to the cold; only 18,000 returned, a third of whom required amputation of their limbs.[6] Other campaigns further south were only temporarily more successful. The Turks briefly occupied Tabriz, the capital of Persian Azerbaijan, and engaged in characteristic looting and massacre. Enver's brother-in-law, Djevdet Bey, however, led an unsuccessful attack on Khoi, northwest of

Tabriz. In the wake of this failure, Djevdet "ordered the cold-blooded killing of about 800 people — mostly old men, women and children — in the Salmas district."[7]

As to the Young Turk's zeal to purify the country, by World War I the nearly 750,000 Bulgarian minority[8] had been absorbed by Bulgaria as a result of the First Balkan War. This left some 2 million Armenians and 1,730,000 Greeks to be somehow eliminated from a 1914 Turkish population of 20 million.[9] The Greeks posed a special problem, for neighboring Greece, which was no little power, watched over Greeks in Turkey. For Turkey to treat her Greeks incautiously might well provoke neutral Greece to join the Allies (which she did in 1917). The Young Turks decided that the best they could do was to deport their Greeks from border and sea coast areas into the interior. Perhaps later, as events allowed, they could eliminate them altogether.

Unlike the Greeks, the Armenians had no independent, co-ethnic nation that guarded their welfare, for Turkey, Russia, and Persia had earlier incorporated the historical territory of Armenia (after the war, a much smaller Armenia would declare an independence lasting only a few years). The European Powers had expressed concern over past massacres of the Armenians and pressured the Ottoman Empire into agreeing to their special treatment. Now with World War I underway and Turkey fighting alongside Germany, the Young Turks had deprived the Armenians of British and Russian support, and made sure that Germany would look the other way. The Armenians were completely at the mercy of the Young Turks.

There was a convenient excuse for eliminating the Armenians. Most of them lived near the eastern border with Russia, and Armenian Russians were fighting in Russian forces. If Russia were to invade the region, Turkey's eastern Armenians might revolt and join the Russians, while those elsewhere in the country could be a subversive force. No matter that Armenian draftees were fighting valiantly in the army and that Armenians had shown their patriotism in other ways.[10] The Young Turks were determined to eliminate their Armenians and all else was pretext.

At the highest level of government and the ruling party, the Young Turks made a clear decision to annihilate the Armenians, and they carefully planned how they would do this. They implemented this genocide through a special secret organization run by the highest government officials, supervised by select members of the Young Turk Committee, and manned mainly by convicts released from jail.[11]

The evidence of this campaign is overwhelming. Consider the following matter-of-fact minutes of a secret meeting of the Young Turk rulers:

DR. NAZIM [Minister of Education] — Let us think well. Why did we bring about this revolution? What was our aim? Was it to dethrone Sultan Hamid and his men and take their places? I don't think it was for this.

It was to revive Turkism that I became your comrade, brother and fellow-traveler. I only want that the Turk shall live. And I want him to live only on these lands, and be independent. With the exception of the Turks, let all the other elements be exterminated, no matter to what religion or faith they belong. This country must be purged of alien elements. The Turks must do the purging.
...

HASAN FEHMI — Your servant is prepared to present a holy edict in this respect. Don't look upon me as a turbaned Softa (religious fanatic). I was a man of poor means, scarcely able to eke out a living. I was given the right of freedom and I became a Deputy to the Parliament. I am the teacher and the representative of 50,000 students of the schools. Let me explain. Since the collective society is endangered, the individual becomes sacrificed. This is Kaidahi Fiykiyeh (the principle of Islam philosophy). Therefore they must all be killed, men, women and children, without discrimination. To put this idea into effect, I have another suggestion. With your permission, let me explain. By reason of general mobilization, we took into the army all those who carry arms. We send them (the Armenians) to the front line of the battle. Then we will take them in a cross-fire between the Russians in front, and our special forces from behind. Having thus removed the menfolk, we give the order to our Salih (believers) to exterminate the remainder of women and children, the oldsters and the sick and the maimed in one full sweep. Our believers exterminate them and seize their properties and take their daughters to their beds.... Don't you find my suggestion the best and the most acceptable way of dealing with them?
...

DJAVID [Minister of Finance] — ... I will now take the vote.

At the order of Talaat, the votes are collected and counted. The result was that the resolution to exterminate the Armenians, provided not a single Armenian should be left alive, was passed unanimously.[12]

Lest these astounding minutes be considered Armenian disinformation, we also have the words of Talaat to the American Ambassador Henry Morgenthau. Writes Morgenthau, Talaat

> told me that the Union and Progress Committee had carefully considered the matter in all its details and that the policy which was being pursued was that which they had officially adopted ... the deportations [the primary mechanism of extermination] ... were the result of prolonged and careful deliberation.[13]

At another time Ambassador Morgenthau suggested to Enver that the government probably was not to blame for the massacres. Enver then responded in an offended manner: "You are greatly mistaken. We have this country absolutely under our control. I have no desire to shift the blame on to our underlings and I am entirely willing to accept the responsibility myself for everything that has taken place. The Cabinet itself has ordered the deportations."[14]

Then there are the actual orders that Talaat transmitted by telegram to governors and other officials. These came into Allied hands during the war and are no less profoundly shocking in their cold-blooded directness about some 2 million human lives. One signed "Talaat, the Minister of Interior" and dated 15 May 1915, says,

> It has been previously communicated that the government by the order of the Assembly (Jemiet) has decided to exterminate entirely all the Armenians living in Turkey. Those who oppose this order can no longer function as part of the government. Without regard to women, children and invalids, however tragic may be the means of transportation, an end must be put to their existence.[15]

As to carrying out these orders, the Young Turks had a problem of organization not unlike that the Nazis faced in liquidating the Jews. Although concentrated in the northeast, Armenians lived throughout Turkey; in some places they dominated districts, such as Van, and inhabited their own towns and villages. They had their own political party and vigorous political leadership. Moreover, many Armenians had survived previous massacres. Few held illusions about the hatred and brutality that the government could unleash against them. If forewarned they could well mount a spirited defense, as was later proven at Van[16] and Musa Dagh, where 4,000 Armenians withstood the onslaught of superior Turkish forces until relieved after 40 days by a French naval unit.[17]

For some time the Young Turks prepared for this genocide. Throughout the empire, they selected new police chiefs and governors on the basis of their devotion to the Young Turk cause, briefed them in the capitol, gave them secret instructions for liquidating the Armenians when ordered, and appointed them to villages, towns, and districts inhabited by Armenians. When the Young Turks finally decided to carry through the genocide, compliant or enthusiastic officials were in place and procedures prepared. The telegraphed order, "Take care of the Armenians," triggered their merciless slaughter.[18]

This genocide was a clever, multistage process. First to die must be the able-bodied men who could resist. The Turks already had drafted into the army some 200,000 to 250,000 of them. They were easily available for slaughter.[19] In February 1915 all army commanders received the following enciphered telegram signed "Deputy Commander General and Minister of War Enver."

In view of the present situation the total extermination of the Armenian race has been decided by an Imperial order. The following operations are to be performed to that effect:

1. All Ottoman subjects over the age of five years bearing the name Armenian and residing in the country should be taken out of the city and killed.

2. All Armenians serving in the Imperial armies should be separated from their divisions, without creating incidents, taken into solitary places, away from the public eyes, and shot.

3. All Armenian officers in the army should be imprisoned in their respective military camps until further notice.

Forty-eight hours after the above instructions are transmitted to the commanders of the army specific orders will be issued for their execution. Aside from preliminary preparations no action should be taken in that regard.[20]

In obeying this and subsequent orders, the army transferred its Armenian soldiers to labor battalions. It then worked them to death;

killed them by exposure, hunger, and disease in the winter snows; or
simply divided them into groups, tied those within each group
together, marched them off to some secluded spot, and shot them.
Sometimes, with the promise of loot, Kurdish tribes would attack the
bound Armenian soldiers as the Turks forced them along isolated
roads. Overall, the Turks thus murdered 200,000 or more draftees[21]
for simply being Armenian.

Exterminating Armenians in the army still left many males who
could fight and might have the weapons to do so. Moreover, the
Armenian leadership still could organize a rebellion. So the Young
Turks designed three additional stages in preparation for the final mass
genocide. Under the guise of wartime necessity and to protect against
possible sabotage and rebellion by Armenians, the first stage was to
demand throughout all towns and villages that Armenians turn in their
arms or face severe penalties. Turk soldiers and police ransacked
Armenian homes, and many suspected of having weapons were shot
or horribly tortured. This created such terror that Armenians bought or
begged from Turkish friends weapons that they could turn in to
authorities. This terroristic search provided the government a cover for
softening up the Armenians and for beginning the series of civilian
massacres that led to the final stage.

Next, in late April in Constantinople, Turks arrested and jailed 235
of the most respected Armenian leaders — politicians, doctors,
lawyers, educators, churchmen, writers — and subsequently deported
them to the interior, never to return.[22] In the days that followed, the
Turks picked up hundreds more who similarly disappeared, and
eventually they forced about 5,000 Armenian laborers, doorkeepers,
messengers, and the like to the same fate.[23]

Finally the Turks could deal with the remaining able-bodied
Armenian men and launch the ultimate genocide. They did this as a
one-two punch, moving from villages and towns closest to the battle
lines with Russia, to the west and southward. The technique was
generally the same from village to village and town to town, although
in some places the police grew impatient and simply slaughtered any
Armenian males they came across on the streets. First a town crier or
bulletin would call for all Armenian males over age 15 to appear by a
certain time in the town square or in front of the central government
building. Once they had gathered, the authorities then imprisoned

them all. After a day or so, soldiers and police roped the prisoners together in batches, marched them out to a secluded spot, and slaughtered them.

With a few more days' delay for preparation, the authorities then put the ultimate extermination into effect. Their goal was not only to complete the genocide, but also to generate funds, provide homes for Moslem refugees, save ammunition, and give the civil war on the Armenians the appearance of legality. By now, the Turks had reduced Armenian families to women and children, the very old, and the enfeebled — who could hardly offer much resistance. So again, the town crier went to work. All Armenians were to prepare for deportation to some unknown district. The only women exempt would be those who converted to Islam, found Turkish husbands to ratify the conversion by marriage, and turned their children over to a government orphanage that would bring them up as Moslems.

While the authorities sometimes carried out deportations with little warning, they usually gave a week or so for Armenians to settle their affairs. This was a joke. The Turks forbade the frantic Armenian women from selling their real property or livestock, and as soon as the women were gone the officials usually gave, the property to Moslem immigrants. The Armenians were forced to sell most of their family property for virtually nothing, often to government officials. But the authorities were not without mercy: they often hired or requisitioned oxcarts and drivers to carry the Armenians' remaining belongings, one cart per family.

The Turks then gathered Armenian families into convoys of as few as 200 or as many as 4,000 women, children, and old people and, guarding them with soldiers and police, set their deportation into motion. Within a few days or even hours of starting, however, the carters refused to go further and turned back, leaving the families to carry what they could.

The already pitiful deportees now faced, by design, several enemies. One was nature itself. The deportees often struggled in the heat and drought of the summer over rough country whose wells and springs were far apart.

Then there were the Turk guards who supposedly protected the convoys but instead preyed on them, sometimes even forbidding their charges to drink water when they came to wells or streams. Impatient to end their task, they first killed the stragglers and those who fell by the wayside, and then resorted to the outright massacre of those who had not yet died of hunger, thirst, disease, or exposure.

Moslem villagers were another enemy. Forewarned about approaching convoys and sometimes commanded to appear with weapons, they plundered the convoys as they straggled through their villages, raping and killing at will. After being repeatedly raped, some of the prettier Armenian girls survived only because they were taken, forcibly into a Moslem harem.

Some convoys had to make their way across mountains. Then, invited by messengers to have fun, Kurdish tribes would swoop down to do their own style of looting, raping, and killing, carrying off whichever women pleased their eyes.

Finally, the Turks invited brigands, and former Moslem prisoners released for the purpose, to attack the convoys. With the connivance of the guards, they did so enthusiastically.

In some cases the authorities were impatient with this process and simply used their troops to slaughter a whole convoy. In one case, they deployed the army's 86th Cavalry Brigade, ostensibly to keep order among Kurds. Instead it attacked large convoys from Erzindjan, stripped the deportees of their clothes, and led them naked to Kemakh Gorge. There

some Armenians were bayoneted to death. Most, however, had their hands tied behind them and were thrown into a ravine where the Euphrates flows between two rock walls. This method of extermination was quick and expedient, as large numbers of people — 20,000 to 25,000 — had to be eliminated. Roughly half of the Armenian population of Erzindjan were murdered at Kemakh Gorge.[24]

Not all convoys were on foot. The Turks transported some Armenians, especially those from cities in the northwest, by rail in overcrowded cattle cars. These Armenians fared no better. Rail congestion during wartime made for slow travel; and when the line was blocked, the guards forced the deportees out into the open for days or weeks with little or no food or water. Where there were two breaks in the Baghdad railway, the Turks made the deportees trudge across the Taurus and Amanus mountain ranges on foot, after having waited for months in concentration camps. They died by the thousands from epidemics, exposure, and hunger. Turks and mountain Kurds murdered thousands more.

The techniques of genocide varied regionally. In some places the Turks simply annihilated all the Armenian inhabitants of nearby villages and towns. For instance, they killed 60,000 at Moush and surrounding villages[25] and at least another 55,000 in attacks on Armenian villages in Van province.[26] In Constantinople, Smyrna, and Alleppo, however, foreign consuls and ambassadors prevented the Turks from deporting and massacring Armenians, thus saving about 200,000 from immediate annihilation.[27]

This genocide operated from the top down. Many local Turks did not support it. Indeed, some local officials refused to obey the orders and were deposed. And at least part of the Moslem population, according to the German court testimony of Dr. Johannes Lepsius, the German Red Cross official in Turkey at the time, "manifestly disapproved of the mass measures."[28] In some areas authorities had to use terror and force to make the Moslem population participate in the genocide. The Third Army commander, for example, ordered his soldiers to execute any Turk who aided an Armenian, to perform the execution in the front of the Turk's house, and then to burn down the house. Any official who helped an Armenian would be court martialed.[29] Whatever resistance there may have been among the local Turks and officials, however, the orders of the Young Turks were sufficiently obeyed to achieve their incredible purpose. Turks did massacre Armenians, they did dispatch convoys, and they did largely complete the process of killing them off.

Eyewitness accounts convey the resulting agony of these people. Rafael De Nogales, a Venezuelan who became an Inspector-General of the Turkish Forces in Armenia, wrote:

I saw through the windows of the sub-government house a caravan of several hundred Christian women and children resting in the market-place. Their sunken cheeks and cavernous eyes bore the stamp of death. Among the women, almost all of whom were young, were some mothers with children, or, rather, childish skeletons, in their arms. One of them was mad. She knelt beside the half-putrefied cadaver of a new-born babe. Another woman had fallen to the ground, rigid and lifeless. Her two little girls, believing her asleep, sobbed convulsively as they tried in vain to awaken her. By her side, dying in a scarlet pool, was yet another, beautiful and very young, the victim of a soldier of the escort. The velvety eyes of the dying girl, who bore every evidence of refinement, mirrored an immense and indescribable agony.

...

When the hour struck for departure, one after another of those filthy, ragged skeletons struggled to its feet and, taking its place in that mass of misery that shrieked silently to heaven, tottered off, guarded by a group of bearded gendarmes.[30]

A particularly moving experience was recounted by a soldier named Shahln Bey who had participated in one of these massacres. During the massacre, he said,

I saw an Armenian girl whom I knew, and who was very beautiful. I called her by name, and said "Come. I will save you and you shall marry a young man of your country, a Turk or a Kurd." She refused, and said: "If you wish to do me a kindness I will ask one thing which you may do for me." I told her I would do whatever she wished, and she said: "I have a brother, younger than myself, here amongst these people. I pray you kill him before you kill me, so that in dying I may not be anxious in mind about him." She pointed him out and I called him. When he came, she said to him, "My brother, farewell. I kiss you for the last time, but we shall meet, if it be God's will, in the next world, and He will soon avenge us for what we have suffered." They kissed each other, and the boy delivered himself to me. I must needs obey my orders, so I struck him one blow with an axe, split his skull, and he fell dead. Then she said: "I thank you with all my heart, and shall ask you one more favour." She put her hands over her eyes and said: "Strike as you have struck my brother, one blow, and do not torture me." So I struck one blow and killed her, and to this day I grieve over her beauty and youth, and her wonderful courage.[31]

By foot or rail, the Young Turks initially deported possibly 1,400,000 Armenians overall.[32] Weeks or months of exposure, thirst, hunger, murder, and abduction reduced their number to only the very strong and ugly. At the end even they were skeletons, without water, food or possessions, often naked to the sky. Of the 18,000 Armenians the Turks deported from Malatia, the number that made it to Aleppo, a dispersal center along the route, was ... 150. Out of 5,000 from Harpout, no more than 213 arrived.[33] On average, possibly only 10 percent survived, as the deputy director general of the Settlement of

Refugees informed his superior. In telegram No. 57, dated 10 January 1916, he reported that

> after investigation it has been confirmed that ten percent of the Armenian deportees have reached their place of exile. The rest have perished on the way by starvation and natural illness. You are informed that similar results will be accomplished by employing severe means against the survivors.[34]

Maybe even 15 percent survived. Reporting to the American embassy from the Turkish interior, consul Jesse Jackson wrote in September 1915 that

> at least 100,000 [deportees] have arrived afoot ... many having left their homes before Easter, deprived of all their worldly possessions, without money, sparsely clad, some naked from the treatment by their escorts and the despoiling population en route.... So severe has been the treatment that careful estimates place the number of survivors at only 15 percent of those originally deported. On this basis, the number of those surviving even this far being less than 150,000 up to September 21, there seems to have been about 1 million persons lost up to this date.[35]

The deportees' destination? A place where the Armenians could settle down and recreate their life, as the Turks officially informed the world? Not if the Young Turks could avoid it. At the convoy's end, the few survivors found themselves imprisoned in concentration camps located in the inhospitable northern and eastern boundaries of the Mesopotamian desert. These camps were their own hell. Already weakened, survivors readily died of starvation, exposure, and disease. And when the camps got too full from arriving convoys, the Turks took these miserable remnants of human beings into the desert and killed them.

This unbelievable history of the Young Turk genocide would not be complete without mentioning the special pleasure many officials took in torturing the Armenians. This torture came up in a discussion American Ambassador Morgenthau had with a "responsible Turkish official." According to the ambassador,

> he made no secret of the fact that the Government had instigated them, and, like all Turks of the official classes, he enthusiastically approved this treatment of the detested race. This official told me that all these details

were matters of nightly discussion at the headquarters of the Union and Progress Committee. Each new method of inflicting pain was hailed as a splendid discovery, and the regular attendants were constantly ransacking their brains in the effort to devise some new torment. He told me that they even delved into the records of the Spanish Inquisition and other historic institutions of torture and adopted all the suggestions found there. He did not tell me who carried off the prize in this gruesome competition, but common reputation throughout Armenia gave a pre-eminent infamy to Djevdet Bey ... who had invented what was perhaps the masterpiece of all — that of nailing horseshoes to the feet of his Armenian victims.[36]

By massacre and deportation, how many Armenians did the Young Turks wipe out? Table 10.1 lists the overall war dead as well as the domestic and foreign (that outside of Turkey's borders) democide committed by the Young Turks from 1909 to 1918. It also shows the number of deaths caused by regimes that preceded and followed the Young Turks. Table 10.2 recalculates this toll to show the Armenian and Greek totals. Turks had carried out isolated massacres of Armenians before 1915, when they launched the genocide. While the defeat of Turkey in October 1918 ended the Young Turk government and its genocide, the postwar nationalist forces of Mustafer Kemal also carried out massive massacres and deportations of Armenians and other Christians, killing hundreds of thousands of them. Tables 10.1 and 10.2 also record these events.

The size and speed of the Young Turks' ethnic cleansing are unparalleled in modern Turkish history. They alone most likely murdered no fewer than 300,000 and most probably around 1,400,000 — nearly 70 percent — of their Armenians ... in one year. Their kill rate thus surpassed Hitler's, who annihilated only about 38 percent of the Jews, and in the space of five years.

What happened to survivors? Many fled with other Christians into Turkey's southern or Arab provinces; nearly an equal number escaped into Russian Armenia,[37] many soon to die there of massacre, starvation, and disease (deaths for which the Young Turks were surely responsible). The Young Turks' efforts notwithstanding, 150,000 Armenians remained alive in western Armenia,[38] and more in Constantinople and Turkey's western provinces.

Those that survived by fleeing abroad faced yet another hell. They had

TABLE 10.1
Turkey's Dead, 1900–1923

Type of Killing [a]	From	To	Dead (000)
Democide [b]	1900	1923	2,782
By Young Turks	1909	1918	1,889
domestic	1909	1918	1,758
Armenians	1915	1918	1,404
Greeks	1915	1918	84
Other Christians [c]	1909	1918	107 [d]
Leb./Syrians [e]	1914	1918	163
foreign	1915	1918	131
Armenians	1915	1918	83
Nestorians	1915	1918	47
Azerbaijanis	1915		1
By nationalists	1918	1923	878
domestic	1918	1923	703
Armenians	1918	1923	440
Greeks	1918	1923	264
foreign	1918	1923	175
Armenians	1918	1923	175
By Greek army	1919	1923	15
of Moslem Turks	1919	1923	15 [d]
Massacres [g]	1900	1923	120
Under Abdul Hamid	1900	1917	15
Under Young Turks	1909	1918	105
of Armenians	1909		30
of Moslem Turks/Kurds [f]	1915	1918	75
War Dead	1900	1923	872
Famine/Disease [g]	1900	1923	1,350
Total Dead	1900	1923	5,124
Total Domestic Dead	1900	1923	4,818

a All data is from *Statistics of Democide* and are rounded-off mid-values in a low-high range. Values may not add up due to rounding.

b No information could be found on democidal killing other than genocide during this period.

c May include Armenians, Greeks, and Nestorians.

d A low.

e Forced famine in Turkish Lebanon and Syria.

f By Armenian irregulars.

g Nondemocidal.

lost the right to live as a community in the lands of their ancestors; they lost their personal property and belongings. They left behind the schools, churches, community centers, ancient fortresses, and medieval cathedrals, witnesses to a long history. Survivors were forced to begin a new life truncated, deprived of a link with their past, subject to upheavals in the new lands where they suddenly found themselves as foreigners. The remnants of the largely peasant and rural population were now a wretched group of squatters on the outskirts of cities poorly equipped to handle an increase in population.[39]

How can we possibly understand the utterly incredible decision to exterminate some 2 million Armenians? Surely massacres and wanton mass murder had become endemic in this part of the world. As the Ottoman Empire crumbled through defeat in foreign wars and internal rebellions, the desire for national self-determination and identity — nationalism — infected all national groups in the region. Bulgarians, Serbians, and European Greeks fought for and gained their independence in the nineteenth and early twentieth centuries. They then found their own minorities increasingly hostile. These they tried to eliminate through forced population exchange and deportation, with hundreds of thousands being moved around from one land to another

TABLE 10.2
Turkey's Armenian and Greek Genocide
(From table 10.1)

Victims	Number (000)
Armenians killed	2,102
By Young Turks	1,487
domestic	1,404
foreign	83
By nationalists	614
domestic	440
foreign	175
Greeks killed	347
By Young Turks	84
By nationalists	264
Total killed	2,449

more than once. Many died; many were killed. Elsewhere in the Balkans, the Greeks, Turks, Bulgarians, and Serbians also massacred each other, and the world seemed hardly to notice.

As already mentioned, the spirit of nationalism also infected the Young Turks. They believed in the classic Turk, in a Golden Age during which the Turks manifested all the Great Virtues. They glorified Turkism and, like the Nazis, believed in themselves as a master race. They desired a new Turkey that would unite all ethnic Turks into one great nation, undistracted and unweakened by rebellious minorities. This new nation, they believed, would be a basic force on world history. In all this, religion was only instrumental. Being "practically all atheists,"[40] the Young Turks only used Islam to incite the Moslem masses against Turkey's Armenians.

It was these Armenians that the Young Turks saw as a severe obstacle standing in the way of this united and pure Great Turkey. They believed Armenians to be clannish and haughty, always vociferously agitating for a territorial independence that would take yet another major chunk out of Turkey. Moreover, the European Powers, and particularly troubling, neighboring Russia, continually intervened in Turkish affairs to protect the Armenians, forcing Turkey to sign humiliating agreements to this effect. In 1913, the Russo-German agreement imposed on Turkey internal reforms that the Armenians had demanded. This angered the Young Turks, who unsuccessfully demanded that their Armenians reject them.[41]

Not only did the Armenians compromise the sovereignty of Turkey by promoting foreign meddling, but they were rebellious and strategically located. The great majority lived in Eastern Anatolia, vastly outnumbering local Muslims along the border with Russia, Turkey's historical enemy. Indeed, since the Turko-Russian border bisected most of the historical Armenian homeland, Turkey's Armenians identified with those across the border, and many Armenian Russians served in the Russian army that the Turks were fighting in 1915. Understandably, the Turks thought sabotage and insurrection behind the Turko-Russian front was a clear danger (even in a democracy like the United States, during the Second World War, U.S. citizens of Japanese descent were deported forcibly from the West Coast to interior camps). For the jingoistic and racist Young Turks this was an unbearable situation.

Added to this genocidal stew was the economic and professional success and dominance of the Armenians. They were the main businessmen, tradesmen, and intellectuals — the middle-class — in Turkey. Armenians directed 60 percent of Turkish imports, 40 percent of exports, and 80 percent of domestic commerce.[42] In some areas, Armenians were the only carpenters, tentmakers, masons, smiths, weavers, shoemakers, potters, jewelers, lawyers, pharmacists, and doctors. Furthermore, they were a distinctive religious, cultural, and political group, as Jews had been in Germany when the Nazis came to power. This superimposition of ethnicity, culture, religion, historical experiences, occupations, economic success, and minority status would be a dangerous brew in any country.

Finally, the outbreak of World War I and Turkey's alliance with Germany changed the balance of power that had one protected the Armenians. The Germans had the power and influence in Turkey to stop the genocide, but refused to do so. The German government was willing to make only *pro forma* protests, regardless of what the Turks did to the Armenians. Germany's war with Russia, Britain, and France left the Armenians no other protectors. Moreover, while war isolated the Armenians and would curtail off the genocide, Turkey's mobilization for war and induction of the most able-bodied Armenians into the army, where the Turks could easily liquidate them, provided the instruments of genocide. And there were no democratic checks and balances. The Young Turks exercised absolute power over Turkey. Soon after the outbreak of war, and having suffered rout after rout, the Young Turks believed that their defeat was near. They feared the consequences of surrender and the inevitable large-scale intervention in Turkey by the victors. In early 1915, the time seemed ripe to get rid of the Armenians. The decision for genocide followed.

As to the why and how this was done, the perspective of a Turk captain is revealing. As recounted later, a deported Armenian bishop (who survived only because of the gold he had for bribes — *bakhsheesh*) asked a Turk military police captain guarding his convoy several questions:

> "I asked the Captain if it were true that only Armenian men were to be killed and not the women and children. 'Well,' he replied, 'if we kill only the men and not the women and children, then in fifty years there will be a

couple of million Armenians. We have to kill women and children so that there will be no internal or external trouble.'"

The bishop pursued the question, asking why the women and children in the towns had not been killed. The captain was very forthcoming and explained that was forbidden because in 1895–96 Sultan Abdul Hamid had ordered that everyone in the towns had to be killed. But when Europe and the entire civilized world found out, they did not tolerate it. Now, continued the captain, no one would be left alive as witnesses to come before some future court.

"I now asked the Captain why he allowed these women and children to [be deported] to Aleppo and he replied: 'If we had killed these women and children in the towns, we would not have known where their riches were, whether buried in the ground or otherwise hidden. That is why we allowed precious items such as jewelry to be taken. But after we had proceeded for about four hours, we came into a valley. With us were some thirty Turkish women who began to go through the clothing of the Armenian women and girls and took away the money and jewelry. It took them four days.'"[43]

Did not this killing provoke among these rulers at least sadness, if not terrible guilt? Hardly. As Ambassador Morgenthau says,

In all my talks on the Armenians the Minister of War [Talaat] treated the whole matter more or less casually; he could discuss the fate of a race in a parenthesis, and refer to the massacre of children as nonchalantly as we would speak of the weather.[44]

When Talaat did get serious about the Armenian genocide, it was to squeeze the maximum money out it. To quote another of Ambassador Morgenthau's interviews with Talaat: "I wish," Talaat said,

that you would get the American life insurance companies to send us a complete list of their Armenian policy holders. They are practically all dead now and have left no heirs to collect the money. It of course all escheats to the State. The Government is the beneficiary now. Will you do so?[45]

Finally, I should briefly mention the Young Turk slaughter of Armenians, Nestorians, and other Christians during their futile invasion of Caucasia and Northern Persia. In Urmia during 1915, for example, they killed several thousand Christians; and throughout the region they also exterminated most of the Nestorians, perhaps 47,000 of them. With defeat near in the final year of the war, the Turks did not let up on their slaughter. In Baku and the environs they massacred some 30,000 Armenians.[46] In all, during the May to September 1918 invasion of Caucasia, the Turks may have killed 50,000 to 100,000 Armenians.[47]

Nor should we ignore the Christians of Turkey's Syria and Lebanon. Lacking direct means to exterminate all the Christians living there, the Young Turks purposely created a famine that achieved the death of at least 100,000 people.[48]

As mentioned, the Young Turks also committed genocide against the Greeks in Turkey, but for fear of Greece they did so with much more restraint than they showed the Armenians. Beginning in the spring of 1914, the Turks terrorized West Anatolian Greek communities, driving Greeks from their homes, taking their property, and murdering many.[49] They deported over 100,000 from the Mediterranean littoral to Greek Islands and the interior;[50] and once World War I began, they deported possibly 100,000 more from the Black Sea and Sea of Marmora. Everywhere the Turks robbed Greeks of their possessions, raped young girls and took them into harems, kidnapped boys for Moslem households, and forced the remaining Greeks into convoys, moving them away from coastal or strategically important areas. In all, the Turks possibly expelled as many as 1 million Greeks from their ancestral homes.[51] Although these deportations were hardly as brutal or as deadly as for the Armenian deportees, one estimate is that during the war 240,000 to 300,000 northeastern Greeks perished from hunger and exposure.[52] Further, as with the Armenian soldiers in the army, the Turks isolated Greek soldiers in labor battalions and treated them brutally; thousands died from starvation and severe winter cold.[53]

Those Greeks that survived terror, deportations, and the army, yet were unable to flee the country to Greece, could only look forward to eventual extermination. As Count Wolff-Metternich, the German ambassador in Constantinople in 1918, reported, "the Young Turk 'pack of hounds' was preparing impatiently for the moment when Greece would turn against Turkey, at which time the Greeks would be destroyed like the Armenians."[54] Fortunately for the Greeks, the

Young Turks lost the war before they could organize a Greek extermination. Nonetheless, as shown in table 10.2, they did manage to murder about 84,000 of their Greek citizens.

As totaled in table 10.1, these plus the Armenians and others that the Young Turks killed at home and abroad during and before the war, comprise a staggering murder of almost 1,900,000 men, women, and children. In Turkey alone, the Young Turks killed almost 9 percent of Turkey's total population, for the most part in 1915. Virtually all these people were murdered because of their ethnicity. It was genocide.

This bloody regime ended in humiliating military defeat. By October 1918, Turkey's situation on the war front had become militarily hopeless. Her army was disintegrating, military desertions were widespread, morale at home was abysmal, and the Allies had virtually defeated Germany in the west. One last defeat, this time by the Bulgarian army at Nablus, did it. The Young Turks could hold no more illusions; their regime collapsed.

Germany helped Talaat and Enver, among others, to escape and a new government under Sultan Muhammad VI took power. It appointed an Extraordinary Military Tribunal to investigate and document the Armenian massacres and found the Young Turks guilty of carrying out a policy of annihilation among other things (Raphael Lemkin had yet to invent the term genocide).[55] It sentenced the leaders, Talaat, Enver, Jemal, and Nazim to death in absentia.[56]

This did not end the killing of Armenians and Greeks. After the war, France, Great Britain, and Greece occupied portions of Turkey. This outraged the Turkish people, and the pro-Allies policies of the postwar Turkish government further fueled the anger. Sharing this feeling, the army inspector for the eastern provinces, Mustapha Kemal Pasha (otherwise known as Kemal Atatürk), left Constantinople in May 1919, ostensibly for an inspection trip. Upon reaching the eastern provinces, however, he resigned his position and established a rebel nationalist government. Under his presidency, a national congress met in Erzerum to organize resistance to foreign occupation — in effect to the Sultan's government. It proved successful. The Sultan forcibly tried to suppress the rebellion, but to no avail. In October 1919 he gave in, appointed a new cabinet, and held new parliamentary elections. The nationalists then won a big victory and prepared to exercise power in Constantinople.

This the British could not abide. In January 1920 they tightened their occupation, exiled twenty-four generals, ministers, deputies, and others to Malta, and in April made the Sultan appoint a new government. The new government denounced the nationalists as rebels and dissolved Parliament. In response, the nationalists held new elections, set up a new parliament in Ankara, and built up an army. The rebellion gained strength after the Allies forced a treaty on Turkey at Sèvres that politically subordinated Turkey to Britain, France, and Greece.

Although the nationalists initially had the resources of only three provinces, the country as a whole supported them. Within a few years they persuaded the Constantinople government to join them, forcing the Sultan to flee on a British ship. In the July 1923 Treaty of Lausanne signed by the nationalists, the former Allied Powers finally recognized Turkey's sovereignty and independence.

During these years of foreign occupation and rebellion, the nationalists fought France, losing at least 40,000 men; Greece, in which they probably lost a further 55,000 ; and the newly independent Armenian Republic, perhaps suffering around 1,000 more dead.

Along with a number of other Russian national groups, Armenia declared its independence in 1918 when Russia temporarily broke up during the civil war that followed the 1917 Bolshevik coup. It soon fought a minor border war with newly independent Georgia and had a violent conflict with Azerbaijan. It suffered Tatar rebellions and massacres of Armenians. It had to endure a severe winter (1918–19) that, along with a famine, further disrupted a regional economy (already near collapse due to the Young Turks' last-gasp invasion a half year before) and killed almost 20 percent of the population.

Worst of all was the war that the nationalists thrust upon the new Armenian nation. This began when the nationalist army took over some border areas in September 1920, particularly Olti. When Armenia tried to repel the Turks, the Turks used this as a pretext for a general offensive that easily defeated the Armenians, and by mid-November they had to accept armistice terms. In his subsequent treatment of the Armenians, nationalist General Karabekir was ordered to

undertake all the necessary measures to achieve "the political and physical elimination of Armenia." ... He is advised to be circumspect and gradual in the pursuit of the goal which "reflects the real intent of the Cabinet." ...

Most significant, the General is told to employ all available means in order to lull the victims which may be achieved by "deceiving ... the Armenians and fooling the Europeans" who are concerned with their fate.[57]

Although to this end the nationalist troops did not go about exterminating all Armenians under their military control, they did kill many. In Kars they murdered over 10,000,[58] maybe even 25,000.[59] An official memorandum to the Soviet government of Georgia detailed the nationalist occupation of Alexandropol and its district:

> Of the men, 30,000 were murdered, 20,000 were wounded, 16,000 were captives, and 10,000 died from hunger. Of the women, 15,000 were murdered, 5,000 were wounded, 3,000 were taken away as slaves, and 1,000 died from hunger. Of the children, 5,000 were murdered, 3,000 were wounded, and 10,000 died from starvation.[60]

Another contemporary Soviet reports further documents conditions in Alexandropol and Kars:

> Those people who were saved from massacre are condemned to starvation and untold privation, since the districts of Kars and Alexandropol are in total economic ruin. The Turks have taken away all the bread, rice and other foodstuffs from these places. They have left behind not even one single animal, whether cow, horse or sheep — all are herded in droves towards Erzerum [in Turkey]. Parallel with this deathly economic breakdown are the relentless massacres which the Turks have perpetrated in these same regions from the very first moment they invaded them.... The Armenian population of Alexandropol and of some tens of towns in various regions of Armenia have been put to the sword.[61]

These massacres amount to 71,000 Armenians that the Turkish nationalists murdered in and around Alexandropol or that died from the famine that the Turks created. And the districts of Alexandropol and Kars were not unique. Armenians in "some tens of towns in various regions of Armenia have been put to the sword."[62] In one town after another, reports yet another Soviet document, the streets were

> filled with dead bodies. This is nothing yet; it all becomes far worse when the soldiers harass their prisoners and punish the people in more horrible ways. Not content with this, they seek more pleasure by subjecting them to

a variety of tortures. They force parents to hand over to these executioners their eight-year-old daughters and twenty- to twenty-five-year-old sons. They rape the girls and murder the young men — all this in the presence of parents. This is the way they conducted themselves in all the towns. Young girls and women up to the age of forty are snatched away, no one knows where to, while men up to forty-five years of age are murdered. These towns are depopulated.[63]

We should add to the Armenian toll those massacres the nationalists provoked the Kurds or Azerbaijanis to carry out in Armenia or elsewhere in Caucasia, and those people that the Turks killed in Caucasia before they invaded Armenia. Overall, in this foreign genocide the Turkish Nationalists probably murdered 175,000 Armenians, as shown in table 10.2, maybe even as many as 243,000.

Of course, the nationalists murdered Armenians at home as well, although not as systematically as had the Young Turks. By massacre, deadly interior deportation, or forced immigration abroad, the nationalists tried to eliminate Armenian survivors under their control, many of them returned deportees and refugees. In Adana alone during 1919 the nationalists may have killed 50,000 Armenians.[64] Another 20,000 were massacred in Marash during February 1920, according to the report of a British Admiral (Reuters estimated the dead as 70,000).[65] About the same time, the nationalists killed still another 7,600 to 9,000 Armenians in Hadjun.[66]

The best known of the Turk's postwar massacres was that of Armenians and Greeks at Smyrna (now Izmir) in September 1922 after the nationalists recaptured it from the Greek army.[67] Turkish soldiers and Moslem mobs shot and hacked to death Armenians, Greeks, and other Christians in the streets and systematically set fire to their quarters. Fleeing before the soldiers, Moslems, and fire, hundreds of thousands of Christians ended up in a huddled, screaming mass on the city's wide waterfront. At first, the Turks forbade foreign ships in the harbor to pick up these terrorized survivors, but then, under pressure especially from Britain, France, and the United States, they finally allowed the ships to rescue all except males 17 to 45 years old, whom they aimed to deport into the interior — along with all those not rescued within several days. This "was regarded as a short life sentence to slavery under brutal masters, ended by mysterious death."[68] One cannot imagine the sheer emotional pain of those families the Turks forcibly separated on the piers, the women and children to board a ship to safety, the husbands and sons to be marched off to eventual death.

In total, the nationalists massacred over 100,000 Christians in Smyrna itself.[69] Adding those they deported into the interior to disappear forever, the nationalists killed a likely 190,000 altogether, the vast majority Greeks.

As these numbers make clear, what the Young Turks were afraid to do systematically to the Greeks the nationalists accomplished once war with Greece cleared the way. Those Greeks whom the nationalists did not massacre had their property confiscated and were herded, sometimes "barefoot and starving in the depth of winter,"[70] to ports to await deportation to Greece. In Trebizond (or Trabzond) province, the Pontic Greeks were "savagely persecuted … until the community was virtually wiped out."[71] For Aiden's Greek quarter, "a miniature European city," returning Greek forces found that the Turks had either massacred the Greeks or taken them into the interior and captivity.[72]

By November 1922, the European Powers sanctified the inevitable and approved a planned population swap between Turkey and Greece. Ultimately, the nationalists deported to Greece 1,250,000 Greeks in return for 390,000 Moslems.[73] As shown in table 10.2, left behind by the Greek deportees, including those killed in the Smyrna massacre and deportations, were 264,000 Greek dead — the likely total murdered by the nationalists.

As the Turks would hasten to add, the Greek army carried out its own massacres in Turkey's provinces along the Aegean Coast. The historian Arnold Toynbee personally interviewed villagers and investigated atrocities and massacres behind Greek lines before and after the Greek offensive of July 1921. From his report,[74] I counted thirty-two villages that had all their inhabitants massacred and another twenty-two partially. This was not simple communal violence — local Greeks did this with at least the tacit permission if not the connivance of the army. Moreover, after the Greek offensive was defeated they tried to devastate the land and "to exterminate the Turkish inhabitants of districts which it was no longer convenient for the Greek army to hold."[75] In Smyrna alone during the Greek occupation, one news dispatch claimed that over 4,000 Moslems were "butchered."[76] All told the Greeks likely killed at least 15,000 Turks.

Finally we can sum up the overall nationalist genocide. It totals almost 880,000 Armenian and Greek deaths, as we can see from table 10.1. Through this genocide and the forced deportation of the Greeks, the nationalists completed the Young Turk's program — the Turkification of Turkey and the elimination of a pretext for Great Power meddling. The Young Turks' policies were also those of the nationalists, although carried out with less bloodshed and greater cleverness. Through war, genocide, deportation, and the flight of refugees, both regimes reduced Turkey's 1914 population from around 20,000,000 to 13,660,000 in 1927, as counted by Turkey's first full census.[77] Figure 10.1 displays the relative role of war, genocide, and famine in this demographic catastrophe.

In 1922 only about 100,000 Armenians[78] — 5 percent of the probable 1914 population — were left alive in Turkey, mainly in a few major cities. The Turkish census of 1960 uncovered only two Armenian speakers in the city of Van, the former center of Turkish Armenia;[79] presently, fewer than 25,000 Armenians live in Turkey.[80]

Since the post-World War I years, few remember or write about the Greek democide. I know of no work in English focusing on it. But numerous scholars have studied the Armenian genocide and since the 1960s it has become particularly well publicized, as vengeful expatriate Armenians and their angry offspring escalated terrorism against Turk diplomats, murdering over twenty-two in nearly as many countries. Perhaps general appreciation of this genocide is now second only to that of the Jews.

To this day, Turkey absolutely denies that her past governments committed any genocide or mass murder. In this she is aided by the silence of those nations whose archives amply document it. Among them is the United States, which, despite the official contemporary reports of its ambassador and consular officials,[81] now adamantly refuses to recognize this clear genocide. Turkey is a member of NATO, was deemed essential for defense of the southern tier against Soviet aggression during the Cold War, and has since that time been deemed an important Western friend in a hostile and volatile region. Moreover, with the new independence of Armenia, Georgia, and Azerbaijan in the Caucasus, Turkey is seen as essential to the resolution of ethnic conflicts in the region. That such interests take precedence over historical truth and the recognition of Turkey's past mass murder is *realpolitics*; such is the moral bankruptcy of this diplomacy. Long-run U.S. interests in a stable and secure democratic world are better served by clarity of moral principles and resolve than by short-run expediency. Simply consider the moral message communicated to the world by purposely ignoring the Young Turk genocide of nearly 1,500,000 Armenians.

FIGURE 10.1
Deaths from Turkey's Genocide, War, and Famine, 1900–1923
(From table 10.1)

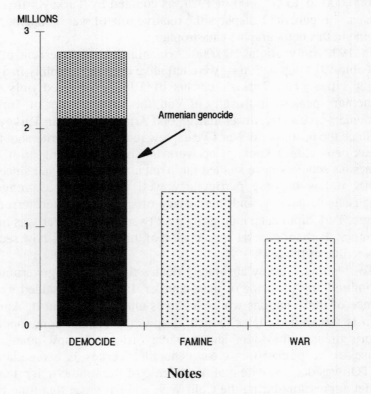

Notes

1.   Quoted from Boyajian 1972, 320. This telegram was included in the preface to the book *La Passion de la Cilicie 1919–1922* by the governor of Adana, Paul de Veou. I have read Orel and Yuca's 1983 analysis of the Talaat's telegrams printed in Andonian 1920 and which have been widely quoted. Based on the Turkish archives and the true format of telegrams of the time, Orel and Yuca argue that these alleged telegrams published by Andonian could only be

forgeries. Dadrian 1986, however, argues that they are authentic. Regardless, Orel and Yuca do not claim that all published telegrams from Talaat or from others helping to substantiate the Armenian genocide are falsifications.

2. Adalian 1991, 99, Hovannisian 1986a, 25, and Boyajian 1972, 83, 287.
3. See Gürün 1985, 165.
4. See Lang 1981, 14; Dekmejian 1986, 89; and Boyajian 1972, viii, 48, 83. I cannot define this as genocide. In Adana, the massacres occurred in two waves, one as the countercoup was underway in Constantinople, the other about ten days later as Young Turk soldiers regained control of the city (Sarkisian and Sahakian 1965, 20). It is a question as to whether the Young Turks had the time and interest to then organize or provoke an attack on the Armenians, and the literature on this is contradictory. For some evidence that the Young Turks were responsible, see Sarkisian and Sahakian 1965, 21–22.
5. Emin 1930, 51.
6. Sachar 1969, 50.
7. Walker 1980, 205.
8. Karpat 1985, 168.
9. These population figures are consolidated from a variety of estimates in *Statistics of Democide.*
10. There had been a small uprising at Koms, near Moush, but a commission of inquiry found the Turk police responsible. Then there was an armed uprising at Van in April 1915. After Djevedet Bey's campaign to the east proved futile, he initiated massacres and a reign of terror throughout his eastern province of Van, of which he was governor, and then issued a general order calling for the extermination of all Armenians. The day following this order, the Armenians, who had been building up their defenses in the city of Van, used what weapons they had to defend their quarters against Turkish soldiers and police (Walker 1980, 207). This rebellion is often cited as an example of the danger the Armenians posed to the defense of Turkey and as justification for their deportation from this region. Rather, it was an uprising by an Armenian community against the national campaign of total extermination the Young Turks had just begun.
11. Libaridian 1987, 205.
12. This is extracted in Nazer 1968a, 60–62 from Mevlan Zadeh Rifat's *The Inner Facet of the Turkish Revolution* in Turkish.
13. Morgenthau 1919, 333. The authenticity of Morgenthau's report on the Armenian genocide and relevant conversations with Talaat and other Young Turks has been disputed by Heath Lowry (1990). Lowry is an American expert on Turkey with the Institute of Turkish Studies in Washington, D.C., and denies the Armenian genocide took place. He argues that Morgenthau's account of times, places, and conversations are often inconsistent with his "diary," letters, and other personal documents. Moreover, Lowry claims that Morgenthau's book was written primarily by the Pulitzer Prize-winning journalist, biographer, and historian Burton J. Hendrick, and that others around Morgenthau, especially the Armenian Hagop S. Andonian, played an influential role in its writing. In spite of Lowry's claim that his questioning of Morgenthau's veracity should not be interpreted as an attack on the Armenian charge of genocide, he certainly does try to invalidate Morgenthau's evidence for the genocide. Since those parts of Morgenthau's story bearing on the genocide are consistent with so many other sources of information

about it—newsmen, other American diplomats, German diplomats and military personnel, Italian diplomats, other autobiographies, German and Turkish court testimony, Young Turk documents, reports of Turkish officials in the government, and refugees—I will continue to give the Story credence until more neutral studies of it confirm Lowry's arguments. For annotated bibliographies of sources on this genocide, see Smith 1991, Dadrian 1991a and 1991b, and Totten 1991.

14. Ibid., 351–52.
15. Reproduced in Boyajian 1972, 320.
16. See note 9.
17. Lang 1981, 26.
18. Ibid., 20.
19. Sachar 1969, 98; Libaridian 1987, 207.
20. Published in Boyajian 1972, 333–34.
21. Libaridian 1987, 204.
22. Boyajian 1972, 288–89.
23. Walker 1980, 209.
24. Mazian 1990, 92–93. See also Walker 1980, 213.
25. Walker 1980, 212.
26. Ibid., 208–9.
27. Boyajian 1972, 285.
28. Alexander 1991, 136. This testimony was given during the German trial of the Armenian Soghomon Tehlirian, who in March 1921 assassinated Talaat in Munich.
29. Ibid., 136.
30. De Nogales 1926, 130–31.
31. Mazian 1990, 100.
32. Boyajian 1972, 283, quoting Johannes Lepsius' court testimony. This is also the figure consolidated from a number of estimates in *Statistics of Democide*.
33. Toynbee 1916, 650.
34. The telegram is published in Boyajian 1972, 328.
35. Alexander 1991, 110.
36. Morgenthau 1919, 307.
37. Libaridian 1987, 206.
38. Ibid.
39. Ibid.
40. Morgenthau 1919, 323.
41. Ibid., 288.
42. Kuper 1986, 56–57.
43. Alexander 1991, 146–47.
44. Ibid., 353.
45. Morgenthau 1919, 339. This caused Morgenthau to lose his temper. "You will get no such list from me, " he said, and undiplomatically got up and left Talaat.
46. Gross 1972, 47n. 6.
47. Walker 1980, 230.
48. Glaser and Possony 1979, 526.
49. Toynbee 1922, 140.
50. Morgenthau 1919, 328; Barton 1930, 63.
51. Morgenthau 1919, 325.
52. Sachar 1969, 309.

53. Morgenthau 1919, 324.
54. Alexander 1991, 139. This is from the testimony of Johannes Lepsius during the Talaat assassination trial. Germany had been an ally of Turkey and was hardly disposed to manufacture anti-Turk propaganda.
55. Lemkin 1944.
56. See Alexander 1991, 123, 125, 128; and Dadrian 1991b.
57. Dadrian 1991a, 101.
58. Boyajian 1972, 142.
59. Walker 1980, 272.
60. Sarkisian and Sahakian 1965, 55.
61. Walker 1980, 320n.
62. Ibid.
63. Ibid.
64. Gross 1972, 47n. 6.
65. Gürün 1985, 278.
66. Boyajian 1972, 154–55.
67. For a book-length description of this massacre, see Housepian 1966.
68. Lovejoy 1933, 150.
69. Boyajian 1972, 156; Lang 1981, 37; Housepian 1966, 190n.
70. Ladas 1932, 429.
71. Walker 1980, 345.
72. Toynbee 1922, 151–52.
73. Housepian 1966, 208.
74. Toynbee 1922.
75. Ibid., 316.
76. Housepian 1966, 153.
77. Emin 1930, 298.
78. Lang 1981, 37.
79. Ibid., 37–38.
80. Kuper 1986, 52.
81. According to Alexander 1991, 105, "The reports to [American Ambassador] Morgenthau, which he forwarded to the State Department, from three consuls in particular—Leslie A. Davis in Harput, Oscar S. Heizer in Trebizond, and Jesse B. Jackson in Aleppo—constitute the most accurate documentation of the deportations and massacres from official American sources." Then there is the Ambassador's own book (1919).

11

1,670,000 Murdered
The Vietnamese War State

> *It is better to kill ten innocent people than to let one enemy escape.*
>
> —Dr. Nguyen Manh Tuong,
> Speech to the National Congress of the
> Fatherland Front, Hanoi, October 1956

Perhaps of all countries, democide in Vietnam and by the Vietnamese is the most difficult to unravel and assess. It is mixed in with six wars spanning forty-three years (the Indochina War, the Vietnam War, the Cambodian War, the subsequent guerrilla war in Cambodia, the guerrilla war in Laos, and the Sino-Vietnamese War), one of them involving the United States; a nearly twenty-one-year formal division of the country into two sovereign North and South parts; the full communization of the North; occupation of neighboring countries by both the North and South; defeat, absorption, and communization of the South; and the massive flight by sea of

241

Vietnamese. As best as I can determine, through all this, close to 3,800,000 Vietnamese lost their lives from political violence, or nearly one out of every ten men, women, and children.[1] Of these, about 1,250,000, or nearly a third of those killed, were murdered. Table 11.1 provides the mortality statistics.

France took over all of Indochina in the late nineteenth century, making Vietnam one of its colonies. There had been some rebellions against the French, most notably the 1930–31 communist-led uprising in which 10,000 Vietnamese were killed.[2] But it was not until World War II that the French hold was shaken. When France was defeated by Germany, the remaining French Vichy regime was allowed nominal control over a French garrison of 50,000 in Vietnam. The Japanese allies of Germany had applied military pressure to the French garrison for facilities and bases in Vietnam even before France fell, and in negotiations with the Vichy government, Japan later achieved control over Vietnam's important airports and port facilities. In December 1941, the day of the attack on Pearl Harbor, Japan surrounded French forces in Vietnam and gave them an ultimatum: cooperate or be destroyed. With no outside help possible, and with even the appearance of French control at stake, the French accepted full Japanese use of Vietnam as a base and staging area. In effect, the French and Japanese operated as co-colonists of the country. As the end of the war approached and Japan became increasingly concerned about setting up an "impregnable defense" of its empire, it became disenchanted with this relationship and, in a surprise coup d'état in March 1945, took over Vietnam by brutal force, massacring many French in the process.[3]

Even before this coup it was obvious to many Vietnamese that Japan would eventually lose the war and have to leave Vietnam. Vietnamese nationalists and communists thus envisioned their country's independence and worked toward that end. With the defeat of Japan in August 1945, both groups moved to take over Vietnam. The communists, or Viet Minh as they were called (this is a short term for the Vietnam Independence League that the communist Ho Chi Minh formed in 1941 to fight the French), were especially well organized. Although only about 5,000 in number,[4] they succeeded in dominating the major cities in the North. In September 1945, their undisputed leader, Ho Chi Minh declared the independence and sovereignty of the Democratic Republic of Vietnam while carrying out guerrilla warfare against French forces.

France was not about to allow a de facto break-up of its empire and gradually mobilized its forces to recapture Vietnam. With the help of

TABLE 11.1
Vietnamese War Dead and Democide, 1945–87

Type of Killing [a]	From	To	Dead (000)
War/Rebellion [b]	1945	1987	2,510
Indochina War	1945	1954	512
Vietnam War	1960	1975	1,747
N. Viet./V. Cong	1960	1975	1,062
S. Vietnam	1960	1975	684
Other [c]	1991	1987	251
Democide [d]	1945	1987	1,813
By North Vietnam	1945	1987	1,669
domestic	1945	1987	944
foreign	1945	1987	725
in S. Vietnam	1954	1975	164
in Cambodia	1970	1987	461
in Laos	1975	1987	87
other	1945	1987	13
By South Vietnam	1954	1975	90
domestic	1954	1975	89
foreign	1970	1973	1 [e]
By Others	1945	1987	54
United States	1960	1972	6
Cambodia	1975	1979	35 [e]
South Korea	1965	1973	3 [e]
France	1945	1954	10
Total Domestic Dead	1945	1987	3,761

a All figures are from *Statistics of Democide* and are mid-values in a low-high range. Values may not add up due to rounding.

b Figures for Vietnamese war dead, excluding democide.

c Includes wars with China and Cambodia and guerrilla wars in South Vietnam, Laos, and Cambodia.

d. Includes democidal military action (e.g., bombing).

e This is a low.

the British (formally there to disarm the Japanese, but actually also providing organizational and political support for the French — their fellow colonialists in the region), of French troops released from internment by the British and Japanese, and of Japanese troops and planes, France reasserted authority over most of the South. Neither the Viet Minh in the North nor the French desired all-out war, however. Still in effective control of areas in the North, Ho Chi Minh tried to negotiate some kind of autonomy in a French Union. A preliminary agreement to that effect was signed in March 1946. By then 1,200 French soldiers had been killed.[5]

As Ho was in Paris to negotiate the final agreement, Admiral d'Argenlieu, the French High Commissioner for Indochina and a staunch colonialist, recognized a puppet pro-French regime in the South. He then met with its officials and those of Laos and Cambodia as though the Democratic Republic of Vietnam did not exist. Finally, burying Vietnamese hopes, France adopted a new constitution that refused to recognize members of the French Union as fully independent (they could not control their own foreign affairs, for example). As a result, Hanoi published its own constitution — in effect another declaration of independence. It covered all Vietnam and recognized no French authority.

Negotiations could no longer bridge French colonial aims and Viet Minh nationalist aspirations. A truce that had been in effect for months was broken, and in December 1946, with 60,000 trained troops,[6] the Viet Minh launched attacks on French garrisons throughout Vietnam. All-out war began.

The war rallied Vietnamese around the Viet Minh, especially in the north. Having massacred the most important noncommunist nationalists (to be described below), the Viet Minh remained the only coherent force fighting for Vietnam against foreign imperialism.

The number of Viet Minh activists quadrupled to 20,000 in 1946 and then increased more than tenfold to 210,000 three years later.[7] By the end of 1948, they had gained control over half the population and villages of Vietnam.[8] By 1951 they were a huge communist organization of 760,000 activists. Under Ho Chi Minh's minister of defense, General Vo Nguyen Giap, Viet Minh's military forces doubled and redoubled similarly, and he eventually commanded 350,000 regulars and guerrillas. At their peak, French forces numbered over 400,000 troops, including 20,000 Foreign Legionnaires and over 300,000 Vietnamese soldiers.[9] This bloody war, which each year cost almost 7 percent of French forces (compared to the 2.5 percent loss rate for South Vietnam and 1.8 percent for U.S. forces in the subsequent Vietnam War),[10] only came to an end with the defeat of the French at Dien Bien Phu in May 1954.

This defeat reset the stage for the Geneva Conference, then being brokered by the British, Soviets, and Chinese to deal with Korean and Vietnamese issues, and which also involved the French, Viet Minh, Laos, and Cambodia (the United States had been involved but withdrew over a deadlock involving Korea). As a result of the French defeat, a cease-fire was agreed to and France accepted the independence of Vietnam. The final Geneva Agreements of July 1954 also established a cease-fire line at the 17th Parallel that effectively partitioned the country into North and South Vietnam and later would define the demilitarized zone (DMZ) between them. It allowed for a 300-day period for the two-way free movement of pro- or anticommunist forces and other Vietnamese. And it called for free elections in 1956 to unite the country.

Aside from France agreeing to the sovereign independence of Vietnam, Hanoi was not too concerned about the other arrangements. It believed that in effect it had won all Vietnam, and according to its agents, opposition to Hanoi in the South, particularly by that much hated French and Japanese collaborator Prince Bao Dai, would soon collapse. Even though his government had been recognized as early as February 1950 by the United States and Britain, and by August the United States had started to provide military aid to him and the French, four years later Bao Dai's rule still was shaky. The South was plagued with private militias and independent armies, some organized by secret societies and autonomous religious groups (such as the Cao Dai with 1,500,000 to 2,000,000 members and an army of 30,000).[11] No government unification or coherent opposition to the communists then seemed possible, even under the "strong" Premier Ngo Dinh Diem that Bao Dai had just selected and to whom he reluctantly had given full authority over the army and government administration.

The human cost of the Viet Minh victory was enormous. Even before the Vietnam War was imposed on the people, nearly 510,000 — maybe even more than twice that number — died in battle or due to the fighting. Probably half of those killed were civilians. And this does not even take into account the democide.

As the Viet Minh struggled against the French, they also fought a vicious hidden war against their noncommunist nationalist competitors. They assassinated, executed, and massacred whole groups of nationalists, including relatives, friends, women, and children. Nationalists were not the only victims: "class enemies" were also "punished," and communist ranks were purified of Trotskyites and others who deviated from accepted scripture. Thousands among the most educated and brightest Vietnamese were wiped out in the years 1945 to 1947 that it took the communists to firmly establish their power.[12] James Pinckney Harrison gives us a feel for this purge:

> The terror ... continued, and from mid-1945 through 1946 the Communists did away, not only with Ta Thu Thao and Huyn Phu So, but with five other Trotskyist leaders — with Pham Quyhn [Quynh], Bao Dai's prime minister from 1932 until March 1945; with the founder of the Constitutionalist Party, Bui Quang Chieu; with Ngo Dinh Diem's brother Ngo Dinh Khoi; and with various other non-Communist Nationalists. Some sources speak of Communist executions of some 5,000 and imprisonment of another 25,000 Nationalist rivals at this time, but according to Troung [Truong] Chinh, the Party should have eliminated more "enemies of the revolution" than it did. In September 1946, he wrote that, except in Quang Ngai province, revolutionaries had been "conciliatory to the point of weakness, for forgetting [Lenin's dictum] that a 'victorious power must be a dictatorial one,'" and adding that "for a new-born revolutionary power to be lenient with counter-revolutionaries is tantamount to committing suicide."[13]

By 1953 virtually all the countryside and many cities and towns in the north were under communist Viet Minh control, and a French defeat and formal independence could well be anticipated. The communists now could think more seriously of social revolution, particularly to the eventual nationalization of all land. But first they had to extend their power over the countryside.

It would be a mistake to consider the resulting "land reform" movement that consumed the next three years as an act of egalitarianism. Land ownership among the peasants was widespread, and in the vital Red River Delta 98 percent of the peasants owned the land they worked;[14] throughout the north, about two-thirds owned the land they farmed.[15] Moreover, few outside the Mekong Delta region owned more than two or three hectares (nearly 5 to a little over 7 acres).[16]

As it was for the People's Republic of China in 1950–53, "land reform" had two basic purposes. One was to consolidate communist power over the peasants by destroying their natural, centuries-old source of countervailing authority in the villages and hamlets, particularly that of the larger landowners and wealthier peasants. The second was to clear away potentially effective opposition to the ultimate collectivization of all land.

The technique followed the communist Chinese model. First, marshal the far more numerous poor peasants against their few better-off and locally more powerful neighbors by taking the land and property of the better off and giving it to the poor peasants. This would give the mass of poor peasants a stake in the struggle and rally their support for the revolution. Moreover, if many of the "landlords" and "rich" are also killed, this will terrorize the remainder into obedience — as the ancient Chinese maxim says, "Kill just one and frighten ten thousand others."[17] Then, once this struggle was won against these actual or potential "enemies of the revolution," the communists could turn on the peasant mass and nationalize and collectivize its newly gained land. Divided, without organization or leadership, the natural local leaders eliminated, having seen what happened to the "landlords" and "rich," the peasants would be too terrorized to resist.

As the party carried it out, "land reform" involved two so-called "sky-splitting and earth-shaking" mass campaigns,[18] one after the other. The first was the largely two-year Land Rent Reduction Campaign that began in 1953 in Viet Minh-controlled areas. It involved two successive population classification decrees, one in 1953 and the other, a more refined version, in 1955. Both required the rural folk to pigeonhole every member of every village into one of a hierarchy of classes, with the poorest wage-earning or landless peasant class at the bottom; the landlords at the top, with the rich peasants right below them; and the weak, average, and strong middle-level peasants forming three middle classes.

The communists then demanded that the poor peasants liquidate the landlords. With the "help" of communist cadre, some landlords were shot while others were imprisoned or otherwise punished, sometimes by having their land taken away. But apparently not enough were liquidated. Unhappy about the few "landlords" so dealt with in each village, the communists pointed out "that according to the scientific calculations made by 'our Chinese comrade advisers' who had thoroughly investigated land ownership in the villages (a flying team of Chinese advisers was, in fact, moving rapidly from village to village), a much greater number of exploiters should have been found."[19] They demanded that peasants reconsider the population classification decree and reclassify their neighbors. Now "rich" and "strong middle-level" peasants had to be redefined as "landlords." This multiplied by about five the number that were to be executed.[20]

The new classification, however, also condemned not only the better-off peasants but also the more productive and enterprising of them. The differences between landlords, or rich or strong middle-class peasants, on the one hand, and the poorer or smaller land-owning peasants on the other, was often a matter of fine distinctions, sometimes simply separating the harder working and more successful peasants from the others. This hardly fazed the cadre, however, since the goal was to carry out a social revolution; whether class differences had to be forced or invented did not matter. To make it even more likely that they find the requisite number of sacrificial victims, the communists then defined a new category, "landlord mentality" signifying, incredibly, evil by lineage. A person in this category was anyone whose ancestors had been "landlords" or who sometime in the past had possessed land or livestock.[21]

Murder by classification was often made final by a bullet, but many of these "evil" ones also died in prison, by suicide, or as the result of an "isolation policy." Whole "landlord" families would be ostracized and boycotted by demand of the state. The population as a whole was forbidden to have anything to do with them. Even talking to them was prohibited, and children were encouraged to throw stones at them. They were not allowed to work. Quite simply and understandably, the "majority of them died of starvation, children and old people first, and eventually the others."[22] Admitted the high communist Nguyen Manh Tuong in a 1956 speech to the National Congress of the Fatherland Front in Hanoi, "While destroying the landowning class, we condemned numberless old people and children to a horrible death."[23]

The overall toll of this pitiless campaign can only be guessed at. According to French Professor M. Gérard Tongas, who lived in Hanoi throughout this period, 100,000 Vietnamese were thus murdered.[24] This may well be an underestimate.

The purpose of the Land Rent Reduction Campaign was to soften up the countryside for the radical seizure of the land of those who had "too much," and its temporary transfer to those who had "too little," thus preparing for eventual collectivization. With the elimination of the "landlords" and the "rich" — the "most reactionary" peasants — and after a delay to allow for the political and economic reorganization of the villages, Hanoi launched its Land Reform Campaign.

Land and other possessions were brutally stripped from those with even moderate-sized plots and given to peasants with either very little or nothing at all. But in North Vietnam peasants with as much as an acre of land were few; even fewer, however classified by the population decree, fit the classic Marxist idea of "landlord." Nonetheless and however defined, "landlords" that had survived and kept their land through the previous campaign now were forced to vacate their homes and abandon their land and possessions. Also to be confiscated were the land and possessions of "French colonialists, and other imperialist aggressors, and of Vietnamese traitors, reactionaries and cruel bullies."[25] Ultimately this meant that anyone in communist disfavor could be robbed of all his possessions.

The expropriation of property and its transfer to the poorer peasants was often done with some ceremony. This might involve the beating of drums, a speech by some comrade announcing the evils of the victims and the confiscation of their property, shouting of the required ritualistic "Long live..." and "Down with...," and ending with removal of all the movable possessions, such as farm animals, pets, farm implements, household furniture and goods, pots and pans, and other cooking utensils. Distribution of the confiscated land might also involve great ceremony, with the usual flags, slogans, and shouting. Each peasant then would be given a certificate of land ownership. If we can believe Radio Hanoi, one-fifth of an acre thus went to each of 325,000 families.[26]

A particularly shocking device of these two savage campaigns was murder by quota. In applying each population classification decree, Hanoi demanded that at least one "landlord" be killed per village. But, as mentioned, on first application the poor peasants were found insufficiently dedicated, and too few "evil" ones were exterminated.

So, during the Land Reform Campaign the communist Central Committee raised the quota from one to five per village.[27] That is, the peasants of each village in North Vietnam were ordered to define at least five "landlords" for execution, even if the land in the village was already being shared communally.[28] And five executions was a minimum.

The party's Politburo believed that 95 percent of the land was owned by the wealthiest 5 percent of the people. Therefore, of course, 5 percent of the folk in each village and hamlet had to be eliminated: five in a village of 100, twenty-five in a village of 500 and fifty in a village of 1,000. I do not know how they handled the numbers when 5 percent of a village of 50 yielded 2.5 people. I suspect that since by communist theory it was better to kill the innocent then let the guilty go free, they always rounded upward. In any case, each village had its special "land reform" team whose job it was to do the killing, once its report was approved by provincial party headquarters.[29]

The number that were murdered in or died from these two "sky-splitting and earth-shaking campaigns" from 1953 to 1956 may have been huge. Some estimate it as high as 500,000 Vietnamese;[30] even a high estimate of 600,000 has been mentioned.[31] But there are also very low estimates, such as 800,[32] 5,000[33] or 15,000[34] dead, killed, or victims. Given the minimum quota of five "landlords" in each of 15,000 villages,[35] and considering those that committed suicide or families that died from official ostracism, probably the correct figure is more like 150,000 dead.

But this is not all. In 1953 the party also carried out a Political Struggle Campaign of terror. This was a very short-lived and explosive campaign to prepare the way for "land reform." Its aim was to eliminate those still remaining who had helped the French, who were anticommunist or not sympathetic enough, and who were unreliable or questionable communist cadre. In a replay of Stalin's Great Terror, people would be arrested for some excuse, such as not paying taxes, and then painfully tortured until they "confessed" to membership in fictional anticommunist associations and plots with certain others, names supplied. These in turn would be arrested and tortured. Of course, this typical communist technique provided the "legal" foundation for finally arresting and executing the "reactionaries" the party was after.

Such terror went on in every village, for if the social revolution was to proceed, those who did or might question it had to be liquidated. After about two weeks of this terror as many as three to five people had been killed per village.[36] But it was getting out of hand: peasants were fleeing the villages; the party itself could be in danger. Having achieved their purpose, the communists formally ended the terror and, as they would do after "land reform," publicly admitted their mistakes. Even President Ho Chi Minh apologized for failing to lead the people properly. This was hardly sincere, however, for a month later he sent cadre into the Fifth Zone, the part of South Vietnam controlled by the communists, to repeat the terror.

The terror lived on as a form of repression and social prophylaxis, and there were periodic purges of communist cadre. Many of the cadre had joined the party in its early years and had bourgeois backgrounds; they or their families would eventually be classified as landlords. "Land reform" thus provided an excuse for a national purge of the party, of which the vanguard were the poor and landless peasants, whose denunciations often extended to the rank and file of the party. Anyway, party officials had difficulty finding the requisite number of bodies to meet their quota for each village, so it helped to include objectionable party members.

Aside from these purges, the political repression and associated terror reached its peak in 1956 at the same time that "land reform" was ending. In this year, about 70,000 Vietnamese may have been murdered from repression alone.[37]

Apparently concerned that the accelerating terror and killing associated with these and other campaigns might weaken or destroy the Communist Party's hold on the country, the party then launched the Rectification of Errors Campaign. As usual, it confessed again that mistakes had been made, and it fired many top officials that had directed "land reform." From his firsthand observations during this period, Hoang Van Chi, a former member of the Vietnamese resistance movement against the French and a nationalist, had this to say.

This confession, together with the spectacular removal of those responsible for the movement, has led many outside observers to believe that the confessed errors were genuine mistakes, and that there was a sincere effort on the part of the North Vietnamese leaders to correct them.

A few even have gone so far as to conclude that the whole process had been a complete failure. This was far from true, for the so-called Rectification of Errors campaign was another bluff to be added to an already long list.

Rectification of Errors was indeed an integral part of the well-planned process of Land Reform and, as such, it had been conceived long before as a necessary conclusion to Land Reform.... [R]ight from the very beginning, in 1953, the party had engaged in the so-called Political Struggle ... to pave the way for Land Reform, i.e., to move step by step from a normal situation to that of terror. This time the process was reversed. After three years of sustained violence, the party wished to return to a normal situation as smoothly as possible. They did this by resorting to the Rectification of Errors campaign. It was inevitable that the party should suffer a certain loss of prestige but it was prepared to accept this small sacrifice.[38]

As part of this "forgiveness" period, many prisoners were released, including former communist cadre, who, for the most part, had been arrested for deviationism, bourgeois tendencies, or "landlordism." Since those who had done the finger pointing were often new party cadre, as the old cadre returned to their villages there was much conflict between them and these new, much more radical cadre, especially if they had replaced the former cadre or been responsible for their arrest and punishment. Many scores were settled, revenge exacted, and untold numbers of communist cadre thus murdered.

To be expected amid all this terror, killing, expropriation, and social chaos, the peasants also rose up, particularly during the deadly years 1955–57. For example in November 1956, Ho Chi Minh's home province of Nghe An, saw open rebellion, and rioting and insurrection spread throughout much of the province. It took a whole division of troops almost a month to reimpose communist control. Rebellions also broke out elsewhere. The worst of these, near Vinh, involved protests by those who had been prevented from moving South during the 300-day window opened by the Geneva Agreements.[39] The following year, armed rebellions took place in Phat Diem, Than Hoa, and near Hanoi;[40] they were bloodily suppressed by the army. While communist order was being restored, many peasants were killed, many executed, and many others deported. In the uprisings of November 1956, perhaps 2,000 were executed,[41] possibly 6,000[42] killed or deported. Overall, from 1955 to 1956 those who lost their lives from rebellion may have numbered between 10,000 and 15,000.[43]

Clearly, the period from 1953 to 1956 was a politically tumultuous one for North Vietnam. It saw the end of the Indochina War and the signing of the Geneva Agreements, which established the independence of Vietnam and its separation into two Vietnams. It saw the mass exchange of populations between them, with some 727,000 to 1 million North Vietnamese refugees (about 60 percent Catholics) moving to the South, and nearly 50,000 to 100,000[44] primarily Viet Minh guerrillas, families, and sympathizers moving to the North. And it saw the victorious communists socially and economically reconstruct the North, wiping out actual or potential opposition. The Political Struggle, Land Rent Reduction, and Land Reform campaigns were the major weapons in this social revolution. All told, from 1953 to 1956 the communists likely killed 195,000 to 865,000 North Vietnamese. I conservatively estimate the toll as around 360,000 men, women, and children.

This democide, however, does not take into account the 24,000, at least, that died from prison or forced labor. Nor does it include the likely 5,000 French Union POWs who died as a result of inhumane treatment in POW camps or who perished on the 500-mile 7,000-prisoner death march after the French defeat at Dien Bien Phu, or the approximately 1,000 seriously wounded who were left to die.[45] These figures raise the toll to some 415,000 people that were murdered or died.

While in the North the communists were engaged in their lethal mass campaign, in the South Premier Ngo Dinh Diem achieved several military victories against the autonomous sects and armies that had bedeviled the Bao Dai regime. In April 1955 he then turned on Prince Bao Dai himself and, through an extralegal assembly meeting, had a new government declared, with himself as head. In October he held a sham referendum to endorse this bloodless coup (in one area he got 98 percent of the vote).[46]

Things were not going quite as Hanoi had planned. The Bao Dai regime was supposed to disintegrate, but with the help of Diem it appeared to be growing stronger, and then with Diem's coup it was replaced by what appeared to be an even more effective and dedicated anticommunist government. Perhaps some nudging would help. So, as early as 1955, Hanoi permitted those Viet Minh remaining in the South to carry out a low-level guerrilla war against the new regime, with the goal of expanding their area of control and of thwarting Diem's attempt to rid the countryside of those Vietnamese who were communists (they were called "Viet Cong"). At the time, nothing more appeared necessary since the regime was still thought unlikely to survive.

Once the communists had successfully extended and consolidated their own power in the North, they more seriously focused on the South. In late 1956, the Politburo reevaluated the likelihood of Diem's collapse. It decided that more revolutionary techniques would have to be applied to bring him down and temporarily replace his regime with a congenial and transition pro-unification government. There remained violent discontent in the South: those sects and regions striving to keep their autonomy still rebelled against government control; Diem's own version of "land reform" was alienating masses of peasants, who saw it only as a way the rich got richer; and attempts to win the support of mountain people only embittered them when they were deported en masse "for their own protection." But this discontent was disunited and lacking in direction. So the North moved to provide antigovernment rebels, dissidents, and guerrillas that had once fought against the French with organization and leadership, and particularly with the aim of overthrowing that "reactionary" Diem. Thousands of former Viet Minh still remained inactive in the South and had only to dig up their weapons.

During the following months, terrorism and related assassinations significantly increased in the South.[47] Mainly under Hanoi's direction, officials and civilians who were anticommunist or who created trouble for the communists were assassinated or abducted. Often these victims were simply the best officials, or civilians who were extraordinary in some way and thus too good an example to the people. For the communists, a corrupt and incompetent official was always to be desired; the dishonest and criminal created disaffection and an environment for communist proselytizing. In 1957 alone over 700 low-level officials were thus murdered, around 3,750 were killed in the following three years.[48]

Beginning in 1958, Hanoi also secretly returned to South Vietnam those military and political cadres who had been regrouped to the

North after the Geneva Agreements. But the guerrilla war against the South was still at a relatively low level, and Diem appeared to be growing stronger. With U.S. advisors and military aid, his army would soon be a well-trained and -equipped force of over 135,000 men. Clearly, the communists now had to undertake a full-scale armed struggle to "smash" the Saigon regime. The decision to do so was made during the January 1959 communist Fifteenth Conference of the Central Committee meeting in Hanoi.[49] The appropriate policies soon were issued, underlined by Ho Chi Minh's appeal in May "to unify the country by appropriate means" and his clear call for the "liberation" of South Vietnam.[50]

Hanoi then prepared for the infiltration of South Vietnam's regular troops and military supplies. It moved to establish bases on the Cambodian border at Tay Ninh (northwest of Saigon) and east of Ratanakiri province in the South's Central Highlands. And it built the first "trail" of the so-called Ho Chi Minh Trail (code-named "Line B-59" — the "B" stood for the battlefield in South Vietnam and the "59" for 1959, the year it was built)[51] through Eastern Laos and Cambodia and thence at several points into South Vietnam. Through use of the trail and its subsequent extensions and modifications, the communists built up their forces in the South. In 1960, Hanoi killer squads increased the rate at which they were assassinating officials and village heads, killing perhaps nearly 3,000 over the two years ending in 1961.[52] By this time, Hanoi had also infiltrated 10,000 regular soldiers and a substantial number of the 40,000 guerrillas then operating against the Diem regime.[53]

Moreover, from July 1959 to June 1960, Hanoi carried out the Concerted Uprising Campaign, whose goal was to expand direct communist control over Southern territory. This was to be done by "breaking up the machinery of oppression," that is by disorganizing Diem's strategic hamlet program (aimed at separating villagers from communist agents) and assassinating South Vietnam's real centers of authority outside the cities — the hamlet and village officials. In this way, the communists hoped to gradually spread their control over the countryside and eventually lay siege to the cities.[54]

The start of North Vietnam's war against the South, and therefore the Vietnam War, might therefore be set at 1959, or even 1958. I date it, however, as beginning in January 1960, when General Giap unambiguously involved Hanoi in war against the South. "[T]he North," he declared, "has become a large rear echelon of our army. The North is the revolutionary base for the whole country."[55] The following September, the Communist Party's Third Congress meeting in Hanoi decided to create a broadly defined political front, a façade for its war against the South. Several months later the Saigon media reported the formation of the National Liberation Front.[56]

The tempo and scale of war and terror from then on increased materially, and by 1964 thirty to forty-five main-force battalions of North Vietnam troops, comprising 35,000 guerrillas and 80,000 irregulars,[57] had gained control over most of the South. One source claims that in 1964 the Viet Cong taxed the population in forty-one out of the South's forty-four provinces and prevented government access to 80 percent of its territory.[58] The National Liberation Front claimed it controlled 8 million of the South's 13 million people, and three-fourths of the country.[59] With all these losses and its troops by then dispirited, it seemed only a matter of time before Saigon would succumb to the communists. Nor did extraordinary U.S. military aid and 23,000 "advisors"[60] prove enough to even stabilize government defenses. The collapse of the South that Hanoi had been predicting since 1954 seemed imminent.

Manifestly, only massive U.S. involvement held hope of saving the South from communism. And, so it appeared to President Johnson's administration. If the foreign policy of containment meant anything, if U.S. defense treaty commitments were to be credible, the United States must save the South. In August of 1964, the excuse was given: North Vietnam patrol boats attacked two U.S. destroyers patrolling international waters across the Gulf of Tonkin (or appeared to attack them in what may have been mistaken radar blips of the ship's wake for torpedo boats; in any case, torpedo boats had clearly launched an attack against one of the same destroyers in these waters two days before). Johnson moved swiftly. While launching retaliatory air attacks against the boat's bases, he also presented Congress with the Gulf of Tonkin resolution. Although falling short of a declaration of war it would give the President a blank check to fully join the Vietnam War in defense of the South. With President Johnson and much of the elite establishment in Washington leading the charge and with strong public support shown by the polls, Congress promptly passed the resolution.

Hundreds of thousands of U.S. troops and massive supplies of light and heavy military equipment poured into South Vietnam. This formidable American effort, which reached its peak of 543,400 troops in April 1969,[61] shored up the South Vietnam government and achieved a military victory on the ground. The Viet Cong were badly defeated after their abortive countrywide Tet Offensive of January to February 1968, losing 32,000 guerrillas. More important, the Viet Cong revolutionary infrastructure that had been built up in the villages and urban areas surfaced during the Tet Offensive and was in many places virtually destroyed.[62] Overall, possibly some 50,000 National Liberation Front cadre were lost.[63] Moreover, by 1968 South Vietnam's military was considerably restrengthened by U.S. aid and training, numbered around 819,000,[64] and regained control over a considerable portion of the country's population.

The year 1968 was the turning point in the war, but not in the direction one might suppose. By then, the propaganda of communist front groups in the West, and particularly in the United States, was pervasive, especially when recycled by Hanoi's sympathizers and those opposed to the war (often in the press[65] and through mass demonstrations and "political theater"). With between 200 to nearly 300 U.S. dead returning home from Vietnam in body bags every week, deep cleavages already had appeared in U.S. public and particularly elite opinion.

By 1968, what held the war's support base together in the United States was the administration's promise that the war was being won, that there "was light at the end of the tunnel." America needed only to "stay the course." But the rosy assurances were made to appear lies by the Viet Cong's obvious ability to launch the 1968 countrywide Tet Offensive (Tet is the Vietnamese New Year celebrations taking place during the first seven days of the lunar calendar's first month). While few Americans saw the magnitude of the Viet Cong's defeat, they did see, as universally displayed in the news media, the Viet Cong's bloody street-by-street occupation of the large city of Hue and the battle to evict them, the battles in the streets of many other cities, and the attack on the American Embassy in Saigon. That was it. This offensive, coupled with Hanoi's largely successful struggle for the hearts and minds of American intellectuals, won the only battle that mattered — the political one. The elite establishment's support, and that of Congress, for the war was finally and irretrievably shattered. The war now appeared unwinnable, or in any case unsustainable by the American people.

From that time on it was only a matter of when and how the United States would withdraw from the war. Under President Nixon, partly elected by his promise to bring the war to an end, U.S. troops were gradually withdrawn, and efforts to reach a political settlement with North Vietnam were redoubled. The resulting Paris Peace Agreement and cease-fire was signed with Hanoi in January 1973, and the last U.S. troops were withdrawn the following March.

This peace agreement, in which, among other things, the North recognized the sovereignty of South Vietnam, turned out to be merely a fig leaf for the American defeat. Regardless of what promises the United States had made to the South about not letting it fall, or threats to the North about violations of the Agreement, the United States had not only withdrawn militarily but in spirit as well. While Hanoi openly violated the agreement and prepared its forces for the final offensive against the South, the U.S. Congress in June voted to deny President Nixon any funds for any use of the military in or around or over Indochina. And Congress disastrously reduced military aid to Saigon's forces — from $2.27 billion in fiscal year 1973 to $700 million in fiscal year 1975.

Ironically, for a war that was fought so much in the shadows — by guerrillas and unconventional forces, by assassination and abduction, by subversion and terror, and by front groups and propaganda — it was ended by a massive, conventional military offensive. At first only part of a two-year strategy to defeat the South, Hanoi was surprised when it routed the forces of the South during its attack on the Central Highlands in early March. Hanoi immediately deployed additional forces east to the coast and then south toward Saigon. In disarray through incompetent leadership at the very top and in the field, with whole divisions disintegrating through lack of coordination and leadership, the South's forces could only put up spotty resistance. Saigon fell in April 1975.

Over the fifteen years of war, North Vietnamese forces or their Viet Cong front continued their terror campaign against South Vietnamese civilians, amounting to 24,756 incidents just from 1965 to 1972.[66] This number covers terrorist executions, as when the Viet Cong would enter a government village at night, round up officials and civilians on a list, brutally torture and kill them, and then disappear into the jungle. But it does not take into account the continuous day-by-day terror in the Southern provinces they controlled. The Viet Cong arrested people even for such crimes as having close relatives who worked for the government or were unsympathetic to the communists. Note one captured Viet Cong roster of those arrested from 1965 to early 1967 in seven villages of the Duc Pho district, Quang Ngai province. Among those labeled government agents, spies, policemen, soldiers, and the like, were people characterized as "distorting Communism," "sympathizing" with the enemy, "spreading rumors to belittle," "spoke evil of" or "attacked revolutionary policy," "opposing the denunciation campaign," "opposed cadre," "wife of an enemy soldier," "husband is an enemy tyrant," "his son joined the enemy army," and the like.[67] Many of these people faced execution, along with others tagged as "tyrants" and "spies." One list of such executed during 1963 to 1964 in Phu Yen province included members of South Vietnam political parties, "a 'number one cruel village policeman'; an individual who had 'left the liberated area' and who was 'cruel and stubborn;' and a district agent who had 'incited Catholics to counter the Revolution.'"[68]

Even the wives or relatives of South Vietnamese soldiers were sometimes assassinated. A captured Viet Cong document, for example, revealed that in Binh Tan district the wives of two government officials were murdered; murdered also in Duc Hoa district, according to another captured report, were the dependents of two South Vietnamese military men.[69]

The communists refused to call assassinations and such executions acts of terror. Rather, they labeled them acts of "justice," "retribution," or "revolution." These were not directed at ordinary peasants, social workers, teachers, simple village chiefs, and other such, but at objects shaped by the appropriate revolutionary rhetoric. As pointed out by Douglas Pike, then a U.S. Foreign Service officer specializing in Asia, such victims were

> seldom shot or decapitated; he is *punished* or the *Front has exercised its power.* The victim is never a civil servant but a *puppet repressor*, or a *cruel element*; never a policeman but a *secret agent* or a *lackey henchman....* One is not a member of a political or religious group

opposing the communists but a *key reactionary* or *recalcitrant elements* (when more than one) in an *oppressive organization*. Always *cruel fascists* are *brought to justice* or *criminal acts against patriots avenged* or the *Front has carried out its severe verdict against the aggressors*, not that non-combatants have been slaughtered.[70]

As Professor Guenter Lewy adds, "Most of the hapless victims were peasants, teachers, social workers and the like who had sided with the [government of South Vietnam], but by dehumanizing them in this way the use of terror could be rationalized."[71]

The Viet Cong carried out a particularly gruesome massacre when they temporarily occupied the old city of Hue during the Tet Offensive. They brought with them prepared lists of victims that they sought out and arrested. In short time the victims were shot, beheaded, buried alive, or tortured to death. Hundreds of such victims were found in nineteen mass graves around Hue. According to the report of a joint U.S. and South Vietnamese investigation,

many bodies were found bound together in groups of 10 or 15, eyes open, with dirt or cloth stuffed in their mouths.

Some of the uncovered bodies had bullet wounds. A Buddhist monk in a nearby pagoda was said to have reported hearing "nightly executions by pistol and rifle shots in a plowed field behind the pagoda ... with victims pleading for mercy." However, nearly half the bodies uncovered in the graves "were found in conditions indicating that they had been buried alive." One such victim was an 80-year-old teacher, who had been buried alive because he was "accused of having a son in the army." Several cadavers had also been beheaded. Many of the men and women who had been executed appeared "to be government employees or citizens linked to the South Vietnamese regime"; one of the victims was identified as a prominent leader of the [Vietnamese National Party]. However, some of those killed were non-Vietnamese, including several French priests and four German faculty members of the Hue University medical school.[72]

The communists themselves estimated they thus killed around 3,000.[73]

Throughout the war, all such killing was planned and systematically conducted by Hanoi. As part of its own organization and through its operatives placed in key positions, Hanoi's Ministry of Public Security ran the Viet Cong Security Service, whose members in the years around 1968 reached over 25,000. It was this organization that throughout the South determined who would be assassinated, executed, murdered, and otherwise punished, and then carried out the dirty work.[74]

I have already indicated how the Security Service selected South Vietnamese for extermination. As to the underlying theory of selection, note what Stephen T. Hosmer reveals.

> In its planning of repression, the Security Service gives first priority to "ringleaders," "leading tyrants," and "the most stubborn elements" in the above target categories. Persons so characterized not only include key civilian officials and military officers but also lower-ranking personnel who are adjudged to have committed serious "crimes against the people" or who have obstructed the development of the Communist movement in a particular area. Thus, a local policeman might be labeled a "leading tyrant" in a particular village and put high on the list of persons to be assassinated. And [a South Vietnamese Army] noncommissioned officer might be branded a "wicked tyrant," deserving of execution "on the spot" if captured. Indeed, lower-level personnel, because of their larger numbers and easier accessibility, make up the great bulk of the victims of repression.[75]

Aside from those assassinated or arrested and executed, many civilians were also killed by North Vietnamese or Viet Cong mines or booby-traps. In Thua-Thien province in 1968, for example, a water buffalo tripped a booby trap and killed the twelve-year-old boy walking alongside; a civilian clearing the area around a grave site was killed by another.[76] As for mines, special ones made to only explode from the weight of a bus were placed on civilian bus routes. This was no little matter, since buses were a major means of transportation between villages. In one case, for example, twenty-five civilians were killed and five wounded when a bus hit a mine.[77]

Moreover, civilians were fired upon directly. Buses and other civilian traffic were often raked by automatic fire or mortared from the roadside, or traffic would be ambushed and civilians killed indiscriminately. Moreover, cities, hamlets, and villages in government areas were shelled and mortared. For example, civilian areas in Saigon were twice attacked with rockets in March 1969, killing fifty-five people and wounding 117.

Then there was the Viet Cong practice of swimming in a civilian sea. They would set up their bunkers in villages and attack from the midst of helpless civilians. Using innocent civilians to protect oneself is in itself a war crime and makes the Viet Cong and thus Hanoi criminally responsible for the resulting civilian dead.[78] It is a form of democide. However they would also directly attack villages and hamlets, kill the inhabitants, including children, in order to panic civilians in the area and cause social chaos that the communists then could exploit. A particularly gruesome example was their December 1967 attack with flame throwers on Dak Son, a Montagnard hamlet. They killed 252 Montagnards. In a similar attack in June the next year against the Son Tra hamlet in Quang Ngai province, they murdered 78 civilians.[79] And during the evening of June 1970, a battalion of North Vietnam army sappers with local Viet Cong guides

> invaded the village of Phuthan some 18 miles south of Danang ... and, methodically dropping grenades and satchel charges into the mouths of bunkers, killed an estimated 100 civilians "with the precision of a deadly corps de ballet." An American marine told Laurence Stern of the *Washington Post*, who was at the grisly site, to get all the pictures possible "because I am sick and tired of everyone talking about just American atrocities."[80]

To show that the government could not provide protection, that there was no escaping the communists, and that refugees should return or flee to communist-controlled areas, even refugee camps or columns of refugees fleeing battle areas were attacked. This particularly criminal policy was practiced throughout the war. In just four months during 1968, for instance, the North Vietnamese and Viet Cong launched forty-five such attacks on refugee sites in two military zones alone. In two months these attacks killed more than fifty-three refugees, wounding 112.[81] In one such attack on the Kon Horing highlander refugee camp in Kontum province, they left 68 dead refugees.[82] All this killing of refugees was by order of high Communist Party officials. For the early 1969 attacks, for example, the party's Decision No. 9 directed that the main targets for attack were to be refugee camps.[83]

Regardless of what civilian areas or population centers the communists attacked, it was their policy to leave wounded civilians to die from their wounds, no doubt often slowly and painfully.[84]

As morally reprehensible as all this was, even more abominable was the use of quotas. Given Hanoi's use of quotas in its "land reform," that they also used them in their war on the South should not be surprising. As an example, consider a secret 1969 Viet Cong directive for the Can Duoc District Unit, Subregion 3, which specified for the month of June the following quotas for the units it covered: "kill at least one chief or assistant chief in each of the following Public Security Service, District National Police Service, Open Air Service, Information Service, Pacification Teams," and a "District Chief or an Assistant District Chief," and "exterminate three wicked tyrants living in district seats or wards." As to village units, they "must kill three enemy."[85]

Captured Viet Cong documents revealed that quotas played a role even in military operations. In capturing and taking over the capital of Ben Tre province, for example, such a document ordered that they must "kill from three to five [reactionary elements] and put out of action from five to ten others on each street, in each bloc of houses. Loosen the enemy's oppressive control machinery, destroy 70% of the inter-family chiefs and 100% of the administrative personnel in the area."[86] Other documents and sources reveal quotas as well. In the Quang Da Special Zone, a sapper unit was ordered to kill 100 "tyrants"; another force in Thua Thien province had to "completely destroy ... 200 tyrants."[87]

Often such quotas were imposed at the village and hamlet level. Note the targets assigned by the command committee of the Chau Duc District Unit of Ba Bien province for the upcoming Tet Offensive: "Break the enemy grip. Destroy the three village administrative personnel in Phu My, Phuoc Thai Phuoc Hoa Villages along Highway No. 5. Kill the 10 hamlet administrative personnel, 3 people's council [members] and other [personnel of] the reactionary political organizations."[88] In some cases the quota to be killed per village was as high as twenty-five, particularly regarding the government personnel to be exterminated.[89] Sometimes the quotas were even given in the aggregate for whole areas. Just for the coast in the Viet Cong's Sub-Region 5, higher authority instructed them to "kill 1,400 persons (including 150 tyrants [South Vietnam government officials]) ... and annihilate ... four pacification groups."[90]

As should be clear from the various examples of communist democide in South Vietnam, Hanoi did not leave all this dirty work to its Viet Cong front. One final example should nail this down. During the North's Easter offensive in 1973 when North Vietnam's

> 711th Division took the Hoai-An and Tam-Quan districts of Binh-Dinh without resistance early in May, some of the people, whose pro [Viet Cong] sentiments had been hardened by the brutal Korean occupation that had just ended, welcomed the North Vietnamese. They were to be bitterly disillusioned. [Government] officials were hunted down and tried in kangaroo courts. A hundred [government] village and hamlet cadres in Hoai-An were summarily executed. In Tam-Quan 48 people were buried alive. Able-bodied inhabitants were taken for forced labor into the jungle, where an estimated 80 died. Younger women were permitted to volunteer "for promotion of soldiers' morale." By the time the [government's] 22nd Division liberated the area three months later, all the goodwill with which the Communists had been received was gone; the lesson of northern Binh-Dinh was not lost in Saigon and elsewhere.[91]

A count of the total number of civilians, government officials, or South Vietnam soldiers (while surrendering or as POWs) that were murdered is, of course, impossible. Saigon, however, did keep some record for part of the war of civilians and officials that were assassinated in the countryside. From this and other sources[92] I estimate that from 19,000 to 113,000 were so assassinated, probably around 66,000 civilians and officials. Keep in mind that these were noncombatants. They were South Vietnamese who possibly because of the good job they were doing in a village, their honesty, industriousness, or leadership, or because of their beliefs or outspokenness, were murdered — sometimes with the greatest cruelty and pain. When this number is added to those killed by communist mines, shelling, and in others ways, the total democide by Hanoi in the South was possibly around 164,000 South Vietnamese. Over the course of the guerrilla and Vietnam War this would be about one out of every ninety-eight South Vietnamese men, women, and children.[93]

Not to be denied is that the various South Vietnamese regimes also murdered civilians and captured guerrillas and North Vietnamese. Although not as methodically conducted, as planned at the highest levels, or done under quotas, it was democide nonetheless. In the early years of the war, the Diem regime tried to "resettle" and "relocate" people, euphemisms for forcefully deporting entire village and regional populations to more secure parts of the country. The ostensible purpose was to better protect these people from the communists and to set up fire-free areas where anyone who moved could be assumed a communist. Presumably, these deportees[94] would also be provided better homes and fields to plant, and won over to the government's side. None of this proved true. But in any case, these deportations, often brutally and hastily carried out, killed many people, either in the process or as a result of the relocation itself. For one minority group of Montagnards, for example,

> The relocations were extremely traumatic ..., particularly those made during the cold winter months. About 208 of the 2,050 people moved to Plei De Groi [camp] and 56 of the 760 relocated to Plei Bang Ba [camp] ... died between mid-December 1970 and April 1971. The high death rate became a cause célèbre, and many medical teams and high-ranking officials ... visited the camps during those months and afterwards. There were congressional inquiries. Extra food, medicines, and other supplies were rushed in. The deaths were attributed to exhaustion, exposure, physical and psychological trauma during the moves, pneumonia and other respiratory diseases during the early period, and enteric infections and malaria during the later months. Malnutrition, both primary at first, and secondary (to diarrheas) was a factor....What happened at these two camps was probably duplicated, although perhaps in a less severe fashion and with less public notice, at many other relocation sites.[95]

Consider also that out of 6,000 Roglai, a minority ethnic group that had lived in the mountains and was deported in 1959, some 600 died in the next few years.[96] Since the total number of Vietnamese deported throughout the war runs well over 1 million (almost 873,700 were deported from 1961 to 1964 alone),[97] the associated deaths must have been in the tens of thousands. These deaths, and that the peasants were forced to leave their precious land and graves, in some cases even their possessions and animals, hardly endeared the government to them. When the new areas were more difficult to live in, the field to farm a much greater distance to walk, and above all, not even more secure, one can understand the failure of these relocation programs.

Moreover, the Diem regime and those that succeeded it in rapid succession after he was assassinated in a coup d'état during November 1963, carried out their own terror campaigns against communists and procommunists. Thousands were arrested, and many died in prison or were executed. In an attempt to unify government control in the early years, military and police sweeps had been made of semiautonomous religious sects or locally independent militias or armies. Political opponents and nonconformists were murdered.

One has to be very careful when estimating the number of communists or political opponents killed in such operations or in Saigon's prisons. Condemning the South for its massacres, atrocities, alleged huge prison populations, and prison torture and deaths (and the United States for atrocities), was a communist industry during the war, with many communist agents posing as responsible critics. For example,

> in the summer of 1973 a Paris-educated Redemptorist priest in Saigon, Father Chan Tin, charged in a mimeographed handout that as of 1 June 1973 the [government] was detaining 202,000 political prisoners. Chan Tin said that he headed an organization called "Committee to Investigate Mistreatment of Political Prisoners." Western newsmen and Americans visiting Vietnam reported him to be a man deeply concerned with human suffering. In September 1973 some of Hanoi's friends in Washington, operating the "Indochina Resource Center," presented Chan Tin's charges and figures to a congressional committee where they appeared to make an impression. After the fall of Saigon in 1975 it turned out that Chan Tin and several other Catholic priests had been part of the VC underground in Saigon. "They presented themselves as exponents of the Third Force," writes a well-informed European journalist with left-wing political leanings, Tiziano Terzani, who stayed in Saigon after the communist takeover, "but in reality they were part of an operation whose purpose was to back up the struggle of the National Liberation Front."[98]

With this in mind, it is also clear that throughout the war South Vietnam military treated captured communist soldiers or guerrillas with little respect. They were often, if not usually in the early years, tortured for information and then killed, or if wounded, simply left to die. While perhaps not ordered at the top, such killing must have been done with the acquiescence if not nodding agreement of the South's high command. As the war progressed, the United States brought considerable pressure to bear on the government to more humanely treat its prisoners; to a degree, such apparently occurred.

Nor for the South Vietnamese were noncombatants immune. Villages were often bombed and shelled indiscriminately and, when civilians were mixed in with enemy guerrillas, little distinction was usually made. For example, in February 1964, the Viet Cong captured Ven-Cau village in Tay Ninh province. Although the village had a population of 6,000 people, government forces still bombed and shelled it. As a result, they killed forty-six civilians, wounded sixty more, destroyed 670 homes, caused 2,000 refugees to flee,[99] and killed eleven Viet Cong. Although occurring a few months after the anti-Diem coup, such indiscriminate military action reflected an attitude toward civilian lives all too common in the Diem years.

In such ways and in other forms of democide mentioned, the Diem regime probably murdered 39,000 Vietnamese. The successor regimes were little better. Executions, torture, the killing of POWs, and indiscriminate bombing and shelling continued. Through American pressure, public opposition, and the recognition that much of this killing was counterproductive, such democide lessened over the years of the war. Nonetheless, these post-Diem regimes themselves probably murdered some 50,000 Vietnamese. When the democide of all South Vietnamese governments is added up from 1954 to the fall of Saigon in April 1975, the toll comes to 57,000 to 284,000 Vietnamese, or a likely 89,000. While this number is 54 percent of the North Vietnamese democide in the South, both Hanoi and Saigon during the war were in the same murderous league.

Although much lesser in extent and different in nature, the democide of U.S. forces in South Vietnam must be recognized. Unlike the communists and to a much greater degree than the South Vietnamese army, the Americans did in general try to make a distinction between combatants and noncombatants. This was evidenced for example in the treatment of wounded enemy soldiers, guerrillas, and civilians. Whereas communist forces would leave enemy wounded to die from their wounds, including civilians who had not given allegiance to them, U.S. forces generally made an effort to treat and evacuate to hospitals any wounded, regardless of what side they were on.[100] Says Guenter Lewy who has made much study of this matter:

> The American record in Vietnam with regard to observance of the law of war is not a succession of war crimes and does not support charges of a

systematic and willful violation of existing agreements for standards of human decency in time of war, as many critics of the American involvement have alleged. Such charges were based on a distorted picture of the actual battlefield situation, on ignorance of existing rules of engagement, and on a tendency to construe every mistake of judgment as a wanton breach of the law of war. Further, many of these critics had only the most rudimentary understanding of international law and freely indulged in fanciful interpretations of conventions and treaties so as to make the American record look as bad as possible. Finally, there were the communist propagandists who unleashed a torrent of largely unsubstantiated charges with the hope that at least some of the lies would stick. This is indeed what happened.

If the American record is not one of gross illegality, neither has it been a model of observance of the law of war. Impeccable [rules of engagement], based on applicable legal provisions, were issued, but their observance was often inadequate and the American command failed to take reasonable steps to make sure that they would be properly enforced.[101]

But there is also no doubt that democide was committed. The My Lai massacre, in which about 347 innocent peasant women and children were massacred by U.S. soldiers,[102] is well known. Other massacres probably occurred as well. Also, it cannot be doubted that U.S. soldiers killed North Vietnamese troops and Viet Cong who were trying to surrender. When Lt. James B. Duffy was court-martialed for ordering that a prisoner be killed (he was found guilty),

evidence was presented indicating that a policy of "no prisoners" was in effect for at least a part of U.S. ground forces in South Vietnam. Four officers testified under oath to this effect. According to First Lt. John Kruger, "Our policy was that once contact was made we kept firing until everything in the kill zone was killed. We did not take prisoners." And First Lt. Ralph Krueger testified, "My policy was that a man does not surrender during a fire-fight. If a VC comes out of a fight to give himself up, that man is dead."[103]

From this and other testimony, letters, and news reports, the evidence is that U.S. soldiers did torture and kill prisoners, shoot communists trying to surrender, machine-gun from hovering helicopters peasants running away, disproportionately bomb and shell villages suspected of helping the Viet Cong or from which some sniper fire may have come, and so on. As Louis Wiesner points out, "The U.S. and Vietnamese press and other observers reported hundreds of cases in which inhabited places were destroyed from the air or by ground troops because of sniper fire coming from them or because they were suspected of harboring the enemy, and other instances in which people were shot simply because they ran or otherwise acted in a manner considered suspicious."[104] Moreover, "Some [U.S.] soldiers openly admitted without any remorse that they had killed civilians, and airmen were directed to strafe peasants in the fields simply because they were running away or attempting to hide."[105]

A measure of such killing of noncombatants is the number of weapons captured as a ratio of the "enemy" killed in action. The normal ratio killed to weapons captured was 3 to 1. In one seven-month operation begun in December 1968 and focused on the densely populated provinces in the upper Delta, the U.S. Ninth Infantry Division reported killing 10,883 "enemy" in mainly small-scale ground and air actions (such as by helicopter gunships). However, only 748 weapons were captured, or a ratio of killed to weapons of 14.5 to 1. (In some actions the ratio was as high as 50 to 1.) Observers of these actions verified what is obvious from such ratios — not all killed were active Viet Cong.[106]

In defense, it is often pointed out that this was a "dirty war"; "guerrillas fought in the midst of civilians," alleged atrocities were committed in the "heat of battle," "when one's buddies were killed by grenades tossed by civilians, how could one respect civilian immunity," and so on. Moreover, civilians did plant mines, prepare booby traps, and willingly or unwillingly help build bunkers and carry supplies. By the international conventions defining the laws of war, those specifically involved in such activities can become military objectives. Of course, it usually was impossible to tell which civilians helped the enemy and which did not. But this did not make all civilians fair game. Note that such excuses could have been given by the German soldiers in Yugoslavia or the Ukraine during World War II, or for Japanese soldiers in the Philippines or North China. When they killed civilians recklessly or wantonly, however, it was counted as democide. And so should such actions by Americans if it can be shown that this was with the explicit or implicit approval or knowledge of the high command, as it had been in the case of the Germans or Japanese.

However, this killing exceeded or was in spite of orders to the contrary. Those in command, and in particular General William C. Westmoreland (commander, Military Assistance Command, Vietnam, from 1964 to 1968, when he became army chief of staff), had issued explicit rules of warfare based on the applicable treaties and conventions governing it, such as the Geneva Conventions. These rules covered the treatment of prisoners and the rules of engagement that were to protect noncombatants. Although republished every six months, however, they were not well distributed to lower levels, and battalion and company officers had different ideas about the rules. According to a senior embassy official investigating alleged excesses, one battalion commander even admitted that "he had never read any such rules and wasn't certain that there were copies of written instructions on the subject at his headquarters."[107]

Declaratory policy is one thing, getting it understood down the chain of command is another, and applying it in the rapid action, noise, confusion, fear, and reflex shooting of combat is still something else. When in the heat of battle your life and that of your friends is at stake, fine distinctions are difficult to remember, never mind to apply. Moreover, how the rules covered specific situations (say a Viet Cong unit hiding among a group of refugees, a grenade lobbed from a bus at U.S. soldiers along the road, or civilians hiding in a Viet Cong bunker) were not always clear. This notwithstanding, in the first years of U.S. involvement, the rules meant to protect noncombatants were often and blatantly violated by lower-level U.S. officers and their men. "Whatever evidence is available ... shows that knowledge and full understanding of the [rules of engagement] were generally inadequate and that this deficiency led to avoidable civilian casualties and, as in the My Lai incident, was a contributory cause of war crimes."[108]

This violation was such that it raises the question of the high command's culpability in Vietnam, including General Westmoreland. After reviewing the applicable laws of war, relevant orders and instructions of the U.S. high command, and evidence of American atrocities, Lewy concludes that the

> question of whether Westmoreland *should* have known that in the Vietnam environment inadequate understanding of the [rules of engagement] could

and would lead to violations of the law of war must be answered in the affirmative. There is no evidence that [the high command] knew of the My Lai massacre, but [it] was undoubtedly aware of the high civilian casualties resulting from fighting in and around hamlets and villages, of the existence of command pressure for a high body count and of the belief of many soldiers in the "mere-gook rule" — that the lives of Vietnamese were cheap and not protected by the law of war.
...

New training manuals issued by the Army after the My Lai incident explicitly addressed these and related problems. Military personnel now were put on notice that "if you disobey the rules of engagement, you can be tried and punished for disobedience of orders. The disobedience may also be a war crime for which you can be tried and punished." Such instructions should, of course, have been issued earlier, and the fact that such corrective measures were not taken until a major incident had revealed the existing disregard of the [rules of engagement] indicates at least dereliction of duty or perhaps even criminal negligence on the part of [the High Command] and General Westmoreland.[109]

If, contrary to the rules of engagement, a soldier massacres civilians, and his superiors are unaware of it, this is murder by an individual but not democide (which requires some form of actual or practical intentionality[110] on the part of government or its responsible agents). If this is covered up by low-level officers in the field whose command responsibilities are minor, they are accessories to murder and this is a dereliction of duty, but it is not democide. However, if command authorities, those giving orders from secure headquarters and responsible for major military operations in the field, cover it up or gave orders resulting in the massacre, it is democide. Of course, there is an area of ambiguity between murder and democide. But it should also be clear that lieutenants commanding a platoon, or captains a company, and who act on their own initiative in combat, are not committing democide. Generals, however, who command large operations, carry significant responsibility for a state and directly represent its policies on the battlefield. Their decisions, or lack of them, can result in democide.

These distinctions for such a war as in Vietnam are critical. But they are also critical for such similarly dirty combat as took place in the Philippine War at the beginning of this century, in which democide was carried out methodically by the U.S. high command and surely tens of thousands of Filipinos were murdered by U.S. soldiers. The same is true for a more conventional war like World War II, in which American area bombing of German and Japanese cities killed more hundreds of thousands of noncombatants. (In the Pacific, especially, U.S. soldiers often shot Japanese trying to surrender, and in both the European and Pacific theater, enemy sailors and troops trying to escape in the water from a sinking ship were sometimes machine-gunned).[111]

Numerous publications are available describing U.S. atrocities in the Vietnam War. Some are communist[112] or sympathetic to Hanoi or its façades: the National Liberation Front, the Alliance of National, Democratic, and Peace Forces, or the Provisional Revolutionary Government of South Vietnam.[113] And there are many more publications on the other side that mention none, except perhaps for the notorious My Lai massacre.[114] There have been "international tribunals" set up by those who were more inclined to question the war aims and behavior of the United States than of the North Vietnamese or Viet Cong, but their publications sometimes provide helpful clues to what kind of murder may have been committed, especially in the testimony of former U.S. officers and soldiers.[115]

One thing gradually emerges from the communist literature and from that sympathetic to the communists. Even though they were all attempting to display (or in the case of Hanoi's organs, exaggerate or disinform) the full extent of U.S. atrocities, massacres, and indiscriminate bombing of civilians, they provided virtually no overall estimates of those murdered. And, although the "massacres" they list are outrageous in themselves, were they true, the accumulated totals from their examples are relatively small compared to the intensity and blanket nature of the accusations and the numbers murdered by the Vietnamese themselves. Even then, what many of these sources label as atrocities or massacres may, by the Geneva Conventions and other accepted rules of warfare, be legitimate military actions or accidents of war. As, for example, in burning down a village if in fact it sits on top of Viet Cong bunkers; or an attack on civilian river junks that are actually carrying Viet Cong supplies; or bombs that hang up on their rack and then fall on a North Vietnam hospital near antiaircraft batteries (a communist ploy was to place some of these batteries close to sensitive civilian buildings or on river dikes that if destroyed would drown tens of thousands of civilians).

Nonetheless, taking all such figures at face value, and counting those killed in all incidents covered in one report of testimony of the Committee to Denounce U.S. Puppets' War Crimes in Indochina,[116] yields over 5,482 killed just by U.S. forces in over two years. Another report, *U.S. Imperialists' "Burn all, Destroy All. Kill All" policy in South Vietnam,*[117] gives 4,650 killed in Da Nang and five districts in over a year. Then there was the massive U.S. defoliation of mainly uninhabited parts of South Vietnam that from 1961 to 1970 may have killed 1,622, according to the North Vietnamese.[118] And in Tay Nang province, the National Liberation Front claimed that 500 civilians were killed in U.S. (tear) gas attacks during ten months of 1969.[119]

The use of tear gas is not prohibited by international law or the U.S. rules of engagement, nor is there a general moral injunction against its employment to clear tunnels, bunkers, and the like. Nonetheless, innocent civilians did die from it, which is clear from a 1967 letter written by Dr. Alje Vennema, director of the Canadian Medical Service in Vietnam, who worked in the civilian tuberculosis hospital at Quang Ngai. In the letter, he wrote:

During the last three years I have examined and treated a number of patients, men, women and children, who had been exposed to a type of war gas [the tear gas CS].... After contact with them for more than three minutes one has to leave the room in order not to get ill. The patient usually gives a history of having been hiding in a cave or tunnel or bunker or shelter into which a canister of gas was thrown in order to force them to leave their hiding place. Those patients that have come to my attention were very ill with signs and symptoms of gas poisoning similar to those that I have seen in veterans from the First World War treated at Queen Mary Veterans Hospital in Montreal.... The mortality rate in adults is about ten percent, while the mortality rate in children is about ninety percent.[120]

As to the incredibly heavy bombing during the war (about 14 million tons of bombs and shells were dropped on Vietnam, or six times the bomb tonnage the United States dropped in World War II),[121] that which fell on North Vietnam must be distinguished from the bombing in the South. In the former case, influenced by Hanoi's propaganda, which was widely disseminated by its friends, the impression during the war was that the United States was carpet bombing civilians and purposely attacking hospitals, schools, and other civilian targets. But this was not so.

The most important fact of this bombing was the scrupulous care with which targets were selected and bombed. Indeed, these matters were not left to local commanders. They were determined by the Pentagon and White House, and even President Johnson carefully orchestrated the bombing's what, when, and how. Particularly, the greatest care was taken to limit attacks to purely military targets, even when it endangered the lives of U.S. pilots (and U.S. pilots repeatedly protested these restrictions). Indeed, so Lewy notes, "many pilots were shot down because the rules of engagement required approach angles and other tactics designed to reduce civilian casualties rather than to afford maximum protection to the attacking planes."[122] Civilians were killed, possibly 65,000 of them,[123] but these deaths were collateral to bombing military targets and often resulted from pilots' trying to dodge the North's vigorous air defenses, including missiles. Doubtlessly, purely civilian homes and buildings were hit. At least in one case widely publicized by Hanoi, a hospital 1,000 yards from an airstrip and military barracks, for example, was hit by bombs that had hung up on a bomber's rack.[124] But these were accidents of war (mistakes in targeting, poor aim, malfunctioning equipment, and the like) and not intentional.[125]

One prime example of restraint was the North's dikes that held back the waters in the Red River Delta. Had these been targeted not only would Hanoi's economy have been thoroughly disrupted, but also the resulting flood might have wiped out nearly 1 million innocent North Vietnamese.[126] Hanoi had put antiaircraft guns on top of the dikes, but orders from as high as the President were that the dikes were not to be bombed, even though the gun emplacements made them lawful military targets.

U.S. bombing of South Vietnam was quite different. It was often tactical rather than strategic and frequently under local command. Ground troops could call in air strikes on supposed enemy concentrations or movements and direct the bombing of villages and hamlets that presumably contained enemy bunkers or camps, or serviced the enemy in some way. These attacks were subject to limited overview, and considerable discretion was allowed by command authorities. In many cases innocent and helpless noncombatants were indiscriminately killed.

In one case, Viet Cong were seen near Manquang, a village in the vicinity of the U.S. base at Danang. An airstrike on the village was ordered, and according to a Reuters dispatch, forty-five villagers, among them thirty-seven school children, were killed. Villagers carrying coffins tried to march to Danang in protest but were stopped by Vietnamese troops.[127] Another dispatch from John T. Wheeler of the Associated Press reports on the bombing of Ba Gia, most of whose population were anticommunist and from the North. Apparently it had been attacked because the Viet Cong had captured a government stronghold nearby. Even though considered a progovernment village, it was hit three days in a row by bombs, cannon fire, and rockets from the air. As troops subsequently entered Ba Gia in fruitless search for Viet Cong, they were greeted by "the wailing of women and the stench of burned bodies."

> Four men carrying a pallet with a wounded man stared hatefully at American advisers accompanying the Vietnamese Marines, seeming to accuse the Americans of the death and destruction.
>
> Sitting in the middle of a dirt road was a women cradling a baby and flanked by two other small children. Her cries of anguish caused some of the Vietnamese troops to turn aside. Surveying the shattered stucco and bamboo homes and the machinegunned Catholic church, one U.S. advisor said: "That's why we are going to lose this stupid damn war. Senseless, it's just senseless."
> ...
> Asked how many had been killed and wounded, villagers shrugged and replied, "Many."[128]

Such bombing, apparently disproportionate to any expected military gains, was the direct responsibility of command authorities.

In a devastating series of articles that provoked a high-level investigation, Jonathan Shell reported observing preplanned and immediate airstrikes in which

> populated areas were ruthlessly attacked and whole hamlets destroyed because enemy fire had been sighted from them, or simply because they were considered VC territory, on the justification that the people had been warned by leaflets or loudspeaker to get out. The [forward air control] pilots had various empirical ways of deciding when people on the ground

were VC and could therefore be killed, for example, hiding, "pretending to
be working" in the fields; "There's a V.C. havin' his supper. There
shouldn't be anyone down there. He shouldn't be there." "In the
mountains, just about anything that moves is considered to be V.C. No one
has got any reason to be there." The ground troops were equally
indiscriminate in deciding who was a VC and in calling for air strikes
against areas from which they observed or suspected enemy fire, including
in one instance two churches that were in the middle of a preplanned strike
area but from which no fire had been observed. The [forward air control]
pilot double checked with the ground commander before calling in the
strike against them and later Schell observed the airmen to be visibly
embarrassed about the strike. The churches were listed as two permanent
military structures in the [forward air control] pilot's bomb damage report
to ... headquarters.[129]

Of course, shelling by mortar and artillery of villages and hamlets
was even less supervised from the top, although the published rules of
engagement were supposed to govern. Nevertheless, some of this
shelling was also excessive, some out of all proportion to the military
significance or target involved, and some out of whimsy. How many
civilian casualties were caused by this shelling is unknown, of course.
Overall, over each of the four years from 1966 to 1970, some 43, 38,
31, and 22 percent of all civilian casualties admitted to South
Vietnam's Ministry of Health hospitals were due to shelling and
bombing (mine and mortar casualties, which one may assume were
mainly due to the Viet Cong or North Vietnamese, were separately
classified). The amount of such "friendly" fire can be seen in another
way. A survey of the South Vietnamese population asked, "Were any
friendly artillery or air strikes directed in or near the inhabited area of
this village this month?" The percents of the population answering yes
for each December of 1969 to 1971 were 27.1, 16.3, and 10.8.[130] The
decline is attributable to the gradual withdrawal of U.S. forces from
Vietnam, and from offensive military action for those remaining.
  U.S. democide in this war is most difficult to calculate. No source
estimates such a toll; as mentioned, not even the communists or those
who pointed out atrocities and accused the United States of war crimes
gave an overall accounting that I could find. Nor are even such meager
and questionable estimates available in the sources of information on
Allied bombing and shelling in the South. From what qualitative

information is available, and from figures on hospital admissions and causes of civilian casualties, I calculate that Allied bombing and shelling most likely caused 90,000 to 180,000 civilian deaths. It appears that a likely 5 to 10 percent of this was democidal, and that of this the United States was responsible for 10 to 25 percent. This means that democidal U.S. bombing — bombing consistent with orders from high command or known to be indiscriminate by high command and allowed to continue — likely killed from 500 to 5,000 Vietnamese civilians.

Treating the scanty and suspect statistics on U.S. massacres, atrocities, and other kinds of democide in the same way, and adding the resulting calculation to the estimated number killed because of bombing and shelling, I must conclude that the U.S. democide in Vietnam seems to have killed at least 4,000 Vietnamese civilians, POWs, or enemy seeking to surrender, maybe as many as 10,000 Vietnamese. A prudent figure may be 5,500 overall.

Besides the United States, South Korean forces in Vietnam also committed democide. They became known for their brutal thoroughness, a reputation partly gained from their treatment of captured guerrillas or those trying to surrender, and their reckless and sometimes intentional killing of civilians. In Quang Nam province, for instance, when a Korean troop carrier ran over a mine and some sniper fire came from the neighboring hamlet of Phong Nhi, Koreans called for an artillery strike on the hamlet. They then moved through it, firing on and hurling grenades at the surviving civilians. All told, they murdered over 80 villagers, mostly women and children.[131] The communists allege that they also massacred 500 in Tuy Hoa I district, that with U.S. troops they killed nearly 1,000 in the Son Tinh and Binh Son districts,[132] and that perhaps a total of 2,102 were killed (according to incomplete statistics) on a variety of other massacres from October 1968 through 1970.[133] While some of these claims are probably disinformation or exaggerated, doubtlessly some such killing did occur as in Phong Nhi. Taking all these and other possible cases into account, I estimate the Korean democide at at least 3,000 Vietnamese civilians and enemy POWs.

Obviously, the Vietnamese suffered grievously during the war, which can only be partially measured by the overall democide toll and war dead. Nevertheless, on these scales alone the human cost was horrendous. Slightly over 2,100,000 North and South Vietnamese were killed, or murdered: approximately one out of every seventeen.[134] From 1954 to the end of the Vietnam War, the democide in the South by its own regimes, or by the North Vietnamese, Americans, or Koreans, probably accounts for 261,000 of the total dead — slightly over 12 percent. Most of this democide, over 62 percent, likely was committed by Hanoi and its guerrilla front, the Viet Cong.

After the South surrendered to the North in April 1975, and the North had consolidated its military control over Saigon and the most vital sections of the South, the North moved to disband and absorb the most important personnel of the Viet Cong, the National Liberation Front, and the Provisional Revolutionary Government (whose pronouncements and declarations had been credible to so many in the West as an independent third force). If there is any doubt about the true nature of such groups, consider what the Northern party historian Nguyen Khac-Vien points out about the Provisional Revolutionary Government: it "was always simply a group emanating from [Hanoi]. If we [Hanoi] had pretended otherwise for such a long period, it was only because during the war we were not obliged to unveil our cards."[135]

The killing did not end. Not in Cambodia. Not in Laos. Not in Vietnam. Vietnamese armies fought in Laos to consolidate their control. They fought against the Khmer Rouge army in Cambodia and, with victory in January 1979 and the installation of a puppet regime in Phnom Penh, they fought a nearly decade-long war against both the Cambodian Khmer Rouge and anticommunist guerrillas.[136] This alone cost 150,000 Vietnamese lives.[137] In 1979, they fought a border war against China, which had invaded Vietnam across its northern border in order to "teach it a lesson" over its satellization of Cambodia and hug of the Soviet Union. This probably cost at least another 8,000 Vietnamese lives,[138] and perhaps another 500 died in postwar border clashes and artillery duels.[139] They also fought internal rebellions in the South, where perhaps 12,000 to 15,000 insurgents mined roads, laid booby traps, threw grenades in Saigon, and possibly fought pitched battles against communist troops.[140] And they fought armed remnants of the National Liberation Front, many of whom believed that they had been betrayed by Hanoi's complete and utter takeover of the South after victory. One archeology team sent by the North Vietnam Institute of Social Research to do research in Ha Tien, Minh Hai province, had to return after only two days there. The archaeologists explained that "our armed units are fighting against an NLF Unit, and so a member of the District Committee advised us to come back immediately to Saigon."[141]

In these post-Vietnam years, over 160,000 more Vietnamese likely died from war and rebellion. This is no small number. It is over three times the 47,321 U.S. battle dead from the Vietnam War.[142] In no way, then, did peace come to the Vietnamese people, nor to Laos and Cambodia. And, pitifully, neither did democide end in Vietnam nor for her neighbors. This is quantified in table 11.2, where the number killed after the Vietnam War in these three countries exceeds by over 1 million those killed during the war. As shown in figure 11.1, most of this postwar killing is due to democide.

To the post-1975 Vietnamese war dead must be added those murdered by the triumphant communist regime. After victory, under the pretense of giving them a month or less of lectures, the communists rounded up former South Vietnamese government officials, military officers, party leaders, police, and supporting intellectuals and imprisoned them in "re-education" camps. Presumably they were all to be indoctrinated in communist thoughts and ways, and to discover the "errors" of their old behavior and beliefs. In reality, these were concentration camps whose purpose was to systematically weed out of the new society true "enemies of the people," that is potential critics and opposition, and to take the victor's revenge on his die-hard enemies.

But the camps were not limited to those who had been the South Vietnam government's "henchmen" and "puppets." They were also the destination of those former South Vietnam antiwar or antigovernment opponents who were arrested after the war. Such was the former faculty of law dean at Saigon University who had been critical of the former government. Even at age seventy, the nationalist scholar and writer Ho Huu Tong was sent to the camps. He had survived imprisonment by the French and Diem regimes, but died in the camps when the communists refused to give him medical care.[143] More tragic still were the common folk sent to the camps for having stupidly joked about communism, idly criticized the new regime, showed insufficient sympathy for Northern rule, or otherwise displayed "improper" attitudes. At any one time in the early years, some 150,000[144] to 500,000[145] Vietnamese apparently suffered in these camps.

Like the Stalinist gulag, living conditions in these camps were such that

> the prisoners' health speedily deteriorates. Former prisoners who are now refugees report that many of their fellow inmates died of malnutrition. Well attested cases include those of [South Vietnam Army] Majors Luan, Van, and Phong at Vinh Quang Camp, Vinh Phu Province, in North Vietnam. In all other camps from which reports are available, including Gia Trung, Gia Ray, Ben Gia, and Xuyen Moc, the situation would appear

FIGURE 11.1
Comparison of Vietnam War and Post-Vietnam War Deaths in
Vietnam, Laos, and Cambodia, 1954–87
(Data from table 11.2)

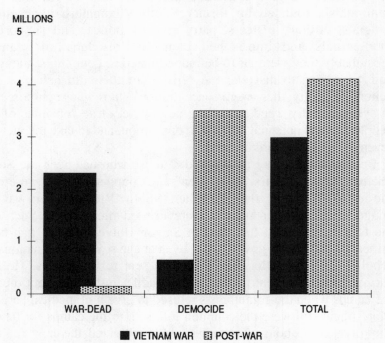

to be similar. Without relatives' food parcels, which get through only because camp authorities are bribed, many prisoners would not have survived.[146]

But inhuman conditions and constant "thought reform" are not all the prisoners had to worry about. There was tortuous physical punishment for minor violations or insufficient obedience, or for inadequate dedication to changing one's beliefs. Moreover,

> every camp has a loudspeaker system that is used without warning to summon prisoners who did not show enthusiasm for their work or who, according to informants, made unfavorable remarks about the revolution. They are ordered to report to the camp headquarters at midnight. Such prisoners never come back. Usually, a few hours after they have been summoned, the other prisoners hear rifle fire in the nearby jungle. Perhaps these are mock executions, and the "executed" prisoners are secretly moved to other camps; perhaps they are not. I have inquired of ex-prisoners and they cannot tell me. I do know, however, that these midnight arrests have an effect on the prison population that is absolutely terrifying. Even in his dreams, a prisoner is haunted by the thought that he may be summoned and taken away like his friends.[147]

The poet Nguyen Chi Thien, who by 1980 had spent over sixteen years in prison camps, must also have been expressing the feelings of "re-education" camp inmates in a poem he called "From Ape to Man" that was smuggled out of the camps to the West:[148]

> From ape to man, millions of years gone by.
> From man to ape, how many years?
> Mankind, please come to visit
> The concentration camps in the heart of the thickest Jungles!
> Naked prisoners, taking baths together in herds,
> Living in ill-smelling darkness with lice and mosquitoes,
> Fighting each other for a piece of manioc or sweet potato,
> Chained, shot, dragged, slit up at will by their captors,
> Beaten up and thrown away for the rats to gnaw at their breath!
> This kind of ape is not fast but very slow in action, indeed
> Quite different from that of remote prehistory.
> They are hungry, they are thin as toothpicks,
> And yet they produce resources for the nation all year long.
> Mankind, please come and visit!

In sum, "re-education" was a label for revenge, punishment, and social prophylaxis. But unlike the Khmer Rouge who were too public about their mass killing, the Vietnamese regime cleverly and at first successfully hid it from the outside world. In dealing with "war criminals" and high members of the South Vietnamese government, they claimed that "re-education" was a humane alternative to a blood

TABLE 11.2
Vietnam War and Postwar Dead, 1954–87 [a]

Period	Dead (000)
Preguerrilla and Vietnam War, 1954–75	2,932
War Dead [b]	2,265
Vietnam	1,804
Laos	32
Cambodia	429
Democide	637
Vietnam	311
Laos	38
Cambodia	288
Other Related	30
Cambodian Famine	30
Post-Vietnam War, 1975–87	4,157
War Dead	149
Vietnam [c]	10
Laos	54
Cambodia	85 [e]
Democide [a]	3,508
Vietnam	528
Laos	130
Cambodia	2,850
Other Related	500
Cambodian Famine/diseased	250
Boat People	250

a All figures from or calculated from those in *Statistics of Democide*.
b For or by all parties.
c Vietnam dead in Laos and Cambodia included under those nations.
d Nondemocidal.
e Low.

bath. Explained Foreign Minister Nguyen Co Thach, "It's not good to kill as Pol Pot did.... When you kill you lose the sense of family."[149] But in private they boasted about their blood letting to those they trusted. This was pointed out by Nguyen Cong Hoan, a member of the Buddhist antiwar opposition in South Vietnam during the war and of the postwar Vietnam National Assembly until his defection. "The party leaders themselves have told me," he says, "that they are very proud of their talent for deceiving world opinion. 'We've been worse than Pol Pot,' they joke. 'But the outside world knows nothing.'"[150]

Many notables met their end in the camps. I have already mentioned the famous writer Ho Huu Tong. I might also mention the former senator and vice-president of the South Vietnamese Senate, Hoang Xuan Tuu; the former senator and political independent Tran The Minh; the attorney and former president of the Saigon Bar Association, Tran Van Tuyen; pre-1954 commander-in-chief of the Catholic anticommunist forces in the Autonomous Region of the Bui Chu and Phat Diem dioceses in North Vietnam, Father Hoang Quynh; and the senior monk of the An Quang Church and vice-president of the Unified Buddhist Church, Thich Thien Minh, who had during the war worked for a cease-fire and a policy of national reconciliation.[151]

Based on a 1985 statement by Foreign Minister Nguyen Co Thach,[152] 2,500,000 people may ultimately have passed through these "re-education" camps. One estimate is that at least 200,000 people also died or were killed in them.[153] This is probably a high, however. Taking account of the death toll in the similar Stalinist and Maoist gulags, a more likely figure is around 95,000.

For those who were less an actual or potential threat to the regime, who were just excess population in the cities or had committed minor infractions, the "new economic zones" were waiting. Accepting the blandishments of the regime or wishing to escape the deteriorating conditions of the cities, some also volunteered for these zones. Most, however, were forcibly sent. Work in these zones was hard and living conditions harsh — in some places deadly. But one had no choice: work or try to escape. But if caught, one faced an even worse fate: prison, a "re-education" camp, or execution. No numbers are available on the resulting deaths in these zones. Judging from their description and the toll at forced labor in the Soviet Union and China, possibly 48,000 Vietnamese thus lost their lives, maybe even 155,000.

One could be sent for "re-education" and die there from the abysmal treatment; one could be sent to a "new economic zone" and possibly perish there from the labor, exposure, or disease. Or one could be marked for execution on some communist list, or summarily executed for anticommunist behavior. Jacqueline Desbarats and Karl Jackson carried out a survey of Vietnamese refugees in the United States and unexpectedly found that about one-third had seen executions or had detailed information on them. Thinking that they might be dealing with a biased sample of refugees, the two researchers traveled to France to interview refugees there. They found the same story. From the refugee reports, they calculated that at least 65,000 South Vietnamese had been executed.[154] Desbarats believes that these strictly extrajudicial executions might even have been as many as 100,000.[155] Nguyen Cong Hoan, a former official of the new postwar government of Vietnam, estimates that in perhaps one year after the war, from 50,000 to 100,000 people were executed outright.[156] Others put the toll at either at least[157] or at most[158] 250,000. Many of these estimates may include those executed in the "re-education" camps. Separately from these, of the "pick them up and shoot them" type of execution, the various reports and estimates suggest that some 100,000 people were killed overall. In the months after "liberation," the victims were most commonly high officers of the previous regime; after 1975, they were usually "antigovernment resisters," which could be nothing more than not registering for "re-education."[159]

Throughout the Indochina and Vietnam wars, with all the associated killing and democide, Vietnamese generally refused to leave their country. Not even when many were forced to flee for their lives from vicious battles (in 1974 alone, there were 417,300 such refugees).[160] Even then they returned to their home villages when they could. Vietnamese are loathe to give up their family, ancestral roots, and traditional customs. But after "liberation" they were faced with a new terror: that of the "re-education" camps; of the "new economic zones;" of torture and execution for who knows what; of conscription to fight another of Vietnam's wars; of formal ostracism and a slow death from starvation, exposure, or disease. As the communists tightened their hold on the South, there was more intervention in all forms of life, more rules, more enforcement; it became "a new and even more insidious warfare, this time a warfare practiced by the liberators against their own people."[161] In this new police state no one moved without state permission. People spied on one another and had become accustomed to state control over all aspects of their lives — education, employment, the amount of food rations, the goods allotted for personal use, the amount of goods to be produced on the job.[162]

This was not all. Suddenly, in March 1978

all private trade in South Vietnam was abolished. Merchants were directed to shift to productive activities or to join collectively owned or joint private-state enterprises. All goods held by private merchants were to be purchased by the state. Youth assault squads were mobilized the night before the announcement to confiscate goods before they could be dispersed.... By the end of the year, 30,000 private firms had been abolished and government control over the urban economy in South Vietnam had been established.[163]

The alarm, dismay, and dread, the trembling fear thus created, also extended to Northerners, particularly those of Chinese ethnicity. In 1976, the party began to expel thousands of ethnic Chinese, calling them "fifth columnists," a rhetoric that forecast more serious consequences. Indeed, as relations with China soured, this soon became a label used to indict all such Chinese, North or South. In the North, ethnic Chinese living in the provinces, especially in important areas bordering China, were deported, while their homes were burned and property stolen. Others in the cities suddenly found themselves without jobs and the subject of sharp discrimination.

Understandably, more and more Vietnamese, ethnic Chinese, and other minorities began to seriously consider escaping the country. But there were few options. China to the North was also communist and, in any case, if one were not ethnic Chinese, one could be forcibly returned. Laos was a Vietnamese satellite. From 1975 through 1978, Cambodia was under rule of a Khmer Rouge that hated and killed Vietnamese; after the short 1978–79 Cambodian-Vietnamese war, Cambodia also became Vietnam's satellite. That left trying to get across at least several hundred miles of open ocean to reach Hong Kong, the Philippines, Malaysia, or Indonesia, or hoping that some passing ship would pick one up. But this was dangerous. Aside from the problem of finding someone with a boat and the risk of being swindled out of one's life savings, being turned in to the communists, or captured while trying to escape, few seaworthy boats were available. And not many knew how to navigate the open ocean. Some of this risk was alleviated when, for an often-quoted amount of $2,000 in gold or hard currency, government officials or quasi-government organizations secretly aided those Vietnamese, especially ethnic Chinese, seeking to escape.

Getting out of the country was only part of it. The primary danger was on the ocean. Once out in the South China Sea, often in old, unseaworthy, and overloaded boats, some simply not constructed for deep ocean travel, these escapees were subject to deadly storms. And they were prey for Cambodian and Thai fishermen turned savage pirates. Typically, these pirates would pull alongside a boat, brandish their weapons, forcibly board it, rob the escapees of their valuables, selectively rape the women and girls, kill those who tried to interfere, and take a few of the women with them when they left. Mercifully, they sometimes would allow those still living to continue. Sometimes they would kill everyone or sink the boat and leave all on it to drown.

This piracy went on day after day, week after week, and year after year. In 1989 these pirates were still operating. For example, the UN high commissioner for refugees in Kuala Lumpur, Malaysia, reported in May 1989 that

> seven pirates armed with shotguns and hammers killed 130 Vietnamese refugees and set fire to their boat off the Malaysian coast.... The attackers shot and bludgeoned refugees to death after raping several women.... Other boat people died of exhaustion after floating in the sea clinging to bodies of fellow refugees.[164]

If the refugees did make it to another shore, they might be forced again out into the ocean in a rickety boat (as did Malaysia), possibly this time to face certain death. If allowed to remain, there was life in squalid refugee camps and maybe, eventually, acceptance by some country whose culture and land would be alien.

Yet at first thousands, then tens of thousands, and then hundreds of thousands of what became known as the "boat people" so fled their homes, relatives, friends, and country. And they fled largely during a time of peace. This is truly a testament to the kind of life imposed on them.

In 1978–79, this flight reached incredible numbers. In just one month in 1979, 60,000 Vietnamese risked pirates, storms, and other sources of death on the high seas, often in ridiculous boats, to reach Thailand, Malaysia, Hong Kong, Indonesia, Macao, the Philippines, and even Japan.[165] According to the UN High Commission on Refugees, as of 1984 a total of 929,600 Vietnamese actually reached the country of first asylum.[166] The U.S. Department of State estimates that from 1975 to 1985, 1 million Vietnamese fled Vietnam.[167] Desbarats and Jackson believe that through 1984 that number is a minimum.[168] For the years possibly including 1987, Braddock puts the number much higher, claiming that those who fled and survived were no fewer than 1,700,000.[169] From these and other estimates, it seems that probably 1,500,000 attempted the dangerous escape from Vietnam by sea, possibly even 2 million.

The toll on the ocean is, of course, unknown. There are percentage estimates of these dead, however, which vary from 20 to 70 percent of the boat people, the latter from an official of Ho Chi Minh city (former Saigon).[170] Many refugee officials believe that up to 50 percent died on the ocean;[171] the Australian Immigration Minister Michael MacKeller gave about 50 percent as his estimate.[172] Some give actual numbers of dead. One source claims that 300,000 to 1 million died in the period from 1975 to about 1979.[173] One ranking American official believed the toll was 30,000 to 50,000 per month up to 1979.[174] For the period up to April 1988, the United States Committee for Refugees estimates that 500,000 died.[175]

Such figures and other estimates of the percentage that died[176] suggest that from 100,000 to 1,400,000 Vietnamese drowned at sea or died of other unnatural causes. A prudent estimate seems to be 500,000. If, of this number, we only count those fleeing under communist pressure for their lives, which I conservatively calculate at about half of them, then the deaths of 250,000 boat people constitute democide.

As described in chapter 9, Vietnam also appears responsible for the death of 461,000 Cambodians from 1970 to 1987 (virtually all of them after 1978) and from 1979 to 1987 another 87,000 in Laos.[177] Adding these to the figures for the post-Vietnam War democide in Vietnam, Vietnam likely murdered about 1,040,000 people. Just this post-Vietnam War toll makes Vietnam one of this century's megamurderers.

However, we still have the democide committed by Hanoi during the Indochina War and the Vietnam War. Including this number,

Hanoi is probably responsible for the murder of almost 1,700,000 people, nearly 1,100,000 of them Vietnamese. The figure might even be close to a high of 3,700,000 dead, with Vietnamese around a likely 2,800,000 of them. As shown in table 11.3, this means that from 1945 to 1987 the Vietnamese communists probably murdered nearly 1.3 percent of Vietnam's population, about one out of every 75 Vietnamese men, women, and children. On an annual basis, this was about one out of every 1,000 Vietnamese per year for each of slightly more than forty-four years. Also listed in table 11.3 is the democide rate for South Vietnam, which did its share of murdering Vietnamese.

One might note that the rate for South Vietnam compares well (if one can say such a thing about democide) with the record of the Soviet Union from 1917 to 1987, in which for every year of communist rule one out of every 222 people was killed. Japan's rate under the militarists' government was one out of every 370 people per year in countries occupied by Japan. For communist China, one out of every 556 Chinese was murdered by the party annually. Of course, in this century none of the regimes in these countries come close to the killing of the Khmer Rouge, which annually was one out of every twelve Cambodians.

Why the democide by Hanoi of probably close to 1,700,000 Vietnamese and others? The reason is little different from that for the other communist megamurderers: It was the Marxist imperative. The

TABLE 11.3
Vietnam: Comparative Democide Rates [a]

Governments/Periods	Years	Democide Rates (%) [b]	
		Overall	Annual
N. Vietnam [c]	1945–87	1.33	.10
Indochina War Period	1945–56	3.27	.29
Vietnam War Period	1957–75	.26	.01
Post-Vietnam War Period	1975–87	.90	.07
S. Vietnam	1954–75	1.10	.05

a All figures are from *Statistics of Democide*. Domestic democide only.

b Mid-rates in a low-high range. The overall rate is the percent of the population killed; the annual rate is the percent of the population killed per year.

c Includes democide in South Vietnam.

revolution had to move forward, the utopia had to be realized. This required, in communist eyes, that actual and potential opponents be eliminated and that, like cogs in a machine, those that remain obey commands from the party, absolutely. No competing power structure could remain; not religious leaders, not village and hamlet leaders, not alternative voices. Nor could land or productive machinery be allowed in private hands, for these might be used in a way contrary to the communist restructuring of society. Anyway, capitalists were "evil." And for a whole society of millions of individuals, each with different interests and values, nothing of the most fundamental social engineering and reconstruction envisioned by the communists could be carried out without casualties. After all, this was a war on exploitation, poverty, and inequality, and in wars people are killed. Again, "You can't make an omelet without breaking eggs."

As for democide in the Vietnam War, this was after all a revolutionary war, a war ultimately for utopia. And, as in the war on domestic capitalism and feudalism, whatever is expedient, whatever is necessary to win the war, must be done no matter the number of civilians sacrificed.

And certainly the imperatives of Power played their role. Power Aggrandizes Itself is a lesson of history. Those who have power seek more power, and more power demands even more to protect itself. Nor can one deny that envy of the rich and productive, or individual greed, played a role, especially among lower cadre. But among the top communists it is clear that Marxism, as it became interpreted by the Soviets and Chinese, and the dynamics of Power set in motion by the Vietnamese communists, were paramount.

As far as the South Vietnamese regimes were concerned, their killing of probably 89,000 Vietnamese was in part surely driven by their anticommunism. But, unlike with Marxism, this is not separable from the imperatives of Power. The existence of the South Vietnamese government was at stake, as were the lives of at least its high officials and officers. Power was challenged, and Power responded as Power does. While Saigon's power was not absolute — as it was for Hanoi — it could still operate without the usual restraints that democracies place on power. Officials and officers could arrest tens of thousands of opponents, many alleged communists could be killed in regional military and police sweeps, and POWs could be mistreated, tortured,

and killed. The United States nagged and threatened the South
Vietnamese regimes about this, and this restraint did work to a degree
in the later years of the war.

As for the U.S. democide toll of apparently 6,000 Vietnamese, three
factors were mainly involved. One was that this was largely an
unconventional guerrilla war where the guerrillas hid among and used
civilians. It should

> be recognized that the VC's practice ... of "clutching the people to their
> breast" and of converting hamlets into fortified strongholds was one of the
> main reasons for the occurrence of combat in populated areas. The existing
> law of war was not written to encompass this kind of warfare; to the extent
> that it does apply to insurgency warfare it prohibits such tactics, for it
> seeks to achieve maximum distinction between combatants and innocent
> civilians. Resistance fighters must carry arms openly and have "a fixed
> distinctive sign recognizable at a distance"; the civilian population may
> not be used as a shield — "the presence of a protected person may not be
> used to render certain points or areas immune from military operations."
> ... [B]y carrying the war into the hamlets and by failing properly to
> identify their combatants, the VC exposed the civilian population to grave
> harm.[178]

That these Viet Cong tactics themselves constituted a war crime does
not excuse U.S. soldiers from, as the heat and confusion of combat
allowed, being more careful of whom they killed.

Second, and related to this, was that, particularly in the early years
of the war, U.S. officers and soldiers were inadequately trained in the
laws of war and the rules of engagement promulgated by the military
command to protect civilians. This serious negligence of the high
command does not itself define democide, but did contribute to it.

And third, U.S. soldiers came to look on the Vietnamese as
"gooks," as inferior beings whose lives were cheap: "The only good
gook is a dead gook." Such feelings are hardly consistent with a
general respect for Vietnamese civilian lives, or for the rules of
engagement meant to protect those lives in actual combat. And this
also is a fault of the high command, which should have made sure that
all soldiers were acquainted with Vietnamese history and culture, and
that any negative stereotyping was punished. Of course, it was the
primary job of the U.S. military to win the war, but if one wants to be

utilitarian about protecting innocent lives, I argue that respect for the civilians for whom Americans were fighting was not inconsistent with winning their hearts and minds, and that this well could have been communicated to all U.S. forces in Vietnam. As Wiesner points out,

> Resentment meant that the people would not inform the Allied troops about enemy movements or cooperate in other ways. In a people's war, hearts and minds were lost to the [South Vietnamese] side and sometimes gained by the enemy. The Viet-Cong and the North Vietnamese lost no opportunity to make propaganda, both in Viet-Nam and in the wider world, out of Allied destructiveness. Although both the Geneva Conventions and the rules of engagement of the United States armed forces imposed strict limitations on the use of firepower against unarmed civilians, it seems clear that those regulations were commonly and widely ignored or violated.[179]

In sum, the Vietnamese have suffered through horrible wars and horrible democide. Probably nearly 3,800,000 of them were thus killed over forty-three years. Of these, 1,250,000 of them were murdered by South Vietnamese regimes, by Frenchmen, Americans, Koreans, and Khmer Rouge, and particularly by the Vietnamese communists ruling in Hanoi — they alone wiped out about 1,100,000 Vietnamese.

Notes

1. Vietnam's population for 1967, the mid-year of the period, was 36,820,000 (Demographic Yearbook 1971, 135).
2. *The Aftermath: Asia* 1983, 168.
3. Ibid., 167.
4. Harrison 1982, 115.
5. *The Aftermath: Asia* 1983, 171.
6. Ibid., 172.
7. Harrison 1982, 115.
8. Duiker 1981, 136.
9. Harrison 1982, 115–16.
10. Shawcross 1986, 172.
11. Bonds 1979, 58.
12. In the mid-1930s, Ho Chi Minh actually started assassinating nationalists who opposed the communists. See Turner 1975.
13. Harrison 1982, 103–4.
14. Wiesner 1988, 299.
15. O'Ballance 1981, 15.
16. Wiesner 1988, 299.

17. Chi 1964, 212.
18. Ibid., 166.
19. Ibid.
20. Ibid.
21. O'Ballance 1981, 15.
22. Chi 1964, 190.
23. Ibid.
24. Ibid., 166.
25. Ibid., 197–98.
26. O'Ballance 1981, 15.
27. Chi 1964, 166.
28. Ibid., 212.
29. Canh 1983, 122.
30. Culbertson 1978, 683; Wiesner 1988, 300, citing President Nixon; Chi 1964, 72, 205.
31. Fitzgerald 1973, 299.
32. Porter 1972, 29, 54–55. For a thorough refutation of Porter's figure and analysis, see Turner 1972.
33. Moise 1976, 78.
34. Harff and Gurr 1988, 364.
35. Pike 1978, 108.
36. Chi 1964, 95.
37. Bradsher 1976, A–10.
38. Chi 1964, 210–11.
39. Pike 1978, 111.
40. O'Ballance 1981, 16.
41. Pike 1978, 111, citing Bernard Fall.
42. Fall 1966, 157; Bonds 1979, 56.
43. Nutt 1972, 34, citing Clark Clifford.
44. Pike 1978, 160; Bonds 1979, 56. One estimate from S.S.N. Murti is that 86,900 soldiers and 43,000 civilians had been regrouped to the North during 1954 to 1955 (Thayer 1989, 18).
45. Lewy 1978, 341.
46. Bonds 1979, 60.
47. Duiker 1981, 180.
48. Calculated from Fall 1966, 360.
49. Lewy 1978, 15
50. Canh 1983, 8.
51. Ibid., 9.
52. O'Ballance 1981, 41.
53. Canh 1983, 9.
54. Ibid., 8.
55. Lewy 1978, 17.
56. Ibid., 15. Defining the war as beginning in 1960 is also statistically conservative since my calculations are based on extrapolating many estimates for shorter durations to the whole war period. In a personal communication, Robert Turner writes that he would date the start of the Vietnam War as of May 1959, since it is now recognized that this as when the decision was made to resume the struggle in the South. See also Turner 1975, 180.

57. Duiker 1981, 228.
58. O'Neill 1969, 7.
59. O'Ballance 1981, 68.
60. O'Neill 1969, 7.
61. Thayer 1985, 34.
62. Duiker 1981, 269.
63. Becker 1986, 352.
64. Thayer 1985, 34.
65. Elegant 1982.
66. Calculated from Thayer 1985, 44.
67. Hosmer 1970, 61.
68. Ibid., 70.
69. Ibid., 144n. 8.
70. Lewy 1978, 273.
71. Ibid.
72. Hosmer 1970, 49.
73. Ibid., 28.
74. Ibid., 6.
75. Ibid., 9.
76. Wiesner 1988, 225.
77. Ibid., 227.
78. The fundamental customary principles of international law bearing on this have been codified in Article 51 paragraph 7 to Protocol I added to the Geneva Conventions in 1977. See Bothe, Partsch, and Solf 1982, 297–318.
79. Lewy 1978, 276
80. Ibid.
81. Wiesner 1988, 225.
82. Ibid., 225–26.
83. Ibid., 227.
84. Ibid., 125.
85. Hosmer 1970, 10.
86. Ibid., 27.
87. Ibid.
88. Ibid., 28.
89. Ibid.
90. Andradé 1990, 272.
91. Wiesner 1988, 260.
92. For example, see Bonds 1979, 127; Hosmer 1970, 44; Lewy 1978, 272, 454; and Thayer 1985, 51.
93. Based on a 1965 population of 16,120,000 given in *Demographic Yearbook* 1971, 135.
94. In no source that I have read have these "relocated" Vietnamese been called deportees. Yet this concept, which has been applied in the literature on the Soviet Union to the deportation of whole ethnic groups, including whole nations, from one part of the Soviet Union to another (e.g., see Conquest 1970), surely applies to Vietnam.
95. Wiesner 1988, 250.
96. Ibid., 24.
97. Ibid., 346.

98. Lewy 1978, 294–95.
99. Wiesner 1988, 61.
100. Ibid., 125.
101. Lewy 1978, 268.
102. This number massacred was established by a final American Army investigation (Bonds 1979, 180). I have seen figures as high as 500 (Harrison 1982, 194, citing figures compiled by Gabriel Kolko and L. Schwartz).
103. Herman 1970, 67.
104. Wiesner 1988, 60–61.
105. Ibid., 356.
106. Lewy 1978, 142.
107. Ibid., 234.
108. Ibid., 239.
109. Ibid., 241.
110. I define practical intentionality as that resulting in actions that cause deaths in such a way as to be intended. See chapter 2.
111. See, for example, Dower 1983 and de Zayas 1989.
112. Such as *U.S. War Crimes in Vietnam* 1967, *The American Crime of Genocide in South Viet Nam* 1968, and *U.S. Imperialists' "Burn All, Destroy All, Kill All" Policy in South Vietnam* 1967.
113. Such as Herman 1970, Harrison 1982, or Rose and Rose 1972.
114. See, for example, Thayer 1985 and O'Ballance 1981.
115. Few, if any, U.S. military or civil prosecutions resulted from these testimonies, which seriously questions their validity and truthfulness. See *U.S. War Crimes in Vietnam* 1968, *The American Crime of Genocide in South Viet Nam* 1968, *U.S. Imperialists' "Burn All, Destroy All, Kill All" Policy in South Vietnam* 1967, Browning and Forman 1972, and Duffett 1968. See also *The Dellums Committee Hearings on War Crimes in Vietnam* 1972.
116. "Wholesale Massacre in South Vietnam Since the Son My Case" 1972, 261–69. For roughly the same period, counts of those "massacres" given as examples for U.S. and "puppet" forces adds up to 2,668 killed; for "puppet" forces alone the total is 4,505.
117. 1967, 31
118. Lewy 1978, 262. These people presumably died from inhaling the defoliants.
119. This gas could in fact be deadly if concentrated dosages were used on people in confined areas, such as a cave or bunker.
120. Rose and Rose 1972, 44–45.
121. Chanda 1990, 84.
122. Lewy 1978, 403.
123. Ibid., 451.
124. Wiesner 1988, 305.
125. See Lewy 1978, 397, 403.
126. O'Ballance 1981, 170.
127. Norden 1966, 25
128. Ibid., 25–26.
129. Wiesner 1988, 115.
130. Lewy 1978, 447, 449.
131. Ibid., 327.
132. *U.S. Imperialists' "Burn All, Destroy All, Kill All" Policy in South Vietnam*

1967, 15, 28–29.
133. "Wholesale Massacre in South Vietnam Since the Son My Case" 1972, 279–81.
134. Based on 1965 population of 35,120,000 for all Vietnam (Demographic Yearbook 1971, 135).
135. Tang 1985, 268.
136. See chapter 9.
137. Brogan 1989, 570.
138. Small and Singer 1982, 95.
139. This is half of the total dead listed for both sides in Ball and Leitenberg 1991, 26.
140. Bradsher 1977, 1.
141. Canh 1983, 15.
142. *The World Almanac and Book of Facts* 1986, 333.
143. Becker 1986, 363.
144. Lewy 1978, 278.
145. Gelinas 1977; Culbertson 1978, 683.
146. Canh 1983, 212.
147. Ibid., 213.
148. Ibid., 224–25.
149. Becker 1986, 363.
150. Canh 1983, 207.
151. Ibid., 215–17.
152. Desbarats 1990, 196. She spells the name "Nguyen Co Tach."
153. Ramaer 1986, 22.
154. Desbarats and Jackson 1985.
155. Desbarats 1990, 197.
156. Evans 1977, 661.
157. Ramaer 1986, 22.
158. "The Current Death Toll of International Communism" 1979, 9.
159. Desbarats and Jackson 1985; Desbarats 1990, 196.
160. Wiesner 1988, 346.
161. Tang 1985, 289.
162. Becker 1986, 364–65.
163. Duiker 1981, 334.
164. *Honolulu Star-Bulletin* 5 May 1989, p. A–9.
165. Hugo 1987, 242.
166. Becker 1986, 462n. 355.
167. Vietnam: Under Two Regimes 1985.
168. Desbarats and Jackson 1985, 23.
169. Braddock 1988, 50.
170. According to *Newsweek* (2 July 1979, p. 48), the estimates vary from 20 to 50 percent; for the 70 percent estimates, see Lewis 1979.
171. Jeffries 1980, J–16; Lewis 1979, A–8.
172. *Honolulu Star-Bulletin* 17 July 1979.
173. "The Current Death Toll of International Communism" 1979, 10.
174. *Time* 7 July 1979:36.
175. Wiesner 1988, 344.
176. Such as those in Rubenstein 1983, 186; Applegate 1988, 19; and Jeffries 1980, J–16.

177. The figure for Vietnam's democide in Laos is from *Statistics of Democide.*
178. Lewy 1978, 230–31.
179. Wiesner 1988, 356, 422n. 75.

12

1,585,000 Murdered
Poland's Ethnic Cleansing

The uprooting of millions was too many and would be morally wrong.

—Winston Churchill at the Potsdam Conference

If the conscience of men ever again becomes sensitive, these expulsions will be remembered to the undying shame of all who committed or connived at them.

—Victor Gollancz, *Our Threatened Values*

As the Red Army pounded the Wehrmacht back toward Germany's eastern territories in October 1944, some 4 to 5 million Germans fled[1] or were forced by the Nazis to evacuate. Millions of young, old, maimed, and sick refugees, along with their carts, horses, and all sorts of belongings, clogged the roads; 500,000 alone formed haphazard caravans across an ice-covered lagoon to reach Baltic ports.[2]

297

Thousands were cut down by Soviet artillery and strafing planes, machine-gunned on the roads, and run over by tanks ... or disappeared into holes in the ice created by bombs. Thousands more that tried to escape on overcrowded ships were killed when these ships were sunk by planes or submarines. One ship, the *Wilhelm Gustloff,* was torpedoed and sunk with the loss of about 7,700 lives[3] (compare this to the loss of 1,503 lives on the sinking of the *Titanic*). About 25,000 refugees were drowned in the Baltic alone.[4] Tens of thousands more died from exposure and sickness. Overall, possibly 1 million German civilians perished during this evacuation and flight,[5] an incredible toll in human lives. And this does not count the tens of thousands of refugees that died from British and U.S. bombing of Germany's eastern cities, such as refugee-filled Dresden in February 1945.[6]

Many of the surviving refugees made it across the border of postwar Germany; some found temporary havens in Silesia, Pomerania, and other German territories; others were overtaken in flight by the Red Army. It did not much matter. As the war neared its end, millions of these refugees and those that refused to flee were subjected to Red Army looting, indiscriminate beating, murder, and rape. Even then, like the return flow of a wave breaking on a beach, millions of Germans tried to return to their former homes or areas. In the land they passed through and returned to, famine was widespread, social and health services totally disrupted. Signs warned refugees that they would starve to death if they lingered.

For these returning Germans and those that had found havens in the eastern territories from the war or had remained, the "greatest forcible dislocation of persons in European history"[7] was yet to come. Within a few years of the war's end, an incredible 15 million Reichdeutsch and ethnic German civilians would be thrown out of Poland, the Baltic States, Memel, Czechoslovakia, Hungary, Rumania, Yugoslavia, and the eastern areas of Germany (this is as though the Netherlands, Afghanistan, or Greece were totally emptied of all humans by force). Almost 1,900,000 Germans would die or be killed in this process (in addition to those who died during the wartime evacuation and flight), most by actions of the Poles, Czechs, and Yugoslavs. The numbers expelled and the death toll are shown in table 12.1.

Encouraged by Soviet forces, domestic extremists, and the new national governments, these expulsions and the treatment of

Reichdeutsch and ethnic Germans leading up to them were at first savage and deadly: time and again, Germans, who for generations had lived in a town or village or on land they owned, were grabbed, looted, beaten, raped, and then often corralled until they could be forced into unheated freight cars and expelled to Germany — sometimes without food or water for a trip taking many days, even weeks. The Potsdam Conference among the Allies in November 1945 tried to legalize these expulsions and make them more humane, but had little impact until 1946, when the organized expulsions became fairly orderly.

The expulsions by the Poles from Germany's former eastern territories and Poland proper were the largest, amounting to 8 million Reichdeutsch and ethnic Germans. In compensation for taking Poland's eastern marshes and other areas in the east, the Soviets gave the Poles the former free city of Danzig (which had been supervised by the League of Nations), German East Prussia, Eastern Pomerania, Eastern Brandenburg, and Silesia. These Oder-Neisse provinces (excluding Danzig) had for centuries been a big chunk of the German homeland.[8]

TABLE 12.1
German Expulsion Democide [a]

Nations/Areas	Expelled (000) [b]	Democide (000) [c]
Czechoslovakia	2,900	197
Hungary	240	0
Poland (New) [d]	8,000	1,583
Germany's Eastland [e]	7,144	1,450
Poland (Old) [f]	750	133
Rumania	166	0
Yugoslavia	250	82
Total Eastern Europe	15,000	1,863

a Most probable mid-values in a low-high range. All data is from *Statistics of Democide.*

b Numbers do not add up to the total due to overlap and consolidation and omission of some areas.

c Numbers will not add up due to a reordering of Yugoslavia's values. See *Statistics of Democide.*

d Post-World War II Poland.

e Germany's former Eastern areas plus Danzig.

f Pre-1939 Poland.

They comprised 39,400 square miles (three times larger than Belgium and about the size of Austria), or 24 percent of 1937 Germany.[9] According to the German Federal Ministry for Expellees, Refugees, and War Victims, 9,575,000 Germans lived in these eastern territories in 1939[10] (about 15 percent of Germany's population).[11] Perhaps no more than a couple of hundred thousand Poles lived there too.[12]

As this huge area came under Polish administration, Germans were forced from their homes, their property expropriated. They were often beaten, robbed of what few positions they had taken with them, and raped; resistance could mean death. Many were stuffed into freight or open coal cars, shipped off, and dumped somewhere in occupied Germany. According to the Berlin correspondent of *The Times* (London), in 1945 one group of evicted Germans was transported in cattle cars from Danzig without water, food, or even straw on which to lie. When they finally reached Berlin, twenty were dead out of the eighty-three jammed into two of the trucks.[13]

These expulsions gradually became more regularized, sometimes in the style of the infamous Soviet deportations of their Volga Germans, Crimean Tatars, Chechens, Ingushi, and other national groups to Siberia or other inhospitable areas in the east.[14] Similarly, in postwar Germany's eastern territories under Polish administration and in Poland proper, whole German neighborhoods or villages were now given a few hours, sometimes a half hour, or only a few minutes, to pack a bag. They would then be collected, taken to a train station, shoved aboard cars, and freighted to an occupation zone in Germany — never to be allowed to return. Their homes, land, animals, and whatever other property remained were all assumed by the authorities and distributed among Poles brought in to repopulate former German land and cities. In fact, this provided the new communist-controlled Polish government an incredible wealth of former German property with which to reward its supporters and buy support from the peasants.

Hundreds of thousands of Germans were killed while awaiting expulsion; possibly even over 1 million.[15] Numbers of them were imprisoned in lethal camps. "Conditions in many ... approached those of the murderous Nazi period, in which sadism was given free rein and internees were left to starve slowly to death."[16] Note, for example, that of the 8,064 Germans in Camp Lamsdorf in Upper Silesia, 6,488 (including 628 children) died from starvation, disease, hard labor, and physical maltreatment. No doubt "tens of thousands" similarly died in other Polish internment camps.[17]

But these camps and the expulsions were only part of the horror. Millions of Germans who did not flee or were yet to be expelled were deprived of their very means of survival: Livestock was taken by the Soviet occupation troops and Poles; cereals, foodstuffs, and seed crops were looted; even farm machinery and implements were confiscated. And because of the mass flight of Germans before the Red Army there also was a severe shortage of agricultural workers. All this meant famine among the Germans. Poles could purchase food in Polish shops; Germans had to rely on the black market,[18] and after they had sold to Poles for a pittance whatever goods they saved from the looters, there was virtually no way for them to earn more Polish złoty (the only legal currency).

Consider the plight of Germans in Breslau (now Wrocław), Silesia, as documented by its archdiocese. There,

> where the number of Germans who had remained behind was about 300,000, it has been officially ascertained that more than ninety per cent of the babies, a very large percentage of infants, many young mothers and old persons died of starvation. As a result of the shortage of fats, dysentery broke out and claimed many victims, all the more so as the medical supplies which had not been confiscated or stolen were soon exhausted. Since the dispensaries usually only sold their goods in exchange for zloty ..., the majority of Germans were not in a position to buy any medical supplies. For the same reason it was practically impossible for them to obtain hospital treatment as a deposit of 200 Zloty ... had to be paid upon admission to a hospital. The Germans were obliged to sell the few possessions they had managed to save, such as linen, clothing, electric stoves, jewelry, etc., to the Poles in order to obtain zloty with which to buy a little food. It must be remembered that from May 8th [1945] onwards the Germans had been obliged to get along without receiving any Polish money (in the form of wage or salary) and without any official allocations of food rations. The misery and distress of the population in the towns was indescribable.
> ...
> It is obvious that, under the circumstances, many persons were at their wit's end. The number of suicides increased at an alarming rate; in fact, there would have been even more suicides in Breslau had the gas supply been available.

...

The same conditions with slight variations also prevailed in the remaining German eastern territories under Polish administration. Famine raged throughout the country.[19]

To be sure, the Poles had suffered greatly under the Nazi occupation from September 1939 to the winter of 1944–45. Poles had been beaten, tortured, and murdered, their homes and cities destroyed (600,000 Poles had been expelled from Warsaw,[20] and the city was completely leveled after the Warsaw uprising of 1944). Intellectuals, professionals, and political elite were murdered to deprive the Poles of any leadership. The most infamous German death camps had been located in Poland. And the half of the country that the Nazis seized (by agreement with Hitler, Stalin grabbed the other half) was itself divided into two parts, one comprising territories incorporated into the Reich. In 1941–43, the Germans expelled 1,800,000 Poles from this former Polish land, including 700,000 who were sent to Germany for forced labor.[21] Altogether the Nazi evictions in occupied Poland affected about 4 to 5 million Poles.[22] Overall, through their savage occupation policies, executions, mass murder, and death camps, the Nazis killed about 5,400,000 Poles (one out of every six to seven — see table 12.2), 3 million of them Jews.[23]

It is easy to understand, while not one bit justifying, why after the war Poles would take revenge for this horror on the first defenseless Germans under their control. Few could argue with the Polish courier, Jan Karski, who told President Roosevelt,

I would rather be frank with you, Mr. President. Nothing on earth will stop the Poles from taking some kind of revenge on the Germans after the Nazi collapse. There will be some terrorism, probably short-lived, but it will be unavoidable. And I think this will be a sort of encouragement for all the Germans in Poland to go west, to Germany proper, where they belong.[24]

It is even more important to recognize that there were also many Poles who treated German civilians with kindness and tried to protect them against the vengefulness of other Poles, often at their own risk.

As the early disorganized expulsions from Poland and other countries disgorged Germans into the American and British zones of Germany, the Western Allies became increasingly concerned about the inhumane nature of the expulsions and the impact on their zones of this influx of expellees. Germany itself was in a chaotic state. Whole cities had been destroyed by bombing or battle; the nation's economic and social infrastructure was in ruins. Millions were homeless and without work; food was scarce, and in many urban areas there was a near disastrous famine. And health and medical services could not possibly handle the additional millions of starving, ill-clothed, homeless, and sick German refugees, evacuees, and expellees.

Death was easy and frequent. Bodies lying in the street or along the roads and railroad tracks were no strange sight, mothers hugging dead children to their breast not uncommon. One Western reporter writing from Berlin pointed out that while the expected death rate was eleven or twelve per thousand; the actual was sixty-one per thousand in the first month of the Allied occupation — about six times what had been expected.[25] But this doesn't tell the whole story, for it was the very young that suffered the most. Of 609 infants less than a year old during this first month in Berlin, 361 died.[26] Into this postwar, manmade human catastrophe that was postwar Germany continued to be jettisoned 20,000 weak, hungry, and homeless per day in the summer of 1945,[27] many soon to die.

After every day seeing in Berlin the results of these expulsions, American political advisor Robert Murphy cabled the U.S. Department of State in October 1945.

Here is retribution on a large scale, but practiced not on the *Parteibonzen*, but on women and children, the poor, the infirm.... Knowledge that they are the victims of a harsh political decision carried out with the utmost ruthlessness and disregard for humanity does not cushion the effect. The mind reverts to other mass deportations which horrified the world and brought upon the Nazis the odium which they so deserved. Those mass deportations engineered by the Nazis provided part of the moral basis on which we waged war and which gave strength to our cause. Now the situation is reversed. We find ourselves in the invidious position of being partners in this German enterprise and as partners inevitably sharing the responsibility.[28]

Of course, many countries had been devastated by the war, and conditions throughout Europe were abysmal. France, Great Britain, and the United States were reluctant to divert needed food, clothing, tents, medicine, and other supplies from elsewhere in Europe to those who had been such brutal enemies just a few months previously. But as conditions deteriorated in occupied Germany and thousands died from starvation or disease during the terrible winter of 1945–46,[29] the Allies relented and allowed private international relief agencies to provide food and clothing.

At a summit conference well before this, the United States and Britain had tried to limit and organize the massive flow of expellees into their zones and to ameliorate the ruinous conditions of their transport. The meeting took place between Truman, Churchill (at first; he was succeeded later by Labor Party leader Clement Attlee when he lost Britain's first postwar general election), and Stalin in July 1945 at Potsdam, a town 17 miles from Berlin. One of the main issues they had to settle was what Poland's new borders would be. Stalin pushed hard for extending Poland's borders west to the Oder-Neisse rivers, which, as mentioned, would encompass a large chunk of Germany. This was strongly resisted until a last-minute package was worked out that provisionally (until a final peace settlement) accepted the Soviet definition of Poland's western frontier in exchange for concessions on the German reparations Stalin demanded; and it was agreed that this region would be under Polish administration.

How many Germans in fact remained in this Oder-Neisse territory was one of the critical questions regarding both Poland's new borders and the expulsions. Truman and Churchill were told by the Polish delegation that there were only 1,500,000 Germans left[30] (out of a prewar population of over 9,575,200);[31] Stalin simply said that there were none — all those surviving the war had run away.[32] Even the Americans gave a very low estimate of 2 million still remaining.[33] Churchill, however, saw the true dimension of the issue. He predicted that 8 to 9 million would have to be expelled.[34] As it was, possibly as many as nearly 8,169,000 Germans[35] from these territories alone would be dumped into already overcrowded and famished regions of occupied Germany, virtually all within two years.

Truman and Churchill had initially been opposed to such expulsions; Churchill especially had "grave moral scruples about vast movements of population."[36] But it became clear that, with or without authority, expulsions would be carried out; Poland and Czechoslovakia insisted on it. Moreover, there was the argument that this was a way of eliminating a major source of future conflict and aggression in this part of Europe. Doubtlessly some thought was given to the pro-Nazi agitation of many Sudeten Germans in Czechoslovakia in the mid 1930s — agitations that paved the way for Hitler's demands on the country and its takeover in 1939 — and prewar German-Polish conflicts in Silesia and Danzig. Perhaps with such in mind and to regularize and civilize what looked inevitable, the United States and Great Britain reluctantly agreed to these mass "transfers," but insisted on writing into the protocol that they "should be effected in an orderly and humane manner." Similar transfers from Czechoslovakia and Hungary were also legalized, with the numbers, pacing, and procedures left up to the Allied Control Council in Germany.

This Potsdam Agreement underwrote the largest mass expulsion of a population in history. Eventually, the forced removal of Germans from their homeland would total possibly 11,603,400 expellees,[37] perhaps even 18 million,[38] most probably the 15 million[39] shown in table 21.1. In its favor, the agreement did promote better treatment of most of the Germans during their expulsion. Excesses were less, and expelled Germans began to arrive in Allied zones in better condition. Nonetheless, in late 1945 and early 1946 living conditions in Germany were still dangerous to human life. Expellees who would have easily survived had they remained in their homes and on their farms in Silesia, Prussia, Sudentenland, or other areas of expulsion, found in Germany that they were in deadly competition for the very basic necessities of life.

Getting any accurate count of the death toll in the Polish expulsions is impossible. Germans were murdered by Poles before and during expulsion; Germans died from the expulsion process or as a result of it in Germany. Few public records were kept, of course, and calculation of the mortality has to depend on pre- and postexpulsion population figures in the expulsion area and the number of expellees in Germany. But this also is clouded by the mass flight and evacuation of Germans during the war, and the attempt of many to return to their homes as the war was ending.

No wonder then that the estimates among Germans themselves for the human cost of the expulsion from the German eastern territories varies from 800,000 to 3,200,000 dead.[40] Even lower figures are available. A Polish publication estimated that 556,000 Germans and

Poles died in these territories from all causes during this period.[41] The West German Federal Ministry for Expellees, Refugees, and War Victims calculated the loss from 1945 to 1950 as 1,225,000 for Germany's eastern areas.[42] The German Statistisches Bundesamt in Wiesbaden put the number at 1,339,000 for just the Oder-Neisse territories.[43] Weighing a variety of such estimates, I calculate the dead for the eastern territories and old Poland as 415,000 to almost 3,100,000, probably around 1,600,000 Reichdeutsch and ethnic Germans, as given in table 12.1. In my view, this toll is the direct and indirect responsibility of the new Polish government (although aided, abetted, and promoted by the Soviets): it is Polish democide.

Czechs were no less revengeful after their occupation by Nazi forces. They were not about to forget the Nazi executions and atrocities, the massacres of whole villages, the killing in total of 213,000 Czechs; or the role that many Sudeten Germans had played in Hitler's takeover of Czechoslovakia. The feeling of numerous Czechs against the Sudeten Germans was expressed by Eduard Benes, leader of the Czech government-in-exile, who said in a radio speech, "We must get rid of all those Germans who plunged a dagger into the back of Czechoslovakia state in 1938." The end of the war provided the new Czech government with an opportunity to take revenge and rid itself of a long-troublesome minority.

In the early postwar months, the Czechs treated the Sudeten Germans before and during their expulsion with extreme brutality and violence, which at least one writer claims "can be compared in severity only to the persecution of the Jews by Hitler."[44] Sometimes without regard to whether the Germans had been pro- or anti-Nazi, they would be grabbed off the streets or ejected from their homes, herded together, looted, beaten, raped, or shot. Many survivors were forced into concentration camps where large numbers died from further beatings, torture, and other mistreatment. Without any sanitary arrangements, the barracks in these camps "swarmed with vermin and the food was less than in German concentration camps." Indeed, "in many cases the food supply and other conditions were considerably worse in these Czech concentration camps, established after the end of the war, than at Dachau or Buchenwald."[45] According to an October 1945 letter to the *Manchester Guardian* from R. R. Stokes, a British member of Parliament and minister who visited these camps, the

German inmates got about 750 calories a day, consisting mainly of black coffee and bread for breakfast and supper, and vegetable soup for lunch. This is less than what prisoners received at Belsen.[46]

If not put into camps, many Germans were forced into slave labor on Czech farms or factories until eventually expelled. Others were force-marched with clubs and rifle butts to border collection areas to suffer further hunger, exposure, disease, and beatings before finally being thrown across the border into occupied Germany. Sometimes many were simply massacred on the spot. For example, after an explosion of a munitions depot in a village near Aussig in July 1945, the Czech militia slaughtered 1,000 to 2,700 Sudeten Germans in the town.[47]

To get a feel for the barbarity of such killings and the treatment of the survivors, the report of an investigation by Arno Behrisch (a former secretary of the German Social Democratic Party in Saxony) and his wife should suffice. During June 1945 in Saaz, Czech authorities summoned all German males between the ages of 13 and 63 to the marketplace at 6 A.M. Those who arrived late were "terribly beaten up with whips, clubs and planks."[48] Those who protested were shot. Then 5,000 boys and men were fast-marched eleven miles away to the town of Postelberg, with laggards shot along the way. Once there, the survivors were forced to lie flat on the ground of a barracks yard, encouraged by volleys fired over their heads every hour by their Czech guards. Those who moved were beaten. In the morning, a command in Czech was misunderstood to mean "get up," which some of the men tried to do. "At once the guards opened fire and whole rows of the victims were mown down with tommy-guns." The wounded were finished off.

While many men were crowded into stables for the next night, hundreds had to remain in the yard. No food was given to any of them for three days, while shooting of individual prisoners continued day and night. Finally, those Germans who were communists or former inmates of German concentration camps were sent back to Saaz, while the rest, including many boys, were kept for special treatment. Former Nazis, SS-men, and policemen were forced into the stables, which were so crowded and unventilated that some of the men grew hysterical or fainted from lack of air. When the prisoners tried to leave through an open door, the guards fired shots through two small holes in the walls. Several died; more were shot in the morning. Later, the horse troughs were filled with water and the Germans were forced to keep their heads underwater; those who raised them were bludgeoned. Then, practically every two hours groups of Germans would be taken out to be beaten further by guards and civilians using sticks, clubs, whips, and cables. Some were bludgeoned to death.

In one case, a truck full of Czechs arrived with rubber truncheons and whips to carry out the beatings. The Germans had to undress and stand still for an hour while being battered and whipped. Those who fainted were revived with cold water for more pummeling.

Czechs smashed the genitals of some men by stamping on them with their boots. The cries of the tortured were frightful. Five boys, aged 13 to 16, were beaten murderously because they had moved a few steps from their place. The children groaned and yelled for their mothers. Then the five children were stood up against the wall and the Czechs raised their rifles. The boys cried: "Don't fire, let us live!" A volley was fired and the five boys fell to the ground.

Beatings, different kinds of torture, and shooting continued for days. Some survivors were finally sent to concentration camps or forced labor; the remainder were marched back to Saaz while being battered along the way. The horror they had survived had lasted for nine days.

In Saaz, the first group of Germans to be expelled consisted of those who were unable to work, such as invalids. They could take no belongings, not even artificial limbs. "At the station of Komotau a girl was fetched out from one carriage, taken to the compartment of the escorting soldiers and raped." Rather than being transported the whole distance to Germany, the expellees were dropped off at Ober-Georgenthal, 30 miles across the mountains from the German-Saxon frontier. They then were forced to march over the mountains the remaining distance, with disabled former soldiers in particular being beaten along the way. It is surprising that only one woman died during the march.

The next day, in Saaz, the 14,000 remaining women were ordered to appear at a barracks, where they were herded into barrack buildings, stables, garages, and the barracks yard itself. When night fell, in one of the rooms where the women were, hordes of Czech guards entered ... and mass rape started. By flashing torches the victims were selected and raped on the spot. There were terrible cries.... Women and girls were also taken away and never seen again. These mean acts were repeated night after night. There was no sanitation and soon diseases started. There was no food for the first three days, and very little afterwards. The women had been ordered to bring their house keys along with them; they were taken away and given to Czechs for looting the houses. Within two days 40 babies had died in their mothers' arms in the barracks. The women were kept there for many weeks and the number of deaths increased. Babies died every day, up to 15 a day.

Many of these women were finally sent to forced labor, for which they received no pay and where they would be imprisoned at night in barns and stables. Eventually, all the survivors were expelled to Germany.

There is much more to this sorry report of inhumanity, but enough.[49] Overall, the number of Saaz Germans thus murdered was over 2,000, the pain and suffering immeasurable. As should be made clear, Czechs were not exceptionally savage in their pre-expulsion treatment of their Germans; similar examples could be given for Poles[50] and Yugoslavs (particularly Serbs).[51]

As in the Polish expulsions, the transportation of the expellees from Czechoslovakia involved its own dangers. Just consider one transport of Sudeten Germans from Troppau in Czech Silesia. It carried 4,200 women, children, and aged for eighteen days. Only 1,350 were left when it arrived in Berlin.[52]

These deadly pre-Potsdam expulsions were centrally directed by the Czechs. "Expulsion orders were issued as public proclamations by local and district National Committees. The methods were alike in different places, which shows that this important measure was organized in agreement with the central government."[53] Moreover, several government decrees clearly envisioned and promoted the expulsion of Germans as a group.[54] However, the government did subsequently punish some of those responsible for the more extreme horrors and tried to regularize the expulsions, which eventually was done under the Potsdam Agreement.

Out of a population of 3,391,000[55] to 3,453,000[56] Germans at the end of the war, some 200,000 to 300,000 were expelled from Czechoslovakia in the disorganized pre-Potsdam months[57] and almost all the remainder in the year following. Only an officially reported 192,000 ethnic Germans remained when the expulsions were declared completed in 1947.[58]

Some Czech scholars argue that only a few thousand died during the expulsions, and those due to the brutality of some in the internment camps who were later punished.[59] Former Sudeten Germans, however, allege that hundreds of thousands were killed. Some writers estimate the toll as high as 500,000,[60] 600,000,[61] and even 800,000,[62] but these are excessive. However, given the savage pre-expulsion treatment of many Germans, the inhuman nature of their transport (sometimes taking many days, without cover, food, or water), and the awful conditions in Germany at this time, far more reasonable is the German Federal Ministry for Expellees, Refugees, and War Victims' estimate of 267,000 dead or missing.[63] I calculate the toll as 68,000 to 510,000 German dead, most likely the nearly 200,000 listed in table 12.1.

Both Rumania and Hungary also expelled hundreds of thousands of their ethnic Germans, especially under strong Soviet pressure in the case of a reluctant Hungary. And although some of the expellees arriving in Germany were in bad condition, and doubtlessly some died as a result, probably no significant number perished or were killed before or during the expulsion.

It was a different story for Yugoslavia. Nazi occupying forces had murdered 625,000 Yugoslavs, particularly Serbs,[64] and a vicious civil war that had divided the country in several ways was coming to a bloody conclusion at the same time that Germany was meeting defeat. This will be covered in chapter 14. Here I only need note that vengefulness and violent retaliation were century-old Balkan principles. As Nazi soldiers surrendered near or after the war's end, they were often unmercifully killed. Sometimes little distinction was made between surrendering German soldiers and ethnic Germans who had lived in the country for generations. Many would be simply killed offhandedly.

In 1939 there were 537,000[65] to 750,000[66] ethnic Germans, out of which some 25,000 were evacuated by the Nazis or fled. Another 117,000 were deported in 1944–45 by the Soviets to forced labor in the Soviet Union. Of those that remained, between 150,000[67] and 300,000[68] ethnic Germans were expelled, with possibly 82,000 dying or being killed in the process. No more than 100,000 ethnic Germans remained in July 1947[69] or thereabouts.[70]

And so for all Eastern Europe, from about 530,000 to close to 3,700,000 Reichdeutsch, German Poles, Sudeten Germans and other German Czechs, and German Yugoslavs were murdered within a few years. A prudent estimate is that almost 1,900,000 were killed, as shown in table 12.1

The overall and nation-specific democide rates are listed in table 12.2. Of all ethnic Germans in the expulsion regions, about 11 percent were killed. What is equally telling is the democide rates for the overall national populations of the expelling countries. Given the annual rate for Poland, her government killed per year 1 out of every 40 German men, women, and children under its administration. Compare this to the democide of the Nazis, who for Germany and all of occupied Europe murdered 1 out of every 110 people per year, including Jews.[71] Note that Czechs wreaked far greater vengeance, were that purely the motive, on their Germans than the democide that they suffered under the Nazis: one German out of every 175 people per year killed in Czechoslovakia versus one Czech murdered by the Nazis out of every 278 people. Poles and Yugoslavs, however, suffered far more democide from the Nazis, relatively, than that they inflicted on their German minority.

No matter. By any definition of the term, what the Czechs, Poles, and Yugoslavs did to their Germans was genocide: "The manner of the Expulsions, as well as the Expulsions as a policy, violated numerous norms of international law and civilized humanity. This was indeed the final genocide of World War Two."[72] No doubt the Western Allies bear some responsibility for this through their legalization of the expulsions in the Potsdam Agreement and the initial horrendous conditions they allowed in their zones of occupation in Germany. Surely the Soviets bear even more responsibility for encouraging and even in some cases pressuring for these expulsions. But the first responsibility for all these deaths lies with the Poles, Czechs, and Yugoslavs. Their governments promoted and then decreed the expulsions; and their nationals carried out what in a November 1946 *New York Times* article the journalist Anne O'Hare McCormick called "the most inhuman decision ever made by governments dedicated to the defense of human rights."[73]

Certainly, as mentioned, revenge upon the Germans for Nazi crimes had much to do with this democide. So did greed — the opportunity to loot and expropriate large tracts of farmland and successful businesses. So did politics — the chance for these early, unstable governments to pay off or buy support from the population. And so did the desire of the Czech and Polish governments to rid themselves of a minority that could instigate or be the tool of intervention by a future German government, whose coming nature and policies could only be guessed at from an unpromising history. And surely, regardless of the policies of these governments, there would have been individual atrocities against the Germans and perhaps some local expulsions for those close to the border with Germany.

But given all this, the countrywide expulsions could not have been carried out without the power of the national governments. And it was the assumption of near total Power in these early years that made it possible for the governing elite to wantonly commit this most basic violation of human rights and international law.

TABLE 12.2
Germany Expulsion Democide Rates [a]

	Democide Rate %	
Nations	1945–50	Annual
Czechoslovakian Expulsions	1.53	.57
Nazi Democide in Czechoslovakia	2.09	.36
New Poland Expulsions	6.62	2.47
Nazi Democide in Poland	36.00	6.26
Yugoslavian Expulsions	.51	.19
Nazi democide in Yugoslavia	4.17	1.00
Of Expulsions Overall [b]	11.24	4.22
Nazi Democide Overall [c]	5.46	.91

a All figures are from *Statistics of Democide*. Based on national populations. Nazi rates are of the Nazi democide and are based on Rummel 1992, table A.

b For Eastern European Ethic/German population.

c For Germany and occupied Europe.

Notes

1. de Zayas 1979, xx.
2. Whiting 1982, 198.
3. McWhirter and McWhirter 1977, 435.
4. Whiting 1982, 199.
5. de Zayas 1979, 103.
6. The number of civilians killed in this bombing is much in dispute. For various estimates, see *Statistics of Democide.*
7. G. C. Paikert quoted in Bühler 1990, 103. Although this quote refers to the expulsion of the German population from the Oder-Neisse territories, it must apply even more forcibly to the expulsions from all of Eastern Europe.
8. von Wilpert 1964, 19, claims that this area has been part of the German homeland for over 700 years. However, Germany was not really one country until Otto von Bismarck united it in 1871. Before that Germany, had been fragmented into various states; even in the seventeenth century it consisted of some 300 principalities, free cities, and bishoprics.
9. Szaz 1960, 1.
10. de Zayas 1979, xxv.
11. Schechtman 1963, 11.
12. So say the Germans. Poles claim a million lived there (Wiskemann, 1956, 121).
13. Gollancz 1948, 141.
14. Conquest 1970.
15. Szaz 1960, 126.
16. de Zayas 1979, 124.
17. Ibid., 125–26, 128.
18. Kaps 1952/53, 69. It is true that most of the initial expropriation and looting was carried out by Soviet occupation forces. However, once the Polish administration was in place, it executed its own confiscations while doing virtually nothing to ameliorate the resulting disastrous conditions of the Germans; indeed, their policies seemed aimed at aggravating them.
19. Kaps 1952/53, 69.
20. Schimitzek 1966, 335.
21. Zielinski 1961, 48–49.
22. Schimitzek 1966, 335.
23. See chapter 6.
24. Wiskemann 1956, 89n. 1.
25. Gollancz 1948, 140.
26. Ibid.
27. Botting 1983, 82.
28. de Zayas 1988, 25–26.
29. It remains an open question whether these deaths were democide by the Allies. It depends on whether vital relief diverted from Germany did indeed save lives elsewhere or simply punished the German population for the Nazi horrors.
30. de Zayas 1979, 86.
31. Schoenberg 1970, 33.
32. de Zayas 1979, 86.
33. Wiskemann 1956, 107.

34. Ibid.
35. Bühler 1990, 104.
36. Botting 1983, 81.
37. Schoenberg 1970, 33.
38. Glaser and Possony 1979, 85.
39. "Expellees and Refugees" 1950, 5; de Zayas 1979, xix.
40. Schimitzek 1966, 14.
41. Ibid., 168.
42. de Zayas 1979, xxv.
43. Schoenberg 1970, 33.
44. Gluckstein 1952, 194.
45. Turnwald 1953, xxii–xxiii.
46. The letter retranslated from the German is published in Ibid., app. 7.
47. de Zayas 1979, 97.
48. This and subsequent related quotes are from Gluckstein 1952, 195–99.
49. For other reports of Czech atrocities, see *Documents on the Expulsion of the Sudenten Germans* 1953.
50. See, for example, Kaps 1952/53.
51. See documents in Prcela and Guldescu 1970. Ethnic Germans were just one group among the many that the victorious partisans tortured and killed, including German POWs, Ustashi, Croatian government officials and soldiers, Chetniks, Slovenian Home Guards and officials, anticommunists, and anyone with the slightest hint of Nazi or Ustashi collaboration. See chapter 14.
52. Gluckstein 1952, 199–200. No doubt referring to the same tragedy, de Zayas 1979, 113–14 quotes F. A. Voigt that, of 2,400 transported, 1,050 perished.
53. Turnwald 1953, xxi.
54. Ibid., xxiv.
55. Documents ..., IV, 1960, 128n
56. Schoenberg 1970, 33.
57. Bouscaren 1963, 58.
58. Wiskemann 1956, 129.
59. See Luza 1964, 269n. 10.
60. Ibid., 293.
61. Radspieler 1955, 20.
62. Luza 1964, 289n. 56.
63. de Zayas 1979, xxv.
64. See chapter 14.
65. de Zayas 1979, xxv.
66. Radspieler 1955, n.1 to table, 35.
67. Holler 1963, 10
68. Glaser and Possony 1979, 528.
69. Bouscaren 1963, 61.
70. Schechtman 1953, 163.
71. See chapter 6.
72. Bühler 1990, 97–98.
73. *New York Times* 13 November 1946, p.26. Quoted in de Zayas 1979, 89.

13

1,503,000 Murdered
The Pakistani Cutthroat State

Kill three million of them and the rest will eat out of our hands.

—Yahya Khan, President of Pakistan

In 1971, the self-appointed president of Pakistan and commander-in-chief of the army General Agha Mohammed Yahya Khan and his top generals prepared a careful and systematic military, economic, and political operation against East Pakistan (now Bangladesh). They planned to murder that country's Bengali intellectual, cultural, and political elite. They planned to indiscriminately murder hundreds of thousands of its Hindus and drive the rest into India. And they planned to destroy its economic base to insure that it would be subordinate to West Pakistan for at least a generation to come. This despicable and cutthroat plan was outright genocide.

After a well-organized military buildup in East Pakistan, the military launched its campaign. Within 267 days it killed about

315

1,500,000 people, turned another 10 million into refugees who fled to India, provoked a war with India, incited a countergenocide of 150,000 non-Bengalis, and lost East Pakistan.

East and West Pakistan were created in 1947 when the British partitioned India into Hindu India and Moslem Pakistan. Solely based on religion, Pakistan was divided into east and west wings separated by nearly 1,000 miles. From the beginning, West Pakistan assumed domination over the East. In the civil service and military, Bengalis from East Pakistan were clearly in the minority. The Bengali language was denied national status. The piety of Moslems in East Pakistan was deprecated. And economically, in all that mattered, East Pakistan was treated as though a colony. Even though it had 54 percent of the population, it got only 35 percent of that spent on development. Its trade surplus was used to cover the deficits of West Pakistan, thus draining resources from East Pakistan. And income per capita in West Pakistan was 61 percent higher.[1]

As a result, Bengalis increasingly sought through political means to force West Pakistan to recognize and correct this inequality. Led by Sheikh Mujibur Rahman, the Awami League of East Pakistan made equality with West Pakistan its core platform and grew in power as more and more Bengalis became outraged by West Pakistan's treatment of them. The league proposed a six-point program that included giving East Pakistan control over its trade and foreign aid allocation, and taxation. It envisioned ending the domination by the central government over the distribution of resources. In effect, it called for autonomy.

Two momentous events ultimately triggered the genocide. First was the killer cyclone and associated floods that hit East Pakistan in November 1970. With winds possibly reaching 150 miles per hour, it was the most devastating in memory. An official body count gave 207,000 dead, but it did not include the tens of thousands who were washed out to sea, buried in the mud, or died on outlying and remote islands. The actual toll may have reached over 500,000.[2]

Shocked by this disaster, the international community rapidly responded, and international aid flowed into East Pakistan. Bengalis angrily noted, however, that help from West Pakistan was slow, reluctantly given, and minimal.

That did it. Not only were Bengalis being deprived of their fair share of resources, but when in dire need they were largely ignored and given little sympathy by their supposed brethren. Fortunately, the upcoming national parliamentary elections in December gave the Bengalis a mechanism for expressing their rage, and the six-point program of the Awami League gave them an alternative.

For the moment, the military dictators of Pakistan seemed content to retire from front stage, turn Pakistan over to civilian and constitutional rule, and use their considerable power from behind the scenes. The elections would determine the composition of the Constituent National Assembly, which in turn would have 120 days to write a new constitution (which would require Yahya Khan's approval, of course). Incredibly to the military and other Punjabi elite, dissatisfaction with West Pakistan was such that the Awami League won a landslide victory, taking 167 of the 169 seats in the Assembly reserved for East Pakistan. This gave it an absolute majority of the legislature's 313 seats, and thus gave Sheikh Mujibur Rahman the power to write into the new constitution the Awami League's autonomy program. Sheikh Mujib himself might become prime minister.

Faced with this electoral coup from below, central government and military leaders tried to pressure Sheikh Mujib to compromise, especially to leave with the central government control over East Pakistan trade and aid. However, Sheikh Mujib refused. So Zulfiqar Ali Bhutto, who headed the powerful West Pakistani People's Party (it got around 80 seats in the election), announced that his party would boycott the Assembly. Doubtlessly choreographed beforehand, on 1 March 1971, Yahya Khan suddenly gave the boycott as an excuse to indefinitely postpone the Assembly meeting then scheduled for two days later.

The failure of West Pakistan to respond to the November disaster in East Pakistan was bad enough. Now to deny it the honest victory it had won at the polls was a political quake that rocked East Pakistan. It shattered any expectation of fair play within Pakistan's current political structure and made absolutely clear that the Bengalis would have to wrest independence from Pakistan. Within minutes of hearing General Khan's announcement canceling the Assembly meeting, in Dacca (the capital of East Pakistan),

shops, offices, restaurants and bazaars had emptied. No meeting had been announced — there was no time for it — but long lines of people were seen making their way to the Paltan Maidan, the traditional forum for public dissent. They were grimfaced and they carried bamboo poles, iron rods, hockey sticks, even coconut fronds stripped of their greenery.

Astonished foreigners, West Pakistanis among them, were witnessing a spontaneous outburst of anger the like of which could not have been achieved by a thousand anarchists spouting venom from a thousand soapboxes. The events in Dacca were repeated elsewhere in the province.

Bangla Desh was born that day in the hearts of its angry people.[3]

Bloody pro-independence demonstrations and disturbances were precipitated in East Pakistan, which the army tried to control through force. It fired on demonstrators, killing an admitted 172 but perhaps really nearer 2,000.[4] In the night, isolated soldiers were also killed by Bengalis and their weapons taken. Moreover, Bengalis attacked and massacred Biharis and other non-Bengalis suspected of supporting West Pakistan.

To the dismay of many Bengalis, Sheikh Mujibur Rahman refused to declare independence. Not only was he the unqualified leader of the Bengali masses, but he was universally seen among them as the agent of their freedom. Had he asked, hundreds of thousands would have followed him to the province's headquarters to demand the governor's surrender. Lives would have been lost, but the aroused masses and the support of mutinying Bengalis of the East Pakistan Rifles probably would have overpowered the limited military forces then in East Pakistan. Over a million lives subsequently lost to the army would have been saved, the suffering of more tens of millions avoided, and independence still achieved.

But instead of declaring independence immediately and seizing it from the government, Sheikh Mujib announced a civil disobedience movement "to achieve self-determination." He ordered a general strike against West Pakistan that was so completely obeyed that in effect the Awami League became a de facto government of East Pakistan. It issued dozens of decrees, ordered exceptions to the strike where necessary, and suspended the payment of all forms of taxes. For the Bengalis, the word of Sheikh Mujib and the league was law.

At the same time, Sheikh Mujib expressed his willingness to meet with the president of Pakistan to negotiate a new status for what was now being called Bangladesh. From Yahya Khan's perspective, the threat of a declaration of independence was imminent. This was a crisis of unanticipated severity. But plans had already been laid and a decision to act on them made. Caught between allowing Mujib to assume power over Pakistan and having East Pakistan rebel and declare its independence, Yahya and his four top Generals had met back in February and devised a simple solution to the Awami League's victory at the polls. Surely the soft and degenerate Bengalis could not stand up to the strong Punjabi with his history of military skill and valor. As General Tikka Khan declared subsequently, "Give me enough force and I'll crush them in 48 hours."[5]

The plan of the *top political and military leadership of the state of Pakistan* was to arrest Sheikh Mujib for later disposition, kill other leaders and organizers of the Awami League, arrest or kill Bengalis in the army stationed in East Pakistan, kill or arrest all the top intellectuals and Bengali civil servants working there, kill most of the university students (who provided the rationale, energy, and organization for the pro-independence demonstrations), destroy the old shanty towns and city blocks in Dacca and kill their inhabitants (a home of mass support for the Awami League), and throughout East Pakistan kill a significant number of the 10 million Hindus, forcing the rest to flee across the border into India.

All this would be launched in Dacca by surprise. No ultimatum would be given the Awami League, there would be no curfew, and the shock of West Pakistan's success and cold-blooded efficiency presumably would create terror and paralyze opposition throughout East Pakistan. At its leisure, the army could then complete its deadly task in other cities and towns. Preparations would go forward under the cover of negotiations with Mujib, and disturbances would be provoked to provide an excuse for a military buildup.[6] As with the Nazi's "Final Solution," an innocuous covering rhetoric was employed: this would be a "cleansing" operation.

On 22 February 1971, even before he indefinitely postponed the Assembly meeting, Yahya and his generals made the final decision to implement the plan.[7] From then on the secret preparations were underway, including writing down the addresses of those to be murdered, building up overwhelming military force in East Pakistan, and infiltrating a special commando group to provoke unrest. As to the smoke screen for these preparations, Yahya flew to Dacca to negotiate with Sheikh Mujib, ostensibly about a new constitution and future relations between the two sections of Pakistan. Over three weeks would be consumed by these talks — enough time to complete the air and sea movement of heavy equipment, munitions, and three divisions of West Pakistan troops to East Pakistan, and to break up and disarm the mainly Bengali army units. When done, the new governor of East Pakistan, General Tikka Kahn, would have six divisions with which to do the "cleansing."[8]

Of course, the Bengalis knew about this buildup. They agitated, demonstrated, and rioted against it. They physically tried to prevent West Pakistan ships from unloading. Thousands of Bengalis were killed as West Pakistan troops put down the demonstrations and broke through human blockades. But Mujib gave strict instructions against violence. He was determined to achieve a political settlement, if possible, through the use of nonviolence, in which he believed, and he continued to engage in fruitless talks with Yahya Kahn. But the army's preparations were obvious, and finally Sheikh Mujib warned the masses "to turn every house in East Bengal into a fortress."[9] He also established throughout the province revolutionary committees. Apparently, however, he had no contingency plans or concrete arrangements for an all-out attack by the military.

The Pakistan army was ready on March 25. President Yahya Kahn suddenly flew from Dacca to West Pakistan without notifying Sheikh Mujib. At 11 P.M. that night the army carried out its plan to the letter. Among the first targets were the Bengali East Pakistan Rifles and armed police. Some soldiers were able to put up a fight, but it was hopeless. Those caught were disarmed and slaughtered, along with any of their families that were within reach.[10] Among just the police, 4,000 to 10,000 would die in this and the following days.[11]

Other army units fanned out through the city with addresses of Awami Leaguers and supporters to be killed. Many had fled days before, however, believing that an army crackdown and arrest was imminent. Those the soldiers caught they killed, along with the wives, children, and any other relations that had been with them.

Then there was Sheikh Mujib himself, a top priority for the army. He bravely refused to go into hiding as had some other top members of the league. Even when by oversight the army neglected to attack the telephone exchange and Mujib was warned by phone that the army had launched attacks throughout the city, he still remained in his home and waited for the troops to arrive, although certain he would be shot. In the meantime, he was able to call the telegraph office and have the following declaration sent out on all wires: "The Pakistani Army has attacked police lines at Rajar Bagh and East Pakistan Army Rifles headquarters at Pilkhana at midnight. Gather strength to resist and prepare for a war of independence."[12] The civil war had begun.

Surprisingly, Sheikh Mujib was not executed but kept in isolation during subsequent events. Rather than make him a martyr, Yahya thought that once the province was "cleansed," Mujib might be a pacifying influence if given some power — under the guidance of Yahya, of course.

That first night, army units also attacked the University of Dacca. Four American-built M-2 tanks shelled student dormitories at close range, killing many men and women students.[13] Those students who survived until the morning were forced to dig mass graves for the dead and then themselves were lined up and shot.[14] The attitude of the murderers is chillingly displayed in messages intercepted between army headquarters and soldiers at the university.

What do you think would be the approximate number of casualties at the university — just give me approximate number in your view. What will be the number killed or wounded or captured? Just give me rough figures.

Wait. Approximately 300.

Well done. 300 killed? Anybody wounded or captured?

I believe only in one thing — 300 killed.

Yes. I agree with you that is much easier. No, nothing asked. Nothing done, you do not have to explain anything. Once again well done. Once again I would like to give you *shabash* and to all the boys, including Aziz, who was with you for the wonderful job done in this area. I am very pleased.[15]

The army also sought the university's leading department heads and professors, murdering thirty-two of them in the following two days.[16] Notable business leaders were also murdered, including

Jogesh Chandra Ghose, 86, an invalid chemist who was the founder of the Sadhana Ausadhalaya, a famous chemical factory of Pakistan. He was

dragged from his bed and shot by soldiers who later looted the house....
[And] Ranada Prasad Saha, 80, one of East Pakistan's leading jute
exporters and philanthropists; he had built a modern hospital offering free
medical care at Mirzapur, 40 miles north of Dacca.[17]

Civil servants were also rounded up, even those that had been
conscientious workers for Pakistan's bureaucracy. Many were tortured
and killed in concentration camps.[18]

Nor could Dacca's newspapers be ignored, of course. The army
shelled the newspaper buildings and shot anyone who ran out. Over
400 people were caught in the offices of one of the newspapers, the
daily *Ittefaq*. All died.[19]

Not all were killed according to name, address, and occupation.
People were indiscriminately shot or bayoneted on the streets. So were
those families awakened in their homes and attracted outside by the
fires.[20] But the most horrible of all was the army's attack the
following day on the poor shanty-town area of Dacca's old city. Over
1 million people lived there, along a jungle of winding narrow streets
and alleys, and they were strong supporters of Sheikh Mujib. For
twelve hours soldiers systematically razed one area of the old city or
another. Gasoline was poured around blocks and ignited. People trying
to escape the flames were shot down. Streetside squatter colonies were
especially vulnerable and were destroyed by tanks. As the massacre
proceeded, whole families were killed together. One can easily picture
the horror and panic of these poor people as they jumped from
windows or ran out of buildings and down streets and alleys to escape
the flames, bullets, and tanks.[21] It was no accident that this was
mainly a Hindu section — it was part of the plan to kill large numbers
of these "infidels" and to terrorize the rest into fleeing the province.

Overall, in the first days of slaughter in Dacca, possibly 7,000, to
10,000 civilians,[22] or 15,000 overall,[23] maybe even as many as
50,000,[24] were killed. If we just take the lower estimate of 10,000 as
the number burned to death or shot in cold blood in Dacca, this alone
would make it an incredible, premeditated act of mass murder. But
within months the death toll throughout the province would be over
100 times this number. This, done by the authorities of an
internationally recognized government.

Remember, the military had planned that their merciless purge of
Dacca would discourage resistance elsewhere. After all, there was no

effective military opposition or guerrilla movement, and the Awami League would be decapitated. Moreover, the blood bath in Dacca should have created widespread paralyzing fear of the army. And if there were a rebellion, Governor and General Tikka Khan believed that he could crush it in 72 hours. But he and Yahya Kahn badly miscalculated, for some Bengali military and police units survived and became the nucleus of resistance forces, while many other enraged Bengalis volunteered to fight for an independent Bangladesh. In a short time, the Pakistan army in East Pakistan found itself engaged in a full-fledged guerrilla war.

The atrocities committed in Dacca were more than equaled elsewhere. In particular, in what became province-wide acts of genocide,[25] Hindus were sought out and killed on the spot. As a matter of course, soldiers would check males for the obligated circumcision among Moslems. If circumcised, they might live; if not, sure death. Women and children were no less victims, but this the army would self-righteously deny. As the Pakistan journalist Anthony Mascarenhas was to hear in Comilla, "We are only killing the men; the women and children go free. We are soldiers not cowards to kill them."[26] One would think that murdering an unarmed man was a heroic act.

Buddhists and Christians also were killed because of their religion, but the soldiers were less fanatic about this. They often contented themselves with simply burning down Christian villages, as they did in Loodaria, Nalchata, and Laripara near Dacca. Even Buddhist monasteries were not exempt. In the village of Pahartali Chaumuhani, an old monastery was put to the torch, but not before troops looted its sacred and valuable possessions.[27] Even "impure" Moslems were sought out and murdered. Among imprisoned Moslems, for example, those who were unable to quote Kalma from the Koran were killed.[28]

But religion is one thing, economics another. To cripple its industrial production and assure that East Pakistan would remain a de facto colony, the army killed skilled and unskilled workers and destroyed industrial units. According to the post-independence report of the Bangladesh Government Inquiry Committee, nearly one-third of all workers were murdered.[29] Since there were nearly 2 million workers,[30] this would mean the premeditated murder of around 666,000 in just nine months.

As the soldiers advanced and consolidated control over one district or town after another, atrocities were repeated ad nauseam. Bengalis were spared no torture, no way in which their lives could not be stolen from them. Some accounts seem simply the stuff of propaganda but come from reputable sources or eyewitnesses. In a letter to *The Guardian* of London, for example, the Reverends John Hastings and John Clapham cite instances of babies tossed in the air and caught on bayonets, women bayoneted vertically, children sliced up like meat, and the heads of others smashed.[31] A correspondent of *The Daily Mirror* reported from the province that soldiers had buried two boys "in mud that came up past their noses and the crows did the rest."[32]

There was one kind of atrocity that seems unique to the Pakistani army and should be mentioned. According to *Newsweek*, an army major in the village of Haluaghat announced to assembled Bengalis that blood was needed for wounded soldiers and he requested donors. Apparently those that volunteered donated blood alright — all of it until they died.[33] This murder by blood extraction apparently happened at a number of places.

Example after example of these kinds of atrocities and massacres could be given, but let the words of Anthony Mascarenhas be their summary.

> For six days as I traveled with the officers of the 9th Division headquarters at Comilla I witnessed at close quarters the extent of the killing. I saw Hindus, hunted from village to village and door to door, shot offhand after a cursory "short-arm inspection" showed they were uncircumcised. I have heard the screams of men bludgeoned to death in the compound of the Circuit House (civil administrative headquarters) in Comilla. I have seen truckloads of other human targets and those who had the humanity to try to help them hauled off "for disposal" under the cover of darkness and curfew. I have witnessed the brutality of "kill and burn missions" as the army units after clearing out the rebels pursued the pogrom in the towns and the villages.
>
> I have seen whole villages devastated by "punitive action."
>
> And in the officers mess at night I have listened incredulously as otherwise brave and honourable men proudly chewed over the day's kill.
>
> "How many did you get ?"
>
> The answers are seared in my memory.[34]

Hundreds of thousands of Bengalis were also arrested — some for minor infractions, some for interrogation, some on suspicion, some because sabotage or attacks on soldiers had occurred within perhaps a half a mile or so. The way in which their fate was determined is well communicated by Mascarenhas.

> Sitting in the office of Major Agha, Martial Law Administrator of Comilla City, on the morning of April 19, I saw the off-hand manner in which sentences were meted out. A Bihari sub-inspector of police had walked in with a list of prisoners being held in the police lock-up. Agha looked it over. Then, with a flick of his pencil, he casually ticked off four names on the list.
>
> "Bring these four to me this evening for disposal," he said. He looked at the list again. The pencil flicked once more…. "And bring this thief along with them."
>
> The death sentence had been pronounced over a glass of coconut milk. I was informed that two of the prisoners were Hindus, the third a "student," and the fourth an Awami League organizer. The "thief," it transpired, was a lad named Sebastian who had been caught moving the household effects of a Hindu friend to his own house.
>
> Later that evening I saw these men, their hands and legs tied loosely with a single rope, being led down the road to the Circuit House compound. A little after curfew, which was at 6 o'clock, a flock of squawking mynah birds were disturbed in their play by the thwacking sound of wooden clubs meeting bone and flesh.[35]

The army even operated its own death camps. At the village of Hariharpara was one of a number blessed by nature with an automatic corpse disposal system. It was on the banks of the Buriganga River not far from Dacca. Here people could be slaughtered en masse. Those arrested or picked up in Dacca and surrounding villages — men, women, and children — would have their hands tied behind them and usually brought here in trucks. The prison itself was a large riverside warehouse that belonged to the Pakistan National Oil Company. There were no trials, no interrogation. The processing of the arrivals was simple. Seven or eight of them would be roped together, led to the river's edge, and in the light of an arc lamp forced to wade out into knee deep water. And then, from above them on a pier jutting out into the water alongside, executioners would shoot down on the starkly lighted forms. Group upon group would be so executed. In the morning, boatmen hooked and dragged the roped clusters of bodies out to midstream and cut the ropes to allow the individual bodies to float downstream.[36] In this one place possibly 20,000 people were murdered[37] — a toll equivalent to the crashing of 100 jumbo airliners. Similar camps operated elsewhere along the banks of East Pakistan's rivers.

Throughout the province, the army practiced a simple technique of pacification. As used in Dacca that first horrible day, soldiers would surround a hamlet, village, town, or city block. Then, whether slums or thatched huts or residential houses, they would pour gasoline around the homes, ignite it, and shoot or bayonet people trying to escape the flames.[38] Thus, in the district of Comilla the army burned down Dhaleswar and other villages. It burned nine villages in the Manickganj subdivision and killed an estimated 300 people. In Tripura, it burned down more villages and killed many of their residents. In Rajshahi, eye witnesses reported that soldiers used flame throwers on people to burn them to death and shot those trying to escape their burning houses.[39]

The Pakistan military even massed its heavy weapons to pour death and destruction on unarmed Bengali civilians. Cities and towns were reduced to rubble by artillery and tank fire, shelling by warships off shore, and bombing by the air force. Even major cities, such as Chittagong, Khulna Comilla, Jessore, Rangpur, Rajshahi, Mymensingh, and Sylhet, were not exempt; nor were hospitals and medical centers within them; nor were churches, temples, and mosques.[40] Reportedly napalm was also used, such as against Sylhet and villagers of Nurnagar.[41] Often after such attacks the soldiers would occupy the devastated area, rape and kill those who had survived and could not run away, and loot what valuables they could find, including from banks and jewelry shops.

The Pakistan army also systematically continued to search for and murder Awami League members and supporters. An official postwar accounting by the new Bangladesh government found that 17,000 members of the league were killed.[42] Even those whose only crime was to have voted for the league were at risk. At a tea estate, for example, Pakistan troops asked people whom they had voted for and shot 200 of those who, apparently unaware of the consequences, said the Awami League.[43]

No sooner had the army taken over areas of the country than it found its logistics subject to attacks and its small army units ambushed. Bridges were downed, warehouses blown up, roads blocked, and convoys machine-gunned. Army reprisals were Draconian. In one instance, after sabotage near Dacca, soldiers went to a suburb over a mile away and shot anyone they saw — 200 people.[44]

The cold-blooded nature of this and other killings is told by Mascarenhas, for whom the following colloquy with a Pakistan major over the imminent killing of a prisoner, Abdul Bari, was the final straw leading to his seeking refuge in England and the writing and publication of his exposé on Pakistan's democide.

Abdul Bari had run out of luck. Like thousands of other people in East Bengal, he had made the mistake — the fatal mistake — of running within sight of a Pakistani army patrol.

He was 24 years old, a slight man surrounded by soldiers. He was trembling, because he was about to be shot.

"Normally we would have killed him as he ran," I was informed chattily by Major Rathore, the G-2 Ops. of the 9th Division, as we stood on the outskirts of a tiny village near Mudafarganj, about 20 miles south of Comilla. "But we are checking him out for your sake. You are new here and I see you have a squeamish stomach."

"Why kill him ?" I asked with mounting concern.

"Because he might be a Hindu or he might be a rebel, perhaps a student or an Awami Leaguer. They know we are sorting them out and they betray themselves by running."

"But why are you killing them? And why pick on the Hindus?" I persisted.

"Must I remind you." Rathore said severely, "how they have tried to destroy Pakistan? Now under the cover of the fighting we have an excellent opportunity of finishing them off."[45]

Like the Japanese during World War II and the Red Army in its victorious march through Eastern Europe in 1945, the West Pakistanis were singularly devoted to raping any women in sight. Many were repeatedly raped in their homes or on the streets and then killed. Many were taken to military installations where they were kept and raped repeatedly, in some cases until they died. According to one report, for example, 700 naked women were liberated from the army cantonment at Moinamati.[46] Of those women that survived the war, perhaps 200,000 or more may have been raped, at least according to a postwar figure that gained wide currency.[47]

As the army's program of fire and death laid waste to towns and villages, millions of terrorized Bengalis sought refuge across the border in India. There, these miserable people wandered across fields, slept under trees and in schools, collected and squatted on hills and along rivers and roads, hopelessly begged villagers and passersby for food and help, and struggled to survive. The Indian government tried to help. By July it had set up 650 refugee camps, 633 State Transit camps, and seventeen Central Transit Camps, all striving with the help of international organizations to care for an impossible 7 million refugees. They could not, of course, and many refugees died from exposure and disease, especially cholera. As estimated by relief workers, the death toll at one point reached 1,000 a day.[48] The monsoon rains did not help. As told by Mathis Bromberger, a German doctor helping at one of these camps,

> there were thousands of people standing out in the open here all night in the rain. Women were with babies in their arms. They could not lie down because the water came up to their knees in places. There was not enough shelter and in the morning there were always many sick and dying of pneumonia. We could not get out serious cholera cases to the hospital. And there was no one to take away the dead. They just lay around on the ground or in the water. High pressure syringes have speeded vaccination and reduced the cholera threat, but camp health officials have already counted about 500 dead and an estimated 35,000 have been stricken by the convulsive vomiting and diarrhea that accompany the diseases. Now officials fear that pneumonia, diphtheria and tuberculosis will also begin to take a toll among the weakened refugees.[49]

Senator Edward Kennedy toured some of these camps and on return to Washington reported at a press conference what he saw.

> You see infants with their skin hanging loosely in folds from their tiny bones — lacking the strength even to lift their hands. You see children with legs and feet swollen with oedema and malnutrition, limp in the arms

of their mothers. You see babies going blind for lack of vitamins, or covered with sores that will not heal. You see in the eyes of their parents the despair of ever having their children well again. And, most difficult of all, you see the corpse of the child who died just the night before.[50]

That millions of these poor people, mainly Hindus, fled to India was as planned. This would reduce the population of East Pakistan to less than that in West Pakistan and eliminate the infidels.

But what the military did not anticipate was the wide-scale resistance in East Pakistan and the military support India gave to it. Flooded by millions of refugees in just four months, the Indian government suddenly was faced with feeding and caring for the equivalent of a nation the size of Austria. Moreover, as amply and vividly reported in Indian and international newspapers at the time, West Pakistan was clearly guilty of genocide against the Hindus and mass murder of the Bengalis. Finally, West Pakistan was India's traditional enemy against whom she had already fought two wars in a generation. She could hardly be unhappy over the prospect of a divided Pakistan.

Soon after the Dacca massacre, India began to provide rifles, ammunition, and light equipment to the Bengalis along the length of her long border with East Pakistan. Moreover, she provided extensive training to guerrillas. All this did more than help — it was critical. By November, the rebel guerrillas — called Mukti Bahini (freedom army) — had wrested from the army control over 25 percent of East Pakistan,[51] a success that led the Pakistan army to seek out those especially likely to join the resistance — young boys. Sweeps were conducted of young men who were never seen again. Bodies of youths would be found in fields, floating down rivers, or near army camps. As can be imagined, this terrorized all young men and their families within reach of the army. Most between the ages of fifteen and twenty-five began to flee from one village to another and toward India. Many of those reluctant to leave their homes were forced to flee by mothers and sisters concerned for their safety.[52]

As the civil war progressed, India not only provided training and military aid to the Mukti Bahini, but in November engaged Pakistani troops and forced them out of some border areas. Moreover, India warned Yahya Kahn that if she were attacked the war would be fought on Pakistani territory. Clearly, India had become an active participant.

And the threat had teeth. An attack on India would be difficult; a defense against her even more so. Pakistan had a one-to-three inferiority in arms, and its troops in East Pakistan were tired from a civil war with what had become an armed and organized liberation army of 100,000 guerrillas.[53] But Yahya Kahn thought he would have at least the political support of the United States and China in any war with India. Indeed, secret discussions within the U.S. administration revealed that President Nixon favored the Pakistanis. Accordingly, U.S. heavy armaments continued to be supplied to Pakistan, in spite of public denials and the massacres in East Pakistan .

Seeing by December 3 that war with India was all but certain, and modeling its attack on India after Israel's successful preemptive strike that began the 1967 Israel-Arab War, Pakistan launched simultaneous surprise bombing strikes on India's major air bases. India was surprised alright, but pleasantly so. The attacks did not seriously weaken her military capability, and she could now pursue with all force the liberation of East Pakistan. India had been planning this since mid-November anyway,[54] but now it could be vigorously pursued under the cover of a wider Indo-Pakistan War that Pakistan clearly was guilty of starting.

While meeting and holding Pakistan's forces on her western border, India invaded East Pakistan. For its defense, the Pakistani army had nearly 100,000 weary soldiers, which were no match for the combined forces of the Bengali Mukti Bahini and the fresh well-supplied Indian army of over 200,000 troops. As a result, the Indian army advanced rapidly into East Pakistan and by 16 December surrounded Dacca. Hopelessly outnumbered, Pakistani forces in East Pakistan surrendered the next day.

But first the Pakistani army had to carry out one final act of frustration and vengeance. With lists in hand, soldiers and paramilitary forces sought out hundreds of Bengali intellectuals that for one reason or another they had so far allowed to survive. Those they picked up in Dacca, Khulna, and Sylhet, among other places, they savagely tortured and murdered, some 250 in Dacca alone,[55] perhaps 2,000 overall.[56] Among the more gruesome mutilations, "The heart of a heart-specialist was taken out, the eyes of an eye-specialist were extracted, the fingers of a writer were chopped off and the throat of an artist was cut."[57]

One of the conditions of Pakistan's surrender in East Pakistan was the formal recognition of Bangladesh's independence. In short time Sheikh Mujibur Rahman was released from prison and returned triumphantly to Bangladesh. Destruction in the country was vast; property losses alone amounted to 60 percent of Bangladesh's Gross Domestic Product.[58] According to a UN report, the Pakistani army had leveled most of rural Bangladesh — 70 percent of its villages were destroyed.[59]

But most of all, the human death toll over only 267 days was incredible. Just to give for five out of the eighteen districts some incomplete statistics published in Bangladesh newspapers or by an Inquiry Committee, the Pakistani army killed 100,000 Bengalis in Dacca, 150,000 in Khulna, 75,000 in Jessore, 95,000 in Comilla, and 100,000 in Chittagong. For eighteen districts the total is 1,247,000 killed.[60] This was an incomplete count, and to this day no one really knows the final toll. Some estimates of the democide are much lower — one is of 300,000 dead[61] — but most range from 1 million[62] to 3 million.[63] In a David Frost television interview, Sheikh Mujib himself claimed that 3 million had been killed.[64] Based on these and other estimates, it is likely that 300,000 to 3,000,000 men, women, and children were murdered, most probably the 1,500,000 given in table 13.1.

As the democide rates in table 13.1 show, the Pakistani army and allied paramilitary groups killed about one out of every sixty-one people in Pakistan overall; one out of every twenty-five Bengalis, Hindus, and others in East Pakistan. If the rate of killing for all of Pakistan is annualized over the years the Yahya martial law regime was in power (March 1969 to December 1971), then this one regime was more lethal than that of the Soviet Union, China under the communists, or Japan under the military (even through World War II). That is, Yahya Kahn, a name still largely unknown outside of Pakistan and Bangladesh, killed in cold blood proportionally per year more people than Lenin, Stalin, or Mao Tse-tung. Of course, he must bow to Hitler and Pol Pot.

Sadly, our consideration of the democide in East Pakistan does not stop here. The Bengalis themselves were responsible for the wide-scale killing of Biharis and others, particularly those speaking Urdu (a minority but official literary language of West Pakistan). Non-Bengalis numbered 5 to 6 million[65] and, as the fierce demonstrations and protests for independence peaked in March, as the general strike against West Pakistan became absolute, non-Bengalis were seen as Pakistan supporters, spies, and anti-Bangladesh. Even before the army launched its massacre in Dacca, non-Bengalis were being attacked and killed by mutinous Bengali troops, police, and armed Awami League supporters. For example, the approximately 40 percent of the East Pakistan Rifles that consisted of non-Bengalis were isolated and killed.[66]

Throughout East Pakistan, non-Bengali communities were assaulted, their members mutilated, tortured, and butchered. Let the words of Mascarenhas, whose vigorous condemnation of the Pakistan democide in East Pakistan established his credentials, speak to this:

> Thousands of families of unfortunate [Bihari] Muslims ... were mercilessly wiped out. Women were raped, or had their breasts torn out with specially-fashioned knives. Children did not escape the horror: the lucky ones were killed with their parents; but many thousands of others must go through what life remains for them with eyes gouged out and limbs roughly amputated. More than 20,000 bodies of non-Bengalis have been found in the main towns, such as Chittagong, Khulna and Jessore. The real

TABLE 13.1
Pakistan Dead, March-December 1971 [a]

Type of Killing	Dead (000)	Democide Rates (%) [d]	
		Overall	Annual
War/Rebellion [b]	75		
Democide	1,650		
By Pakistan army [c]	1,500		
All Pakistan	1,500	1.64	.58
East Pakistan	1,500	4.00	
By Awami League	150	.20	
Total Dead	1,725		

a All figures are from *Statistics of Democide* and are mid-values in a low-high range. Values may not sum due to rounding.

b Figure for civil and international Pakistan war dead, excluding democide.

c Includes democidal famine/disease and military action (e.g., bombing).

d Annual rate is for March 1969-December 1971, the life of the Yahya Khan Regime.

toll, I was told everywhere in East Bengal, may have been as high as 100,000; for thousands of non-Bengalis have vanished without a trace.[67]

Nor was it possible for these non-Bengalis to show their allegiance and join the guerrillas. They were outcasts and were to be killed. Particularly chilling is the report by the journalist Peter Hazelhurst of what Bengali Major Osman Choudhury of the East Pakistan Rifles said in a meeting with journalists, "If we get a Bihari, we kill him. We are also raiding their houses and killing them."[68]

There is no need here to give examples of the horrible atrocities afflicted on these people — brutalities that matched in sadistic imagination and inhuman cruelty that which was being carried out by the army on Bengalis. Suffice to point out that in March alone perhaps over 5,000 non-Bengalis were brutally killed in Dacca,[69] over 50,000 in Chittagong,[70] between 12,000 to 20,000 in Jessore,[71] and over 5,000 in Rangpur,[72] just to mention a few places. In April and throughout the war, the killing continued. And after the Pakistani army launched its democide, the Bengalis also exterminated with "gusto"[73] those accused of collaborating with the army.

Rather than being democide, was not this simply unpremeditated, nongovernment communal mob violence that has so often inflicted this part of the world? The answer lies in the role of the Awami League. When Sheikh Mujibur Rahman initiated his campaign of nonviolence against West Pakistan, his Awami League became a government parallel to that which already existed in East Pakistan. It issued decrees, gave orders, and, most important, was obeyed. The civil service operated under the command of the league. Taxes were collected by it.[74] Moreover, in obedience to the Awami League, East Pakistan's chief justice would not give the oath of office to the newly commissioned military governor, General Tikka Khan. West Pakistan's rule did not extend beyond its military camps and bayonets.

While it is also clear that violent actions taken against non-Bengalis were contrary to Sheikh Mujib's orders,[75] nonetheless much of the killing was done by those ostensibly under the command of the Awami League — mutinous Bengalis of the East Pakistan Rifles, police, and armed Awami League members and supporters. No doubt much mob action by fanatic Bengali nationalists also occurred, and armed volunteers and some officers of the league did try to prevent violence.[76] But those Bengalis who had the arms and should have prevented the violence or protected the non-Bengalis often did not. Sheikh was not fully in control of the events he put in motion nor the Awami League "government" he had set up. The mass-murder of the non-Bengalis is therefore the responsibility of the Awami League and should be considered genocide. Regardless of status, sex, age, or past support of the league, people were killed simply because they were Biharis or other non-Bengalis, often by those very people who exercised local authority and to whom the victims had looked for law and order.[77]

In total, probably 50,000 to 500,000 non-Bengalis, including at least 5,000 collaborators, were thus killed. As given in table 13.1, a prudent estimate is that the Bengalis murdered about 150,000 people overall.

This massive bloodletting by all parties in Bangladesh affected its politics for the following decades. The country has experienced military coup after military coup, some of them bloody. Because of corruption and incompetence in Sheikh Mujib's government and his assumption of authoritarian rule, he became a most hated public figure. Not without cheers, he and his family were killed in one of these coups in 1975. General Zia Moshtaque, who took over from him, survived all but the last of twenty-one coups and mutinies. Moreover, these changing Bangladesh regimes also have been responsible for democide. For example, from 1972 to August 1974, 6,000 political opponents were murdered.[78]

One serious question has been left hanging. Why did the ruling elite of Pakistan embark on a cold, calculating democide of its fellow citizens in East Pakistan? Indeed, how is that its officers and soldiers would carry this out with dispatch and proudly ask each other in their mess at night "How many did you get?"[79] They even kept a record of who had scored best.[80]

First, there were critical differences between the two parts of Pakistan. They were in fact distinct nations, different in language, dress, food, fashion, sports, and, fundamentally, ethnicity. Moreover, West Pakistan saw itself as a Moslem nation and part of the Middle East; East Pakistan identified with Southeast Asia. Easterners and Westerners apparently found little in common; friendships and marriages were infrequent between them. Even the Moslem religion, which one would think would have united them, was looked at differently. Many West Pakistanis believed that the culture in East Pakistan was in fact a Hindu culture,[81] that Bengali Moslems were only relatively recent converts to Islam, and that their faith was skin deep — that they were in reality heretics, Hindus in disguise. This was in fact one of the justifications given soldiers for killing them.[82] Among the largely Punjabi soldiers doing the killing, Bengalis were therefore a group not only beyond their moral universe but subhuman and deserving of brutal treatment and death. Bengalis were often compared with monkeys and chickens. Said Pakistan General Niazi, "It was a low lying land of low lying people."[83] The Hindus among the Bengalis were as Jews to the Nazis: scum and vermin that best be exterminated. As to the Moslem Bengalis, they were to live only on the sufferance of the soldiers: any infraction, any suspicion cast on them, any need for reprisal, could mean their death. And the soldiers were free to kill at will. The journalist Dan Coggin quoted one Punjabi captain as telling him, "We can kill anyone for anything. We are accountable to no one."[84] This is the arrogance of Power.

And power was the major factor that set all this killing in motion. East Pakistan was challenging the comfortable structure of power that existed among the military, politicians, and government bureaucracy. West Pakistan was caught between accepting the outcome of the election and the governance of the hated Awami League of East Pakistan and inferior Bengalis, and secession of the province. In one case, she would lose personal power to lesser men; in the other, power over resources and men. Since the East Pakistani were scum worthy of no moral consideration, the elite could without compunction plan on a third solution: genocide, mass murder, and repression of all secessionists and opposition elements. The president of Pakistan, Yahya Kahn, and his coterie of generals, were dictators. They had the power to kill indiscriminately without fear of being brought before a national or international court. Their power was threatened by infidels 1,000 miles away. The democide followed. As senior military and civil officers told Mascarenhas over and over again,

We are determined to cleanse East Pakistan once and for all of the threat of secession, even if it means killing off two million people and ruling the province as a colony for 30 years.[85]

Notes

1. Mascarenhas 1971, 20.
2. Payne 1973, 9–10.
3. Mascarenhas 1971, 91.
4. Blood 1972, 30.
5. Mascarenhas 1971, 95.
6. On this plan see Chowdhury 1972, 142; Payne 1973, 13; Muhith 1978, 219–20, 224; and Chandra 1971, 139, 145.
7. Payne 1973, 13.
8. Muhith 1978, 219.
9. Mascarenhas 1971, 116.
10. See Chaudhuri 1972, 103.
11. Chowdhury 1972, 99.
12. Payne 1973, 24.
13. Ibid., 16.
14. Muhith 1978, 222.
15. Mohan 1971, 26, from The Times of India News Service.
16. Chowdhury 1972, 99.
17. Chaudhuri 1972, 25.
18. Ibid., 105.
19. Chowdhury 1972, 101.
20. Chandra 1971, 141.
21. See Muhith 1978, 222–23 and Chaudhuri 1972, 25.
22. Chowdhury 1972, 98.
23. Chaudhuri 1972, 31.
24. Muhith 1978, 223.
25. See The International Commission of Jurists 1972, 57.
26. Mascarenhas 1971, 116.
27. Chowdhury 1972, 114.
28. Chaudhuri 1972, 68.
29. Ibid., 137.
30. Ibid., 137n.
31. Chowdhury 1972, 106.
32. Ibid.
33. Ibid., 107–8.
34. Mascarenhas 1972, 120.
35. Ibid., 124.
36. Payne 1973, 55–56; Chowdhury 1972, 121–22.
37. Chowdhury 1972, 122.
38. Ibid., 103.
39. Ibid., 104n. 58.
40. Chaudhuri 1972, 104.
41. Chowdhury 1972, 101.
42. Payne 1973, 58.
43. Quaderi 1972, 151.
44. Mohan 1971, 6.
45. Mascarenhas 1972, 116–17.

46. Chowdhury 1972, 121.
47. See Muhith 1978, 234, and Chaudhuri 1972, 22.
48. Chaudhuri 1972, 78–79.
49. Ibid., 86.
50. Ibid., 87.
51. Payne 1973, 59.
52. Rafiq-Ul-Islam 1981, 183.
53. Muhith 1978, 251.
54. Sisson and Rose 1990, 214.
55. Muhith 1978, 238.
56. The International Commission of Jurists 1972, 44–45.
57. Muhith 1978, 238.
58. Ibid., 238–39.
59. Chaudhuri 1972, 6.
60. Ibid., 199–202.
61. Sisson and Rose 1990, 306n. 24.
62. Eckhardt 1989, 95; Chaudhuri 1972, 22.
63. Muhith 1978, 238; Payne 1973, 29.
64. Chowdhury 1972, 124.
65. *Terror in East Pakistan* n.d., 10–11.
66. Ibid., 4.
67. Mascarenhas 1972, 118.
68. *Terror in East Pakistan* n.d., 11 (italics omitted).
69. Aziz 1974, 15.
70. Ibid., 48.
71. Ibid., 160.
72. Ibid., 150.
73. Muhith 1978, 253.
74. Chaudhuri 1972, 14.
75. Mascarenhas 1971, 104.
76. Muhith 1978, 201.
77. See Aziz 1974, 219.
78. Ahamed 1988, 63.
79. Mascarenhas 1972, 120.
80. Mascarenhas 1971, 118.
81. Mascarenhas 1972, 122.
82. Payne 1973, 53.
83. Muhith 1978, 233–34.
84. Ibid., 225.
85. Mascarenhas 1971, 117; 1972, 118.

14

1,072,000 Murdered
Tito's Slaughterhouse

> *Tito cried out in disgust to his Central Committee:*
> *"Enough of all these death sentences and all this*
> *killing! The death sentence no longer has any effect!*
> *No one fears death anymore!"*
>
> —Milovan Djilas, *Wartime* (449)

No other country suffered during World War II as did Yugoslavia — from diverse foreign occupations, guerrilla and fratricidal warfare, and cold-blooded genocide and mass murder. Invaded in April of 1941 by Nazi Germany, the campaign was brief and particularly savage in line with Hitler's demand that it be done "with unmerciful harshness in order to destroy Yugoslavia militarily and as a national entity."[1] The unprotected capital of Belgrade was indiscriminately bombed, killing from 4,000 to 20,000 people,[2] possibly even 25,000.[3]

In twelve days Yugoslavia was defeated and an armistice signed, at the cost of 151 German[4] and 5,000 Yugoslav battle dead.[5] The Nazis then occupied Serbia, Banat, and over half of Slovenia, while the other regions of the country were annexed or occupied by Hungary, Rumania, Bulgaria, Italy, and Albania. The Nazis also permitted the fascist and terrorist Croat Ante Pavelic and his nationalist Ustashi Party to set up the puppet Independent State of Croatia (in the beginning really a de facto Italian protectorate until Italy's collapse in 1943, after which the Nazis assumed full control). Besides prewar Croatia, the Independent State included the Serbian provinces of Bosnia and Herzegovina, and the districts of Srem and Lika. This carved a region of some 6,250,000 people out of Yugoslavia's 16 million. Almost 40 percent of Croatia consisted of Serbs, which, as we shall see, would later have deadly consequences.

Guerrilla war against the occupying Nazi forces began almost immediately. In the beginning it was carried out by guerrillas led by a colonel on the General Staff of the Yugoslav army, Dragoljub-Draza Mihailovic. Called Chetniks (an official prewar force of volunteers and irregulars trained for warfare behind enemy lines), these guerrillas were largely Serbian, anticommunist, nationalist, and royalist. In the beginning, Mihailovic led one of three Chetnik groups. Of the other two, one supported the Nazi puppet government while the other tended to support the communists. After a fact-finding tour of resistance forces by a joint British-Yugoslav mission, Mihailovic was recognized by the British in October 1941 as the overall Chetnik leader.

The communists had never been an important force in prewar Yugoslavia. The defeat and occupation changed all that. Led by Josip Broz Tito, their secretary general since 1937, the communists were at first inhibited in opposing the Nazi occupation. This was the result of the Hitler-Stalin Pact of 1939. After all, the Soviet Union was a de facto German ally, having divided Poland with the Nazis and continuing to supply the Nazis with raw materials. The communists did, however, prepare for an armed uprising if war were to break out between the two, as it did in June 1941. Then the Comintern called for communists to defend the Soviet Union and defeat fascism; the Yugoslav communists broadcast a call to arms on 4 July and formed a partisan force of their own under Tito. While in the beginning there was some attempt at cooperation between Mihailovic's Chetniks and Tito's partisans, and they did in fact engage in some operations together, they soon were involved in a deadly war against each other, even while fighting the Nazis, other occupying armies, and Ustashi troops. These nationalist and ideological conflicts were aggravated and channeled by historical ethnic and religious animosities and grievances among Slovenes, Croats, Serbs, Montenegrins, Roman Catholics, Eastern Orthodox, and Moslems.

The Nazi occupation of Yugoslavia was savage and genocidal. As is noted in chapter 6, the Nazis killed whatever Jews or Gypsies they could find, executed intellectuals, resisters, communists, and potential opponents, and tens of thousands of hostages and innocent people in retaliation for attacks on Germans. Overall, they murdered from nearly 500,000 to over 830,000 Yugoslavs,[6] probably 625,000, as shown in table 14.1.

Nor were the Hungarian, Italian, and the other occupying armies free of bloodied hands. The Hungarians, particularly, were guilty of

TABLE 14.1
Democide in Yugoslavia

Nation/Group	Years	Democide [a]
Yugoslavian Nation/Groups		
Tito Government	1944–87	1,072,000
Tito Partisans	1941–44	100,000
Total Communist	1941–87	1,172,000
Chetniks	1941–45	100,000
Croat Government	1941–45	655,000
subtotal	1941–87	1,927,000
Occupying Nations		
Nazis	1941–45	625,000
Italians	1941–45	5,000 [b]
Bulgarians	1941–45	10,000 [b]
Hungarians	1941–45	78,000
subtotal	1941–45	718,000
Totals		
Democide	1941–87	2,645,000
Democide	1941–45	2,073,000
Battle dead	1941–45	555,000

a Most prudent estimate in a range of low and high estimates. Data is from *Statistics of Democide*
b This is a low.

massacres no less horrible and barbaric than those of the Nazis. In the town of Novi Sad, for example, during January 1942 possibly some 4,000 Jews and 6,000 Serbs were killed by a "rampaging" Hungarian General Feketehalmi-Zeisler;[7] possibly even more than 15,000 people were slaughtered in the town and vicinity.[8] In total, the Hungarian army probably massacred 66,000 to over 90,000 Yugoslavs.

As large as the number of Jews, Gypsies, Serbs, and others murdered by the Nazis and their allies, as totaled in table 14.1, this toll is almost matched by the new Ustashi regime of Croatia. It rapidly put in place a number of anti-Jewish laws modeled on those of Germany, and in order to facilitate the deportation of Jews to the Nazi extermination camps, it agreed to pay the Nazis blood money of thirty Reichmarks per Jew deported to them.[9] Not content with this, the Ustashi also set about killing any Jews that fell into their own hands, often in a barbaric manner even sickening to Nazi observers. In total, they likely murdered around 28,000 Jews.

Gypsies also were hated and pursued, with probably nearly the same number massacred,[10] or virtually the entire minority.[11]

While this genocide was only limited by the relatively small population of Jews and Gypsies, there was no such natural limit to massacring the Orthodox Serbs, who constituted a population of 2 million[12] or more[13] in Croatia. The Roman Catholic Ustashi set about to brutally murder them, sometimes after vicious torture; they were slaughtered like pigs, burned to death in their churches, hunted down individually and shot, and hung, cut, or sawed to death; they suffered every device to cause pain and steal their life. To give some examples:

> At Korenica hundreds of persons were killed but before they died many of them had their ears and noses cut off and then they were compelled to graze in the meadow. The tortures the most frequently applied were beatings, severing of limbs, goring of eyes and breaking of bones. Cases are related of men being forced to hold red-hot bricks, dance on barbed wire with naked feet and wear a wreath of thorns. Needles were stuck in fingers under the nails, and lighted matches held under their noses.

> Of the murders on the large scale in the village of Korito 103 peasants were severely tortured, tied in bundles and thrown in a pit ... then gasoline was poured over all the bodies and ignited.[14]

Much of such horrible killing was done in Ustashi death camps, particularly Jasehovac. Perhaps about 100,000 Serbs and political opponents were murdered there (Yugoslavia officially claimed 700,000).[15] The flavor of this was communicated by the Chilean minister in Belgrade, who personally checked out this report of atrocities broadcast by a Belgrade network and attests to its accuracy. One eleven-year-old Serbian Orthodox girl was captured while her family escaped to Belgrade and taken to the Jasehovac camp.

The first days our heroine passed in the camp were terrifying. No war, no shelter, no bed, no roof. She was obliged to sleep in the rain on the snow. At first she still possessed her own clothes, but these, too, the Ustashi took. Without clothes and famished, she began her descent into the hell beyond Dante's dreams. The daily "Our Father" was replaced by the formula: give us our daily beating.

This child one day attended a cruel spectacle. Forty students were smothered and then burnt. Another time, the Ustashi drove a hot iron rod into a man's head. Sometimes women were quartered, and to vary the spectacle, arms instead of legs, were torn off.

There were, of course, other diversions for the Ustashi. The best of these diversions consisted of gouging out the eyes of the dying so as to make a "beautiful" collection of how the dying look.

Our heroine passed two whole days bound to a tree. To be more certain that she did not escape, her hair was attached to the trunk. Another time she hung for four hours, head down. Then for two hours she was tied by her hair to a branch where she swung back and forth. Another time she was left head down where she was kept hanging for a whole day. Her hair was also tied to her feet and she was obliged to remain in this position for an entire night. Sometimes, for a change, the Ustashi made a sort of trestle with red hot iron, and forced the children to sit on it astride.

Other torments existed for the adults, befitting their age. Among many was the woman who was about to give birth to a child. The Ustashi played the role of mid-wife, as well as that of the executioner, thrusting the knife into the mother's womb, they extracted the child and put a cat in its place.[16]

The Ustashi soon found that killing and disposing of millions of Serbs was less easy than they thought. They also tried to deport hundreds of thousands to Serbia, which the Nazis opposed at first. But by agreeing to accept Slovenians from annexed Slovenia in return, they managed to expel 200,000 Serbs in the first year before the Nazis stopped it.[17] Consistently, this was done with great cruelty and loss of life. They also sought to forcibly convert remaining Serbs from their Orthodox faith to Catholicism. Often a Serb was faced with three choices: immediate and possibly very painful death, deportation with the loss of all possessions and possibly one's life, or giving up one's faith.

As mentioned, all this was premeditated acts of the fascist Croatian state. It was genocide pure and simple. Croatian rulers, which included at the highest levels the Croatian Catholic hierarchy, some of whom actually participated in the killing, were determined to fully Catholicize and homogenize Croatia (as the Moslem Young Turks during World War I tried to homogenize Turkey by slaughtering all the Christian Armenians and Greeks). Said one Ustashi priest, the Reverend Dijonizije Jurichev,

> In this country, nobody can live except Croatians. We know very well how to deal with those that oppose conversion [to the Roman Catholic faith]. I personally have put an end to whole provinces, killing everyone — chicks and men alike. It gives me no remorse to kill a small child when he stands in the path of the Ustasha.[18]

The Croatian governor of western Bosnia made clear that his was official policy. In a speech, he proclaimed that "all undesirable elements will be exterminated so that no trace will remain." In a meeting the next day he clarified what this meant:

> The highways will be waiting for the Serbs to pass, but the Serbs will be no more there! I have published drastic orders for their total economic destruction, and other orders will follow for their complete annihilation. Do not be weak toward any one of them.... Destroy them wherever you get a chance, and the blessing of our Leaders and mine will be upon you.[19]

However, the most telling insight into the fanatic and bestial nature of this regime comes from the personal experience of the Italian author Curzio Malaparte. During a visit in Zagreb to Ante Pavelic, president of the Ustashi government, Pavelic said, "The Croatian people wish to be ruled with goodness and justice. And I am here to provide them." While he spoke, Malaparte noticed a wicker basket on Pavelic's desk, with the lid slightly raised. It looked like it was full of mussels, or shelled oysters. Malaparte asked if in fact these were Dalmatian oysters. Then, according to Malaparte, "Ante Pavelich removed the lid from the basket and revealed the mussels, that slimy and jellylike mass, and he said, smiling with that good-natured smile of his, 'It is a present from my loyal Ustachis. Forty pounds of human eyes.'"[20]

How many Serbs were thus murdered is in great dispute. Hitler's troubleshooter in the Balkans, Hermann Neubacher, put the dead at 750,000 overall.[21] Tito claimed the number killed (which he attributed to the Nazis) to be at least 500,000 in three months of 1941;[22] Chetnik estimates were 600,000 to 800,000,[23] with Mihailovic[24] himself preferring the 600,000 estimate as of late 1942; and Serbian estimates give the toll as 750,000.[25] Some of the killers themselves thought they murdered 1 million.[26] After considering over two dozen such estimates,[27] I conservatively calculate that probably 600,000 were murdered altogether. This was 25 to 30 percent of all Serbs in Croatian hands.

When the number of Jews and Gypsies murdered is included, the overall genocide was probably 655,000 (as listed in table 14.1) — about 10 percent of Croatia's population; one person out of every forty in the Croatian state per year. As shown in table 14.2, this is more than twice the democide risk for Europeans, including Jews, living under Nazi occupation; and much greater still than the risk of being killed by their own government of citizens living in the Soviet Union or communist China, or of those living under Japanese occupation during World War II. The Croatian fascist regime was proportionally the deadliest during the war and among the most lethal in this century.

Were the sorry story of Yugoslav democide to end here, it would be human catastrophe enough during the war years. But then we have yet to consider the democide of the Chetniks and partisans. During their guerrilla war against the Nazis and partisans, the Chetniks, mainly made up of Serbs, often retaliated against the Croatian genocide by carrying out their own massacres of Croats in Bosnia, Herzegovina, Dalmatia, and elsewhere.[28] Although Mihailovic unsuccessfully tried to prevent any general mass murder of Croats by Chetnik units, he had no sympathy for the Ustashi. In a December 1942 telegram, he declared that "we are exterminating Ustachi whenever we find them."[29] Moslems were also a favorite target. In southeastern Bosnia, particularly about the town of Foca, from December 1941 to January 1942 the Chetniks carried out a number of massacres, likely killing over 2,000 Moslems; and from January to February 1943, 10,000 Moslems were massacred in southeastern Bosnia, including Sandjak.[30] Then there were those partisans, and also Nazis, Italians, and other occupiers, who were taken prisoner. They were usually killed out of hand or after interrogation. Perhaps overall more than 50,000 Croatians, communists, Moslems, and other prisoners were killed by Chetnik forces; possibly 100,000 of them.

To consider now the communist partisans. As mentioned, in the two months of occupation before the invasion of the Soviet Union, the communists did little against the Nazis. They devoted their major efforts to liquidating those hostile to communism, such as murdering several hundred Russian émigrés.[31] After the invasion of the Soviet Union, the partisans took up arms against the Nazis and their allies, including the Ustashi and Slovenian fascists. But their first priority

TABLE 14.2
Comparison of Yugoslavian Democide and Democide Rates

Nation	Years	Democide	Democide Rates [a]	
			Overall	Annual
USSR [b]	1917–87	54,769,000	29.64	.45
Communist China [c]	1949–87	35,236,000	4.49	.12
Nazi Europe [d]	1933–45	20,946,000	5.46	.91
Nationalist China [c]	1928–49	10,214,000	1.24	.18
Japanese Asia [e]	1937–45	5,890,000	0.99	.27
Tito Government [f]	**1944–87**	**1,072,000**	**5.55**	**.12**
Croatia [f]	**1941–45**	**655,000**	**10.48**	**2.50**

a The overall rate is the democide as the percentage of the mid-year population. The annual rate is the overall rate divided by the number of years over which the democide as calculated.

b Citizens only. From Rummel 1990, table 1.1.

c From Rummel 1991, table 1.A. Nationalist rates are the average of three periods.

d From Rummel 1992, table A. Rates are average of 1929–37, 1937–45, and 1945–49 periods.

e From *Statistics of Democide*.

f From *Statistics of Democide*.

remained winning the politico-military war over who would control Yugoslavia after the defeat of the Nazis. They thus continued to target anticommunists and other opponents and fought an off-and-on war against the Chetniks and other domestic enemies in the first year or so. In some cases they would attack Chetnik forces rather than Nazis (as they were sometimes similarly attacked by the Chetniks). And in Slovenia, where the partisans mainly operated, there was a widely acknowledged general program to kill "non-Communist elements."[32] In fact, Politburo member Edvard Kardelj "issued a manifesto threatening all who resisted the Party with liquidation."[33] He claimed two years later that "in four days in September 1943 seven thousand of the White Guard traitors were actually erased from Slovenian soil."[34] This included 700 National Guardsmen, who although surrendering with amnesty in hand at Turjak Castle, were subsequently massacred.[35] Such killing occurred in all areas subject to partisan control or attack. During 1941 in Montenegro, for example, "they staged indiscriminate executions and hurled the bodies into ravines. For this practice the Montenegrin Chetniks pinned a macabre nickname on the partisan rivals: 'Pitman.'"[36]

Throughout Yugoslavia, fear was widespread among the peasants subject to partisan control, for "nobody quite knew why 'they' were killing, what kind of sin was being punished. Some were saying that they were hitting only at landowners, others that they were purging those going to church too often, and some were even worried for fat people because they were allegedly 'bourgeois' and their 'Black Friday' had arrived."[37] As Tito said in an interview reported in a Zagreb newspaper, "This then was civil war. But we did not want to talk about this during the war because it would not have been useful to us."[38]

As certain defeat of the Nazis approached, the partisans stepped up their war against domestic enemies while increasingly ignoring Nazi forces. They also tried to purge their forces of less than enthusiastic communists. Consider Order no. 416 of partisan battalion commander Politkomisar Novak, which issued in 1943 demanded that the understanding of Marxism by conscripts be judged and that "all those who do not know much about the history of Communism and show no interest must be liquidated.... These liquidations must be carried out very discreetly, and you will be held responsible if people get wind of them."[39] Moreover, lists were compiled of opponents who would be eventually exterminated; their numbers added up to tens of thousands.[40]

In all their warfare against the occupation and domestic armies, the partisans showed no more mercy for prisoners of war than did the Chetniks. Such was admitted openly by the partisan leaders. For example, Milovan Djilas, a former member of the central command, noted that in one case when the Italians holding a town surrendered, "All the Italian troops — the entire Third Battalion of the 259th Regiment of the Murge division — were put to death."[41]

The partisans also adopted a reprisal technique used by the Nazis (who calculated that one hundred Yugoslavs would be executed for each German soldier killed; fifty for every one wounded): killing by arithmetic. For every partisan lost, ten "traitors" (that is, "anticommunists") were to be killed.[42] This was part of a general effort to terrorize the population into joining the partisans, or at least refusing to aid their enemies. To this end, in December 1941 the partisans entrapped and murdered a prominent resistance leader; in 1941–42 they killed "well over" 2,000 people.[43] The best of the nationalistic opponents disappeared one by one.[44]

A special technique, also used by partisans in the Soviet Union, was to ambush and kill a few Nazi soldiers or blow up Nazi vehicles, communication lines, or buildings, in order to invite Nazi retaliation on the neighboring population. Hundreds and sometimes thousands of innocents would thus be shot by the Nazis. In one such reprisal for the killing of twelve soldiers in 1941, the Nazis executed from 4,000[45] to 8,000[46] inhabitants of Kragujevac. Often many of the survivors of such massacres and those in the region who heard about them would rush to join the partisans or escape to the hills and forests where the partisans could recruit them. This was also a technique for liquidating opponents or neutralizing hostile areas, and helped to destroy the social order that the partisans wanted to replace with communism. In line with this they would take loot from Nazi convoys and leave some of it in anticommunist areas, thus inviting Nazi reprisals against anticommunists.[47]

Of course, the partisans also targeted for liquidation the usual communist bête noire: the bourgeoisie, landlords, rich, and aristocrats. The following chilling story makes this clear.

Marijan Stilinovic, an old Communist and member of the agit-prop team, had been at Piva in Montenegro, visiting a youth organization. The cell secretary gave a report which mentioned that they had executed a rich peasant. "An informer or a collaborator, I suppose?" asked Stilinovic. "Not at all!" replied the Secretary. "He even donated regularly to our funds. But we had to execute him. You see, he was a kulak! And one day he would have been our enemy!" Stilinovic began to remonstrate, but the Secretary cut him short, pointing to a boy sitting with him. "That is his son — he also voted for his father's execution — you ask him." The boy nodded.[48]

None of this is to deny that the partisans also fought the Nazis valiantly, narrowly escaping being surrounded and annihilated several times. Their ranks were often depleted from battle and disease, to be renewed by fresh recruits. The life expectancy of the average partisan was quite low, considering they suffered by the end of the war at least 300,000 dead,[49] more than their force level of 200,000 at the end of 1944 (by war's end they had an army of 350,000 to 400,000).[50]

Larger in number (over 300,000 in 1941, according to Mihailovic — probably a greatly exaggerated figure)[51] than the partisans during the early years of the occupation, the Chetniks also had the original advantage of being supported by the Yugoslavian government in exile. However, Soviet propaganda and misinformation about the "heroic struggle" of the patriotic and democratic partisans and "collaboration of the reactionary and repressive Chetniks with the Nazis and Italians and refusal to fight" helped to turn the Allies' support to the partisans. But perhaps most effective in persuading the Allies to stop aiding the Chetniks and for British Prime Minister Churchill to finally and completely support Tito were British communist sympathizers and agents, particularly Major James Lugman, deputy chief of the British Special Operations Executive, Yugoslav Section, and Guy Burgess, who headed the Special Talks department of the BBC.[52] They and other moles were able to control and slant the flow of intelligence and information from Yugoslavia and to bias BBC reports in favor of the partisans. Disinformation and agents of influence won a whole country to communism, perhaps the most significant victory for disinformation during the war.[53]

In November 1943, the communist-controlled Anti-Fascist Council for the National Liberation of Yugoslavia (AVNOJ) declared itself the supreme legislative and executive body, with a national committee elected as a temporary government. Tito was made prime minister. Even though by June 1944 Tito controlled less than ten percent of the population,[54] Dr. Subasich, prime minister of the Yugoslav government in exile, under firm British prodding, recognized Tito's National Committee of Liberation as the "provisional administration of the country."[55] And he agreed that those opposing the partisans would be excluded from the future government. A couple of months later, exiled King Peter of Yugoslavia made a broadcast over BBC in which he called on all Yugoslavs to support Tito, labeling as traitors any who would not do so.[56] June 1944 thus dates the formal abdication of whatever rights the government-in-exile had and dates for our purposes here the beginning of the Tito government, which was to continue until Tito's death in 1980.

During the three years preceding legalization of the Tito government, partisans probably murdered some 100,000 people, as listed in table 14.1. Assuming formal national authority after June 1944 did not change partisan methods; it simply gave them legal cover. This was particularly evident when the Soviet Red Army and partisan forces captured Belgrade, the capital of Yugoslavia, in October 1944. The partisans then proceeded to hunt down and kill "collaborators," opponents, and "anticommunists." Milan Grol, a royalist with the empty title of vice-premier, was shattered by what he saw. To friends in London he wrote, "This is not a state; it is a slaughterhouse."[57]

As the war approached its end and Tito's forces took over much of the country, particularly Croatia and its capital of Zagreb, large-scale massacres were carried out. Dr. Giuseppi Massucci, secretary to the Vatican's envoy to the Croatian Episcopate, kept a diary in which he compared Zagreb to a huge cemetery and noted that people were being executed en masse. For 22 November 1945, he wrote:

> Bitter tears are flowing without pause. New punishments continuously send men to death by hanging. The entire land is inundated by streams of tears. After the massacres of several hundred thousand Croatian soldiers and civilians in the first months of the Communist regime, shootings and hangings still are being carried out day in and day out. Evidently this policy of mass execution is that of the new regime rather than a series of acts committed by irresponsible elements. There is no one who does not mourn someone.[58]

All over Yugoslavia, "collaborators" were hunted down and killed. While many of these had in fact helped the occupying armies, or were officials of the various puppet governments or participants in the slaughter of Serbs by the Ustashi, many also were simply those who opposed or might oppose the communists. They were even young boys guilty of only being drafted into one of the puppet militias or armies. For example, over 1,700 young men just recruited into the Croatian army before war's end and left without orders were killed in Virovitica.[59] Sometimes the killing was simply indiscriminate mass murder, as that of 400 inhabitants of Gospic, witnessed by Dusan Vukovic, a former partisan. One Ustashi was skinned alive and hung from a tree with his own skin.[60]

Knowing what fate waited for them, near the end of the war hundreds of thousands of civilians and Chetnik, Ustashi, and Slovenian White Guard soldiers streamed toward the Austrian and Italian borders to surrender to Allied forces. Many in fact succeeded in crossing the border and surrendering to British units. However, at the highest level the British had decided to return most of these refugees to the partisans. For example, in an agreement with the partisans in May 1945, the British Fifth Corps turned over approximately 18,585 such desperate civilians and former soldiers and guerrillas to partisan hands,[61] even though partisan officers who negotiated their return "made no bones about the fact that their purpose in recovering the refugees was to wreak vengeance on them."[62] The Welsh Guards also returned about 5,000 Croats to partisan mercies; other units handed over several thousand more. Most were then massacred; just at one slaughter site covering about a mile in the Forest of Brezovica there were perhaps 5,000 to 10,000 bodies.[63] These numbers alone surpass the infamous 1941 Katyn Forest massacre of 4,255 Polish intellectuals, soldiers, and officers by the Soviet Union.[64] Such massacres no doubt also awaited the 12,196 Croats, 5,480 Serbs, 8,263 Slovenes, and 400 Montenegrins the British Fifth Corps evacuated to Yugoslavia by 1 June 1945.[65]

Then there was the Bleiburg massacre. Over 100,000 Croat troops and civilians who had fled Yugoslavia rather than be captured by the partisans or live under communism had crowded into a large field outside the town of Bleiburg, Austria, near the Yugoslav border. Thinking they were surrendering to the British, they waved, ran up white flags, and gave up their arms. By prior agreement with partisan officers, the British turned all these refugees over to the partisans for return to Yugoslavia. The partisans, however, simply opened fire with machine guns from nearby woods on the unarmed people in the field. The British, who were in nearby Bleiburg Castle, did not participate and were largely unaware of the massacre.[66] Those Croats who survived were herded back into Yugoslavia to be soon massacred there or forced on cross-country death marches.

The British also turned back tens of thousands of other panicked refugees at the line of the River Drava in Austria. Tens, if not hundreds of thousands of others, gave up hope of escaping west once they saw what was happening to those in British hands. Milovan Djilas (member of Tito's Politburo at the time) commented as follows about the Chetniks and their sympathizers, but what he said could have applied to all the refugees, "To be quite frank with you — we didn't at all understand why the British insisted on returning these people."[67]

Whatever the explanation,[68] perhaps overall at least a quarter of a million Croats and tens of thousands of others thus found themselves at Tito's mercy. Partisans and their secret police massacred these people on a scale matching the most terrible atrocities. They were machine-gunned as in the Bleiburg field, shot, stabbed, cut, or beaten to death nearby, or eventually killed after savage death marches, such as by being drowned in rivers or thrown into deep ravines. Just near Kocevje, as reported by a young partisan who defected, executioners boasted about liquidating 30,000 to 40,000 people in eight days (which tallies with reports of other witnesses who escaped).[69] And in May 1945, some 5,000 Serbian Chetniks and 12,000 to 15,000 Croats and Slovenes that were being held in St. Vid were taken into the Kamnik Mountains south of the Austrian frontier and there, at the edge of antitank trenches, killed by machine gun squads. Some 10,000 other prisoners were similarly slaughtered.[70] Tens of thousands more, their numbers dwindling from violent death, were marched for hundreds of miles and, over weeks and even months, through villages and towns whose inhabitants were encouraged to attack them.[71]

Among all the refugees perhaps no more than 5 percent finally survived.[72] The total number murdered may be over 300,000[73] — an incredible number that doesn't even count those Croats, Slovenes, or Serbs who stayed in their villages and towns and were executed there. But if this figure seems much too high, consider the former partisan General Kosta Nadj's admission in the January 1985 Belgrade weekly *Reporter* that of the 150,000 such people given or falling into the hands of just his Third Army, "naturally in the end we liquidated them."[74]

In the ten months between legalization of the Tito government and the end of the war, Tito likely murdered overall from 300,000 to 750,000 Croats, Slovenes, and Serbs, as well as German prisoners of war. And, as we have seen, much killing of collaborators and alleged opponents continued after the war's end in May 1945. But this was only part of the postwar democide by this communist regime.

Anticommunists, of course, continued to be hunted down and murdered long after the war; other standard communist enemies, such as landlords and the rich, often suffered similar fates. Religious leaders and unsympathetic intellectuals were also targets. After the war, 200 nuns and priests were executed (many for complicity in Ustashi massacres).[75] Solid evidence of the Tito government's wanton democide comes from its brief occupation of Trieste, across the border in Italy. Having illegally occupied the city, Tito succumbed to saber rattling by the British and withdrew after 40 days. During this short period, the communists arrested many thousands and possibly killed from 10,000 to 15,000 people in Trieste and neighboring regions (Gorizia, Istria, and Rijeka).[76]

In Yugoslavia, those who opposed or continued to fight against the regime after the war were often termed "renegades" and killed outright when arrested or caught. Djilas expresses the mood of the top communists at this time:

> But court proceedings were not accorded to these outlaws except in special cases. Whether this was due to ideological rigidity, raging hatred, or a fierce desire to settle accounts, who can say? In these circumstances, vagaries operated: the mood of the prosecutors, local relationships, private vendettas. However, I firmly believe that the basic issue was the revolutionary, which is to say nonjudicial, character of absolute authority. Tito believed in legal procedures, but not of the kind that restrict the political decision-making process or challenge the primacy of the state.
> ...
> I was already convinced that in settling accounts with the renegades the governing principle was the primacy and the functioning of the new regime.[77]

In other words, it was a matter of power.

Not to be forgotten are the ethnic Germans. True, some of them collaborated with the Nazis, as did many other Yugoslavs. Most, however, were simple peasants trying to survive through the war years. Systematic genocide was committed against them: all were looted, women were raped, and many were murdered, often most painfully. Tens of thousands were put into concentration camps where they subsequently died. From October 1945 to March 1948, in the camp of Rudolfsgrad alone, 10,000 of 33,000 ethnic German prisoners perished.[78] At least 55,000 overall must have died in such camps or been murdered.[79] The remainder, some 300,000 people, were freighted to and dumped in a destroyed Germany and Austria.[80] Many must have died in Germany as a result of the trip or, subsequently, from rampant starvation and a severe lack of shelter, as described in chapter 12.

The routine killing of "collaborators," opponents, "anticommunists," "renegades," and the like by the OZNA (Committee for the Protection of the People) finally slacked off after late 1945. Tito himself had objected to the toll, crying out against the killing at a Politburo meeting, "excited and aware of what the terrible reality had become."[81]

But the reprieve did not apply to the concentration camps set up throughout the country. Frank Waddams, a British representative who had lived outside of Belgrade, said he knew firsthand of ten "concentration camps," and had talked with inmates from nearly all of them. "'The tale is always the same," he said. "Starvation, overcrowding, brutality and death conditions, which make Dachau and Buchenwald mild by comparison. Many Slovenes who were released from Dachau at the end of the war came home only to find themselves in a Slovene camp within a few days. It is from these people that the news has come that the camps are worse than Dachau."[82] Out of a Slovene population of 1,200,000, Waddams believes that 20,000 to 30,000 were imprisoned.[83]

In 1948, throughout Yugoslavia the communists added a whole new group to the prison and camp population. As a result of Tito's dispute with Stalin over the independence of his regime from Soviet domination and control, Yugoslavia was formally expelled from the Cominform in June 1948. Stalin also had his military prepare itself to invade Yugoslavia sometime in the early 1950s (this invasion was subsequently canceled out of fear that the United States might come to the defense of Yugoslavia, as it had in South Korea when the North invaded the South in 1950).[84] More important to Tito in the short run, the expulsion risked an anti-Tito coup d'état by those Yugoslavian communists who sided with Stalin or sympathized with the Soviet Union. These so-called "Cominformists" became the new enemy.

No matter whether low or high officials, or even former top partisans, these Conformists were rounded up by the thousands. They were often tortured, sometimes killed, and usually sent to concentration camps. Among these was Tito's personal bodyguard, who got life at hard labor; the commander of the security guard of the supreme headquarters; chief of the general staff of the Yugoslav army, who died under mysterious circumstances; the deputy prime minister of Croatia; chairman of the supreme military tribunal; and other generals and colonels, ministers, members of the Central Committee, writers and professors, and so on.[85] Of those tortured in the camps and prisons were "more than twenty ex-ministers of republics, one chairman of the National Assembly, two deputy prime ministers, one hundred people's deputies, five generals, thirty colonels, and thousands of officers and NCOs."[86] To get an even better sense for the magnitude of this national purge, consider the sweep of Montenegro by the secret police (UDBA). Over 8,000 communists were arrested and sent to camps, including Montenegro's entire Central Committee, twenty-two deputy ministers, and five county committees.[87] This is not to say that the purge was limited to party members. Innocent noncommunists were also picked up for one reason or another, as were anticommunists and complainants. In the Montenegro village of Kostanje, a peasant was killed for simply protesting to a UDBA man, "You eat white bread while we have none."[88]

The infamous hell hole to which the "Cominformists" generally were sent was Goli Otok. Located on an island off the Dalmatian coast, it was especially constructed for this purpose. Djilas claims that about 15,000 communist party members and sympathizers were held at one time or another, of which a "substantial number served time simply because of having expressed pro-Soviet sentiments among friends."[89] More than 50,000 political prisoners may have passed through this camp.[90] "Some were entirely innocent."[91] In the camp, for example, was a peasant who, after selling his wheat at the market, went to a tavern for a drink. A stranger asked him: "Uncle, if you have two glasses, one of which is Russia and full, the other of which is Yugoslavia and empty, from which one would you drink?" "From the full one, of course," he answered.

That man had never been involved in politics.

Also at Goli Otok is the colonel who said that Jovanka's [Tito's third wife] legs were sexy. And also the general who was betrayed by his own small children for shooting at the portrait of the supreme commander [Tito].[92]

I have seen no estimates of deaths in the Goli Otok. But we do know that conditions in the camp were horrible. Says Djilas, "Evil and shame — evil beyond compare, unending shame — is what lay in store for the prisoners in the camp. Never mind the foul food, the mindless and exhausting labor in the quarry, the prisoners were subjected to torture, the cruelty of which was matched by its perversity."[93] As to what these conditions did to human beings, Djilas says, "Very few, if any, returned from Goli Otok unscathed. Not so much physically, perhaps, as psychologically and intellectually. Many were bitter, depressed, shattered."[94] No wonder he confesses that "Goli Otok has haunted me both intellectually and morally since my own break with the system, and my reevaluation of it."[95]

The number of Yugoslavs arrested and sent off to such camps, subjected to forced labor, or executed is unknown. Many were dealt with secretly. Many also were tried as "criminals." The possible magnitude of the overall purge can then be appreciated from just the number of "criminal trials" held by the regime. According to the communist newspaper *Borba*, there were 220,000 such trials in 1948, and 160,000 in 1949; perhaps 1 million went through the prisons of the secret police, although some for a very short time.[96] No wonder that during these years, as during the immediate postwar period, "Everyone lived in fear, no one knowing when fabricated charges might be brought against him, leading to imprisonment and trial."[97]

How many prisoners died during these purge years we do not know. Some calculations can be made, however, and if we consider not only these years but the entire period from 1945 to when the regime virtually ended such practices in 1963 (as discussed below), then the overall death toll of the prisons and camps may have been around 60,000, perhaps even over 200,000.

As in the Soviet Union and China during their most repressive and deadly periods, there was unrest in the form of uprisings and rebellions in Yugoslavia. For example, in the winter of 1948–49 there was an armed rebellion against the Tito regime by the regional Communist Party committee in Bjelo Pole, which was led by the secretary and national hero Ilia Bulatovic. The regime had to use tanks and artillery to put it down. Leaders of the rebellion then fled into the forest, where they were hunted down and eventually surrendered. "Yet not a single one made it back into town alive. All were killed on route."[98]

During the same period, 500 to 600 Moslem peasants from different villages rebelled, took over a police station, and disarmed a government official. As they marched to Cazin in Bosnia, they were dispersed by fire from a small group of security officers and committee members. Most returned to their villages, but around thirty fled to the forests where they were hunted down and when caught immediately shot to death.[99] In 1952 a number of villages were burned in more than eight districts, presumably as a result of rebellion.[100]

In light of Western attention and aid, the Tito regime began to liberalize its practices in the early 1950s. By June 1951, for example, it had largely abandoned forced labor in camps.[101] One can roughly date the most repressive and deadly years in Yugoslavia as from 1945 to 1952, but even in 1955 the regime initiated a new wave of terror and executions in Moslem Kossovo, which was showing signs of unrest.[102] In 1966, one of Tito's closest comrades during the war and the former head of the secret police, Aleksandar Rankovic, was dismissed and disgraced. This marks the final move away from the centralist and repressive Stalinist policies,[103] and away from bloody purges, political executions and mass political imprisonment. Even then, some killings still took place, such as the assassination by Yugoslav state security agents of more than twenty political émigrés in the early 1970s.[104]

Overall, in the postwar period the communists likely killed around 570,000 Ustashi, Croat soldiers, Nazi POWs, ethnic Germans, Slovenian White Guards, "anticommunists," communist "Cominformists," "collaborators," Chetniks, intellectuals, bourgeoisie, landlords, "rich" peasants, rebels, critics, and innocents. When added

358   Death by Government

to those the government killed during the war, the democide is almost 1,100,000 people and is shown in table 14.1 for comparison to the other democides in Yugoslavia. It is repeated in table 14.2, which also gives the annual democide rates. The Nazi, Soviet, and communist Chinese (People's Republic of China) annual rates are also given for comparison and plotted in figure 14.1.

As in the case of other Marxist regimes, the Yugoslav democide was a product of a fanatical ideology that justified the exercise of absolute power toward a utopian end. As Djilas put it for the Communist Party, "We are a synthesis of our revolutionary power, of Leninist dogma and Stalin's teaching. Power prevailed; power was our reality."[105] And as he says elsewhere, "Tito was faithful to pure power."[106] How demands of this power permeated policy is clear from Djilas' lament about how dissident communists — the Cominformists — themselves had to be treated.

FIGURE 14.1
Annual Democide Rates in Yugoslavia Compared to Other Countries
(Data from table 14.2)

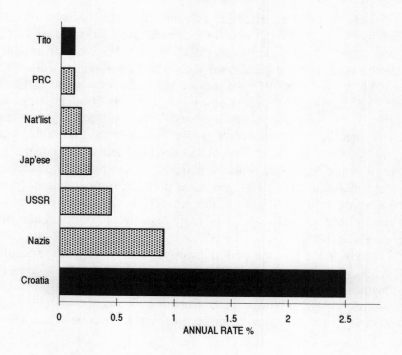

In retrospect and with all the self-criticism of which I am capable, I must admit that we could not have avoided a concentration camp for the Cominformists.... [Otherwise, it] might have led to the disintegration of the Party and to the ascendancy of pro-Soviet forces. It is the misfortune of dictatorial and particularly totalitarian powers that they cannot allow opposition without undermining their own survival.[107]

Ideology and power were also paramount in the Croatian democide. The Ustashi rulers combined a secular fascism on the Nazi model with a rabid Catholicism absolutely intolerant of competing religious doctrine. Indeed, high Catholic officials often called for or were directly involved in the massacre of Orthodox Serbs or their forced conversion.[108] Power was of course both the means to achieve the "true" Croatian state; and an end in itself. Thus, "as tactics individual terror [was] for the attainment of power, and mass terror for consolidation."[109]

Notes

1. Bailey 1978, 25.
2. Ibid., 26.
3. Paris 1961, 46.
4. Jukic 1974, 72.
5. Small and Singer 1982, 91.
6. Rummel 1992, table A, line 1187.
7. Hilberg 1961, 521.
8. Fotitch 1948, 138. During the next year and after the Moscow declaration on war criminals, Hungarian leaders indicted the general and two accomplices for the massacre. They subsequently escaped to Germany where they were given sanctuary (Hilberg 1961, 521).
9. Kuper 1981, 129.
10. A Yugoslavian Inquiry Commission put the number at 28,000 (Poliakov 1971, 266).
11. Fein 1979, 105.
12. Shelah 1990, 74.
13. The Serb population was 2,200,000 according to Paris 1961, 49n. 7; almost 40 percent (2,400,000) of an overall population of 6,000,000, according to Martin 1946, 47.
14. Paris 1961, 106.
15. Mihajlov 1987.
16. Paris 1961, 134–35.
17. Shelah 1990, 77.
18. Ibid., 74.
19. Paris 1961, 81.

20. Fotitch 1948, 121.
21. Paris 1961, 9.
22. Martin 1946, 50.
23. Tomasevich 1975, 261.
24. Gross 1966, 345n. 10.
25. Singleton 1985, 177.
26. Paris 1961, 9, 15.
27. See *Statistics of Democide.*
28. Gluckstein 1952, 152; see also Martin 1946, 62–63.
29. Gross 1966, 345n. 10. According to Gross, the "Albanians estimate roughly abut 50,000 Albanians killed." Reading the context of the footnote, these massacres probably took place in Moslem Kossovo. But, as the author points out, ethnic massacres were a frequent occurrence in Kossovo for centuries and I am unable to tell further from the context whether this toll is for Albanians over centuries, decades, or for the WWII period.
30. Tomasevich 1975, 258.
31. Tolstoy 1986, 17.
32. Ibid., 402n. 13.
33. Ibid., 21.
34. Ibid.
35. Ibid.
36. Bailey 1978, 86.
37. Tolstoy 1986, 402n. 13.
38. Ibid., 402n. 15.
39. Ibid., 21.
40. Ibid.
41. Djilas 1977, 220.
42. Beloff 1985, 76.
43. Tolstoy 1986, 19.
44. Dragnich 1954, 23–24.
45. Ibid.
46. Seton-Watson 1961, 120–21.
47. Dragnich 1954, 23–24.
48. Clissold 1983, 85–86.
49. Bailey 1978, 100. Djilas puts the number of dead at 305,000 (1977, 443).
50. Martin 1990, 272.
51. Tomasevich 1975, 181.
52. Martin 1990, xviii–xix.
53. Recently released secret British and American documents from that period make this clear. See *National Security Record: A Report on the Congress and National Security Affairs* (Washington, D.C.: The Heritage Foundation, April 1985), p. 3.
54. Fotitch 1948, 258.
55. Ibid.
56. Singleton 1985, 202.
57. Beloff 1985, 131–32.
58. Prcela and Guldescu 1970, 122.
59. Willoughby 1970, xii.
60. Tolstoy 1986, 387.
61. Ibid., 140.

62. Ibid., 142.
63. Ibid., 136.
64. FitzGibbon 1975, 446. Robert Conquest gives a figure of 4,143 (1968, 483); J. K. Zawodny puts it at 4,443 (1962, 24).
65. Tolstoy 1986, 204.
66. Ibid. 103–7.
67. Ibid., 139.
68. Tolstoy 1986 lays final blame on then minister resident in the Mediterranean Harold Macmillan.
69. Ibid. 198–99. For extensive documentation on these and other massacres and the death marches by survivors and witnesses, see Prcela and Guldescu 1970.
70. Ibid., 189.
71. Ibid., 387–88. See also Prcela and Guldescu 1970, passim.
72. Jukic 1974, 283.
73. Willoughby 1970, ix.
74. Tolstoy 1986, 409n. 8.
75. Singleton 1985, 215.
76. Gross 1978, 102, 107.
77. Djilas 1980, 78.
78. Paikert 1967, 287.
79. Glaser and Possony 1979, 528.
80. Ibid.
81. Djilas 1980, 77–78. Also see this chapter's epigraph.
82. Beloff 1985, 134.
83. Ibid.
84. According to General Bela Kiraly, who was commander of the army that was to invade Yugoslavia, all preparations were being made to invade the country sometime around 1951. What stopped the invasion was the Korean War. "America stood up. Consequently, the Russians assumed that if they invaded Yugoslavia, Americans would stand up again. I'm absolutely convinced of that because what we did was not military exercises: it was a systematic build-up and a systematic preparation for war, which was supposed to come sometime in 1951 or about then" (Ibid., 148).
85. See Markovski 1984, 4–6.
86. Ibid., 8.
87. Ibid.
88. Ibid.
89. Djilas 1980, 87.
90. Beloff 1985, 146.
91. Djilas 1980, 87.
92. Markovski 1984, 32–33.
93. Djilas 1980, 85.
94. Ibid., 87.
95. Ibid., 81.
96. Beloff 1985, 135.
97. Markovski 1984, 9.
98. Djilas 1980, 80. See also Markovski 1984, 8.
99. Djilas 1980, 79.
100. Markovski 1984, 8.

101.   Carlton 1955, 55.
102.   Qira 1970, 135.
103.   Beloff 1985, 195.
104.   *Political Killings by Governments* 1983, 23.
105.   Djilas 1980, 85.
106.   Ibid., 90.
107.   Ibid., 84.
108.   See Paris 1961, passim.
109.   Gross 1972, 65.

Part IV

4,145,000 Victims
The Suspected Megamurderers

15

1,663,000 Murdered?
Orwellian North Korea

*By the time we had finished with them they were only
the shells of men. There was nothing left in them
except sorrow for what they had done, and love of
Big Brother. It was touching to see how they loved
him.*

—George Orwell, *1984*

*For the great future of Revolution, his deep and
warm love embraces all of us at once! How can we
describe his virtue and sacrifice for the people and
the homeland! Let us keep his love deep in our hearts
and follow him to the victory of Revolution! Even if
we die a billion times, we must be determined to
follow him without any hesitation.*

—North Korean junior high school textbook

At the end of World War II, Soviet and U.S. forces divided Korea
between them along the 38th parallel. With neither the United States,

the Soviet Union, or the Koreans able to agree on how the two Koreas were to be unified, both halves moved toward their own governments. Under the "guidance" of the Soviets, the Korean Communist Party that had been destroyed by the Japanese was reconstituted and began to rule through "people's committees." By 1946 the communists had turned North Korea into a typical communist police state. Understandably, from August 1945 to September 1948 around 800,000 Koreans escaped to the South.[1]

At the head of all this the Soviets placed their Moscow-trained Kim Il-sung, a man whose reputation even among Korean communists was minimal. There was nothing charismatic about him. He appeared to be what he was initially — a Soviet puppet. But he had Soviet power behind him and soon was able to purge both major groups who opposed him: communists from the South, and those who had been in exile in China and were favored by the Chinese communists.

In September 1948, the People's Republic of Korea was proclaimed, and, in communist fashion, Kim Il-sung was elected premier by its Assembly. As soon as Soviet troops left the country and his own control was firmly established through successive top-level purges, he slowly steered North Korea toward neutrality between the Soviets and China.

Since its formal inception to the present, North Korea has become an absolute totalitarian state. In no other country in modern times has control by a party and its ruler been so complete. Everything people do, from birth to death, is strictly controlled, either directly by the party or through its facade, the government. Consider, for example, that the party strongly discourages marriage or sex before the age of twenty-eight, and then gives permission to marry only if it serves the party's purpose. Love, attraction, family background, and other conventional considerations play little role. In fact, the marriage may be denied if the couple is found to be too involved with each other, for dedication to Kim Il-sung must come first.

The common citizen faces a plethora of laws and rules that he transgresses only at the risk of his life. Half the violations covered in the country's criminal code are capital ones.[2]

There are no, not even the most insignificant, independent sources of news or thought. Officials open and read personal mail before sending it on. The party prints all pamphlets, brochures, announcements, newsletters, magazines, and books; it runs all publication houses and newspapers, and it fills virtually all printed material with the "great" sayings and doings of Kim Il-sung. All media and textbooks exclaim that the country is the first and only paradise on earth, and that this is due to the "perfect genius" of the "Great Leader." The party even so fixes radios and television sets that no foreign broadcasts can be heard, and it continuously inspects the receivers so that they cannot be altered.

There are no private businesses; the party distributes all food and other goods. Through its government front, the party owns all the land, and farmers generally work in government "cooperatives." During the "land reform" campaign, the party stripped land from large landowners, much as was done in communist China (although executions were proportionally much fewer — it was too easy to escape to the South at this time). Also as in China, the party allowed the farmers to own the land for only a few years before seizing it. By 1957 the party had forced all farmers to labor in "cooperatives."[3]

The party strictly forbids foreign travel by ordinary citizens, and it allows only the most trusted officials, agents, or students to travel or temporarily live abroad. Even then, they are constantly spied upon. What very few foreigners the party allows into the country depends on what foreign policy Kim is pursuing at the time and the sympathies of the foreigner. The party even tightly controls what foreign sympathizers can see or to whom they can talk, and it almost always accompanies them with watchful "guides" or "translators."

The core of this system is the birth-to-death thought control the party exercises throughout the country and up and down the communist hierarchy. It teaches people to idolize Kim Il-sung and hate his alleged enemies, above all "the Yankee imperialist bastard" United States and its "lackey" South Korean government. It requires everyone to study and discuss Marxist-Leninism, above all to worship the "Great Leader" Kim Il-sung and, overriding every other value, adore his *juche* philosophy that emphasizes political, social, and economic self-reliance. Everywhere, great photos, paintings, and statues, great flag-waving and slogan-yelling demonstrations, great placard-bearing rallies, great poems and works, and great edifices prove the people's great appreciation of the paradise Kim has created and of their deliverance from the horrors of capitalism and imperialism. In

Pyongyang, for example, Kim Il-sung has had erected a gigantic statue of himself, sixty-feet high and gilded in gold. The gold came from residents who "selflessly" donated their gold teeth, rings, and other gold possessions in "acts of heroic loyalty and gratitude for Kim's benevolence."[4]

Failure to so express one's appreciation and loyalty is dangerous, and protest lethal. Even having a minor accident that somehow the party might twist into a reflection on the regime can mean severe punishment. Note what happened to a school teacher:

> One day, one of my students dropped a portrait of Kim Il-sung while cleaning the classroom. This was a big event. Although this was an accident, I, as well as the parents of the student, were held responsible for what had happened. For one month, the parents of the student were criticized by the Party constantly and then were taken to a forced labor camp at Aoji coal mine. I went through a week of criticism from the Party and was expelled from the Party. After that, I was also taken to a forced labor camp.[5]

Even idle comments or expressions can mean severe punishment, including death. One cannot confide even in friends or one's loved one at home. According to a then-Soviet scholar on North Korea, "Everyone informs on each other.... Who would say anything negative when they know they will be collected in a truck and taken off to some unknown destination?"[6] Such happened to an official who mentioned to a friend that the country's sports team lost a game in the Montreal Olympics. The next day he disappeared and eventually was found to have been deported to work in a distant factory.[7] Then there was the case of an older man who, while playing chess, pointed to a pictorial magazine which displayed Kim Il-song holding hands with several girl students and said, "Premier Kim must be enjoying himself!" Somehow, this remark was reported to authorities, the party charged the man with defaming the premier, subjected him to a public trial, and severely punished him.[8]

The party does not leave the uncovering and preventing of such incorrect thoughts and ideas to chance. As revealed by a former Soviet scholar, in order to prevent dissident movements, the party periodically deports to new workplaces 30 to 40 percent of the urban population.[9] And the party also has set up perhaps the world's most extensive domestic spy system, with at least in some places as few as "one agent responsible for five residents."[10]

Those the spies find to have impure ideas they report to the military's Political Security Council. If the council administratively confirms it, then all the possessions of the accused are confiscated, and the accused is dispatched to a prison camp with nothing more than the clothes he is wearing.[11] Those judged to be antiparty may be used also as an example for the masses, and like the Chinese communist public trials, tried in a stadium and condemned to death before thousands of yelling and fist-waving spectators. One such trial held in the Kyongamsa Sports Stadium before 30,000 shouting people was reported by a defector. As soon as the party announced the death penalty for four prisoners,

> several young men in the front rows ran to the six men with axes and shovels. I closed my eyes when I saw them killing the six blindfolded men with the axes and shovels. After the killing, the officials tied the corpses to poles and marched around the city singing songs praising Kim Il-sung.[12]

In the early years of the "people's republic," those the party found to have some independence of mind, as by their possession of a *Bible* or a cross, they often executed; but progress has been made and the party now simply treats them as though mentally sick: they are taken to one of the seventy mental hospitals kept for this purpose.[13]

In addition to spies, the party makes wide use of electronic surveillance techniques. It has planted listening devices in the homes and workplaces of many scientists, technicians, teachers, and other professionals — even communist cadres. One scientists whose home the party bugged through his radio set made the mistake of vocalizing his anger over ten rotten apples among his family's food rations. He complained that high party officials got all the fresh apples and then called Kim Il-sung "a son of a bitch." The party arrested and reportedly executed him.[14] The party even bugs its own spies in this way. One defected to the South when he found that the party had planted a bug in his government-issued car.[15]

Of course, the party has to mobilize mass campaigns of one sort or another to eradicate wrong thinkers, establish correct ideas, or swiftly develop the country, as in the Flying Horse Campaign, Korea's equivalent of China's Great Leap Forward. Kim Il-sung even subjected the party hierarchy and military chain of command, as well as the masses, to periodic and systematic purges. Those purged might be fired from their jobs, sent off to forced labor or concentration camps, or, in notable cases, executed. Previous or present rank or position protects no one except Kim. From 1945 to 1971, Kim Il-sung executed forty-one vice-premiers and higher (another twenty-five were exiled or deported), sixteen division military commanders or higher, and, of those responsible for operations against the South, nine directors or higher.[16]

Beginning in 1956, Kim aimed a massive countrywide purge at "counterrevolutionaries" and, in 1958, through the Concentrated Guidance Campaign, he transformed this into a mass ideological census and registration of the background and political purity of each and every North Korean. Anyone found to be a "counterrevolutionary" might be exiled to a remote area, sent to a labor camp, or executed. "Counterrevolutionaries" included such people as "families of people who escaped to the South, former members of anti-Communist organizations and their families, religious people and their families, former landlords and their families, former businessmen and their families, expelled partisans and their families, returned war prisoners, South Korean natives, draft dodgers, prison inmates and ex-convicts."[17] There was one at least temporary out for these people: If, during a generously allowed period of surrender, these people confessed their subversive activities, they might be mercifully accepted into society. If, after this, they were arrested for some reason, the party subjected them to the typical communist public trial, after which they were executed.[18]

If we can believe a former public security official, during the early years of this mass purge the party resettled, jailed, or executed almost 500,000 people. In the official's own village ninety-eight were executed, 300 sent off the prison, and another 489 families deported.[19]

Apparently not satisfied with the results, beginning in 1964 the party demanded that all citizens re-register. As a result, the party classified everyone into one of three critical life-defining classes, depending on their background and perceived unfriendliness to the regime. Over one-quarter of the whole population, especially those whom the party had previously labeled counterrevolutionaries, was classified as a "hostile class."[20] In 1989, a report by two human rights groups claimed that 4 million North Koreans still were identified as "hostile" and "assigned to hard labor on the margins of society."[21]

People in the middle group, such as those having relatives in the South, were classified as a "wavering" or "uncertain" group.[22] These made up almost half of the population.[23] The top group comprised the remaining near quarter of the people and was the one that the party believed it could trust.

Classification into one of these three groups followed each person and family for the rest of their lives, determining for each and every Korean the education the party would allow them and their children, the job the party would require of them, the punishment the party would meet out for their infractions, and even the food rations the party would permit them.

Of course, all this demanded that the regime have its own gulag. In North Korea this was called "Special Dictatorship Target Areas."[24] Even in 1990, after forty-three years of absolute dictatorship, the party perceives a need for twelve labor or concentration camps with perhaps 152,000 political prisoners,[25] possibly even 200,000.[26] Reportedly, the party has taken up over one out of every 100 square miles of the whole country with these camps.[27]

Conditions in the camps is often life threatening; treatment of the inmates severe and in some cases barbarous. In some camps inmates must grow their own food with what inadequate equipment and poor land is available. No help is given them. Food is thus scarce, and prisoners are often reduced to eating grass. "Many die from malnutrition and disease."[28]

Moreover, housing is not sufficient, with some prisoners living in caves or mud and wood huts. Nor in general is clothing enough for the severe North Korean winters. In spite of all this, in all camps the party forces prisoners to work twelve hours a day and then to meet for two hours of thought-reform classes.

Spies are everywhere. Prisoners reported as lazy may be executed; all those trying to escape are publicly executed, seemingly without exception. At least in some cases, those prisoners the party judges still to be or have become antiparty are also executed. According to one Korean defector, some have been used for target practice by the military.[29]

As an illustration of what life is like in these North Korean camps, consider Yodok camp in Yodok county. The work day for political prisoners begins at 5:30 A.M. and, except for a thirty-minute lunch break, continues until 8:00 P.M. This schedule appears invariable, even if the labor is logging or mining. After work, the camp bosses demand that all prisoners attend ideological classes for an hour, beginning at 10:00 P.M.

For families interned together, food consists of 550 grams (19.4 ounces) a day of corn, sometimes some salt, and occasionally a soy paste; bachelors get 350 grams (12.3 ounces) of maize[30] (in some of the other camps they might get potatoes and other roots).[31] These meager and unhealthy rations may be cut in half for alleged malingering or insufficient ideological enthusiasm. Extra food comes from what frogs and worms prisoners can find, and trapping and raising rats for food has become an industry among them. It should be no surprise that "a great number of inmates die from malnutrition."[32]

Family inmates are forced to build their own quarters out of mud and wood; there is no heating for warmth, regardless of the hard winters; there is no fuel for cooking other than the little wood that can be found. There are no sanitation facilities and no doctors. Of course people try to escape this camp. But all — some fifteen a year — are caught and publicly executed.[33]

Not all in the camp are commoners. Reflective of the waves of party purges, even former higher officials or military are imprisoned there, such as in recent years a former navy commander and his whole family of seven, a former senior accountant of the party and his family of eight, the son of the country's vice-president, and a former ambassador.[34]

All this information about the camp comes from two former inmates who defected to the South. One of them, Kang Chol-hwan, was arrested when he was nine years old and sent to the camp along with his father and grandmother because his grandfather had been accused of spying. He spent ten years in the camp; his grandmother and father died there.[35]

Informants claim that the party also deported political undesirables to the Soviet Union to labor in lumber camps there, with North Korea picking up the earnings from their work.[36] Moreover, at least near one North Korean logging and lumbering operation remote from Soviet settlements, the party operated its own prison — Chegdomyn prison. According to the Moscow correspondent in Khabarovsk, a former member of the North Korean elite and long-time resident in the Soviet Union revealed in an interview that

> the prison is typically medieval. They practice torture there and possibly they execute unruly North Korean citizens. Many employees at the enterprise have vanished without trace. We know of several instances of the mutilated corpses of North Koreans being found in the river which flows through Chegdomyn.[37]

How many people died in this and the other camps is a guess. Judging the conditions better than the Soviet gulag, but as bad as in China, perhaps over 260,000 died since the early years, possibly even nearly three times this.

The party subjects the whole population to periodic forced labor, and transports people at its desire to work on one or another project. Of course, refusal is impossible. Reported one former North Korean,

> Just after I graduated from high school all the residents of Hwanghaebuk-do Province were mobilized to work for the canal project of Songnim city. All the residents had to work for 90 days. Over 100 residents died of disease or work-related accidents. The students had to carry heavy loads on their backs and if the daily objectives were not met, they had to work overtime to meet them.

> Even on Sundays, there was no spare time. If the weekly work objectives were not met, the residents were mobilized to work on Sundays.[38]

All this about North Korea is depressingly familiar, for I could be describing one period or another in other present or past communist systems, such as Stalin's Soviet Union, Mao's China, Hoxha's Albania, or Ceausescu's Rumania. But in Kim Il-sung's Korea, communism has never reached this absoluteness elsewhere. Only Enver Hoxha's Albania — an equally small, homogenous, and isolated country — was able to approach North Korea's self-isolation, internal totalitarian control, and ant-like society.

Aside from internal democide, the party also murdered tens of thousands and possibly hundreds of thousands of people during the Korean War. With Stalin's approval, direction, and promised help,

North Korea invaded South Korea in June 1955, eventually costing the death of probably nearly 2,550,000 people in battle or as a result of the war.[39] An additional almost 500,000 people likely were killed in massacres, executions, or from mistreatment.[40]

Within four months of the invasion by North Korea, the main North Korean forces were driven out of the South by South Korean and American-led United Nations forces, and, within another month, from much of their own North Korean territory. During its occupation of the South, the Korean communists systematically executed many alleged anticommunists, defectors from the North, and South Korean military officers and government officials. They also illegally conscripted around 400,000 South Korean civilians[41] and impressed 50,000 South Korean POWs[42] into their military forces. Judging by North Korean casualties overall, a hundred thousand or so of these South Koreans must have been killed in battle.

Apparently encouraged by Radio broadcasts by Kim Il-sung, as well as secret orders, retreating communist cadres and soldiers executed those political prisoners they had to leave behind[43] and massacred civilians. In Wonju, for example, they slaughtered 1,000 to 2,000 civilians before escaping north.[44] Taejon became known for being among the worst of these massacres: after taking the city, North Koreans arrested from 5,000 to 7,000 people. When U.S. forces began to close in, these prisoners were taken out in batches of 100 to 200 and shot. Only three civilians survived. Forty-two captured U.S. soldiers were killed, and near the Taejon airstrip, 500 South Korean soldiers with their hands tied behind them were found in mass graves.[45] At Sachon, North Koreans torched the jail, burning alive some 300 former officials, police, and landowners.[46] Overall, claims the South Korean government, during their occupation of the South, North Korean soldiers and officials murdered more than 129,000 civilians.[47]

The massive intervention of China enabled the communists to retake the North and establish a stable front across its previous border with the South, which with the end of the war became a permanent demilitarized zone. As United Nations forces retreated back to the South, 685,000 North Koreans fled with them.[48]

When North Korean forces were forced to retreat from much of their own land, some North Korean civilians took revenge for the lives they had been forced to live by killing communists and their supporters, although apparently on a disorganized personal basis.[49] When the Korean communists retook their territory, especially after the war ended, the party sought out and executed those who had attacked communists. It punished others who in some way or another it construed as helping UN forces or being sympathetic to them. There was no statute of limitations on this. In one case, for example, a person who had kept out of trouble until 1959 was then accused during the Concentrated Guidance Campaign of during the war being

> visited by three or four men accompanying the advancing allied forces who had previously been his subordinates. He was immediately arrested, and a public trial was scheduled. Before it could take place, he died in jail, having first slipped out a small note to his family via a released prisoner which said, "When I am put on trial, there will be no chance for me so I want to say good-bye to you."[50]

Shortly after the North Korean reoccupation of their territory, in every village

> open-air kangaroo courts were held, the accused standing trial before the entire populace. Naturally, ancient grudges of a neighborly type, and the hatred produced by a brutal war, came into play. Many accusers undoubtedly exaggerated in telling of the crimes they had witnessed, and these trials, according to certain respondents, embittered villages for years thereafter. Nor did the retribution end quickly. As late as 1959, for example, "war-time crimes" were being uncovered, and people were being punished.[51]

Alleged "lack of patriotism" during the war could mark one's whole family. The party proclaimed such stigma by placing red tuman signs on the gates of those families' houses or other conspicuous places. In some hamlets it so branded nearly 100 percent of the homes.[52]

Throughout the Korean War, communist treatment of captured UN soldiers was worse than that doled out by the Russians. American prisoners, for example, were often shot before they got to a camp or perished on death marches; if they survived to reach a camp, they often soon died from torture, hunger, disease, and exposure. In one 120-mile march, 130 out of 700 POWs died; in another group of

prisoners captured at Kunu-ri, 325 out of 400 died or were killed.[53] By
U.S. Department of Defense statistics, of the 7,140 known American
prisoners, 4,418 came out alive — a 38.1 percent toll.[54] Compare this
to the 1.2 percent of American POWs who died in Nazi captivity
during World War II.[55] Overall, during the Korean War, 5,639
American servicemen died as a result of communist war crimes.[56] The
communists also claimed that they had captured 70,000 South Korean
soldiers, but they only returned 8,000 of them after the war.[57] We do
know that 5,500 were killed in communist captivity.[58]

After the war, Kim Il-sung's murderous nature continued to be
demonstrated to the international community by his support and
training of international terrorists and his own terrorism against the
South and the UN Command. For example, regardless of the innocents
who might be killed, he sent commandos to Rangoon, Burma, in 1983
to bomb President Chun Doo Hwan of South Korea as he met with
Burmese leaders. The bomb missed the president but killed seventeen
members of his official party, including four cabinet ministers and
three Burmese.[59]

Another particularly reprehensible action involved a civilian
airliner. Very upset over being upstaged by the Olympics to be held in
South Korea, Kim Il-sung had two agents plant a bomb on a South
Korean airliner, KAL flight 858, in Baghdad. The plane exploded
while approaching Bangkok, killing all 115 passengers. One of the
agents, a woman, was captured; she subsequently confessed the plot.[60]

Agents were also sent into South Korea to kill the president; they
got within a few hundred feet of his residence before being killed.
They did, however, shoot his wife to death.

In a staged display at Panmunjom (the jointly controlled center of
negotiations and exchange between the UN Command and the North),
communist guards launched an unprovoked attack on two U.S. guards
and killed them with axes.

Although these foreign attacks by the North resulted in a relatively
small number of deaths, they displayed Kim Il-sung's indifference to
the lives of others and his abysmal treatment of his own people.

How many overall have been murdered in or by this Orwellian
society? No overall estimates are available in the literature and there
are only a few estimates for particular events, such as the killing of
American POWs, a specific massacre, or the purge and execution of

higher-ups. From the nature of the system and by analogy with the Soviet Union and the People's Republic of China, I think a reasonable estimated range is from 710,000 to slightly over 3,500,000, with a mid-estimate of almost 1,600,000 people killed, as shown in table 15.1. But this figure and its components, listed in table 15.1, amount to little more than educated guesses, and that is why North Korea only stands accused of megamurder. In this case, Kim's thorough control over all his people and their foreign and domestic communication has protected him and his party from everything but deep suspicion about having committed megamurder. But given the nature of his society, the bits and pieces that have emerged about his purges, labor camps, and executions give strong enough evidence to at least indict him and his party for this crime against humanity.

TABLE 15.1
North Korean Democide, 1948–87

Type of Killing	Democide (000) [a]
Domestic Democide	1,293
purges	10 [b]
"Open Struggle" campaign	10 [b]
"Collective Guidance" campaign	25 [b]
labor concentration camps	265
corvée/hard labor	983
Foreign Democide	370
of South Koreans	363
others	7
Total Democide	1,663
North Korean War Dead	1,401 [c]

a Mid-estimates from *Statistics of Democide.*

b This is a low.

c Includes military action since the Korean War.

Notes

1. Scalapino and Lee 1972, 380.
2. Buchkin 1990, 25.
3. Sin 1991, 295.
4. "Paradise Lost" 1989, 11.
5. George Orwell's *Nineteen Eighty-Four* 1984, 35.
6. "Four More Concentration Camps Created Since 1982" 1990, 18.
7. Chira 1989.
8. Scalapino and Lee 1972, 830n.30.
9. "Four More Concentration Camps Created Since 1982" 1990, 18.
10. George Orwell's *Nineteen Eighty-Four* 1984, 59.
11. Ibid.
12. Ibid., 112.
13. Ibid., 60.
14. "Paradise Lost" 1989, 11–12.
15. Chira 1989.
16. *North Korean Political System in Present Perspective* 1976, 11.
17. Kim 1980, 43.
18. Ibid.
19. Scalapino and Lee 1972, 834n. 36.
20. "Four More Concentration Camps Created Since 1982" 1990, 18.
21. Maass 1989 and McBeth 1989.
22. Chira 1989.
23. "Four More Concentration Camps Created Since 1982" 1990, 18.
24. "North Korea Admits to Operating Labor Camps" 1992, 25.
25. Ibid.
26. "Horrible Conditions of Concentration Camp ..." 1992, 16.
27. "Four More Concentration Camps Created Since 1982" 1990, 18.
28. George Orwell's *Nineteen Eighty-Four* 1984, 59.
29. Ibid., 60.
30. "Horrible Conditions of Concentration Camp ..." 1992, 17.
31. "North Korea Admits to Operating Labor Camps" 1992, 25.
32. "Horrible Conditions of Concentration Camp ..." 1992, 18.
33. Ibid.
34. Ibid., 19.
35. Ibid., 16–17.
36. Scalapino and Lee 1972, 830.
37. Glukinov 1991, 38.
38. George Orwell's *Nineteen Eighty-Four* 1984, 98.
39. From *Statistics of Democide*. That Stalin directed the war, including the drafting of military plans by the Soviet military, has been revealed by historian Gavrill Korotkov, a former political assistant for the former Soviet Far East Army commander at the time the war began. He claims to have found documents showing the detailed planning of the Soviet military (*Honolulu Star-Bulletin* 22 June 1992, p. A–8). For testimony by former Soviet and North Korean officers and officials generally supporting this involvement by the Soviets, see Chullbaum

1991; for supporting academic and historical research, see *The Historical Reillumination on the Korean War* 1990.
40. From *Statistics of Democide.*
41. *Red Atrocities Remembered* 1975, 22
42. Leckie 1962, 331.
43. Nam 1974, 87.
44. Alexander 1986, 226.
45. Ibid. See also Summers 1990, 56, and Hoyt 1984, 184.
46. Hoyt 1984, 182.
47. *Red Atrocities Remembered* 1975, 21.
48. Nam 1974, 87.
49. Scalapino and Lee 1972, 411. Upon return of the party, it admitted "that 'American imperialist robbers' had led Koreans to massacre large numbers of 'progressive people'" (ibid.).
50. Ibid., 832n. 33.
51. Ibid., 832.
52. Ibid., 413.
53. Summers 1990, 213.
54. Lewy 1978, 340.
55. Zawodny 1962, 190.
56. Lewy 1978, 340.
57. Lawson 1964, 128.
58. Leckie 1981, 930.
59. McManaway and Clark 1988, 3.
60. Ibid., 2.

16

1,417,000 Murdered?
Barbarous Mexico

Said a Valle Nacional police officer of Mexican
forced laborers: "They die; they all die. The bosses
never let them go until they're dying."

—John K. Turner, *Barbarous Mexico*

In 1900, Mexico was ruled by Porfirio Díaz, a former general who in 1876 rebelled against President Sebastián Lerdo de Tejada and seized power. He subsequently was elected to the office and, except for one term, was consistently re-elected, sometimes without opposition, until his exile in May 1911. In strictly political terms, his was not a naked dictatorship but a milder form of authoritarian rule. He did not systematically control speech and the press, but there were political limits, and fear of his officials and supporters promoted much self-censorship.

Díaz tried to conciliate various groups, such as the Catholic Church, landed interests, and big business, and he was particularly committed

381

to the economic development of Mexico. He thus promoted foreign investment and ownership, he facilitated the transfer of public lands to private hands, and he helped concentrate the ownership of land for more efficient usage.

However, through these land policies, he ultimately deprived some 5,000 Indian communities of their ancestral land[1] and possibly caused some 1 million families to lose their land.[2] By 1910, fewer than 3,000 families possessed almost half of Mexico's land, most of the remaining land was "virtually uninhabitable,"[3] and over 95 percent of the rural population owned no land at all.[4] Nearly half of the rural population lived on haciendas (large farming or ranching estates or plantations), which together encompassed about 80 percent of the rural communities.[5] Some of these haciendas were huge. That of the Terraza clan in the state of Chihuahua held a little over 6 million acres;[6] a train needed more than one day to cross that of the Escandones family in central Mexico.[7]

Cold statistics tell the story. Deprived of their land, impoverished and unemployed, the mass of Indians and peasants constituted a huge pool for exploitation. And exploited they were. Always subject to some forced labor since colonization, under Díaz they became enslaved within a nationwide system of slave (chattel) and indebted labor. The venal, corrupt, and ruthless took full advantage, as they were protected by links between greedy landowners and pitiless labor contractors on the one hand, and profiteering police and government officials on the other. In some places, such as Valle Nacional, the forced labor system became at least as deadly as that which afflicted the Soviet people at its worst, but within guarded haciendas instead of camps surrounded by barbed wire.

One of the main methods used for enslaving the workers on haciendas was to advance them money. While it was probably a small amount, the worker found it almost impossible to repay, caught, as he was, between the abysmal wages that had resulted from the ready availability of impoverished workers in the countryside and the cost of necessities of life. For example, he could only purchase necessities at the company store, but the bosses often paid their workers in coupons or metal disks that only the company store would accept in exchange for goods. Moreover, debt was by law inherited, so the son also became an indebted slave. And, as with any slave anywhere, if the indebted worker tried to run away, he would be sought by the police, returned if caught, and whipped publicly as a lesson to the others — sometimes even to death.

But the worker could become indebted in ways other than through the hacienda. The poor peon was enmeshed in a system of customs and laws that encouraged, if not required, that he spend more money than he possessed. For example, baptism required a fiesta, a priest, and liquor, the cost of which could only be covered by pledging future wages, as was the case for one's first clothes, one's tools, the cost of a wedding, the birth of a baby. Whether on the hacienda or not, usually to the poor and landless a debt was forever; even to one's children. And once in debt, the worker had no rights while the debt holder had all the power. On the hacienda, this power was over life and death.

Throughout the colonial world of the early twentieth century, peonage and indentured labor were common. In some places, such as the German and Portuguese African colonies, these forced laborers often were worked to death, or they died from mistreatment within months or years. What is unusual about Mexico at this time is the scale of the power over the citizens, whether Indian or Mexican peasant, and its systematic and deadly abuse.

Before going into this democide, I must note that there were good haciendas and bad ones. Among the better ones, the indebted or indentured workers were still forced to work, but they were treated more with the paternalism one would accord personal slaves: they would be whipped to keep discipline and order, but treated also with some civility. On the worst of the haciendas, which were apparently more in line with custom,[8] the peons' lives were usually short and miserable. They were whipped for the slightest infraction; they were whipped when the work slowed; they were whipped sometimes to death when they tried to escape. "Many overseers treated them worse than animals, since they were cheaper to replace, and if an overseer beat a peon to death the local authorities took no action. In Yucatán, the workers on the henéquen plantations (often deportees from other parts of Mexico) worked in chains and were flogged for trifling offenses."[9]

But on many haciendas the peon's misery went far beyond whipping. Wives and daughters would be customarily raped by the bosses, and the prettier ones forced to be their concubines. The bosses provided insufficient nutrition to sustain an adult worker in the field and no change of clothing or bathing facilities. Sanitary conditions were primitive. Disease, exposure, and exhaustion took their toll.

> No planter who knows the real history of the system, or the inside facts of the neighboring plantations, will deny for a moment that the worst stories of the *enganchado* [indebted peon] are true.

> Plantation men do not take the *enganchado* labor because they like it. Nor do they prefer it to any other, even the lowest. But there is a certain advantage in it, as one planter said to the writer, with a queer thrill in his voice: *"When you've got 'em they're yours, and have to do what you want them to do. If they don't, you can kill them."*[10]

Chattel slavery also abounded. Impoverished and landless Indians and other peons would be enticed into signing contracts to work on plantations from which they could never escape. Or they were jailed by the police for trivial or make-believe crimes and then sold as chattels to plantation owners. Or they were just rounded up like cattle and deported to some plantation or another, the survivors to work until they died. Local officials would contract with a hacienda to supply so many workers per year and, in the case of one *jefe politico* (district political boss), when bodies got scarce he fulfilled his contract by grabbing and selling to the hacienda young school boys for fifty pesos each.[11]

While the existence of this slave system is undeniable, orders of magnitude are difficult to find. Out of a rural population of nearly 12 million in 1910,[12] possibly 750,000 were chattel slaves in southern Mexico;[13] possibly over 100,000 on the Yucatán peninsula.[14] Overall, in 1910 debt bondage possibly enslaved some 5 million peons,[15] or about one-third of the total population of Mexico.

How many died because of beatings, mistreatment, or outright killing? First, those Indians enslaved on the haciendas often were especially mistreated and among the first to die. We can see this with the Yaqui Indians, for example, in the interviews conducted by the journalist John Kenneth Turner, whose 1909–1910 investigative reporting on this slavery created a sensation in the United States.[16] He was told by Don Enrique Camara Zavala, the millionaire planter and president of the Camara de Agricola de Yucatán, that "if the Yaquis last out the first year they generally get along all right and make good workers, but the trouble is, *at least two-thirds of them die off in the first twelve months!*" [17] On one farm, Turner found only two Yaqui survivors out of a group of 200 that the farm had bought two years before. One had half his foot eaten off by insects. "I expect I'll have to kill that tiger," said the general manager to Turner. "He'll never be worth anything to me any more."[18]

For another Indian nation, the Mayas, again from Turner: "In Yucatán the Maya slaves die off faster than they are born."[19]

But non-Indian peons were also badly treated, and on some haciendas their life could be brutish and short. Said one American boss of a large plantation near Santa Lucrecia: " I remember a lot of three hundred *enganchados* we received one Spring. *In less than three months we buried more than half of them.*"[20] In the aforementioned Valle Nacional, "all of the slaves, all but a very few — perhaps five percent — pass back to earth within a space of seven or eight months.... And there are fifteen thousand of these Valle Nacional slaves — fifteen thousand new ones every year!"[21] This plantation is not unlike those in many sections of Mexico and particularly in the south, even, says Turner, if it is a "little bit the worst example of chattel slavery that I know of."[22]

I have spent some time doing research on the Soviet gulag,[23] and all this is sickeningly familiar. But is it believable? To this Turner answers explicitly.

This statement [about all except perhaps five percent dying in the first seven or eight months] is almost unbelievable. I would not have believed it; possibly not even after I had seen the whole process of working them and beating them and starving them to death, were it not the fact that the masters themselves told me that it was true.

...

"By the sixth or seventh month they begin to die off like flies at the first winter frost, and after that they're not worth keeping. The cheapest thing to do is to let them die; there are plenty more where they came from."

Word for word, this is a statement made to me by Antonio Pla, general manager of one-third the tobacco lands in Valle Nacional.

"I have been here for more than five years and every month I see hundreds and sometimes thousands of men, women and children start over the road to the valley, but I never see them come back. Of every hundred who go over the road not more than one ever sees this town again." This assertion was made to me by a station agent of the Veracruz al Pacifico railroad.

"There are no survivors of Valle Nacional — no real ones," a government engineer who has charge of the improvement of certain harbors told me. "Now and then one gets out of the valley and gets beyond El Hule. He staggers and begs his way along the weary road toward Cordoba, but he never gets back where he came from. Those people come out of the valley walking corpses, they travel on a little way and then they fall."

This man's work has carried him much into Valle Nacional and he knows more of the country, probably, than does any Mexican not directly interested in the slave trade.

"They die; they all die. The bosses never let them go until they're dying."

Thus declared one of the police officers of the town of Valle Nacional, which is situated in the center of the valley and is supported by it.

And everywhere over and over again I was told the same thing. Even Manuel Lagunas, *presidente* (mayor) of Valle Nacional, protector of the planters and a slave owner himself, said it. Miguel Vidal, secretary of the municipality, said it. The bosses themselves said it. The Indian dwellers of the mountain sides said it. The slaves said it. And when I had seen, as well as heard, I was convinced that it was the truth.[24]

This incredible similarity to the Soviet forced labor system goes beyond the lethal camps and includes deportation. Deportations and accompanying deaths, particularly of Indians, were also a notable aspect of the Mexican slave labor market. For example, at the rate of 500 a month, Yaqui Indians were seized and deported to work on haciendas as slaves. This was even before Díaz decreed that every Yaqui, wherever found and no matter the age, was to be seized by the War Department and deported to Yucatán. They also would end up enslaved on the haciendas. That is, if they survived, for the deportations held their own dangers. In one case, for example

mostly elderly people, women and children, were shipped from Guaymas to San Blas, then herded on foot over mountains to San Marcos, a journey of about fifteen days. From there they went by train to Mexico City and Veracruz and then again by boat to Progreso. Between ten and twenty per cent usually died on the journey. Families were deliberately split up en route to break their spirit even further before they were sent to work on the *henequén* plantations.

...

In February 1908 one boatload of Yucatán bound Yaquis committed mass suicide to avoid being sold into slavery. Colonel Francisco B. Cruz, in charge of the shipment, reported: "Those Indians wanted to cheat us out of our commission money and so they threw their children into the sea and jumped in after them. We lowered boats but it was no use; they all went down before we got to them."[25]

This is all democide, of course. Taking into account what little statistics on these deaths there are and the number enslaved, I guess that in the ten years up to the revolution over 800,000 deportees, Indian slave laborers, ordinary peons, and other workers were probably killed by this system; perhaps even up to 2 million. However, the number could also be only a tenth of this.[26] No one has counted the corpses. Nonetheless, in this country with a population of about 15 million, the relative toll must have been horrendous.

Were this all, it would be enough to thoroughly condemn this reprehensible government. But there is more. Such a system also depended on a certain amount of terror and resulting fear. Each of the states of Mexico had attached to it an *acordada*, a select group of assassins. Personal enemies of the governor or *jefe politicos*, political opponents, critics, or alleged criminals against which there was insufficient evidence, were quietly killed. In one case, the son of a friend of Díaz was made a member of the *acordada*, given two assistants, and told to "kill quietly along the border" at his discretion any person he thought connected to the opposing Liberal Party.[27] But much killing also was public and directly carried out by officials. In 1909, for example, at Tehuitzingo, sixteen people were summarily executed. At Velardena, several people were shot in the street for holding a parade in defiance of the *jefe politico*, and twelve to thirty-two others were forced to dig their own graves with their bare hands before being shot.[28] In the state of Hidalgo,

a group of Indians who resisted the appropriation of their lands were buried up to their necks in the ground they had attempted to defend, and the *rurales* [rural police] galloped over them. Enemies and critics of Díaz became victims of the *ley fuga*, the law of flight, by which *rurales* and the army were permitted to shoot prisoners, afterwards explaining that they had been killed while attempting to escape.... There were more than ten thousand instances of *ley fuga* during Díaz's rule.[29]

Through this *ley fuga* and general terror, from 1900 to 1910 the Díaz regime may have murdered at least 30,000 political opponents, political suspects, critics, alleged criminals, and other undesirables. Probably more.

Quite obviously, Díaz's policies provided opportunity for the venal and corrupt, and security and help for the rich and well placed. As long as they went along with the system, bureaucrats, officials controlling government largess, and the upper middle class and wealthy profited by Díaz's rule while the lower classes did not. The worker, for example, was forbidden to strike.

With the Indians and peasants dispossessed of their land and impoverished; with large numbers of them enslaved on farms and haciendas or with that horror to look forward to; with the industrial worker only marginally better off; and with large numbers of other Mexicans angered by what they saw as foreign exploitation of their country encouraged by Díaz; with a newly developed sense of injustice and exploitation promoted by intellectuals; and with a small, corrupt, and inefficient army; rebellion was bound to occur.[30] And it did. A number of times. But the first successful one and that which launched the revolution was led in the fall of 1910 by Francisco Madero. Upper middle class, believing in a liberal constitutional government, supported by Indians and peasants, and with the important generalship of the former bandit chief Pancho Villa, Madero won major victories against government forces and encouraged other rebellions throughout the country. In May 1911, Díaz fled into exile and Maderos took over the presidency.

In office, Maderos turned out to be ineffective, especially in promoting changes to the system. But he did give peasants and workers free reign to air their grievances and seek change. This, added to the other disorders still plaguing the country, was seen by the elite as endangering property and by the United States as threatening its citizens and their investments. In early 1913, the general commanding the army in Mexico City, Victoriano Huerto, rebelled and, joining hands with other rebels groups, forced Maderos to resign. Huerto then made himself president (Maderos was assassinated four days later).

Huerto's presidency was even worse. He turned out to be not only inefficient but also repressive and dictatorial. His rule is most noteworthy for having instigated the most violent phase of the revolution. As separate movements to restore constitutional government took to the field, Villa's forces among them, civil war broke out in three northern states. In the south, Emiliano Zapata organized and generated a peasant rebellion demanding land reform. In these rebellions, President Wilson of the United States played a strong role. He embargoed arms to Huerto (resulting in the navy's temporarily taking over Veracruz to stop a shipment of German arms) while allowing the constitutionalists to buy them. With constitutionalist forces closing in on him, Huerto escaped into exile in July 1914 and the rebels took over the capital, Mexico City.

But with full government power in their grasp, the constitutionalists could not agree on what was to be done and by whom. Civil war again broke out in December. Finally, by the end of 1915, one of the rebel leaders, Venustiano Carranza, captured control of most of Mexico and, in spite of the refusal of some other rebel leaders, such as Zapata (assassinated in 1918) and Villas, to accept terms, took over the reigns of government and held them until 1920. Under Carranza, a radical liberal constitution was written that, although hardly ever exercised over the next decades, became a program for successive governments. Carranza never brought about the reforms he had promised. And in 1920 he was overthrown by Alvaro Obregón, one of his most effective generals during the civil war, who then was elected president. Although dictatorial, Obregón brought relative stability, order, and change to Mexico.

What is left out of this sketch of the Mexican Revolution is the incredible violence, ruthlessness, and cruelty, on all sides. In the opening years of the revolution in the north, for example, federal (government) forces simply shot all captured rebels. No mercy was shown. When in later years of the war General González was ordered by President Carranza to destroy the "Zapata rabble" in Morelos, he

> systematically began to lay waste to a countryside which had already been ravaged by seven years of civil war. Whole villages were burned; crops were destroyed; women and children were herded into detention camps

and every man González could lay his hands on was hanged. The entire sugar industry of the state was wrecked as González looted what factories and *haciendas* Zapata had left untouched. Even the huge copper vats in the distilleries were melted down and the metal sold.[31]

During the first six months of the rebellion by the constitutionalists, not one of their commanders could be found in federal prison — all those captured had been shot.[32]

Rebels were equally viscous and often extended their butchery to top government supporters and officials. A case in point was their seizure of Guerrero. All captured federal officers were killed; so were the town's top Díaz supporters and officials, including the judge, *jefe politico*, and postal inspector.[33] Whatever city or town they captured, the rebels raped at will. The U.S. ambassador reported that in Durango, for example, fifty women "of good family" killed themselves after rebels raped them.[34]

When rebels captured and held Mexico City in 1914, they pillaged homes and businesses and shot policemen.[35] Villa himself forced "his attentions on a Frenchwoman," creating an international incident.[36] The U.S. State Department learned that 150 people had been accused of political crimes and shot. The rebels also imposed their own sense of criminal justice. Zapata's men hung three people outside the police station, with signs announcing their crime. One was a "thief," a second a "counterfeiter." The sign for the third said "this man was killed by mistake."[37]

Villa's soldiers were particularly prone to use the bullet. They shot suspected spies and counterrevolutionaries; just a hinted "slur on the revolutionary uniform" could mean death.[38] Even innocents were in danger. The British author Charlotte Cameron was in the capital at the time and subsequently wrote, "You may go out fifty times and nothing happens, yet the fifty-first time your life may be forfeit."[39]

From the beginning of the revolution the Villistas had shown a complete disregard for human life. When in 1910 Pancho Villa captured the town of Torreón he killed 200 Chinese, a race he and his followers much despised.[40] Neither did he have any regard for the lives of his own troops. Once, when being interviewed by an American journalist, he was disturbed by a drunken soldier yelling nearby. While continuing his conversation, he "casually pulled his pistol and killed the man from the window."[41] Villa's officers were no better, but among them stands out Fausto Borunda. He always killed his prisoners, and when there were too few of them he would shoot civilians instead. When the Villistas took the town of Durango, for example, there were not many prisoners. So Borunda went from saloon to saloon, picked out a man in each, and asked each if he was a President Huerta sympathizer. When the poor man denied it, of course, Borunda would accuse him of lying and shoot him.[42] But most notorious among this army of killers was Rodolfo Fierro, who, it is said, once personally executed at one time 300 prisoners, "pausing only to massage a bruised trigger finger."[43] Often these rebels were simply bandits and murderers legitimized by a cause. In one especially heinous case, a rebel leader seized a coal train in a tunnel, burned it, and then waited for a passenger train to run into the wreckage so that he could loot the train of gold and the presumably dead and dying passengers of their valuables.[44]

Then there were the forces of Zapata, apparently no less a band of murderers. Said an English widow who with other refugees fled from them: "The Zapatistas treated all alike — masonry, dumb animals and human beings."[45] This may not be quite correct, since dumb animals probably were not tortured.

> Captured landowners and army officers faced agonizing deaths at Zapata's hands. Some victims were crucified on telegraph poles or on giant cactus trees; others were staked out over ants' nests and smeared with honey, or sewn up inside wet hides and left to suffocate as the hides dried in the sun. One of Zapata's favorite execution methods was to stake out a man on a rough framework of branches over the top of a fast-growing maguey cactus. During the night the thorn tipped blossom stalk of the plant would grow a foot or more, driving itself inch by inch through the staked-out victim.[46]

With the collapse of the Díaz regime, many state governors and federal generals became increasingly independent of the central government. During the Carranza presidency they in effect became warlords, some levying their own taxes, some refusing to turn over federal revenues, some ignoring federal laws and orders they did not like. Some became bandits, looting territory or states under their control; some bandits became generals controlling little states of their own. "Even in Mexico City, high military officers continued to loot and kill virtually as they pleased."[47]

My impression is that over all of Mexico for as long as a decade all these warlords and rebel armies must have killed in cold blood at least nearly 400,000 people; perhaps even over 500,000.

Before and during the revolution, a particularly vile conscription system was used. Since the decision as to who would be drafted was in the private hands of the *jefe politico* in each town, graft and bribery were an integral part of the system. Those without the money to buy themselves out of the draft or to bribe officials, those who criticized the regime, those who tried to strike, or those who otherwise angered officials were the ones who ended up in the army.[48] The army served the function of a forced labor camp for undesirables, and for this reason became known as "The National Chain-gang."[49]

During the revolution, press-gang methods were used extensively. In one case, for example, 700 spectators at a bullfight were grabbed for the army; in another case 1,000 spectators in a big crowd watching a fire were similarly seized, including women who were forced to work in ammunition factories.[50] Wrote one woman from Mexico city, "A friend told me this morning that the father, mother, two brothers and sister of one of her servants were taken last week. They scarcely dare, any of them, to go out after dark. Posting a letter may mean, literally, going to the cannon's mouth."[51]

This is, of course, not democide. But it led to democide in the following sense: These soldiers received little training and were thrown into battle as so much expendable equipment — there were always replacements, even criminals, vagabonds, beggars, and Indian peons. They were cannon fodder. In many cases these soldiers would be given little medical care and little food because of the graft among their officers. Some would literally die of starvation; many of disease. One example of this was in the territory of Quintana Roo, where before the revolution an army of 2,000 to 3,000 soldiers was in the field, continuously fighting the Maya Indians. These soldiers were almost all political suspects and thus really armed political prisoners. According to a government physician who served as the chief of sanitary service for the army in this territory,

> During the first two years I was there the death rate was 100 per cent a year, for in that period more than 4,000 soldiers died of starvation and

sickness induced by starvation!

...

General Bravo steals the commissary money and starves the soldiers with the connivance of the federal government. More than 2,000 have died of acute starvation alone during the past seven years, since General Bravo took command.[52]

This is democide. From 1900 through the first year of the revolution, and aside from combat deaths, possibly nearly 145,000 men thus died from conscription and army servitude.

In total, perhaps 2 million Mexicans died in the revolution because of battle, massacre, execution, starvation, and disease;[53] the toll might even be closer to the 3 million population decrease for these years.[54] In any case, nearly 1,200,000 probably died from influenza, typhus, and other diseases. Clearly, this revolution was one of the bloodiest civil wars in our century, only matched by that which followed the Bolshevik coup in Russia and the civil war between the nationalists and communist Chinese.

TABLE 16.1
Mexican Democide, 1900–1920

Kind of Killing	Democide (000) [a]
Federal Government	1,417
Pre-Civil War massacres and executions	30 [b]
Civil War democide	388
Deportation	30
Chattel Slavery/Peonage	825
Conscription	144
Rebels/Bandits/Warlords	420
Total Democide	1,837
Civil War/Rebellion [c]	335

a All estimates are from *Statistics of Democide*. Unless otherwise noted, all estimates are mid-values in a low-high range.

b Estimated low.

c Includes pre-Revolutionary rebellions.

Through its system of peonage and chattel slavery, terror, democidal conscription, revolutionary democide, and political terror, Mexican governments committed murder on a massive scale, surely totaling at least hundreds of thousands of Indians, peons, innocent villagers, captured soldiers, and conscripts. But a more precise toll is unknown and unestimated. As given in *Statistics of Democide*, from partial information and estimates I calculate that from 1900 to 1920 total government democide alone amounted to somewhere between some 600,000 and 3,300,000 Mexicans, perhaps, as shown in table 16.1, closer to 1,400,000 killed. Although these figures amount to little more than educated guesses, I believe that there is enough here to at least indict the Mexican authoritarian governments of 1900 to 1920 for megamurder.

Notes

1. *Encyclopedia Britannica* 1973, 15: 355.
2. Fehrenbach 1973, 464.
3. Atkin 1969, 25.
4. *Encyclopedia Britannica* 1973, 15: 355.
5. Knight 1986, 1: 96.
6. Fehrenbach 1973, 463; Atkin 1969, 25.
7. Fehrenbach 1973, 463.
8. Ibid., 465.
9. Atkin 1969, 29
10. Turner 1969, 197.
11. Ibid., 71.
12. Simpson 1937, 33
13. Turner 1969, 92.
14. Based on ibid., 91, and Tutino 1986, 395.
15. From *Statistics of Democide*.
16. See Sinclair Snow's "Introduction" to Turner 1969.
17. Turner 1969, 49–50.
18. Ibid., 86.
19. Ibid., 54.
20. Ibid., 225.
21. Ibid., 54.
22. Ibid., 56.
23. Rummel 1990.
24. Turner 1969, 54–55.
25. Atkin 1969, 33.
26. See *Statistics of Democide*.
27. Turner 1969, 127.
28. Ibid., 132.

29. Atkin 1969, 14
30. For a serious question raised about the role of exploitation and the mistreatment of workers, see Ruíz 1980, 76–77. He may overstate his case, however. Although there may have been a negative relationship between peasant uprisings and the regions with the greatest exploitation, this does not mean the idea of exploitation did not play an important role among peasants elsewhere and for middle-class liberals and intellectuals. See Hart 1987, 9–10 and Knight 1986, 1: 166.
31. Atkin 1969, 303
32. Lieuwen 1968, 18.
33. Atkin 1969, 62.
34. Lieuwen 1968, 18.
35. Ibid., 27.
36. Fehrenbach 1973, 520–21.
37. Atkin 1969, 236.
38. Fehrenbach 1973, 521.
39. Atkin 1969, 259.
40. Ibid., 62.
41. Ibid., 174.
42. Ibid., 145.
43. Ibid.
44. Ibid., 169.
45. Ibid., 303.
46. Ibid.
47. Ibid., 297. See also Lieuwen 1968, 36–37.
48. Turner 1969, 121 and 124.
49. Ibid., 121.
50. Atkin 1969, 156–57.
51. Ibid., 157. See also Lieuwen 1968, 19–20.
52. Turner 1969, 123.
53. Elliot 1972, 98, 234; Blackey and Paynton 1976, 180.
54. Atkin 1969, xiv.

17

1,066,000 Murdered?
Feudal Russia

Captivity [for prisoners of war] was a struggle harder and more bitter than any other.

—Elsa Brändström,
Among Prisoners of War in Russia & Siberia

In 1900 Russia was ruled by the last of the Russian czars, Nicholas II. In 1894, with the death of his father, Alexander III, he had come to power — a dedicated autocrat opposed to liberal tendencies in Russia. His wife, Princess Alexandra, strongly shared his view. He was also an absolute Russian nationalist who imposed a policy of Russification throughout the empire, which in the west included Poland and Finland. He was also, as were many Russians, anti-Semitic.

Nicholas' anti-Semitism was shared by his officials. The "government consciously, deliberately, knowingly, and overtly supported anti-Semitic activity."[1] The 5 to 7 million Jews in Russia[2] were actively discriminated against economically and culturally. No doubt this alone continued the historical anti-Semitic climate that encouraged and helped legitimize the periodic pogroms that swept Russian cities and towns. In some cases officials were directly involved; in some cases incendiary anti-Jewish propaganda was published on government printing presses; in some cases the police just stood by while Jews and their property were attacked. In many cases the murderers of Jews and responsible officials went unpunished. Nonetheless, although there "is very little hard evidence to show that the government consciously pursued ... a 'pogrom policy,' the circumstantial evidence is damning."[3] In the spring of 1903 somewhere between 47 and 49 Jews were murdered in Kishinev.[4] In 1905 there were massacres in Baku, Kostroma, Rostoff, Odessa, Nakhitchevan, and other places.[5] In Jitomir, over 150 Jews were killed.[6] In 1906 at Belostok some 82 Jews were murdered.[7] From 1900 to the abdication of the czar and the end of the Romanov dynasty in 1917, at least 3,200 Jews must have been killed throughout Russia.[8]

Other kinds of killing and massacres also occurred, such as the shooting down of 200 demonstrating workers in the Lena goldfield.[9] In Armenia in 1903, the governor general of the Caucasus, Prince Golitsyn, tried to nationalize all Armenian Church property. Armenians resisted, and the Cossacks launched a campaign of terror against them.[10] The most important massacre of these years occurred in January of 1905 when in St. Petersburg as many as 1,000 peaceful demonstrators were shot down.[11] This "Bloody Sunday," as it became known, catalyzed what was a revolutionary situation into outright revolution.

Ever since the previous decade, Russia had been in turmoil. Strikes, student demonstrations, and peasant disturbances were frequent. By 1905, revolutionary movements such as the Socialist Revolutionaries and the Social Democrats, of which the Bolsheviks were a faction, were organizing protests, trying to incite the masses, and setting up committees and conferences to detail the direction of reform. As a result of Bloody Sunday, student demonstrations became almost continuous, huge strikes were organized, and peasant uprisings broke out in a number of regions. Bombings and assassinations were widespread.

This culminated in a massive general strike that finally persuaded the czar and his officials to compromise. They issued the so-called

October Manifesto that promised civil liberties, a new duma with actual legislative power to pass and reject all laws, and other reforms. The manifesto went far toward turning the government into a constitutional monarchy. It split the opposition into moderates willing to accept it and radicals believing it hardly went far enough. The radicals fought on — in the next year alone terrorism by the Battle Organization of the Socialist Revolutionaries and the Socialist Revolutionaries-Maximalists caused 1,400 deaths and still another 3,000 in the year following that.[12] But the 1905 revolution was in fact over.

Throughout the years leading up to and following this revolution, the government fought the revolutionaries in one district or another with harsh regulations, newspaper closings, arrests of editors, and, for six months, even summary court martials with almost immediate execution. At least 950[13] to more than 1,000[14] people were killed. The records of overall executions tell the story of these tumultuous years and the government's response. From 1866 to 1900 no more than 94,[15] perhaps as few as 48,[16] people were executed; from 1901 to 1904 nearly 400 people were executed;[17] from 1905 through 1908 the number rose to 2,200;[18] and from 1908 through the remaining years of the monarchy the number executed may have reached 11,000.[19] Judging the level of executions in the latter part of the previous century (an average of one or two executions a year), many of these thousands must have been executed for political offenses and as part of a campaign of severe repression.

Nonetheless, in spite of revolutionary activity and the bombings, assassinations, and disturbances involved, the democide would have been surprisingly low for an empire this huge and diverse and with its bloody history had it not been for World War I and its treatment of ethnic Germans and POWs and the massacre or extermination of rebellious nations and groups in the southern periphery of the empire. In 1915, the duma decided to expropriate all the property of the 150,000 to 200,000 Germans living in Zhitomir Gubernia and deport them to the east. Perhaps as many as 200,000 were deported; under such conditions, 25,000 to almost 140,000 German men, women, and children may have died.[20]

Apparently, the worst killing took place in the Kirghiz Kazak Confederacy, as bitterly denounced by the historian Arnold Toynbee:

During [World War I], while people in England were raking up the
Ottoman Turks' nomadic ancestry in order to account for their murder of
600,000 Armenians, 500,000 Turkish-speaking Central Asian nomads ...
were being exterminated — also under superior orders — by that "justest
of mankind" the Russian muzhik. Men, women, and children were shot
down, or were put to death in a more horrible way by being robbed of their
animals and equipment and then being driven forth in winter time to perish
in mountain or desert. A lucky few escaped across the Chinese frontier.
These atrocities were courageously exposed and denounced by Mr.
Kerensky in the Duma ... , but who listened or cared? Not the [Czar's]
Government, nor the great public in the West.[21]

All these deaths were democide.

Less clear was the killing by Armenian volunteers wearing Russian
uniforms but serving as irregulars with the Russian army. When
Russia invaded the eastern provinces of Turkey during the war, these
Armenian irregulars may have slaughtered tens and perhaps hundreds
of thousands of Moslem Kurds. This is reported by Hassan Arfa,
former chief of staff of the Iranian army (1944–46) and ambassador to
Turkey (1958–61) in his book *The Kurds*:

When the Russian armies invaded Turkey ... their columns were preceded
by battalions of irregular Armenian volunteers, both from the Caucasus
and from Turkey.
...
These Armenian volunteers, on order to avenge their compatriots who had
been massacred by the Kurds, committed all kinds of excesses, more than
six hundred thousand Kurds being killed between 1915 and 1916 in the
eastern vilayets of Turkey.[22]

This probably far overstates the toll, even though quoted elsewhere.[23]
Statistician Ahmen Emin, formerly professor of statistics in
Constantinople University, most likely is closer to the truth with
figures that add up to a massacre of at least nearly 128,000 Moslem
Turks and Kurds.[24] The precise responsibility of the Russian army for
the killing by their irregular forces is unclear, but at least they bear
some onus for these deaths.

None of this democide, however, is sufficient to raise the czar and
his government to megamurder status. It was the Russian treatment of

its prisoners of war during World War I that does so. In the early years of the war, Russia captured large numbers of German, Austro-Hungarian, Czech, and Turkish prisoners, amounting in total for the war to over 2,300,000 POWs. No doubt the Russian people suffered considerably during the war. There were wide-scale shortages of necessities and resulting localized famines; medical services had always been poor and deteriorated during the war, resulting in the spread of disease. Moreover, Russian soldiers themselves suffered from hunger, poor medical care, and unsanitary conditions, perhaps 1,300,000 alone dying of disease during the war.[25] Russia was in no shape, therefore, to treat POWs with the care Britain, for example, was able to accord her prisoners. Nonetheless, even taking this into account, Russian-held POWs were abysmally treated and died in transit to camps and in the camps themselves by the tens of thousands.

Elsa Brändström, the daughter of the Swedish ambassador who served in St. Petersburg before the war, has written a neutral's description of this democide.[26] When the war came she volunteered to help POWs held in Russia and subsequently served in POW camps and hospitals over a period of five and one-half years. Her eyewitness reports clearly point to official responsibility for many POW deaths. Just consider the transportation of these prisoners to camps when they might be locked in cars for weeks. In one case, for example, 200 Turkish POWs suffering from cholera

> were sent north from the Southern Front in sealed wagons, which were not opened until Pensa was reached three weeks later. Sixty men scarcely alive were dragged out of the filth, the others had already succumbed.

> In February 1915 two wagons arrived in Samara with doors and windows boarded up. They were supposed to contain foodstuffs, but inside there were sixty-five Turks of whom eight were still alive.[27]

Weakened by hunger and sickness during the long trip, prisoners then might have to plod 10 to 30 miles to their final camp. And "in the long ranks of men ... now and again one broke down, and, in spite of the help of his comrades, this, his first march into the steppe, was also his last."[28]

Reaching camp provided no security. The conditions in many were lethal. In one, during the winter of 1914–15, over half of the camp's POWs died — 1,300 men — 1,000 of them from typhus.

When the doctors complained about the numbers of deaths to a general who came on a tour of inspection, his answer was that still more men died in the trenches.

Only when the epidemic had reached proportions threatening the Russians themselves with danger, were captive officers allowed to help the men, this ... being otherwise forbidden.[29]

During this same winter in the Novo Nikolayevsk camp, the prisoners were lucky even to be able to sleep on rotten straw and especially to get a blanket. Camp doctors had no medicines or surgical appliances; they had no soap or brushes. Sick and healthy lay together indiscriminately. Often water was not to be had for days or would drip from icicles on to the straw beds. No wonder that when typhus broke out it spread rapidly and prisoners died in huge numbers.

During the melting of the snow, prisoners, the sick and the healthy, might be seen greedily drinking the water that flowed yellow with human excrement from the latrines. Out of the 1,100 men who had originally been in one of these churchyard barracks [earth huts], only 70 left it alive. The mortality in the camp rose and rose until in April 1915, 70 to 80 men died every day.

At the order of a Russian brigade surgeon 1,500 sick prisoners of war were transferred to a stone barracks, where they had to lie without straw on the plank beds or on the cement floor, more than half of them succumbing. Of the 8,600 prisoners brought to the camp during the winter 4,500 died. All the captive doctors and nurses caught typhus and of these 33 per cent died.[30]

Conditions were as bad at many other camps. At the Nargin Island camp, 2,100 out of 3,000 POWs died in six months; 16,000 died at the Omsk camp; 17,000 out of 25,000 in the Totzkoye camp; 45,000 out of 200,000 at the Turkestan camps; and so on. Forced labor also took its toll, with 25,000 out of 70,000 laborers on the Murman railroad dying.[31] This toll is on a par with that for Japanese-held POWs forced to slave on the Burma-Thailand railroad (36 percent for Russia's POWs versus 32 to 35 percent for Japan's), made infamous by the movie *Bridge on the River Kwai*.[32]

Even after the abdication of the czar in March 1917 and the fall of the Romanov dynasty, many POWs continued to die unnecessarily under the successor Kerensky government and the Bolsheviks after their coup in November. Even after the end of the war, many POWs were still held and subjected to barbarous mistreatment, sometimes by former POWs themselves, as by the Czechs who, as they made their way to Siberia trying to escape Russia, would lock up other POWs in concentration camps under Czech guard.[33]

In total, over 158,000 German POWs died while in captivity, over 39 percent of those imprisoned.[34] Considering also the far more numerous Austro-Hungarian and Turkish POWs, altogether 400,000 to 600,000 POWs may have died,[35] probably 500,000. Of these, possibly 400,000 deaths were the responsibility of the czar's government and thus democide.

Taking into account all the democide from 1900 to March 1917, possibly nearly 900,000 to almost 1,500,000 Russians, members of the Russian empire, and foreigners were killed; perhaps slightly over the 1 million shown in table 17.1. But this figure is more uncertain than for the megamurderers described in other chapters. There are too few sources of information to accord Russia this status; there is only sufficient evidence to indict her as a megamurderer.

TABLE 17.1
Russian Democide, 1900–1917

Type of Killing	Democide (000) [a]
Domestic Democide	595
extermination campaign	500
deportations	83
executions	7
Jewish pogroms	2 [b]
other	4
Foreign Democide	475
POWs	400
Turks/Kurds	75
Total Democide	1,070
War/Rebellion	3,556

a All estimates are from *Statistics of Democide*. Estimates are mid-values.
b Estimated low.

Notes

1. Lambroza 1992, 241.
2. Séménoff 1972, 12.
3. Lambroza 1992, 238.
4. Gilbert 1982, 70; Lambroza 1992, 200.
5. Séménoff 1972, 52.
6. Ibid., 56.
7. Ibid., 204.
8. See *Statistics of Democide*.
9. *The Facts on File Encyclopedia of the 20th Century* 1991, 549.
10. Lang 1981, 113.
11. *Encyclopedia Britannica* 1973, 19: 798.
12. Riasanovsky 1977, 458.
13. Dziak 1988, 173.
14. Riasanovsky 1963, 459.
15. Conquest 1978, 229.
16. Dziak 1988, 173.
17. This is based on the figures for 1866 to 1900 and the fact that, according to Solzhenitsyn 1973, 434, no more than 486 people were executed in the years 1876–1904.
18. Solzhenitsyn 1973, 434.
19. Conquest 1978, 230.
20. See Glaser and Possony 1979, 526, and Sheehy and Nahaylo 1980, 18, who give widely different figures. The 150,000 German figure is for Russian Volhynia, called Wolhynia by Glaser and Possony.
21. Toynbee 1922, 342.
22. Arfa 1966, 25–26.
23. For example, see Gürün 1985, 216, and O'Ballance 1973, 19.
24. Emin 1930, 218–19.
25. Dumas and Vedel-Petersen 1923, 137.
26. Brändström 1929.
27. Ibid., 64.
28. Ibid., 67.
29. Ibid., 102.
30. Ibid., 103–4.
31. Ibid., 109–10, 114–16, 139, and 144.
32. See chapter 8.
33. Brändström 1929, 252.
34. de Zayas 1988, 279 n. 41.
35. Speed 1990, 109.

References

Note that this is not a bibliography. The items included here are only those ordinarily cited in this book or as sources for estimates in the supplementary *Statistics of Democide*. Books, articles, and other works used for background or otherwise consulted are not listed. In a few cases, references are still given even though their estimates may have been eliminated from appendix tables published in *Statistics of Democide* because they were redundant against other estimates or were from the same source. References given in *Lethal Politics*, *China's Bloody Century*, and *Democide*, are not repeated here unless also cited in this book or associated appendix tables.

Adalian, Rouben. 1991. "The Armenian Genocide: Context and Legacy." *Social Education* 55 (February): 99-104.

Adamic, Louis. 1943. *My Native Land*. New York: Harper and Brothers.

Afghanistan: Six Years of Soviet Occupation. 1985. U.S. Department of State Special Report no. 135, Washington, D.C. December.

The Aftermath: Asia. 1983. Alexandria, Virginia: Time-Life Books.

Ahamed, Emajuddin. 1988. *Military Rule and the Myth of Democracy*. Dhaka, Bangladesh: The University Press.

Ahmad, Rafiq (Ed.). 1984. *The Assam Massacre 1983 (A Documentary Record)*. Lahore, Pakistan: Center for South Asian Studies, University of the Punjab.

al-Khalil, Samir. 1989. *Republic of Fear: The Politics of Modern Iraq.* Berkeley: University of California Press.

"Albania Accuses Tito of Genocide in Kossowo." 1966. *Central Europe Journal* 14 (December): 399-400.

Albino, Oliver. 1970. *The Sudan: A Southern Viewpoint.* London: Oxford University Press.

Alexander, Andrew. 1990. "Bulgaria ran Brutal Camps for Prisoners." *Honolulu Star-Bulletin* 4 July, p. A-21.

Alexander, Bevin. 1986. *Korea: The First War We Lost.* New York: Hippocrene Books.

Alexander, Edward. 1991. *A Crime of Vengeance: An Armenian Struggle for Justice.* New York: The Free Press.

Ambartsumov, Yevgeny. 1988. "Remembering the Millions that Stalin Destroyed." *Moscow News* (July): 12.

Ambrose, Stephen E. 1991. "Ike and the Disappearing Atrocities." *New York Times Book Review* 24 February.

The American Crime of Genocide in South Viet Nam. 1967. South Viet Nam: Giai Phong Publishing House.

Amiel, Barbara. 1988. "Sovereignty Is Synthetic." *World Press Review* (March): 17-18.

Amnesty Action. 1991. (January/February). Amnesty International.

Anderson, Jack. 1978. "In Cambodia, Obliterating a Culture." *Washington Post* 2 May, p. B12.

Andersson, Hilary. 1992. *Mozambique: A War against the People.* New York: St. Martin's Press.

Andonian, Aram (Ed.). 1920. *The Memoirs of Naim Bey: Turkish Official Documents Relating to the Deportations and Massacres of Armenians.* London: Hodder & Stoughton. (This is a condensed translation of *Documents officiels concernant les massacres arméniens* [Paris: H. Turabian])

Andradé, Dale. 1990. *Ashes to Ashes: The Phoenix Program and the Vietnam War.* Lexington, Massachusetts: Lexington Books.

Antonov-Ovseyenko, Anton. 1981. *The Time of Stalin: Portrait of a Tyranny.* Translated by George Saunders. New York: Harper & Row.

Applegate, William. 1988. "Manial's Refuge Makes It Pearl of the Orient." *The Wall Street Journal* 13 July, p. 19.

Archer, Jules. 1972. *Mao Tse-tung.* New York: Hawthorn Books.

Arendt, Hannah. 1963. *Eichmann in Jerusalem: A Report on the Banality of Evil.* New York: The Viking Press.

Arens, Richard. (Ed.). 1976. *Genocide in Paraguay.* Philadelphia: Temple University Press.

——. 1978. "Death Camps in Paraguay." *American Indian Journal* 4 (July): 3-12.

——. 1982. "The Ache of Paraguay." In *Genocide and Human Rights: A Global Anthology,* (edited) by Jack Nusan Porter. Lanham, Maryland: University Press of America, pp. 218-37.

Arfa, Hassan. 1966. *The Kurds: An Historical and Political Study.* London: Oxford University Press.

Arnold, David. 1988. *Famine: Social Crisis and Historical Change.* Oxford, UK: Basil Blackwell.

Atkin, Ronald. 1969. *Revolution! Mexico 1910-1920.* London: Macmillan.

Avirgan, Tony and Martha Honey. 1982. *War in Uganda: The Legacy of Idi Amin.* Westport, Connecticut: Lawrence Hill.

Aykroyd, W. R. 1974. *The Conquest of Famine.* London: Chatto & Windus.

Aziz, Qutubuddin. 1974. *Blood and Tears.* Karachi: United Press of Pakistan.

Backer, George. 1950. *The Deadly Parallel: Stalin and Ivan the Terrible.* New York: Random House.

Bacque, James. 1989. *Other Losses: An Investigation into the Mass Deaths of German Prisoners.* Toronto, Canada: Stoddard Publishing Company.

Bailes, Howard. 1980. "Military Aspects of the War." In *The South African War: The Anglo-Boer War 1899-1902,* (edited) by Peter Warwick. Burnt Mill, Harlow, Essex, Great Britain: Longman, pp. 65-102.

Bailey, Ronald H. 1978. *Partisans and Guerrillas.* Alexandria, Virginia: Time-Life Books.

——. 1979. *The Air War in Europe.* Alexandria, Virginia: Time-Life Books.

————. 1981. *World War II: Prisoners of War.* Alexandria, Virginia: Time-Life Books.

Bald, Margaret. 1990. "How the CIA Helped Carry out a Massacre of Half-a-million Communists." *Toward Freedom* 39 (October November): 10-11.

Ball, Nicole and Milton Leitenberg. 1991. "Appendix 1. Wars and Conflicts in Developing Countries and Estimates of Related Deaths Since the End of World War II." In *The Post-Cold War World and Its Implications for Military Expenditures in the Developing Countries,* by Robert S. McNamara. Washington, D. C.: World Bank Annual Conference on Development Economics, 25 April.

Bane, Suda Lorena and Ralph Haswell Lutz (Eds.). 1942. *The Blockade of Germany After the Armistice 1918-1919: Selected Documents of the Supreme Council, Superior Blockade Council, American Relief Administration, and Other Wartime Organizations.* Stanford: Stanford University Press.

Bangladesh: Unlawful Killings and Torture in the Chittagong Hill Tracts. 1986. London: Amnesty International Publications.

Banks, Arthur S. 1971. *Cross-Polity Time Series Data.* Cambridge, Massachusetts: The MIT Press.

————. 1972. "Correlates of Democratic Performance." *Comparative Politics* 4 (January): 217-30.

————. (Ed.). 1977. *Political Handbook of the World: 1977: Governments, Regional Issues, and Intergovernmental Organizations as of January 1, 1977.* New York: McGraw-Hill.

Banu, Zenab. 1989. *Politics of Communalism: A Politico-Historical Analysis of Communal Riots in Post-Independence India with Special Reference to the Gujarat and Rajasthan Riots.* Bombay, India: Popular Prakashan.

Baraheni, Reza. 1977. *The Crowned Cannibals: Writings on Repression in Iran.* New York: Random House.

Barron, John and Anthony Paul. 1977. *Peace with Horror: The Untold Story of Communist Genocide in Cambodia.* London: Hodder and Stoughton. American edition titled *Murder of a Gentle Land* (New York: Reader's Digest Press-Thomas Y. Crowell).

Barton, James L. 1930. *Story of Near East Relief (1915-1930): An Interpretation.* New York: Macmillan.

Bauer, Yehuda. 1982. *A History of the Holocaust*. New York: Franklin Watts.

Bawden, C. R. 1968. *The Modern History of Mongolia*. London: Weidenfeld and Nicolson.

Baxter, David M. 1970. "The Serbo-Croatian Antagonism." In *Operation Slaughterhouse: Eyewitness Accounts of Postwar Massacres in Yugoslavia*, (edited) by John Prcela and Stanko Guldescu. Philadelphia: Dorrance & Co., pp. 27-42.

Becker, Elizabeth. 1986. *When the War was Over: Cambodia's Revolution and the Voices of Its People*. New York: Simon & Shuster (A Touchstone Book).

The Beirut Massacre: The Complete Kahan Commission Report. 1983. New York: Karz-Cohl.

Belden, Jack. 1949. *China Shakes the World*. New York: Monthly Review Press.

Bell, J. Bowyer and Ted Robert Gurr. 1979. "Terrorism and Revolution in America." In *Violence in America: Historical & Comparative Perspectives*. Rev. ed. Edited by Hugh Davis Grahams and Ted Robert Gurr. Beverly Hills: Sage Publications, pp. 329-47.

Beloff, Nora. 1985. *Tito's Flawed Legacy: Yugoslavia & the West since 1939*. Boulder, Colorado: Westview Press.

Ben-Tov, Arieh. 1988. *Facing the Holocaust in Budapest: The International Committee of the Red Cross and the Jews in Hungary, 1943-1945*. Dordrecht, The Netherlands: Martinus Nijhoff.

Benevides, Maria-Victoria and Rosa-Maria Fischer Ferreira. 1991. "Popular Responses and Urban Violence: Lynching in Brazil." In *Vigilantism and the State in Modern Latin America: Essays on Extralegal Violence*, (edited) by Martha K. Huggins. New York: Praeger, pp. 33-45.

Berenbaum, Michael (Ed.). 1990. *A Mosaic of Victims: Non-Jews Persecuted and Murdered by the Nazis*. New York: New York University Press.

Bermudez, Joseph S., Jr. 1990. *Terrorism: The North Korean Connection*. New York: Crane Russak.

Bernstein, Jonas. 1988. "Colombia: Making Violence an Occupation." *Insight* (15 August): 34-35.

———. 1990. "Odd Couple of Gulf Crisis: the U.S. and Hafez al-Assad." *Insight* (8 October): 26-27.

Berwick, Dennison. 1992. *Savages: The Life and Killing of the Yanomami*. London: Hutchinson.

Bidwell, Robin. 1983. *The Two Yemens*. Longman Group and Westview Press.

Bigelow, Katherine. 1992. "A Campaign to Deter Genocide: the Bahá'í Experience." In *Genocide Watch*, (edited) by Helen Fein. New Haven: Yale University Press, pp. 189-96.

Bischof Günter and Stephan E. Ambrose. 1992. "Introduction." In *Eisenhower and the German POWs: Facts Against Falsehood*, (edited) by Günter Bischof and Stephan E. Ambrose. Baton Rouge: Louisiana State University Press, pp. 1-25.

Blackey, Robert and Clifford Paynton. 1976. *Revolution and the Revolutionary Ideal*. Cambridge, Massachusetts: Schenkman Publishing.

Blood, Arthur K. 1972. "Conflict in East Pakistan: Background and Prospects." In *Bangladesh Genocide and World Press*, (edited) by Fazlul Quader Quaderi. Dacca, Bangladesh: Begum Dilafroz Quaderi, pp. 24-33. (This is a leaked top-secret report prepared by the American consul general in Dacca).

Bodard, Lucian. 1971. *Green Hill: Massacre of the Brazilian Indians*. Translated by Jennifer Monaghan. New York: Outerbridge & Dienstfrey.

Bonds, Ray (Ed.). 1979. *The Vietnam War: The Illustrated History of the Conflict in Southeast Asia*. New York: Crown Publishers.

Bothe, Michael, Karl Josef Partsch, and Waldemar A. Solf. 1982. *New Rules for Victims of Armed Conflicts: Commentary on the Two 1977 Protocols Additional to the Geneva Conventions of 1949*. Boston: Martinus Nijhoff Publishers.

Botjer, George. 1979. *A Short History of Nationalist China 1919-1949*. New York: G. P. Putnam's Sons.

Botting, Douglas. 1983. *The Aftermath: Europe*. Alexandria, Virginia: Time-Life Books.

Bouscaren, Anthony T. 1963. *International Migrations Since 1945*. New York: Praeger.

Bouthoul, Gaston and René Carrère. 1978. "A list of the 366 major armed conflicts of the period 1740-1974." Compiled and translated by Gernot Köhler. *Peace Research* 10 (July): 83-108.

——. 1979. "Major Armed Conflicts, 1965–1 July 1978." Compiled and translated by Gernot Köhler. *Peace Research* 11 (October): 183-86.

Bowen, Gordon L. 1985. "The political economy of state terrorism: barrier to human rights in Guatemala." In *Human Rights and Third World Development*, (edited) by George W. Shepherd, Jr., and Ved P. Nanda. Westport, Connecticut: Greenwood Press, pp. 83-124.

Bowers, William J. 1984. *Legal Homicide: Death as Punishment in America, 1864-1982*. Boston: Northeastern University Press.

Boyajian, Dickran H. 1972. *Armenia: The Case for a Forgotten Genocide*. Westwood, New Jersey: Educational Book Crafters.

Boyle, J. A. 1968. "Dynastic and political history of the Il-Khans." In *The Cambridge History of Iran: Volume 5: The Saljuq and Mongol Periods*, (edited) by J. A. Boyle. Cambridge, Massachusetts: At The University Press, pp. 303-421.

Brackman, Arnold C. 1987. *The Other Nuremberg: The Untold Story of the Tokyo War Crimes Trials*. New York: William Morrow and Co.

Braddock, Lee. 1988. "Moral Unequivalence: Afghanistan is not the Soviets' Vietnam." *Policy Review* (Summer): 42-51.

Bradsher, Henry S. 1976. "Hanoi Tightens the Screws." *Honolulu Star-Bulletin* 14 June, p. A-10.

——. 1977. "South Viets Mutter as Communists Tighten Control." *Washington Star* 12 February, p. 1.

Braham, Randolph L. 1981. *The Politics of Genocide: The Holocaust in Hungary*. Vols. 1-2. New York: Columbia University Press.

Brändström, Elsa. 1929. *Among Prisoners of War in Russia & Siberia*. Translated by C. Mabel Rickmers. London: Hutchinson & Co.

Brauman, Rony. 1986. "Famine Aid: Were We Duped?" *Reader's Digest* (October): 65-72.

Breiner, Sander J. 1990. *Slaughter of the Innocents: Child Abuse through the Ages and Today*. New York: Plenum Press.

Breitkopf, Andrzej and Andrzej Lesniewski. 1961. "Political Origins of the Transfer of German Population to Germany." In *1939-1950 Population Movements Between the Oder and Bug Rivers*. Warsaw, Poland: Zachodnia Agencja Prasowa, pp. 29-40.

Breytenbach, W. J. 1975. "Inter-Ethnic Conflict in Africa." In *Case Studies on Human Rights and Fundamental Freedoms: A World*

Survey. Vol. 1. Editor-in-chief Willem A. Veenhoven. The Hague: Martinus Nijhoff, pp. 311-31.

Brock, David. 1988. "Making Rights a Right in Cuba." *Insight* (29 February): 8-12.

Brockett, Charles D. 1991. "Sources of State Terrorism in Rural Central America." In *State Organized Terror: The Case of Violent Internal Repression*, (edited) by P. Timothy Bushnell, et al. Boulder, Colorado: Westview Press, pp. 59-76.

Brogan, Patrick. 1989. *World Conflicts: Why and Where They are Happening*. London: Bloomsbury.

Bronkhurst, Daan. 1984. "Extrajudicial Executions, International Alerts and Campaigning." In *Toward the Understanding and Prevention of Genocide: Proceedings of the International Conference on the Holocaust and Genocide*, (edited) by Israel W. Charny. Boulder, Colorado: Westview Press, pp. 281-87.

Brooks, Juanita. c1950. *The Mountain Meadows Massacre*. Stanford: Stanford University Press.

Broome, Richard. 1982. *Aboriginal Australians: Black Response to White Dominance, 1788-1980*. Sydney: George Allen & Unwin.

Brown, Cynthia. 1985. *With Friends Like These: The America's Watch Report on Human Rights and U.S. Policy in Latin America*. New York: Pantheon Books.

Brown, Richard Maxwell. 1969. "The American Vigilante Tradition." In *Violence in America: Historical and Comparative Perspectives: A Report Submitted to the National Commission on the Causes and Prevention of Violence*, (edited) by Hugh Davis Graham and Ted Robert Gurr. New York: Bantam Books, pp. 154-226.

——. 1969a. "Historical Patterns of Violence in America." In *Violence in America: Historical and Comparative Perspectives: A Report Submitted to the National Commission on the Causes and Prevention of Violence*, (edited) by Hugh Davis Graham and Ted Robert Gurr. New York: Bantam Books, pp. 45-84.

——. 1975. *Strain of Violence: Historical Studies of American Violence and Vigilantism*. New York: Oxford University Press.

Brownfeld, Allan C. 1986. "Critique: The Media's Nicaragua." *The World & I* 1 (January): 87-94.

Browning, Christopher R. 1990. "Germans and Serbs: The Emergence of Nazi Antipartisan Policies in 1941." In *A Mosaic of Victims: Non-*

Jews Persecuted and Murdered by the Nazis, (edited) by Michael Berenbaum. New York: New York University Press, pp. 64-73.

Browning, Frank and Dorothy Forman (Eds.). 1972. *The Wasted Nations: Report of the International Commission of Enquiry into United States Crimes in Indochina, June 20-25, 1971.* New York: Harper & Row.

Buchkin, Andrew. 1990. "Koreans Under Communism." *International Journal on World Peace* 7 (December): 15-31.

Budiardjo, Carmel. 1975. "Repression and Political Imprisonment." In *Ten Years' Military Terror in Indonesia,* (edited) by Malcolm Caldwell. Nottingham, Great Britain: Spokesman Books, pp. 95-105.

———. 1976. "The Abuse of Human Rights in Indonesia." In *Case Studies on Human Rights and Fundamental Freedoms: A World Survey.* Vol. 3. Editor-in-chief Willem A. Veenhoven. The Hague: Martinus Nijhoff, pp. 211-41.

——— and Liem Soei Liong. 1984. *The War Against East Timor.* London: Zed Books.

Bühler, Phillip A. 1990. *The Oder-Neisse Line: A Reappraisal under International Law.* New York: Columbia University Press.

Burma: Extrajudicial Execution and Torture of Members of Ethnic Minorities. 1988. London: Amnesty International. May.

Burns, Edward McNall and Philip Lee Ralph. 1955. *World Civilizations from Ancient to Contemporary.* Vols. 1-2. 2nd ed. New York: W. W. Norton & Co.

Burns, John F. 1989. "Afghans Disclose Deaths of 11,000." *New York Times* 9 November, p. 15.

Butterfield, Fox. 1982. *China: Alive in the Bitter Sea.* New York: Times Books.

Buttinger, Joseph. 1967. *Vietnam: A Dragon Embattled: Volume II: Vietnam at War.* New York: Praeger.

Byas, Hugh. 1942. *Government by Assassination.* New York: Alfred A. Knopf.

Cabestrero, Teófilo. 1985. *Blood of the Innocent: Victims of the Contras' War in Nicaragua.* Translated by Robert R. Barr. New York: Orbis Books.

Cadbury, William A. 1969. *Labour in Portuguese West Africa.* 2nd ed. with an added chapter. New York: Negro Universities Press (originally published in 1910).

Caldwell, Malcolm (Ed.). 1975. *Ten Years' Military Terror in Indonesia*. Nottingham, Great Britain: Spokesman Books.

Calzón, Frank. 1979. *Castro's Gulag: The Politics of Terror*. Washington, D.C.: Council for Inter-American Security.

"Cambodia Fact Sheet." 1979. Washington D.C.: Bureau of Public Affairs, Department of State. November.

"Cambodia: The Face of Evil." 1977. *Human Events* (21 May):10-14 (*Human Events* interview with John Barron, senior editor of *Reader's Digest*).

Canh, Nguyen Van. 1983. *Vietnam Under Communism, 1975-1982*. With Earle Cooper. Stanford: Stanford University, Hoover Institution Press,.

Carlton, Richard K. (Ed.). 1955. *Forced Labor in the "People's Democracies."* New York: Praeger.

Cartledge, Paul. 1986. "Might and Right: Thucydides and the Melos Massacre." *History Today* 36 (May): 11-15.

Castellan, Georges. 1992. *History of the Balkans: From Mohammed the Conqueror to Stalin*. Translated by Nicholas Bradley. New York: Columbia University Press.

Cerquone, Joseph. 1987. "Uncertain Harbors: the Plight of Vietnamese Boat People." In *Issue Paper of the U.S. Committee for Refugees*. Washington, D.C.: American Council for Nationalities Service. October.

Ch'i, Hsi-sheng. 1982. *Nationalist China at War: Military Defeats and Political Collapse, 1937-45*. Ann Arbor: The University of Michigan Press.

Chalk, Frank and Kurt Jonassohn. 1988. "The History and Sociology of Genocidal Killings." In *Genocide: A Critical Bibliographic Review*, (edited) by Israel W. Charny, New York: Facts on File, Inc., pp. 39-58.

——. 1990. *The History and Sociology of Genocide: Analysis and Case Studies*. New Haven: Yale University Press.

Chalupa, V. 1959. *Rise and Development of a Totalitarian State*. Leiden, Holland: H. E. Stenfert Kroese N. V.

Chamberlain, Mike. 1982. "The People of East Timor." In *Genocide and Human Rights: A Global Anthology*, (edited) by Jack Nusan Porter. Washington, D.C.: University Press of America, pp. 238-43.

Chamerovzow, Louis Alexis. 1850, "Rajah Brooke and the Borneo Massacre." *The Colonial Intelligencer Supplement* (January): 337-68.

Chand, Attar. 1985. *Politics of Human Rights and Civil Liberties—A Global Survey*. Delhi, India: K. K. Thukral, UDH Publishers.

Chanda, Nayan. 1990. "Indochina." In *After the Wars: Reconstruction in Afghanistan, Indochina, Central America, Southern Africa, and the Horn of Africa*, (edited) by Anthony Lake. New Brunswick, New Jersey: Transaction Publishers, pp. 77-100.

Chandra, Prabodh. 1971. *Bloodbath in Bangladesh*. New Delhi, India: Adarsh Publications.

Charny, Israel W. 1982. *How Can We Commit the Unthinkable? Genocide: The Human Cancer*. Boulder, Colorado: Westview Press.

——. (Ed.). 1984. *Toward the Understanding and Prevention of Genocide: Proceedings of the International Conference on the Holocaust and Genocide*. Boulder, Colorado: Westview Press.

——. "1988. The Study of Genocide." In *Genocide: A Critical Bibliographic Review*, (edited) by Israel W. Charny. New York: Facts on File Publication, pp. 1-19.

——. 1991. "A Proposal of a New Encompassing Definition of Genocide: Including New Legal Categories of Accomplices to Genocide, and Genocide as a Result of Ecological Destruction and Abuse." Invited address to the first Raphael Lemkin Symposium on Genocide, Yale University Law School. February.

Chaudhuri, Kalyan. 1972. *Genocide in Bangladesh*. New Delhi: Orient Longman.

Checinski, Michael. 1983. "Terror and Politics in Communist Poland." In *Research Paper No. 13*. Jerusalem: The Soviet and East European Research Center, the Hebrew University of Jerusalem. October.

Cherne, Leo. 1978. "The Terror in Cambodia." *Wall Street Journal* 10 May.

Chesneaux, Jean. 1973. *Peasant Revolts in China, 1840-1949*. Translated by C. A. Curwen. New York: W. W. Norton.

Chi, Hoang Van. 1964. *From Colonialism to Communism: A Case History of North Vietnam*. New York: Frederick A. Praeger.

Chiang Meng-Lin. 1969. "The Mistreatment of Draftees." In *The Road to Communism: China Since 1912*, (edited) by Dun J. Li. New York: Van Nostrand Reinhold, pp. 223-26.

China Handbook 1937-1945. 1947. Rev. and enlarged with 1946 supplement. Compiled by Chinese Ministry of Information. New York: Macmillan.

Chira, Susan. 1989. "Report: North Korea Marred by Regimentation, Rights Abuse." *New York Times*.[x]

Chona, Mark C. and Jeffrey I. Herbst. 1990. "Southern Africa." In *After the Wars: Reconstruction in Afghanistan, Indochina, Central America, Southern Africa, and the Horn of Africa*, (edited) by Anthony Lake. New Brunswick, New Jersey: Transaction Publishers, pp. 141-66.

Chowdhury, Subrata Roy. 1972. *The Genesis of Bangladesh: A Study in International Legal Norms and Permissive Conscience*. New York: Asia Publishing House.

Chu, Valentin. 1963. *Ta Ta, Tan Tan: The Inside Story of Communist China*. New York: W. W. Norton.

Chullbaum, Kim. 1991. *The Truth About the Korean War—Testimony 40 Years Later*. Seoul, Korea: Eulyoo Publishing.

Clark, Michael K. 1960. *Algeria in Turmoil: The Rebellion: Its Causes, Its Effects, Its Future*. New York: Grosset & Dunlap.

Claude, Richard Pierre. 1987. "The Philippines." In *International Handbook of Human Rights*, (edited) by Jack Donnelly and Rhoda E. Howard. New York: Greenwood Press, pp. 279-300.

Clay, Jason W. and Bonnie K. Holcomb. 1985. *Politics and the Ethiopian Famine 1984-1985*. Cambridge, Massachusetts: Cultural Survival. December.

Clayton, Anthony. 1981. *The Zanzibar Revolution and Its Aftermath*. Hamden, Connecticut: Archon Books.

Clissold, Stephen. 1983. *Djilas: The Progress of a Revolutionary*. New York: Universe Books.

Clubb, Edmund O. 1978. *20th Century China*. 3rd ed. New York: Columbia University Press.

Coale, Ansley J. 1984. *Rapid Population Change in China, 1952-1982*. National Research Council Committee on Population and Demography Report no. 27. Washington, D.C.: National Academy Press.

Cockburn, Alexander. 1987. "Mozambique and Its People: Pawns in a Brutal Struggle." *The Wall Street Journal* 24 December, p. 9.

——. 1989. "Nicaragua, Vietnam and Cuba Praise China? Dead Wrong." *The Wall Street Journal* 15 June, p. A15.

——. 1990. "U.S.-Backed Terrorism Won in Nicaragua, Not Democracy." *The Wall Street Journal* 1 March, p. A17.

Collier, Basil. 1967. *The Second World War: A Military History: From Munich to Hiroshima—In One Volume.* New York: William Morrow & Co.

Collier, Richard. 1968. *The River that God Forgot: The Story of the Amazon Rubber Boom.* New York: E. P. Dutton.

Collins, Larry and Dominique Lapierre. 1975. *Freedom at Midnight.* New York: Simon and Schuster.

Colzón, Frank. 1979. *Castro's Gulag: The Politics of Terror.* Washington: Council for Inter-American Security.

Conquest, Robert. 1968. *The Great Terror: Stalin's Purge of the Thirties.* New York: Macmillan.

——. 1970. *The Nation Killers: The Soviet Deportation of Nationalities.* London: Macmillan.

——. 1971. *The Human Cost of Soviet Communism.* Washington: Committee on the Judiciary, United States Senate, 91st Congress, 2nd Session, 1970; and Staff Consultation, 92nd Congress, 1st Session (July); Subcommittee on Internal Security.

——. 1978. *Kolyma: The Arctic Death Camps.* New York: The Viking Press.

——. 1986. *The Harvest of Sorrow: Soviet Collectivization and the Terror-Famine.* New York: Oxford University Press.

——. 1990. *The Great Terror: A Reassessment.* New York: Oxford University Press.

——, Dana Dalrymple, James Mace, and Michael Novak. 1984. *The Man-Made Famine in Ukraine.* Washington, D.C.: American Enterprise Institute for Public Policy Research.

Contenau, Georges. 1954. *Everyday Life in Babylon and Assyria.* London: Edward Arnold.

Cook, Chris (compiler). 1992. *The Facts on File World Political Almanac.* 2nd ed. New York: Facts on File.

Corruccini, Robert S. and Samvit S. Kaul. 1990. *Halla: Demographic Consequences of the Partition of the Punjab, 1947.* New York: University Press of America.

Coutouvidis, John and Jaime Reynolds. 1986. *Poland 1939-1947.* Great Britain: Leicester University Press.

Cowdrey, Albert E. 1992. "A Question of Numbers." In *Eisenhower and the German POWs: Facts Against Falsehood,* (edited) by Günter Bischof and Stephan E. Ambrose. Baton Rouge: Louisiana State University Press, pp. 78-92.

Cox, Meg. 1989. "Unsettling Parallels to Today's China Snarl Museum Film." *The Wall Street Journal* 30 August, p. 1.

Cribb, Robert (Ed.). 1990. *The Indonesian Killings of 1965-1966.* Monash Papers on Southeast Asia—no. 21. Clayton, Victoria, Australia: Center of Southeast Asian Studies, Monash University.

Cronjé, Suzanne. 1976. *Equatorial Guinea—the Forgotten Dictatorship: Forced Labor and Political Murder in Central Africa.* (Research Report no. 2) London: Anti-Slavery Society.

Crosby, Benjamin L. 1990. "Central America." In *After the Wars: Reconstruction in Afghanistan, Indochina, Central America, Southern Africa, and the Horn of Africa,* (edited) by Anthony Lake. New Brunswick, New Jersey: Transaction Publishers, pp. 103-38.

Crouch, Harold. 1978. *The Army and Politics in Indonesia.* Rev. ed. Ithaca: Cornell University Press.

Cuba: Terror and Death. Once Again a Pirate on the Spanish Main. 1964. Miami, Florida: Agencia de Informaciones Periodísticas.

Culbertson, Todd. 1978. "The Human Cost of World Communism." *Human Events* (19 August): 682-83.

"The Current Death Toll of International Communism." 1979. Paper. London: Foreign Affairs Research Institute.

"Current Issues: Analysis." 1986. *The World & I* (January): 90-94.

Curtin, Philip D. 1969. *The Atlantic Slave Trade: A Census.* Madison: The University of Wisconsin Press.

Czaplicka, M. A. 1918. *The Turks of Central Asia in History and at the Present Time: An Ethnological Enquiry into the Pan-Turanian Problem, and Bibliographical Material Relating to the Early Turks and the Present Turks of Central Asia.* Oxford: At The Clarendon Press.

Dadrian, Vahakn N. 1986. "The Naim-Andonian Documents on the World War I Destruction of the Ottoman-Armenians: The Anatomy of Genocide." *International Journal Middle East Studies* 18(3): 311-60.

———. 1991. "A Textual Analysis of the Key Indictment of the Turkish Military Tribunal Investigating the Armenian Genocide." *Armenian Review* 44 (Spring): 1-36.

———. 1991a. "Documentation of the Armenian Genocide in Turkish Sources." In *Genocide: A Critical Bibliographic Review: Vol. 2*, (edited) by Israel W. Charny. London: Mansell, pp. 86-138.

———. 1991b. "The Documentation of the World War I Armenian Massacres in the Proceedings of the Turkish Military Tribunal." *International Middle East Studies* 23: 549-76.

Dallin, Alexander and George Breslauer. 1970. *Political Terror in Communist Systems*. Stanford: Stanford University Press.

Darsa, Jan. 1991. "Educating about the Holocaust: A Case Study in the Teaching of Genocide." In *Genocide: A Critical Bibliographic Review: Vol. 2*, (edited) by Israel W. Charny. London: Mansell, pp. 175-83.

Davidson, Basil. 1972. *In the Eye of the Storm: Angola's People*. Garden City, New York: Doubleday.

Davies, Nigel. 1981. *Human Sacrifice in History and Today*. New York: William Morrow and Co.

Davis, Sheldon H. 1977. *Victims of the Miracle: Development and the Indians of Brazil*. Cambridge, Massachusetts: Cambridge University Press.

Dawidowicz, Lucy S. 1975. *The War Against the Jews 1933-1945*. New York: Holt, Rinehart and Winston.

De Nogales, Rafael. 1926. *Four Years Beneath the Crescent*. Translated by Muna Lee. New York: Scribner's.

De Sismondi, J. C. L. Simonde. 1826. *History of the Crusades against The Albigenses, in the Thirteenth Century*. London: Wrightman and Cramp.

de Jaegher, Raymond J. and Irene Corbally Kuhn. 1952. *The Enemy Within: An Eyewitness Account of the Communist Conquest of China*. New York: Doubleday.

De St. Jorre, John. 1972. *The Brother's War: Biafra and Nigeria*. Boston: Houghton-Mifflin.

de Zayas, Alfred-Maurice. 1979. *Nemesis at Potsdam: The Anglo-Americans and the Expulsion of the Germans: Background, Execution, Consequences.* Rev. 2nd ed. London: Routledge & Kegan Paul.

———. 1988. "A Historical Survey of Twentieth Century Expulsions." In *Refugees in the Age of Total War*, (edited) by Anna C. Bramwell. London: Unwin Hyman, pp. 15-37.

———. 1989. *The Wehrmacht War Crimes Bureau, 1939-1945.* Lincoln, Nebraska: University of Nebraska Press.

Deak, Istvan. 1992. "Holocaust Heroes." *New York Review* 39 (5 November): 22-26.

Dean, Warren. 1987. *Brazil and the Struggle for Rubber: A Study in Environmental History.* Cambridge, Massachusetts: Cambridge University Press.

Dedijer, Vladimir. 1992. *The Yugoslav Auschwitz and the Vatican: The Croatian Massacre of the Serbs During World War II.* Buffalo, New York: Prometheus Books.

The Defense Monitor Various years. Washington, D.C.: Center for Defense Information.

Dekmejian, R. Hrair. 1986. "Determinants of Genocide: Armenians and Jews as Case Studies." In *The Armenian Genocide in Perspective*, (edited) by Richard G. Hovannisian. New Brunswick, New Jersey: Transaction Book, pp. 85-96.

The Dellums Committee Hearings on War Crimes in Vietnam: An Enquiry into Command Responsibility in Southeast Asia. 1972. New York: Vintage Books.

Del Vecchio, John M. 1990. *For the Sake of All Living Things.* New York: Bantam Books.

Demographic Yearbook. Various years. New York: Statistical Office of the United Nations, Department of Economic Affairs.

Denmark, Robert A. and Mary B. Welfling. 1983. "Terrorism in Sub-Sahara Africa." In *The Politics of Terrorism*, (edited) by Michael Stohl. 2nd ed., rev. and extended. New York: Marcel Dekker, pp. 327-76.

Denikine, General A. 1973. *The White Army.* Translated by Catherine Zvegintzov. Westport, Connecticut: Hyperion Press.

Department of State Current Policy No. 106, 1979. Washington, D.C.: Department of State.

Deriabin, Peter. 1972. *Watchdogs of Terror: Russian Bodyguards from the Tsars to the Commissars.* New Rochelle, New York: Arlington House.

Derrick, Jonathan. 1975. *Africa's Slaves Today.* New York: Schocken Books.

Desbarats, Jacqueline. 1990. "Repression in the Socialist Republic of Vietnam: Executions and Population Relocation." In *The Vietnam Debate: A Fresh Look at the Arguments*, (edited) by John Norton Moore. New York: University Press of America, pp. 193-201.

—— and Karl D. Jackson. 1985. "Research among Vietnam Refugees Reveals a Blood Bath." *The Wall Street Journal* 22 April, p. 23.

Desmond, Edward W. 1986. "Mengistu's Ethiopia: Death by Policy." *Freedom at Issue* (March-April):18-22.

Diem, Bui. 1987. *In The Jaws of History.* Boston: Houghton Mifflin Co.

Disappeared! Technique of Terror. 1986. A report for the Independent Commission on International Humanitarian Issues. London: Zed Books.

Djilas, Milovan. 1977. *Wartime.* Translated by Michael B. Petrovich. New York: Harcourt Brace Jovanovich.

——. 1980. *Tito: The Story from Inside.* Translated by Vasilije Kojic´ and Richard Hayes. New York: Harcourt Brace Jovanovich.

Dobkin, Marjorie Housepian. 1986. "What Genocide? What Holocaust? News from Turkey, 1915-1923: A Case Study." In *The Armenian Genocide in Perspective*, (edited) by Richard G. Hovannisian. New Brunswick, New Jersey: Transaction Books, pp. 97-109.

Documents on the Expulsion of the Germans from Eastern-Central-Europe: The Expulsion of the German Population from Czechoslovakia. 1960. Vol. 4. Bonn, Germany: Federal Ministry for Expellees, Refugees, and War Victims.

Documents on the Expulsion of the Germans from Eastern-Central-Europe: The Expulsion of the German Population from Hungary and Rumania. 1961. Vol. 2/3. Bonn, Germany: Federal Ministry for Expellees, Refugees, and War Victims.

Documents on the Expulsion of the Sudenten Germans. 1953. Translated by Gerda Johannsen. Munich, Germany: University Press, Dr. C. Wolf & Sohn.

Domenico, Roy Palmer. 1991. *Italian Fascist on Trial*. Chapel Hill: University of North Carolina Press.

Domes, Jürgen. 1973. *The Internal Politics of China 1949-1972*. Translated by Rüdiger Machetzki. New York: Praeger.

Dorn, Frank. 1974. *The Sino-Japanese War, 1937-41: From Marco Polo Bridge to Pearl Harbor*. New York: Macmillan.

Dower, John W. and John Junkerman (Eds.). 1985. *The Hiroshima Murals: The Art of Iri Maruki and Toshi Maruki*. New York: Kodansha International.

Dower, John W. 1986. *War Without Mercy: Race and Power in the Pacific War*. New York: Pantheon Books.

Dragnich, Alex N. 1954. *Tito's Promised Land: Yugoslavia*. New Brunswick, New Jersey: Rutgers University Press.

Drechsler, Horst. 1980. "Let Us Die Fighting:" In *The Struggle of the Herero and Nama against German Imperialism (1844-1915)*. London: Zed Press.

duCharme, Douglas. 1987. "Lebanon." In *International Handbook of Human Rights*, (edited) by Jack Donnelly and Rhoda E. Howard. New York: Greenwood Press, pp. 227-52.

Duff, Ernest A. and John F. McCamant. 1976. *Violence and Repression in Latin America*. New York: Free Press.

Duffett, John (Ed.). 1968. *Against the Crime of Silence: Proceedings of the International War Crimes Tribunal*. Flanders, New Jersey: O'Hare Books.

Duffy, James. 1967. *A Question of Slavery*. Oxford: At the Clarendon Press.

———. 1968. *Portuguese Africa*. Cambridge, Massachusetts: Harvard University Press.

Duiker, William J. 1981. *The Communist Road to Power in Vietnam*. Boulder, Colorado: Westview Press.

Dujardin, Jean-Pierre. 1978. "N'oublions jamais oui. Mais n'oublions rien." *Le Figaro Magazine* (18 November): 48-51, 150.

Dumas, Samuel and K. O. Vedel-Petersen. 1923. *Losses of Life Caused by War*. Oxford: The Clarendon Press.

Dunn, J.P., Jr. 1969. *Massacres of the Mountains: A History of the Indian Wars of the Far West 1815-1875*. New York: Capricorn Books.

Dunnigan, James F. and Austin Bay. 1985. *A Quick and Dirty Guide to War: Briefings on Present and Potential Wars*. New York: William Morrow and Co.

Duplaix, Nicole. 1988. "Fleas: The Lethal Weapon." *National Geographic*, (May): 675-94.

Dupuy, R. Ernest and Trevor N. Dupuy. 1970. *The Encyclopedia of Military History: From 3500 B.C. to the Present*. New York: Harper & Row.

Durant, Will. 1950. *The Story of Civilization: The Age of Faith*. New York: Simon and Schuster.

——. 1953. *The Story of Civilization: Part V: The Renaissance*. New York: Simon and Schuster.

——. 1954. *The Story of Civilization: Part I: Our Oriental Heritage*. New York: Simon and Schuster.

——. 1957. *The Story of Civilization: Part VI: The Reformation*. New York: Simon and Schuster.

—— and Ariel. 1961. *The Story of Civilization: Part VIII: The Age of Reason Begins*. New York: Simon and Schuster.

Dushnyck, Walter. 1975. "Human Rights in Communist Ruled East-Central Europe." In *Case Studies on Human Rights and Fundamental Freedoms: A World Survey*. Vol. 1. Editor-in-chief Willem A. Veenhoven. The Hague: Martinus Nijhoff, pp. 379-443.

Duvall, Raymond D. and Michael Stohl. 1983. "Governance by Terror." In *The Politics of Terrorism*, (edited) by Michael Stohl. 2nd ed., rev. and extended. New York: Marcel Dekker, pp. 179-219.

Dyadkin, Iosif G. 1983. *Unnatural Deaths in the USSR, 1928-1954*. Translated by Tania Deruguine. New Brunswick, New Jersey: Transaction Books.

Dziak, John J. 1988. *Chekisty: A History of the KGB*. Lexington, Massachusetts: Lexington Books.

Eagleton, William, Jr. 1963. *The Kurdish Republic of 1946*. New York: Oxford University Press.

Eastland, James O. 1972. "Introduction." In *The Human cost of Communism in Vietnam*. A Compendium Prepared for the Subcommittee of the Committee on the Judiciary to Investigate the Administration of the Internal Security Act and Other Internal Security Laws, United States Senate, 92nd Congress, 2nd Session. Washington, D.C.: U.S. Government Printing Office, pp. 1-10.

Eastman, Lloyd E. 1974. *The Abortive Revolution: China under Nationalist Rule, 1927-1937*. Cambridge, Massachusetts: Harvard University Press.

——. 1980. *China Under Nationalist Rule: Two Essays: The Nanking Decade, 1927-1937, and The War Years, 1937-1945*. Urbana, Illinois: Center for Asian Studies, University of Illinois.

——. 1980a. "Facets of an Ambivalent Relationship: Smuggling, Puppets, and Atrocities During the War, 1937-1945." In *The Chinese and the Japanese: Essays in Political and Cultural Interactions*, (edited) by Akira Iriye. Princeton, New Jersey: Princeton University Press, pp. 275-303.

Eban, Abba. 1983. "Introduction." *The Beirut Massacre: The Complete Kahan Commission Report*. New York: Karz-Cohl, pp. v-xvi.

Eberstadt, Nick. 1988. *The Poverty of Communism*. New Brunswick, New Jersey: Transaction Books.

Eckhardt, William. 1989. "Civilian Deaths in Wartime." *Bulletin of Peace Proposals* 20: 89-98.

——. 1991. "War-related Deaths Since 3000 BC." Paper presented at the Annual Meeting of the International Society for the Comparative Study of Civilizations, Santo Domingo, 30 May-2 June.

—— and Gernot Köhler. 1980. "Structural and Armed Violence in the 20th Century: Magnitudes and Trends." *International Interactions* 6 (4): 347-75.

Edib, Halidé. 1930. *Turkey Faces West: A Turkish View of Recent Changes and Their Origin*. New Haven: Yale University Press.

Edwards, Lyford P. 1927. *The Natural History of Revolution*. Chicago: The University of Chicago Press.

El Salvador's Decade of Terror: Human Rights Since the Assassination of Archbishop Romero. 1991. (Americas Watch) New Haven: Yale University Press.

Elegant, Robert. 1982. *How to Lose a War: The Press and Viet Nam*. Ethics and Public Policy Reprint 35. Washington D.C.: Ethics and Public Policy Center. April. (Formerly appeared in *Encounter* August 1981).

Elliot, Gil. 1972. *Twentieth Century Book of the Dead*. London: Allen Lane The Penguin Press.

Elson, Robert T. 1976. *Prelude to War*. Morristown, New Jersey: Time-Life Books.

Ember, Carol, Melvin Ember, and Bruce Russett. 1991. "Peace Between Participatory Polities: A Cross-Cultural Test of the 'Democracies Rarely Fight Each Other' Hypothesis." HRAF Working Paper PO4, 14 June. (Human Relations Area Files, PO Box 2054, Yale Station, New Haven, CT 06520)

Emin, Ahmed. 1930. *Turkey in the World War*. New Haven: Yale University Press.

Ennew, Judith. 1981. *Debt Bondage: A Survey*. London: Anti-Slavery Society.

Eprile, Cecil. 1974. *War and Peace in the Sudan 1955-1972*. London: David & Charles.

Erlich, Haggai. 1983. *The Struggle Over Eritrea, 1962-1978: War and Revolution in the Horn of Africa*. Stanford: Hoover Institution Press, Stanford University.

Esherick, Joseph W. 1987. *The Origins of the Boxer Uprising*. Berkeley: University of California Press.

Etcheson, Craig. 1984. *The Rise and Demise of Democratic Kampuchea*. Boulder, Colorado: Westview Press.

Evans, Stanton M. 1977. "Westerners Ignore Vietnam 'gulag'." *Human Events*: 661.

"Expellees and Refugees of German Ethnic Origin." 1950. Report of a Special Subcommittee of the Committee on the Judiciary, 81st Congress, HR 2nd Session, Report no. 1841, 24 March.

Fabian, Béla. 1959. "Khrushchev's Broken Promise on Slave Labor in Russia." *U.S. News & World Report* (7 September): 84-85.

The Facts on File Encyclopedia of the 20th Century. 1991. New York: Facts on File.

Fairbairn, Geoffrey. 1974. *Revolutionary Guerrilla Warfare: The Countryside Version*. Harmondsworth, Middlesex: Penguin Books.

Fall, Bernard B. 1966. *The Two Viet-Nams: A Political and Military Analysis*. Rev. ed. n.p.

———. 1966a. *Viet-Nam Witness 1953-66*. n.p.; n.d.

———. 1967. *The Two Viet-Nams: A Political and Military Analysis*. New York: Praeger.

Feder, Don. 1989. "The French Revolution: Prelude to Totalitarianism." *Human Events* (1 July): 16.

Fegley, Randall. 1981. "The Human Rights Commission: The Equatorial Guinea Case." *Human Rights Quarterly* 3 (1): 34-47.

Fehrenbach, T. R. 1973. *Fire and Blood: A History of Mexico*. New York: Macmillan.

Feierabend, Ivo K. and Rosalind L. Feierabend. 1972. "Appendix: Invitation to Further Research—Designs, Data, and Methods." In *Anger, Violence, and Politics: Theories and Insights*, (edited) by Ivo K. Feierabend, Rosalind L. Feierabend, and Ted Robert Gurr. Englewood Cliffs, New Jersey: Prentice-Hall, pp. 369-416.

Feig, Konnilyn. 1990. "Non-Jewish Victims in the Concentration Camps." In *A Mosaic of Victims: Non-Jews Persecuted and Murdered by the Nazis*, (edited) by Michael Berenbaum. New York: New York University Press, pp. 161-78.

Fein, Helen. 1977. *Imperial Crime and Punishment: The Massacre at Jallianwala Bagh and British Judgment, 1919-1920*. Honolulu: University Press of Hawaii.

———. 1979. *Accounting for Genocide: National Responses and Jewish Victimization During the Holocaust*. New York: The Free Press.

———. 1984. "Scenarios of Genocide: Models of Genocide and Critical Responses." In *Toward the Understanding and Prevention of Genocide: Proceedings of the International Conference on the Holocaust and Genocide*, (edited) by Israel W. Charny. Boulder, Colorado: Westview Press, pp. 3-31.

———. 1990. "Lives at Risk: A Study of Violations of Life—Integrity in 50 States in 1987 Based on the Amnesty International 1988 Report." Paper. New York: The Institute for the Study of Genocide, John Jay College of Criminal Justice (CUNY). March.

Fejtö, François. 1957. *Behind the Rape of Hungary*. New York: David McKay Co.

The First Freedom. 1988. A newsletter of the Peubla Institute. 1 (June).

Fisk, Robert. 1990. *Pity the Nation: Lebanon at War*. London: André Deutsch.

FitzGerald, Francis. 1973. *Fire in the Lake: The Vietnamese and the Americans in Vietnam*. New York: Vintage Books.

FitzGibbon, Louis. 1971. *Katyn*. New York: Charles Scribner's Sons.

———. 1975. *Unpitied and Unknown: Katyn ... Bologoye ... Dergachi*. London: Bachman & Turner.

Fluharty, Vernon Lee. 1957. *Dance of the Millions: Military Rule and the Social Revolution in Colombia 1930-1956*. Pittsburgh: University of Pittsburgh Press.

Fodor, Denis J. 1982. *The Neutrals*. Alexandria, Virginia: Time-Life Books.

Forced Back and Forgotten. 1989. New York: Lawyers Committee for Human Rights.

Forster, Edward S. 1941. *A Short History of Modern Greece 1821-1940*. London: Methuen & Co.

Fotitch, Constantin. 1948. *The War We Lost: Yugoslavia's Tragedy and the Failure of the West*. New York: The Viking Press.

"Four More Concentration Camps Created Since 1982—152,000 'Dissidents' Now Incarcerated in 12 North Korean Gulags." 1990. *Vantage Point: Developments in North Korea* 13 (January): 17-24. (South Korean Periodical Report).

Francisco, Luzviminda. 1987. "The Philippine-American War." In *The Philippines Reader: A History of Colonialism, Neocolonialism, Dictatorship, and Resistance*, (edited) by Daniel B. Schirmer and Stephen Rosskamm Shalom. Boston: South End Press, pp. 8-19.

Franke, Richard W. 1976. *East Timor: The Hidden War*. 2nd ed., rev. and extended. New York: East Timor Defense Committee. December.

Frelick, Bill. 1987. "Death in a Boxcar Bound for Ethiopia." *The Wall Street Journal* 25 August, p. 28.

Frelick, Bill. 1992. "Refugees: Contemporary Witnesses to Genocide." In *Genocide Watch*, (edited) by Helen Fein. New Haven: Yale University Press, pp. 45-58.

Fuertes, Sol. 1988. "The Bloody Anarchy in Colombia." *World Press Review* (April): 16.

Fuller, Edmund. 1988. "Death of an Indian Dream." *The Wall Street Journal* 12 December.

Gallo, Max. 1973. *Spain Under Franco*. Translated by Jean Stewart. London: George Allen & Unwin.

Garside, Roger. 1981. *Coming Alive: China After Mao*. New York: McGraw-Hill.

Gates, John Morgan. 1973. *Schoolbooks and Krags: The United States Army in the Philippines, 1898-1902*. Westport, Connecticut: Greenwood Press.

Gelinas, Andre. 1977. "Life in the New Vietnam." *Washington Post* 13 March, p. C4.

Gentile, William. 1981. "Nicaragua Still in Turmoil—2 Years after Leftist Takeover." *The Sunday Star-Bulletin and Advertiser* (Honolulu) 19 July, p. A-16.

George Orwell's Nineteen Eighty-Four: North Korea. 1984. Seoul, Korea: Tower Press.

German African Possessions (Late) 1969. Vol. 17. (Peace Handbooks Issued by the Historical Section of the British Foreign Office) New York: Greenwood Press.

Gilbert, Martin. 1982. *The Macmillan Atlas of the Holocaust.* New York: Macmillan Publishing Co.

Gill, Peter. 1986. *A Year in the Death of Africa: Politics, Bureaucracy and the Famine.* London: Paladin Grafton Books.

Giorgis, Dawit Wolde. 1989. *Red Tears: War, Famine and Revolution in Ethiopia.* Trenton, New Jersey: The Red Sea Press.

Gist. 1979. Washington, D.C.: Bureau of Public Affairs, Department of State. November.

Glaser, Kurt and Stefan T. Possony. 1979. *Victims of Politics: The State of Human Rights.* New York: Columbia University Press.

Global Data Manager. 1990. Macintosh Version 2.3 computer application. Philadelphia, Pennsylvania: World Game Institute.

Gluckstein, Ygael. 1952. *Stalin's Satellites in Europe.* Boston: The Beacon Press.

Glukinov, Stanislav. 1991. "Better in Jail than at Home." In *Information Service on the Unification Question of the Korean Peninsula* (National Unification Board, Seoul, Korea) (April): 33-39.

Goldstein, Robert Justin. 1992. "The Limitations of Using Quantitative Data in Studying Human Rights Abuses." In *Human Rights and Statistics: Getting the Record Straight*, (edited) by Thomas B. Jabine and Richard P. Claude. Philadelphia: University of Pennsylvania Press, pp. 35-61.

Gollancz, Victor. 1948. *Our Threatened Values.* Hinsdale, Illinois: Henry Regnery.

Gorriti, Gustavo. 1990. "The Shining Path Fights on in Peru." *The Wall Street Journal* 20 July, p. A15.

Gough, Kathleen. 1986. "Correspondence." *Bulletin of Concerned Asian Scholars* 18 (July-September): 65-66.

Grant, Michael. 1992. *A Social History of Greece and Rome*. New York: Charles Scribner's Sons.

Graves, Ralph. 1992. "When a Victory Really Gave Us a New World Order." *Smithsonian* 22 (March):88-97.

Grebler, Leo and Wilhelm Winkler. 1940. *The Cost of the World War to Germany and Austria-Hungary*. New Haven: Yale University Press.

Green, Stephen J. 1975. "Afterword." In *The Politics of Starvation*, by Jack Shepherd. New York: Carnegie Endowment for International Peace, pp. 87-98.

Greene, Frederic Davis. 1895. *The Armenian Crisis in Turkey: The Massacre of 1894, Its Antecedents and Significance*. London: Putnam's Sons.

Greenland, Jeremy. 1976. "Ethnic Discrimination in Rwanda and Burundi." In *Case Studies on Human Rights and Fundamental Freedoms: A World Survey*. Vol. 4. Editor-in-chief Willem A. Veenhoven. The Hague: Martinus Nijhoff, pp. 95-133.

Greer, Donald. 1935. *The Incidence of the Terror during the French Revolution: A Statistical Interpretation*. Cambridge, Massachusetts: Harvard University Press.

Gross, Feliks. 1966. *World Politics and Tension Areas*. n.p.: New York University Press.

——. 1972. *Violence in Politics: Terror and Political Assassination in Eastern Europe and Russia*. The Hague, Netherlands: Mouton.

——. 1978. *Ethnics in a Borderland: An Inquiry into the Nature of Ethnicity and Reduction of Ethnic Tensions in a One-Time Genocide Area*. Westport, Connecticut: Greenwood Press.

Gross, Jan Tomasz. 1979. *Polish Society Under German Occupation: The Generalgouvernement, 1939-1944*. Princeton: Princeton University Press.

Grousset, René. 1966. *Conqueror of the World*. Translated by Marian McKeller and Denis Sinor. New York: The Orion Press.

Guantao Jin. 1984. *Behind History*. In Chinese; translated for the author by Hua Shiping. Chengdu: Sichuan People's Publishing House.

Guatemala: A Nation of Prisoners. 1984. New York: An Americas Watch Report.

Guatemala: Human Rights Violations under the Civilian Government. 1989. New York: Amnesty International. June.

"Guatemala 1978: The Massacre at Panzos." 1978. *International Work Group for Indigenous Affairs Document #33*, Denmark.

Guérard, Albert. 1969. *France: A Modern History*. New ed. (rev. and enlarged by Paul A. Gagnon) Ann Arbor: The University of Michigan Press.

Gurr, Ted Robert. 1979. "Political Protest and Rebellion in the 1960s: The United States in World Perspective." In *Violence in America: Historical & Comparative Perspectives*. Rev. ed. Edited by Hugh Davis Grahams and Ted Robert Gurr. Beverly Hills: Sage Publications, pp. 49-76.

———. 1986. "The Political Origins of State Violence and Terror: A Theoretical Analysis." In *Government Violence and Repression: An Agenda for Research*, (edited) by Michael Stohl and George A. Lopez. New York: Greenwood Press, pp. 45-71.

Gürün, Kamuran. 1985. *The Armenian File: The Myth of Innocence Exposed*. London: K. Rustem & Bro. and Weidenfeld & Nicolson Ltd.

Gwertzman, Bernard. 1976. "Up to 50,000 Prisoners Held in Laos Camps." *Honolulu Star-Bulletin* 17 November, p. E-3.

Halliday, Fred and Maxine Molydeux. 1981. *The Ethiopian Revolution*. London: Verso Editions and NLB.

Harbord, James G. 1972. "Report to the 66th Congress of the United States." In *Armenia: The Case for a Forgotten Genocide*. Westwood, by Dickran H. Boyajian. New Jersey: Educational Book Crafters, pp. 160-205.

Harff, Barbara. 1986. "Genocide as state terrorism." In *Government Violence and Repression: An Agenda for Research*, (edited) by Michael Stohl and George A. Lopez. New York: Greenwood Press, pp. 165-87.

———. 1987. "The etiology of genocides." In *Genocide and the Modern Age: Etiology and Case Studies of Mass Death*, (edited) by Isidor Wallimann and Michael N. Dobkowski. New York: Greenwood Press, pp. 41-59.

———. 1989. "Victims of the State: Genocide, Politicides, and Group Repression since 1945." *International Review of Victimology* 1: 23-41.

—— and Ted Robert Gurr. 1988. "Toward Empirical Theory of Genocides and Politicides: Identification and Measurement of Cases since 1945." *International Studies Quarterly* 32: 359-371.

Harrison, Charles. 1976. "Uganda: The Expulsion of the Asians." In *Case Studies on Human Rights and Fundamental Freedoms: A World Survey*. Vol. 4. Editor-in-chief Willem A. Veenhoven. The Hague: Martinus Nijhoff, pp. 287-315.

Harrison, James Pinckney. 1982. *The Endless War: Fifty Years of Struggle in Vietnam*. New York: The Free Press.

Hart, B. H. Liddell. 1934. *A History of the World War 1914-1918*. 2nd, enl. ed. London: Faber & Faber.

——. 1970. *History of the Second World War*. New York: G. P. Putnam's Sons.

Hart, John Mason. 1987. *Revolutionary Mexico: The Coming and Process of the Mexican Revolution*. Berkeley: University of California Press.

Harvey, Karen D. 1991. "Vanquished Americans." *Social Education* 55 (February): 132-33.

Hawk, David. 1982. "The Killing of Cambodia." *New Republic*, (15 November): 17-21.

——. 1984. "Pol Pot's Cambodia: Was It Genocide?" In *Toward the Understanding and Prevention of Genocide: Proceedings of the International Conference on the Holocaust and Genocide*, (edited) by Israel W. Charny. Boulder, Colorado: Westview Press, pp. 51-59.

Heder, Stephen R. 1980. *Kampuchean Occupation and Resistance*. Asian Studies Monographs no. 027, Thailand: Institute of Asian Studies, Chulalongkorn University. January.

Heinsohn, Gunnar and Otto Steiger. 1985. *Die Vernichtung Der Weisen Frauen*. Herbstein: März Verlag GmbH.

Heller, Mikhail. 1988. *Cogs in the Wheel: The Formation of Soviet Man*. New York: Alfred A. Knopf.

—— and Aleksandr Nekrich. 1986. *Utopia in Power: The History of the Soviet Union from 1917 to the Present*. Translated by Phyllis B. Carlos. New York: Summit Books.

Hemming, John. 1987. *Amazon Frontier: The Defeat of the Brazilian Indians*. London: Macmillan.

Henderson, James D. 1985. *When Colombia Bled: A History of the Violencia in Tolima*. University, Alabama: The University of Alabama Press.

Herling, Albert Konrad. 1951. *The Soviet Slave Empire*. New York: Wilfred Funk.

Herman, Edward S. 1970. *Atrocities in Vietnam: Myths and Realities*. Philadelphia: Pilgram Press.

Hilberg, Raul. 1961. *The Destruction of the European Jews*. New York: Harper & Row.

Hildebrand, George and Gareth Porter. 1976. *Cambodia: Starvation and Revolution*. New York: Monthly Review Press.

Hingley, Ronald. 1970. *The Russian Secret Police: Muscovite, Imperial Russian and Soviet Political Security Operations 1565-1970*. London: Hutchinson & Co.

———. 1974. *Joseph Stalin: Man and Legend*. London: Hutchinson & Co.

Hiroshima and Nagasaki: The Physical, Medical, and Social Effects of the Atomic Bombings. 1981. Translated by Eisei Ishikawa and David L. Swain. The Committee for the Compilation of Materials on Damage Caused by the Atomic Bombs in Hiroshima and Nagasaki, New York: Basic Books, Inc.

Hirsch, Herbert and Roger W. Smith. 1991. "The Language of Extermination in Genocide." In *Genocide: A Critical Bibliographic Review: Vol. 2*, (edited) by Israel W. Charny. London: Mansell, pp. 386-403.

The Historical Reillumination on the Korean War. 1990. Seoul, Korea: War Memorial Service—Korea.

Ho Ping-ti. 1959. *Studies on the Population of China, 1368-1953*. Cambridge, Massachusetts: Harvard University Press.

Hodgin, Deanna. 1990. "An Ethnic Inferno in Island Paradise." *Insight* (22 October): 8-18.

Hodgkin, Thomas. 1981. *Vietnam: The Revolutionary Path*. New York: St. Martin's Press.

Hodos, George H. 1987. *Show Trials: Stalinist Purges in Eastern Europe 1948-1954*. New York: Praeger.

Hoig, Stan. 1961. *The Sand Creek Massacre*. Norman: University of Oklahoma Press.

Hoile, David. 1989. *Mozambique: A Nation in Crisis*. Lexington, Georgia: The Claridge Press.

Holler, Joanne E. 1963. *The German Expellees: A Problem of Integration*. Washington, D.C.: Population Research Project, The George Washington University.

Horne, Alistair. 1977. *A Savage War of Peace: Algeria 1954-1962*. New York: The Viking Press.

Horne, Charles F. and Walter R. Austin. 1920. *The Great Events of the Great War*. Vol. 7. n.p.: National Alumni.

Horowitz, Irving Louis. 1976. *Genocide: State Power and Mass Murder*. New Brunswick, New Jersey: Transaction Books.

——. 1980. *Taking Lives: Genocide and State Power*, New Brunswick, New Jersey: Transaction Books.

——. 1989. "Counting Bodies: the Dismal Science of Authorized Terror." *Patterns of Prejudice*, 23 (Summer):4-15.

"Horrible Conditions of Concentration Camp Unmasked by Former Inmates." 1992. *Vantage Point: Developments in North Korea* 15 (November): 16-19. (South Korean Periodical Report)

Hosmer, Stephen. 1970. *Viet Cong Repression and Its Implications for the Future*. Lexington, Massachusetts: D.C. Heath and Company.

Housepian, Marjorie. 1966. *The Smyrna Affair*. New York: Harcourt Brace Jovanovich.

——. 1982. "The Unremembered Genocide." In *Genocide and Human Rights: A Global Anthology*, (edited) by Jack Nusan Porter. Lanham, Maryland: University Press of America, pp. 99-115.

Housepian-Dobkin, Marjorie. 1984. "What Genocide? What Holocaust? News from Turkey, 1915-23: A Case Study." In *Toward the Understanding and Prevention of Genocide: Proceedings of the International Conference on the Holocaust and Genocide*, (edited) by Israel W. Charny. Boulder, Colorado: Westview Press, pp. 100-12.

Hovannisian, Richard G. 1980. *The Armenian Holocaust: A Bibliography Relating to the Deportation, Massacres, and Dispersion of the Armenian People, 1915-1923*. Cambridge, Massachusetts: Armenian Heritage Press.

——. 1984. "Genocide and Denial: The Armenian Case." In *Toward the Understanding and Prevention of Genocide: Proceedings of the International Conference on the Holocaust and Genocide*, (edited) by Israel W. Charny. Boulder, Colorado: Westview Press, pp. 84-99.

———. (Ed.). 1986. *The Armenian Genocide in Perspective*. New Brunswick, New Jersey: Transaction Books.

———. 1986a. "The Historical Dimensions of the Armenian Question, 1878-1923." In *The Armenian Genocide in Perspective*, (edited) by Richard G. Hovannisian. New Brunswick, New Jersey: Transaction Books, pp. 19-41.

———. 1986b. "The Armenian Genocide and Patterns of Denial." In *The Armenian Genocide in Perspective*, (edited) by Richard G. Hovannisian. New Brunswick, New Jersey: Transaction Books, pp. 111-33.

———. 1988. "The Armenian Genocide." In *Genocide: A Critical Bibliographic Review*, (edited) by Israel W. Charny. New York: Facts on File, Inc., pp. 89-115.

Howard, Rhoda E. 1989. "Indonesia and Nigeria: Matched-pair Sampling as a Method of Studying Human Rights Performance." Unpublished paper. Hamilton, Ontario, Canada: Sociology Department, McMaster University. 23 February.

Howorth, Henry H. 1965. *History of the Mongols from the 9th to the 19th Century: Part I: The Mongols Proper and the Kalmuks*. New York: Burt Frankin. (Reprint of 1876 London ed.)

Hoyle, Russ. 1982. "Moving the Miskitos." *Time* (1 March): 22.

Hoyt, Edwin P. 1984. *On to the Yalu*. Briarcliff Manor, New York: Stein and Day Publishers.

Huddleston, Sisley. 1965. *France: The Tragic Years 1939-1947: An Eyewitness Account of War, Occupation and Liberation*. Boston: Western Islands.

Hudson, Michael C. 1970. *Conditions of Political Violence and Instability: A Preliminary Test of Three Hypotheses*. Comparative Politics Series, Series Number 01-005. Vol. 1. Beverly Hills, California: Sage Publications.

Huggins, Martha K. (Ed.). 1991. *Vigilantism and the State in Modern Latin America: Essays on Extralegal Violence*. New York: Praeger.

Hugo, Graeme. 1987. "Postwar Refugee Migration in Southeast Asia: Patterns, Problems, and Policies." In *Refugees: A Third World Dilemma*, (edited) by John R. Rigge. Totowa, New Jersey: Rowman & Littlefield, pp. 237-52.

The Human Cost of Communism in Vietnam. 1972. Committee on the Judiciary, United States Senate, 92d Congress, 2d Session, Washington, U.S. Government Printing Office.

Human Rights in Castro's Cuba. 1986. Special Report no. 153. Washington, D.C.: United States Department of State. December.

Human Rights in Iraq. 1990. (Middle East Watch) New Haven: Yale University Press.

Human Rights in Nicaragua: An Americas Watch Report. 1984. New York: The Americas Watch Committee.

Human Rights Violations in Democratic Kampuchea: A Report Prepared by the United Kingdom Government. 1978. Foreign Policy Documents no. 25. Great Britain. 14 July.

Humbaraci, Arslan. 1974. "Part I." In *Portugal's African Wars: Angola, Guinea Bissao, Mozambique,* by Arslan Humbaraci and Nicole Muchnik. New York: Joseph Okpaku Publishing, pp. 11-73.

Hunczak, Taras. 1990. "The Ukrainian Losses during World War II." In *A Mosaic of Victims: Non-Jews Persecuted and Murdered by the Nazis,* (edited) by Michael Berenbaum. New York: New York University Press, pp. 116-27.

Hutchinson, Martha Crenshaw. 1978. *Revolutionary Terrorism: The FLN in Algeria, 1954-1962.* Stanford: Hoover Institution Press.

Hyman, Harold. 1992. "The Fall of Diên Biên Phú." *Freedom Review* 23 (May-June): 41-43.

Ibarra, Calos Figueroa. 1991. "Guatemala: The Recourse of Fear." In *Vigilantism and the State in Modern Latin America: Essays on Extralegal Violence,* (edited) by Martha K. Huggins. New York: Praeger, pp. 73-83.

Injustice, Persecution, Eviction: A Human Rights Update On Indonesia and East Timor. 1990. New York: Human Rights Watch. March.

The International Commission of Jurists (Geneva). 1972. "Part II: Legal Study of the Events in East Pakistan, 1971." In *Bangladesh Establishment Illegal.* Lahore, Pakistan: Fazalsons Publishers, pp. 1-98.

Internet on the Holocaust and Genocide: An International Information Resource Exchange Towards Understanding, Intervention, and Prevention of Genocide. Various issues. Published by the Institute on the Holocaust and Genocide, P.O.B. 10311, 91102 Jerusalem, Israel.

Investigations into Certain Past Instances of Genocide and Exploration of Policy Options for the Future. 1976. U.S. House of Representatives, Hearings, Committee on International Relations. Ninety-Fourth Congress, 2nd Session, May 11; August 30.

Irvine, Reed and Joseph C. Goulden. 1990. "U.S. Left's 'Big Lie' about El Salvador Deaths." *Human Events* (15 September): 787.

Isaacs, Arnold R., Gordon Hardy, and MacAlister Brown. 1987. *Pawns of War: Cambodia and Laos.* Boston, Massachusetts: Boston Publishing Co.

Ishemo, Shubi L. 1989. "Forced Labour, *Mussoco* (Taxation), Famine and Migration in Lower Zambézia, Mozambique, 1870-1914." In *Forced Labour and Migration: Patterns of Movement within Africa*, (edited) by Abebe Zegeye and Shubi Ishemo. New York: Hans Zell Publishers, pp. 109-58.

Iskander, Maskun. 1990. "Purwodadi: Area of Death." Translated by Robert Cribb. In *The Indonesian Killings of 1965-1966*, (edited) by Robert Cribb. Monash Papers on Southeast Asia—no. 21. Clayton, Victoria, Australia: Center of Southeast Asian Studies, Monash University, pp. 203-13.

Ismael, Tareq Y. and Jacqueline S. Ismael. 1986. *The People's Democratic Republic of Yemen Politics, Economics and Society: The Politics of Socialist Transformation.* London: Francis Pinter Publishers.

Israel in Lebanon. 1983. (Report of the International Commission to inquire into reported violations of international law by Israel during its invasion of the Lebanon) London: Ithaca Press.

Jackson, Gabriel. 1965. *The Spanish Republic and the Civil War 1931-1939.* Princeton, New Jersey: Princeton University Press.

Jackson, Karl D. 1989. "Introduction, The Khmer Rouge in Context." In *Cambodia 1975-1978: Rendezvous with Death*, (edited) by Karl D. Jackson. Princeton, New Jersey: Princeton University Press, pp. 3-11.

Jacobs, Dan. 1987. *The Brutality of Nations.* New York: Alfred A. Knopf.

James, David H. 1951. *The Rise and Fall of the Japanese Empire.* London: George Allen & Unwin.

James, W. Martin III. 1992. *A Political History of the Civil War in Angola 1974-1990.* New Brunswick, New Jersey: Transaction Publishers.

Jansson, Kurt, Michael Harris, and Angela Penrose. 1987. *The Ethiopian Famine*. London: Zed Books.

Japan at War. 1980. Alexandria, Virginia: Time-Life Books.

Jeffries, Brian. 1980. "A Long Look at the Long Exodus from Indochina Nations." *Honolulu Star-Bulletin* 27 November, p. J-16.

Jensen, Holger. 1987. "Mozambique: Winning the War against All Odds." *Insight* (12 January): 33-35.

Johnson, B. L. C. 1975. *Bangladesh*. New York: Barnes & Noble.

Johnson, Paul. 1983. *Modern Times: The World from the Twenties to the Eighties*. New York: Harper & Row.

———. 1991. *Modern Times: The World from the Twenties to the Eighties*. Rev. ed. New York: Harper & Row.

———. 1991a. *The Birth of the Modern: World Society 1815-1830*. New York: HarperCollins.

Jukic, Ilija. 1974. *The Fall of Yugoslavia*. Translated by Dorian Cooke. New York: Harcourt Brace Jovanovich.

Jung Hee-nam. 1990. "Korean Democide under the Decolonization Process 1945-1950." Paper (presented to R.J. Rummel's graduate course, PS740 on "Government Repression and Mass Murder"). Honolulu: University of Hawaii, 2 May.

Juvenal, Claude. 1979. "Equatorial Guinea—After 10 Years of Bloody Rule." *The Sunday Star-Bulletin & Advertiser* 12 August, p. A-12.

Kahin, George McTurnan and Jown W. Lewis. 1967. *The United States in Vietnam: An Analysis in Depth of the History of America's Involvement in Vietnam*. n.p.: A Delta Book.

Kamenetsky, Ihor. 1961. *Secret Nazi Plans for Eastern Europe: A Study of Lebensraum Policies*. New Haven, Connecticut: College and University Press.

Kampuchea: A Demographic Catastrophe. 1980. A Research Paper of the National Foreign Assessment Center, Washington, D.C.: Central Intelligence Agency. January.

Kampuchea: After the Worst: A Report on Current Violations of Human Rights. 1985. New York: Lawyers Committee for Human Rights. August.

Kampuchea in the Seventies: Report of a Finnish Enquiry Commission. 1982. Helsinki, Finland: Kampuchean Enquiry Commission.

Kampuchea: Political Imprisonment and Torture. 1987. London: Amnesty International. June.

Kane, Penny. 1988. *Famine in China, 1959-1961: Demographic and Social Implications*. New York: St. Martin's Press.

Kannyo, Edward. 1987. "Uganda." In *International Handbook of Human Rights*, (edited) by Jack Donnelly and Rhoda E. Howard. New York: Greenwood Press, pp. 385-408.

Kaplan, Robert D. 1988. *Surrender or Starve: The Wars Behind the Famine*. Boulder, Colorado: Westview Press.

——. 1990. "Bloody Romania." *The New Republic* (30 July and 6 August): 12-15.

Kaps, Johannes (Ed.). 1952/53. *The Tragedy of Silesia 1945-46: A Documentary Account with a Special Survey of the Archdiocese of Breslau*. Translated by Gladys H. Hartinger. Munich, Germany: "Christ Unterwegs."

Karpat, Kemal H. 1985. *Ottoman Population 1830-1914: Demographic and Social Characteristics*. Madison: The University of Wisconsin Press.

Katz, Susan. 1986. "Mozambique: A Leader's Legacy: Economic Failure, Growing Rebellion." *Insight* (10 November): 28-30.

Kaufman, Edy and Patricia Weiss Fagen. 1981. "Extrajudicial Executions: An Insight into the Global Dimensions of a Human Rights Violation." *Human Rights Quarterly* 3 (Fall): 81-100.

Kedge, Peter. 1987. "Chinese Promises, Tibetan Reality." *The Wall Street Journal* 12 October, p. 23.

Keller, Edmond J. 1988. *Revolutionary Ethiopia: From Empire to People's Republic*. Bloomington: Indiana University Press.

Kelley, Donald R. 1974. "Martyrs, Myths, and the Massacre: The Background of St. Bartholomew." In *The Massacre of St. Bartholomew: Reappraisals and Documents*, (edited) by Alfred Soman. The Hague: Martinus Nijhoff, pp. 181-202.

Kemasang, A. R. T. 1982. "The 1740 Massacre of Chinese in Java: Curtain Raiser for the Dutch Plantation Economy." *Bulletin of Concerned Asian Scholars* 14 (January-March): 61-71.

Kenez, Peter. 1992. "Pogroms and White Ideology in the Russian Civil War." In *Pogroms: Anti-Jewish Violence in Modern Russian History*, (edited) by John D. Klier and Shlome Lambroza. Cambridge, Massachusetts: Cambridge University Press, pp. 293-313.

Kennett, Lee. 1982. *A History of Strategic Bombing*. New York: Charles Scribner's Sons.

Kenrick, Donald and Grattan Puxon. 1972. *The Destiny of Europe's Gypsies*. New York: Basic Books.

Kerr, E. Bartlett. 1985. *Surrender and Survival: The Experience of American POWs in the Pacific 1941-1945*. New York: William Morrow and Co.

Kertesz, Stephen. 1953. "The Expulsion of the Germans from Hungary: A Study in Postwar Diplomacy." *The Review of Politics* 15 (4): 179-208.

Khmer Rouge Abuses Along the Thai-Cambodian Border. 1989. New York: An Asian Watch Report. February.

Kiernan, Ben. 1982. "The Samlaut Rebellion." In *Peasants and Politics in Kampuchea, 1942-1981*, by Ben Kiernan and Chanthou Boua. London: Zed Press, pp. 166-205.

———. 1982a. "Pol Pot and the Kampuchean Communist Movement." In *Peasants and Politics in Kampuchea, 1942-1981*, by Ben Kiernan and Chanthou Boua. London: Zed Press, pp. 227-317.

———. 1982b. "Kampuchea Stumbles to its Feet." In *Peasants and Politics in Kampuchea, 1942-1981*, by Ben Kiernan and Chanthou Boua. London: Zed Press, pp. 363-85.

———. 1983. "Wild Chickens, Farm Chickens, and Cormorants: Kampuchea's Eastern Zone under Pol Pot." In *Revolution and its Aftermath in Kampuchea: Eight Essays*, (edited) by David P. Chandler and Ben Kiernan. Monograph Series no. 25, New Haven: Yale University Southeast Asia Studies, pp. 136-211.

———. 1985. *How Pol Pot Came to Power: A History of Communism in Kampuchea, 1930-1975*. London: Verso.

———. 1986. "Review Essay: William Shawcross, Declining Cambodia." *Bulletin of the Concerned Asian Scholars* 18 (January-March): 56-63.

———. 1988. "Orphans of Genocide: The Cham Muslims of Kampuchea under Pol Pot." *Bulletin of Concerned Asian Scholars* 20(4): 2-33.

———. 1990. "The Genocide in Cambodia, 1975-79." *Bulletin of Concerned Asian Scholars* 22(2): 35-40.

——— and Chanthou Boua. 1982. *Peasants and Politics in Kampuchea, 1942-1981*. London: Zed Press.

Kifner, John. 1979. "Turkomans Battle Iranian Forces in New Outbreak of Tribal Separatism." *New York Times* 28 March, p. 3.

Kiljunen, Kimmo. 1985. "Power Politics and the Tragedy of Kampuchea During the Seventies." *Bulletin of Concerned Asian Scholars* 17 (April-June): 49-64.

Kim Myong-sik. 1980. *Liquidation in North Korea.* Seoul, Korea: The Institute for North Korea Studies.

Kirkpatrick, Jeane J. 1982. *Dictatorships and Double Standards: Rationalism and Reason in Politics.* New York: Simon and Schuster.

Klafkowski, Alfons. 1963. *The Potsdam Agreement.* Warsaw, Poland: Polish Scientific Publishers.

Klingberg, Frank L. 1966. "Predicting the Termination of War: Battle Casualties and Population Losses." *The Journal of Conflict Resolution* 10 (June): 129-171.

Kloosterboer, W. 1960. *Involuntary Labour Since the Abolition of Slavery: A Survey of Compulsory Labour Throughout the World.* Leiden, Holland: E. J. Brill.

Knight, Alan. 1986. *The Mexican Revolution. Volume 1: Porfirians, Liberals and Peasants.* Cambridge, Massachusetts: Cambridge University Press.

Kogon, Eugen. 1960. *The Theory and Practice of Hell: The German Concentration Camps and the System Behind Them.* Translated by Heinz Norden. New York: The Berkeley Publishing Co.

Kohen, Arnold and John Taylor. 1979. *An Act of Genocide: Indonesia's Invasion of East Timor.* London: TAPOL.

Köhler, Gernot. 1975. "War, the Nation-state Paradigm, and the Imperialism Paradigm: British War Involvements." *Peace Research* 7 (January): 31-42.

Korn, David A. 1990. "Ethiopia on the Brink of Tragedy." *Freedom at Issue* (March-April): 20-22.

Kosyk, Volodymyr. 1962. *Concentration Camps in the USSR.* London: Ukrainian Publishers.

Kousoulas, D. George. 1965. *Revolution and Defeat: The Story of the Greek Communist Party.* London: Oxford University Press.

Kramer, Barry. 1977. "Cambodia's Communist Regime Begins to Purge Its Own Ranks While Continuing a Crack-down." *The Wall Street Journal* 19 October, p. 48.

Kreiger, John. 1992. "Still Waging the Vietnam War." *U.S. News & World Report* (14 September): 48-49.

Kulischer, Eugene M. 1948. *Europe on the Move: War and Population Changes, 1917-47.* New York: Columbia University Press.

Kuper, Leo. 1977. *The Pity of It All: Polarization of Racial and Ethnic Relations.* Minneapolis: University of Minnesota Press.

———. 1981. *Genocide: Its Political Use in the Twentieth Century.* New Haven: Yale University Press.

———. 1982. *International Action Against Genocide: Report No. 53.* London: Minority Rights Group.

———. 1984. "Types of Genocide and Mass Murder." In *Toward the Understanding and Prevention of Genocide: Proceedings of the International Conference on the Holocaust and Genocide,* (edited) by Israel W. Charny. Boulder, Colorado: Westview Press, pp. 32-47.

———. 1985. *The Prevention of Genocide.* New Haven: Yale University Press.

———. 1986. "The Turkish Genocide of Armenians, 1915-1917." In *The Armenian Genocide in Perspective,* (edited) by Richard G. Hovannisian. New Brunswick, New Jersey: Transaction Books, pp. 43-59.

———. 1990. "The Genocidal State: An Ooverview." In *State Violence and Ethnicity,* (edited) by Pierre L. van den Berghe. Niwot, Colorado: University Press of Colorado, pp. 19-51.

———. 1992. "Reflections on the Prevention of Genocide." In *Genocide Watch,* (edited) by Helen Fein. New Haven: Yale University Press, pp. 135-61.

Labin, Suzanne. 1960. *The Anthill: The Human Condition in Communist China.* Translated by Edward Fitzgerald. New York: Praeger.

Ladas, Stephen P. 1932. *The Exchange of Minorities: Bulgaria, Greece and Turkey.* New York: Macmillan.

Ladouce, Laurent. 1988. "Was France the Fatherland of Genocide?" *The World & I* (January): 685-90.

Laffin, John. 1976. "The Arabs as Slavers." In *Case Studies on Human Rights and Fundamental Freedoms: A World Survey.* Vol. 4. Editor-in-chief Willem A. Veenhoven. The Hague: Martinus Nijhoff, pp. 433-59.

Laffin, John. 1986. *War Annual 1.* New York: Brassey's Defense Publishers.

Lake, Anthony. 1990. "After the Wars—What *Kind* of Peace?" In *After the Wars: Reconstruction in Afghanistan, Indochina, Central America, Southern Africa, and the Horn of Africa*, (edited) by Anthony Lake. New Brunswick, New Jersey: Transaction Publishers, pp. 3-29.

Lamb, David. 1978. "A Harsh Re-education in Mozambican Camp." *Sunday Star-Bulletin & Advertiser* (Honolulu) 16 July, p. F-2.

Lambroza, Shlomo. 1992. "The Pogroms of 1903-1906." In *Pogroms: Anti-Jewish Violence in Modern Russian History*, (edited) by John D. Klier and Shlome Lambroza. Cambridge, Massachusetts: Cambridge University Press, pp. 195-247.

Lancaster, Carol J. 1990. "The Horn of Africa." In *After the Wars: Reconstruction in Afghanistan, Indochina, Central America, Southern Africa, and the Horn of Africa*, (edited) by Anthony Lake. New Brunswick, New Jersey: Transaction Publishers, pp. 169-90.

Lancaster, H. O. 1990. *Expectations of Life: A Study in the Demography, Statistics, and History of World Mortality*. New York: Springer-Verlag.

Landy, Paul. 1957. "Hungary since the Revolution." *Problems of Communism* 6 (September-October): 8-15.

Lang, David Marshall. 1981. *The Armenians: A People in Exile*. London: George Allen & Unwin.

Langenberg, Michael van. 1990. "Gestapo and State Power in Indonesia." In *The Indonesian Killings of 1965-1966*, (edited) by Robert Cribb. Monash Papers on Southeast Asia—no. 21. Clayton, Victoria, Australia: Center of Southeast Asian Studies, Monash University, pp. 45-61.

Lawson, Don. 1964. *The United States in the Korean War*. New York: Scholastic Book Services.

Lazo, Mario. 1968. *Dagger in the Heart: American Policy Failures in Cuba*. New York: Funk & Wagnalls.

Le May, G. H. L. 1965. *British Supremacy in South Africa 1899-1907*. Oxford: Clarendon Press.

Leary, Virginia, A. A. Ellis, and Kurt Madlener. 1984. *The Philippines: Human Rights after Martial Law*. Geneva, Switzerland: The International Commission of Jurists.

Leckie, Robert. 1962. *Conflict: The History of the Korean War*. New York: G. P. Putnam's Sons.

Leckie, Robert. 1981. *The Wars of America*. Rev. and updated ed. New York: Harper & Row.

Lecky, W. E. H. 1925. *History of the Rise and Influence of the Spirit of Rationalism in Europe*. Vol. 2. Rev. ed., New York: D. Appleton & Co.

Ledeen, Michael A. and William H. Lewis. 1980. "Carter and the Fall of the Shah: The Inside Story." *The Washington Quarterly* 3 (Spring).

Ledeen, Michael. 1986. "A Defector's Tales of Sandinista Death Squads." *The Wall Street Journal* 19 March, p. 26.

Leggett, George. 1981. *The Checka: Lenin's Political Police*. Oxford: Clarendon Press.

Legters, Lyman. 1984. "The Soviet Gulag: Is It Genocidal?" In *Toward the Understanding and Prevention of Genocide: Proceedings of the International Conference on the Holocaust and Genocide*, (edited) by Israel W. Charny. Boulder, Colorado: Westview Press, pp. 60-66.

Legum, Colin. 1966. "The Massacre of the Proud Ibos." *Observer* 16 (October): 12.

Lemarchand, René. 1970. *Rwanda and Burundi*. New York: Praeger.

——. 1982. "The Hutu-Tutsi Conflict in Burundi," In *Genocide and Human Rights: A Global Anthology*, (edited) by Jack Nusan Porter. Washington, D.C.: University Press of America, pp. 195-217.

——. 1990. "Burundi: Ethnicity and the Genocidal State." *State Violence and Ethnicity*, (edited) by Pierre L. van den Berghe. Niwot, Colorado: University Press of Colorado, pp. 89-111.

——. 1991. "Burundi: A Case of 'Selective Genocide'." *Social Education* 55 (February): 94.

——. 1992. "Burundi: The Politics of Ethnic Amnesia." In *Genocide Watch*, (edited) by Helen Fein. New Haven: Yale University Press, pp. 70-86.

Lemkin, Raphael. 1944. *Axis Rule in Occupied Europe: Laws of Occupation, Analysis of Government, Proposals for Redress*. Washington, D.C.: Carnegie Endowment for International Peace.

Levytsky, Boris. 1971. *The Uses of Terror*. London: Coward, McCann & Geoghegan.

Lewellen, Ted C. 1985. "Structure of Terror: A Systems Analysis of Repression in El Salvador." In *Human Rights and Third World*

Development, (edited) by George W. Shepherd, Jr. and Ved P. Nanda. Westport, Connecticut: Greenwood Press, pp. 59-81.

Lewis, Anthony. 1979. "A Crime against Humanity." *Honolulu Star-Bulletin* 16 June, p. A-8.

Lewy, Guenter. 1978. *America in Vietnam*. New York: Oxford University Press.

Li Cheng-Chung. 1979. *The Question of Human Rights on China Mainland*. Republic of China: World Anti-Communist League, China Chapter. September.

Li, Lincoln. 1975. *The Japanese Army in North China 1937-1941: Problems of Political and Economic Control*. London: Oxford University Press.

Libaridian, Gerard J. 1987. "The Ultimate Repression: The Genocide of the Armenians, 1915-1917." In *Genocide and the Modern Age: Etiology and Case Studies of Mass Death*, (edited) by Isidor Wallimann and Michael N. Dobkowski. New York: Greenwood Press, pp. 203-35.

Librach, Jan. 1964. *The Rise of the Soviet Empire: A Study of Soviet Foreign Policy*. New York: Praeger.

Lieuwen, Edwin. 1968. *Mexican Militarism: The Political Rise and Fall of the Revolutionary Army*. Albuquerque: The University of New Mexico Press.

Linn, Brian McAllister. 1989. *The U.S. Army and Counterinsurgency in the Philippine War, 1899-1902*. Chapel Hill: The University of North Carolina Press.

Lintner, Bertil. 1990. *Outrage: Burma's Struggle for Democracy*. London: White Lotus.

Little Hope: Human Rights in Guatemala January 1984 to January 1985. 1985. New York: Americas Watch Committee. February.

London, Mirium and Ivan D. London. 1976. "The Other China: Hunger: Part I the Three Red Flags of Death." *World View* (May): 4-11.

—— and Ta-ling Lee. 1983. "Bread, Rice, and Freedom: The Peasantry and Agriculture in the USSR and China." *Freedom at Issue*. (May-June): 3-8.

Lopez, George A. 1984. "A Scheme for the Analysis of Government as Terrorist." In *The State as Terrorist: The Dynamics of Governmental Violence and Repression*, (edited) by Michael Stohl and George A. Lopez. Westport, Connecticut: Greenwood Press, pp. 59-81.

Lottman, Herbert R. 1986. *The Purge*. New York: William Morrow and Co.

Louyot, Alain. 1988. "A Journey to the Extremes of Horror." *World Press Review* (September): 21-23.

Lovejoy, Esther Pohl. 1933. *Certain Samaritans*. New York: Macmillan.

Lowry, Heath W. 1985. "The U.S. Congress and Adolf Hitler on the Armenians." *Political Communication and Persuasion* 3(2): 111-39.

Lowry, Heath W. 1990. *The Story Behind Ambassador Morgenthau's Story*. Istanbul, Turkey: The Isis Press.

Luard, Evan. 1978. Speech delivered at the United Nations Commission on Human Rights in Geneva, 3 March 1978. In *Human Rights Violations in Democratic Kampuchea: A Report Prepared by the United Kingdom Government*. Foreign Policy Documents no. 25. Great Britain. 14 July. Annex 1.

Luce, Don. 1972. "A Decade of Atrocity." In *The Wasted Nations: Report of the International Commission of Enquiry into United States Crimes in Indochina, June 20-25, 1971*. Edited by Frank Browning and Dorothy Forman. New York: Harper & Row, pp. 3-20.

Luza, Radomír. 1964. *The Transfer of the Sudenten Germans: A Study of Czech-German Relations, 1933-1962*. New York: New York University Press.

Ma'oz, Moshe and Avner Yaniv. 1986. *Syria Under Assad: Domestic Constraints and Regional Risks*. London: Croom Helm.

Maass, Peter. 1989. "Orwell's Vision: North Korea Moves toward Information-blind Followers." *The Honolulu Advertiser* 21 July, p. A-15.

Macauley, Neil. 1937. *Mandates: Reasons, Results, Remedies*. London: Methuen & Co.

Mace, James E. 1986. "The Man-made Famine of 1933 in Soviet Ukraine." In *Famine in Ukraine 1932-1933*, (edited) by Roman Serbyn and Bohdan Krawchenko. Edmonton: Canadian Institute or Ukrainian Studies, University of Alberta, pp. 1-14.

Mace, James E. 1984. "The Man-made Famine of 1933 in the Soviet Ukraine: What Happened and Why?" In *Toward the Understanding and Prevention of Genocide: Proceedings of the International Conference on the Holocaust and Genocide*, (edited) by Israel W. Charny. Boulder, Colorado: Westview Press, pp. 67-83.

MacFarquhar, Emily. 1988. "The Killing Fields of Mozambique." *U.S. News & World Report* (2 May): 45.

Mackenzie, Richard. 1989. "Rajiv Gandhi's Bloody Inheritance." *Insight* (13 February): 38-40.

Macksey, Kenneth. 1975. *The Partisans of Europe in the Second World War*. New York: Stein and Day.

Madsen, Brigham D. 1985. *The Shoshoni Frontier and the Bear River Massacre*. Salt Lake City: University of Utah Press.

Magstadt, Thomas M.1982. "Ethiopia's Great Terror." *Worldview* 25 (April): 5-6.

——. 1982. "The Great Leap Downward." *Reason*, (July): 46-51.

Maier, Charles S. 1988. *The Unmasterable Past: History, Holocaust and German National Identity*. Cambridge, Massachusetts: Harvard University Press.

Majumdar, R. C. 1963. *The Sepoy Mutiny and the Revolt of 1857*. 2nd ed., rev. and extended. Calcutta, India: Firma K. L. Mukhopadhyay.

Maley, William. 1991. "Social Dynamics and the Disutility of Terror: Afghanistan, 1978-1989." In *State Organized Terror: The Case of Violent Internal Repression*, (edited) by P. Timothy Bushnell, Vladimir Shlapentokh, Christopher K. Vanderpool, and Jeyaratnam Sundram. Boulder, Colorado: Westview Press, pp. 113-31.

Malhuret, Claude. 1985. "Mass Deportations in Ethiopia." In *Médecins Sans Frontières* (confidential report). December.

Mallin, Jay. 1966. *Terror in Viet Nam*. New York: D. Van Nostrand.

Manitzas, Elena S. 1991. "All the Minister's Men: Paramilitary Activity in Peru." In *Vigilantism and the State in Modern Latin America: Essays on Extralegal Violence*, (edited) by Martha K. Huggins. New York: Praeger, pp. 85-103.

Manning, Clarence A. 1953. *Ukraine Under the Soviets*. New York: Bookman Associates.

Manning, Patrick. 1992. "The Slave Trade: The Formal Demography of a Global System." In *The Atlantic Slave Trade: Effects on Economies, Societies, and Peoples in Africa, the Americas, and Europe*, (edited) by Joseph E. Inikori and Stanley L. Engerman. Durham, North Carolina: Duke University Press, pp. 117-41.

Manvell, Roger and Heinrich Fraenkel. 1967. *Incomparable Crime: Mass Extermination in the 20th Century: The Legacy of Guilt.* London: Heinemann.

Markham, Reuben H. 1949. *Rumania Under the Soviet Yoke.* Boston: Meador Publishing Co.

Markovski, Venko. 1984. *Goli Otok: The Island of Death.* New York: Columbia University Press.

Marktheparaks, Bounyadeth. 1986. "America's Forgotten Laotian Allies." *The Wall Street Journal* 28 July, p. 15.

Markusen, Eric. 1987. "Genocide and Total War: A Preliminary Comparison." In *Genocide and the Modern Age: Etiology and Case Studies of Mass Death,* (edited) by Isidor Wallimann and Michael N. Dobkowski. New York: Greenwood Press, pp. 97-123.

Martin, Christopher. 1968. *The Boxer Rebellion.* London: Abelard-Schuman.

Martin, David. 1946. *Ally Betrayed: The Uncensored Story of Tito and Mihailovich.* New York: Prentice-Hall.

——. 1974. *General Amin.* London: Faber and Faber.

——. 1978. "Introduction." In *Patriot or Traitor: The Case of General Mihailovich. Proceedings and Report of the Commission of Enquiry of the Committee for a Fair Trial for Draja Mihailovich.* Stanford University: Hoover Institution Press, pp. 1-179.

——. 1990. *The Web of Disinformation: Churchill's Yugoslav Blunder.* New York: Harcourt Brace Jovanovich.

Martin, Richard. 1988. "Final Act in Long Kampuchean Tragedy?" *Insight,* (1 August): 8-13.

Mascarenhas, Anthony. 1971. *The Rape of Bangla Desh.* Delhi, India: Vikas Publications.

——. 1972. "Genocide: Full Report." In *Bangladesh Genocide and World Press,* (edited) by Fazlul Quader Quaderi. Dacca, Bangladesh: Begum Dilafroz Quaderi, pp. 116-41.

——. 1986. *Bangladesh: A Legacy of Blood.* London: Hodder and Stoughton.

Matthews, Kenneth. 1972. *Memories of a Mountain War: Greece: 1944-1949.* London: Longmans.

Maullin, Richard. 1973. *Soldiers, Guerrillas, and Politics in Colombia.* Lexington, Massachusetts: Lexington Books.

May, Brian. 1978. *The Indonesian Tragedy.* Boston: Routledge & Kegan Paul.

Mazian, Florence. 1990. *Why Genocide? The Armenian and Jewish Experiences in Perspective.* Ames: Iowa State University Press.

McBeth, John. 1989. "Classified Conditions." *Far Eastern Economic Review* (19 January): 27-28.

McBride, George McCutchen. 1923. *The Land Systems of Mexico.* (American Geographic Society Research Series no. 12) New York: American Geographic Society.

McCarthy, Colman. 1988. "Khomeini Turns Wrath Inward on His Own People." *Honolulu Star-Bulletin* 9 December.

McCarthy, Justin. 1983. *Muslims and Minorities: The Population of Ottoman Anatolia and the End of the Empire.* New York: New York University Press.

McEvedy, Colin and Richard Jones. 1978. *Atlas of World Population History.* New York: Facts on File.

McManaway, Clayton C. (deputy to the ambassador at large for counterterrorism) and William Clark, Jr. (deputy assistant secretary for East Asian and Pacific affairs). 1988. "Statements before the Subcommittee on Asian and Pacific Affairs of the House Foreign Affairs Committee." In *U.S. Condemns North Korean Terrorism. Current Policy No. 1042.* Washington, D.C.: United States Department of State.

McWhirter, Norris and Ross McWhirter. 1977. *Guinness Book of World Records.* New York: Bantam Books.

Medvedev, Roy A. 1972. *Let History Judge: The Origins and Consequences of Stalinism.* Translated by Colleen Taylor. New York: Alfred A. Knopf.

Medvedev, Roy A. 1979. *On Stalin and Stalinism.* Translated by Ellen de Kadt. Oxford: Oxford University Press.

Mee, Charles L. 1992. "That Fateful Moment when Two Civilizations Came Face to Face." *Smithsonian* 23 (October): 56-69.

Meisler, Stanley. 1976. "Holocaust in Burundi, 1972." In *Case Studies on Human Rights and Fundamental Freedoms: A World Survey.* Vol. 5. Editor-in-chief Willem A. Veenhoven. The Hague: Martinus Nijhoff, pp. 227-38.

Melko, Matthew. 1973. "Retraction and Modification." *Peace Research* 5 (April): 20.

Melson, Robert. 1986. "Provocation or Nationalism: A Critical Inquiry into the Armenian Genocide of 1915." In *The Armenian Genocide in Perspective*, (edited) by Richard G. Hovannisian. New Brunswick, New Jersey: Transaction Books, pp. 61-84.

Menzel, Paul T. (Ed.). 1971. *Moral Argument and the War in Vietnam: A Collection of Essays*. Nashville, Tennessee: Aurora Publishers.

Mestrovic, Matthew. 1984. "Introduction." In *Goli Otok: The Island of Death*, by Venko Markovski. New York: Columbia University Press, pp. vii-xviii.

Michael, Franz H. and George E. Taylor. 1975. *The Far East in the Modern World*. 3rd ed. Hinsdale, Illinois: The Dryden Press.

Mickolus, Edward. 1983. "International Terrorism." In *The Politics of Terrorism*, (edited) by Michael Stohl. 2nd ed., rev. and extended. New York: Marcel Dekker, pp. 221-53.

Mihajlov, Mihajlo. 1987. "Did Krushchev Lie about Soviet War Casualties?" *Human Events*, (5 September): 13, 16.

The Military Balance 1979-1980. 1979. London: The International Institute for Strategic Studies (also for other years).

Miller, Stuart Creighton. 1982. *"Benevolent Assimilation:" The American Conquest of the Philippines, 1899-1903*. New Haven: Yale University Press.

Miller, William. 1966. *The Ottoman Empire and Its Successors 1801-1927*. New Impression. London: Frank Cass & Co.

Millions on the Move. n.d. Delhi: Publications Division, Ministry of Information, Government of India.

Minear, Larry. 1991. *Humanitarianism under Siege: A Critical Review of Operation Lifeline Sudan*. Trenton, New Jersey: The Red Sea Press.

Misiunas, Romuald J. and Rein Taagepera. 1983. *The Baltic States: Years of Dependence 1940-1980*. Berkeley, California: University of California Press.

Mohan, Jag (Ed.). 1971. *The Black Book of Genocide in Bangla Desh*. New Delhi, India: Geeta Book Center.

Moise, Edwin E. 1976. "Land Reform and Land Reform Errors in North Vietnam." *Pacific Affairs* 49 (Spring): 70-92.

———. 1983. *Land Reform in China and North Vietnam: Consolidating the Revolution at the Village Level*. Chapel Hill: The University of North Carolina Press.

Moon, Penderel. 1961. *Divide and Quit.* London: Chatto & Windus.

Moore, Gary. 1987. "The Agony of Southeast Nicaragua Too Long Overlooked." *The Wall Street Journal* 11 December, p. 21.

Moore, John Norton (Ed.). 1990. *The Vietnam Debate: A Fresh Look at the Arguments.* New York: University Press of America.

Morgenthau, Hans J. and Kenneth W. Thompson. 1985. *Politics Among Nations.* 6th ed., New York: Knopf.

Morgenthau, Henry. 1919. *Ambassador Morgenthau's Story.* Garden City, New York: Doubleday, Page, & Co.

Morrison, Wilbur H. 1982. *Fortress without a Roof: The Allied Bombing of the Third Reich.* New York: St. Martin's Press.

Moser, Tom. 1978. *China-Burma-India.* Alexandria, Virginia: Time-Life Books.

Mosher, Steven W. 1983. *Broken Earth: The Rural Chinese.* New York: The Free Press.

Moss, George Donelson. 1990. *Vietnam: An American Ordeal.* Englewood Cliffs, New Jersey: Prentice Hall.

Muhith. A. M. A. 1978. *Bangladesh: Emergence of a Nation.* Dacca, Bangladesh: Bangladesh Books International.

Mulato, Ernesto. 1979. "Angola—A Call for Courage." *AFL-CIO Free Trade Union News* 34 (May): 9-13.

Mullick, Dhiren. 1972. *Indira Speaks on Genocide War and Bangladesh.* Calcutta: Academic Publishers.

Münzel, Mark. 1976. "Manhunt." In *Genocide in Paraguay,* (edited) by Richard Arens. Philadelphia: Temple University Press, pp. 19-45.

Nam Koon Woo. 1974. *The North Korean Communist Leadership 1945-1965: A Study of Factionalism and Political Consolidation.* University, Alabama: The University of Alabama press.

Naudin, Pierre. 1976. "The Violation of Human Rights in Uganda." In *Case Studies on Human Rights and Fundamental Freedoms: A World Survey.* Vol. 5. Editor-in-chief Willem A. Veenhoven. The Hague: Martinus Nijhoff, pp. 417-31.

Nazer, James (Ed.). 1968. *The Armenian Massacre.* New York: T & T Publishing.

———. 1968a. *The First Genocide of the 20th Century: The Story of the Armenian Massacres in Text and Pictures.* New York: T & T Publishing.

Nettl, J. P. 1951. *The Eastern Zone and Soviet Policy in Germany 1945-50*. New York: Oxford University Press.

Newitt, Malyn. 1981. *Portugal in Africa: The Last Hundred Years*. Harlow, Essex: Longman.

Ngor, Haing. 1987. *A Cambodian Odyssey*. New York: Macmillan.

Nicaragua, Civil Liberties and the Central American Peace Plan. 1988. Washington, D.C.: The Pueblo Institute (a lay Catholic human rights group). January.

1939-1945 War Losses in Poland. 1960. Poland: Zachodnia Agencja Prasowa.

Norden, Eric. 1966. *America's Barbarities in Vietnam*. New Delhi: Mainstream Weekly.

North Korean Political System in Present Perspective. 1976. Seoul, Korea: Research Center for Peace and Unification.

"North Korea Admits to Operating Labor Camps." 1992. *Vantage Point: Developments in North Korea* 15 (July): 24-26. (South Korean Periodical Report)

Novick, Peter. 1968. *The Resistance Versus Vichy: The Purge of Collaborators in Liberation France*. New York: Columbia University Press.

"Nuclear Gulag." c1987. Great Britain: Channel 4 Television, .

Nutt, Anita Lauve. 1972. "On the Question of Communist Reprisals in Vietnam." In *The Human Cost of Communism in Vietnam*. A compendium prepared for the Subcommittee of the Committee on the Judiciary to Investigate the Administration of the Internal Security Act and Other Internal Security Laws, United States Senate, 92nd Congress, 2nd Session. Washington, D.C.: U.S. Government Printing Office, pp. 34-45.

O'Ballance, Edgar. 1966. *The Greek Civil War 1944-1949*. London: Faber and Faber.

———. 1967. *The Algerian Insurrection, 1954-62*. Hamden, Connecticut: Archon Books.

———. 1973. *The Kurdish Revolt 1961-1970*. Hamden, Connecticut: Archon Books.

———. 1981. *The Wars in Vietnam 1954-1980*. New enlarged ed. New York: Hippocrene Books.

———. 1989. *The Cyanide War: Tamil Insurrection in Sri Lanka 1973-88*. London: Brassey's (UK),

O'Connor, Richard. 1973. *The Spirit Soldiers; A Historical Narrative of the Boxer Rebellion*. New York: G. P. Putnam's Sons.

O'Donnell, Charles Peter. 1984. *Bangladesh: Biography of a Muslim Nation*. Boulder, Colorado: Westview Press.

O'Neill, Robert J. 1969. *The Strategy of General Giap Since 1964*. Canberra: A Publication of The Strategic and Defense Studies Center, Australian National University Press.

Ochosa, Orlino A. 1989. *The Tinio Brigade: Anti-American Resistance in the Ilocos Provinces 1899-1901*. Quezon City, Philippines: New Day Publishers.

Offer, Avner. 1989. *The First World War: An Agrarian Interpretation*. Oxford: Clarendon Press.

Ohaegbulom, F. Ugboaja. 1985. "Human Rights and the Refugee Situation in Africa." In *Human Rights and Third World Development*, (edited) by George W. Shepherd, Jr. and Ved P. Nanda. Westport, Connecticut: Greenwood Press, pp. 197-230.

Ojukwu, C. Odumegwu. 1969. *Biafra: Selected Speeches and Random Thoughts of C. Odumegwu Ojukwu*. New York: Harper and Row.

Okey, Robin. 1982. *Eastern Europe 1740-1980: Feudalism to Communism*. Minneapolis: University of Minnesota Press.

Oldenbourg, Zoé. 1961. *Massacre at Montsegur, A History of the Albigensian Crusade*. London: Weidenfeld and Nicolson.

——. 1966. *The Crusades*. Translated by Anne Carter. New York: Pantheon Books.

Omrcanin, Ivo. 1972. *Diplomatic and Political History of Croatia*. Philadelphia: Dorrance & Co.

Orel, Sinasi and Süreyya Yuca. 1983. *The Talât Pasha "Telegrams": Historical Fact or Armenian Fiction?* Nicosia: Northern Cyprus.

Oren, Nissan. 1973. *Revolution Administered: Agrarianism and Communism in Bulgaria*. Baltimore: The Johns Hopkins University Press.

Ottaway, David. 1992. "Doctor Says Police Killed Nearly 200 in S. Africa." *Honolulu Star-Bulletin* 27 July, p. D-1.

Overmans, Rüdiger. 1992. "German Historiography, the War Losses, and the Prisoners of War." In *Eisenhower and the German POWs: Facts Against Falsehood*, (edited) by Günter Bischof and Stephan E. Ambrose. Baton Rouge: Louisiana State University Press, pp. 128-69.

Paikert, G.C. 1967. *The Danube Swabians: German Populations in Hungary, Rumania and Yugoslavia and Hitler's Impact on Their Patterns*. The Hague: Martinus Nijhoff.

Pakenham, Thomas. 1979. *The Boer War*. New York: Random House.

Pal, R. B. 1953. *International Military Tribunal for the Far East: Dissentient Judgment*. Calcutta, India: Sanyal.

Palmer, Colin. 1992. "African Slave Trade: The Cruelest Commerce." *National Geographic* (September): 63-91.

Palmer, W. (Ed.). 1906. *Hazell's Annual for 1906: A Cyclopaedia Record of Men and Topics of the Day*. London: Hazell, Watson, Viney.

Palmier, Leslie. 1973. *Communists in Indonesia*. New York: Doubleday.

Panin, Dimitri. 1976. *The Notebooks of Sologdin*. Translated by John Moore. New York: Harcourt Brace Jovanovich.

"Paradise Lost?—Why North Koreans Really Defect." 1989. *Vantage Point: Developments in North Korea* 12 (May): 11-15 (South Korean Periodical Report).

Paris, Edmond. 1961. *Genocide in Satellite Croatia, 1941-1945: A Record of Racial and Religious Persecutions and Massacres*. Translated by Lois Perkins. Chicago, Illinois: The American Institute for Balkan Affairs.

Parker, Geoffrey. 1977. *The Dutch Revolt*. Ithaca, New York: Cornell University Press.

Parker, Thomas F. 1974. *Violence in the U.S.* Vol. 1: *1956-67*. New York: Facts on File.

Parks, Michael. 1977. "Ethiopia: A Revolution Deteriorating into Civil War." *Baltimore Sun* 15 May, p. K-3.

——. 1978. "Laos Mired in Fight with Hill Tribesmen." *Baltimore Sun* 31 October, p. 7.

Parmelee, Maurice. 1924. *Blockade and Sea Power: The Blockade, 1914-1919, and Its Significance for a World State*. New York: Thomas Y. Crowell.

Patten, Steve. 1980. "Cambodia's Tyrants Eye a Comeback." *U.S. News & World Report* (20 October): 35-36.

Patterson, Orlando. 1982. *Slavery and Social Death: A Comparative Study*. Cambridge, Massachusetts: Harvard University Press.

Paul, David W. 1981. *Czechoslovakia: Profile of a Socialist Republic at the Crossroads of Europe*. Boulder, Colorado: Westview Press.

Paxton, Robert O. 1972. *Vichy France: Old Guard and New Order, 1940-1944*. New York: Alfred A. Knopf.

Payne, Robert. 1973. *Massacre, The Tragedy of Bangladesh and the Phenomenon of Mass Slaughter throughout History*. New York: Macmillan.

Peck, Graham. 1967. *Two Kinds of Time*. 2nd ed., rev. and extended. Boston: Houghton Mifflin Co.

Pelenski, Jaroslaw. 1988. "The Cossack Insurrections in Jewish-Ukrainian Relations." In *Ukrainian-Jewish Relations in Historical Perspective*, (edited) by Peter J. Potichnyj and Howard Aster. Edmonton: Canadian Institute of Ukrainian Studies, University of Alberta, pp. 31-42.

Pelikán, Jirí (Ed.). 1971. *The Czechoslovakia Political Trials 1950-1954: The Suppressed Report of the Debcek Government's Commission of Enquiry, 1968*. Stanford: Stanford University Press.

Pelissier, Roger. 1967. *The Awakening of China: 1793-1949*. Edited and translated by Martin Kieffer. New York: Putnam.

Pepper, Suzanne. 1978. *Civil War in China: The Political Struggle, 1945-1949*. Berkeley: University of California Press.

Peru Under Fire: Human Rights Since the Return of Democracy. 1992. (Americas Watch) New Haven: Yale University Press.

Petrov, Vladimir and Evdokia Petrov. 1956. *Empire of Fear*. New York: Praeger.

Petrushevsky, I. P. 1968. "The Socio-economic Conditions of Iran under the Il-Khans." In *The Cambridge History of Iran: Volume 5: The Saljuq and Mongol Periods*, (edited) by J. A. Boyle. Cambridge, Massachusetts: At The University Press, pp. 483-537.

Pfeffer, Richard M. (Ed.). 1968. *No More Vietnams: The War and the Future of American Foreign Policy*. New York: Harper & Row.

Phan Quang Dan. 1988. "Forward." In *Victims and Survivors: Displaced Persons and Other War Victims in Viet-Nam, 1954-1975*, by Louis Wiesner. New York: Greenwood Press, pp. xiii-xvi.

The Philippines: Violations of the Laws of War by Both Sides. 1990. (An Asia Watch Report) New York: Human Rights Watch. August.

Piccigallo, Philip R. 1982. *The Japanese on Trial: Allied War Crimes Operations in the East, 1945-1951.* Austin: University of Texas Press.

Pike, Clarence Edward. 1979. *Famine: The Story of the Great Bengal Famine of 1943, of Famines Before and Famines Since and How Their Threat Can Be Thwarted.* Cornwall, Ontario, Canada: Vesta Publications.

Pike, Douglas. 1970. *The Viet-Cong Strategy of Terror.* Prepared by Douglas Pike for the United States Mission, Viet-Nam.

——. 1978. *History of Vietnamese Communism, 1925-1976.* Standford, California: Hoover Institution Press.

Pinheiro, Paulo Sérgio. 1991. "Police and Political Crisis: The Case of the Military Police." In *Vigilantism and the State in Modern Latin America: Essays on Extralegal Violence,* (edited) by Martha K. Huggins. New York: Praeger, pp. 167-88.

Pion-Berlin, David. 1991. "The Ideological Governance of Perception in the Use of State Terror in Latin America: The Case of Argentina." In *State Organized Terror: The Case of Violent Internal Repression,* (edited) by P. Timothy Bushnell, et al. Boulder, Colorado: Westview Press, pp. 135-52.

"Pipeline: Largest East-West Transaction." 1982. *Washington Times* 19 May. Included in the *Congressional Record,* 97th Congress, Second Session: Vol. 128–Part 9, 26 May, pp. 11,950-11,951.

Piyadasa, L. (Ed.). 1988. *Sri Lanka: The Unfinished Quest for Peace.* London: Marram Books.

Platt, Adam. 1987. "A Pioneering Democracy Struggles with Disillusion." *Insight* (18 May): 10-14.

Pletka, Danielle. 1991. "Under the Iron Fist: Inside Assad's Syria." *Insight* (5 August): 28-31.

Podhoretz, Norman. 1990. "Questions and Errors of Fact: The Myths and Realities of Vietnam." *The Vietnam Debate: A Fresh Look at the Arguments,* (edited) by John Norton Moore. New York: University Press of America, pp. 23-29.

Poliakov, Léon. 1971. *Harvest of Hate: The Nazi Program for the Destruction of the Jews of Europe.* Westport, Connecticut: Greenwood Press.

Polish Acts of Atrocity against the German Minority in Poland: Compilation Founded on Documentary Evidence and Published for

the German Foreign Office. 1940. 2nd ed., rev. and extended, with
Important addenda. New York: German Library of Information.

Political Killings by Governments: An Amnesty International Report.
1983. London: Amnesty International.

Ponchaud, François. 1977. *Cambodia Year Zero.* Translated by Nancy
Amphoux. New York: Holt, Rinehart and Winston.

Ponlatowska, Elena. 1975. *Massacre in Mexico.* Translated by Helen
R. Lane. New York: The Viking Press.

Porter, D. Gareth. 1972. *The Myth of the Bloodbath: North Vietnam's
Land Reform Reconsidered.* Ithaca: Cornell University IREA
Project.

Porter, Jack Nusan. 1982. "Introduction: What Is Genocide? Notes
toward a Definition." In *Genocide and Human Rights: A Global
Anthology,* (edited) by Jack Nusan Porter. Washington, D.C.:
University Press of America, pp. 2-32.

Possony, Stefen T. 1975. "From Gulag to Guitk: Political Prisons in
the USSR Today." In *Case Studies on Human Rights and
Fundamental Freedoms: A World Survey.* Vol. 1. Editor-in-chief
Willem A. Veenhoven. The Hague: Martinus Nijhoff.

Powell, G. Bingham, Jr. 1982. *Contemporary Democracies:
Participation, Stability, and Violence.* Cambridge, Massachusetts:
Harvard University Press.

Power, G. Bingham, Jr. 1981. "Party Systems and Political System
Performance: Voting Participation, Government Stability and Mass
Violence in Contemporary Democracies." *The American Political
Science Review* 75: 861-79.

Prachand, S.L.M. 1979. *Mob Violence in India.* Chandigarh: Abhishek
Publications.

Prcela, John and Stanko Guldescu (Eds.). 1970. *Operation
Slaughterhouse: Eyewitness Accounts of Postwar Massacres in
Yugoslavia.* Philadelphia: Dorrance & Co.

Pritchard, R. John and Sonia Magbanua Zaide (Eds.). 1981. *The Tokyo
War Crimes Trial: Vols. 1-22.* New York: Garland Publishing.

Prosterman, Roy L. 1972. *Surviving to 3000: An Introduction to the
Study of Lethal Conflict.* Belmont, California: Wadsworth
Publishing.

Prpic, George J. 1967. *Fifty Years of World Communism: 1917-1967: A Selective Chronology*. Cleveland, Ohio: Institute for Soviet and East European Studies, John Carroll University.

Puddington, Arch. 1987. "The Khmer Rouge File." *The American Spectator* (July): 18-20.

Pumipiglas. 1986. Quezon City, Philippines: Task Force Detainees of the Philippines, Association of Major Religious Superiors in the Philippines.

Purcell, Victor. 1962. *China*. London: Ernest Benn.

———. 1963. *The Boxer Uprising: A Background Study*. Cambridge, Massachusetts: At the University Press.

Qira, Zijadin. 1970. *Cell Number 31*. New York: Vantage Press.

Quaderi, Fazlul Quader (Ed.). 1972. *Bangladesh Genocide and World Press*. Dacca, Bangladesh: Begum Dilafroz Quaderi.

Quigley, Harold S. 1962. *China's Politics in Perspective*. Minneapolis: The University of Minnesota Press.

Rabkin, Rhoda. 1987. "Cuba." In *International Handbook of Human Rights*, (edited) by Jack Donnelly and Rhoda E. Howard. New York: Greenwood Press, pp. 99-116.

Race, Jeffrey. 1972. *War Comes to Long An: Revolutionary Conflict in a Vietnamese Province*. Berkeley: University of California Press.

Radspieler, Tony. 1955. *The Ethnic German Refugee in Austria 1945-1954*. The Hague: Martinus Nijhoff.

Rafiq-Ul-Islam, Bir Uttam. 1981. *A Tale of Millions*. Dacca: Bangladesh Books International.

Ramaer, J. C. 1986. *Soviet Communism: The Essentials*. 2nd ed., rev. and extended. Translated by G. E. Luton. Verdediging, Belgium: Stichting Vrijheid, Vrede.

Ramos-Horta, Jose. 1987. *Funu: The Unfinished Saga of East Timor*. Trenton, New Jersey: The Red Sea Press.

Ransdell, Eric. 1992. "The More Things Change." *U.S. News & World Report* (5 October): 56, 69.

Read, James Morgan. 1941. *Atrocity Propaganda 1914-1919*. New Haven: Yale University Press.

Red Atrocities Remembered. 1975. (Korea Policy Series no. 25). Seoul, Korea: Korean Overseas Information Service. June.

Reel, A. Frank. 1971. *The Case of General Yamashita*. New York: Octagon Books.

Refugee and Civilian War Casualty Problems in Indochina. 1970. A Staff Report, Subcommittee to Investigate Problems Connected with Refugees and Escapees of The Committee on the Judiciary, United States Senate, 91st Congress, 2nd Session. September 28.

Reid, Robert. 1989. *The Peterloo Massacre.* London: Heinemann.

Reiss, R.A. 1916. *How Austria-Hungary Waged War in Serbia: Personal Investigations of a Neutral.* Translated by J. S. (sic). Paris: Librairie Armand Colin.

———. n.d. *Report Upon the Atrocities Committed by the Austro-Hungarian Army During the First Invasion of Serbia: Submitted to the Serbian Government.* Translated by F. S. Copeland. London: Simpkin, Marshall, Hamilton, Kent & Co.

Reiter, Randy B., M. V. Zunzunegui, and Jose Quiroga. 1992. "Guidelines for Field Reporting of Basic Human Rights Violations." In *Human Rights and Statistics: Getting the Record Straight,* (edited) by Thomas B. Jabine and Richard P. Claude. Philadelphia: University of Pennsylvania Press, pp. 90-126.

Reitlinger, Gerald. 1961. *The Final Solution: The Attempt to Exterminate the Jews of Europe 1939-1945.* New York: A.S. Barnes.

Report of the National Advisory Commission on Civil Disorders. 1968. *The New York Times* edition. New York: E. P. Dutton.

Report on Human Rights in El Salvador. 1982. Compiled by Americas Watch Committee and the American Civil Liberties Union. New York: Vintage Books.

"The Resistance Can Win in Mozambique." 1986. *National Security Record* (The Heritage Foundation) (June):1-6.

Revel, Jean-François and Rosanne Klass. 1986. "Agony in Afghanistan." *Reader's Digest* (March): 133-37.

Reynolds, Henry (Ed). 1972. *Aborigines and Settlers: The Australian Experience 1788-1939.* New South Wales: Cassell Australia.

Riasanovsky, Nicholas V. 1977. *A History of Russia.* 3rd ed. New York: Oxford University Press.

Rice, Edward E. 1972. *Mao's Way.* Berkeley: University of California Press.

Richardson, Lewis Fry. 1960. *Statistics of Deadly Quarrels.* Pittsburgh and Chicago: The Boxwood Press and Quadrangle Books.

Rioux, Jean-Pierre. 1987. *The Fourth Republic, 1944-1958.* Translated by Godfrey Rogers. Cambridge, Massachusetts: Cambridge University Press.

Rizvi, Sajid. 1979. "Iran Troops Battle Kurds." *Honolulu Star-Bulletin* 22 August, p. A-5.

Roberts, David. 1992. "Geronimo." *National Geographic* 182 (October): 46-71.

Rogge, John R. 1985. *Too Many, Too Long: Sudan's Twenty-Year Refugee Dilemma.* Totowa, New Jersey: Rowman & Allanheld.

Rogger, Hans. 1992. "Conclusion and Overview." In *Pogroms: Anti-Jewish Violence in Modern Russian History,* (edited) by John D. Klier and Shlome Lambroza. Cambridge, Massachusetts: Cambridge University Press, pp. 314-72.

Rose, Hilary and Steven Rose. 1972. "Gas an Imperialist Technology." In *The Wasted Nations: Report of the International Commission of Enquiry into United States Crimes in Indochina, June 20-25, 1971,* (edited) by Frank Browning and Dorothy Forman. New York: Harper & Row, pp. 38-49.

Roth, Russell. 1981. *America's "Indian Wars" in the Philippines 1899-1935.* W. Hanover, Massachusetts: The Christopher Publishing House.

Roucek, Joseph S. and Kenneth V. Lottich. 1964. *Behind the Iron Curtain: The Soviet Satellite States—East European Nationalisms and Education.* Caldwell, Idaho: Caxton Printers.

Roumani, Maurice M. 1976. "The Case of the Jews from Arab Countries: A Neglected Issue." In *Case Studies on Human Rights and Fundamental Freedoms: A World Survey.* Vol. 5. Editor-in-chief Willem A. Veenhoven. The Hague: Martinus Nijhoff, pp. 69-100.

Roy, A. n.d. *Genocide of Hindus & Buddhists in East Pakistan.* Delhi, India: Kranti Prakashan.

Roy, Olivier. 1990. *Islam and Resistance in Afghanistan.* 2nd ed., rev. and extended. Cambridge, Massachusetts: Cambridge University Press.

Ruark, Robert. 1965. "Introduction." In *The Fabric of Terror: Three Days in Angola,* by Bernardo Teixeira. New York: The Devin-Adair Co., pp. vii-x.

Rubenstein, Richard L. 1983. *The Age of Triage: Fear and Hope in an Over-crowded World*. Boston: Beacon Press.

Rubin, Barnett R. 1987. "Human Rights in Afghanistan." In *Afghanistan: The Great Game Revisited*, (edited) by Rosanne Klass. New York: Freedom House, pp. 335-58.

——. 1987a. "India." In *International Handbook of Human Rights*, (edited) by Jack Donnelly and Rhoda E. Howard. New York: Greenwood Press, pp. 135-60.

Ruíz, Ramón Eduardo. 1980. *The Great Rebellion: Mexico, 1905-1924*. New York: W. W. Norton.

Rule by Fear: Paraguay After Thirty Years Under Stroessner. 1985. New York: An Americas Watch Report. January.

Rummel, R. J. 1975-81. *Understanding Conflict and War*. Vols. 1-5. Beverly Hills, California: Sage Publications.

——. 1979. *National Attributes and Behavior*. Beverly Hills, California: Sage Publications.

——. 1983. "Libertarianism and International Violence." *The Journal of Conflict Resolution* 27 (March): 27-71.

——. 1984. "Libertarianism, Violence within States, and the Polarity Principle." *Comparative Politics* 16 (July): 443-62.

——. 1985. "A Test of Libertarian Propositions on Violence." *The Journal of Conflict Resolution* 29 (September): 419-55.

——. 1990. *Lethal Politics: Soviet Genocide and Mass Murder Since 1917*. New Brunswick, New Jersey: Transaction Publishers.

——. 1990a. *The Conflict Helix: Principles and Practices of Interpersonal, Social, and International Conflict and Cooperation*. New Brunswick, New Jersey: Transaction Publishers.

——. 1991. *China's Bloody Century: Genocide and Mass Murder since 1900*. New Brunswick, New Jersey: Transaction Publishers.

——. 1992. *Democide: Nazi Genocide and Mass Murder*. New Brunswick, New Jersey: Transaction Publishers.

——. Forthcoming. *Statistics of Democide: Estimates, Sources, and Calculations on 20th-Century Genocide and Mass Murder*. New Jersey: Transaction Publishers.

Ruo-Wang, Bao and Rudolph Chelminski. c1977. *Prisoner of Mao*. Penguin Books.

Rupen, Robert. 1979. *How Mongolia is Really Ruled: A Political History of the Mongolian People's Republic, 1900-1978.* Stanford, California: Hoover Institution Press.

Russell, D. E. H. 1974. *Rebellion, Revolution, and Armed Force: A Comparative Study of Fifteen Countries with Special Emphasis on Cuba and South Africa.* New York: Academic Press.

Russell, Don. 1973. "How Many Indians Were Killed?" *The American West* 10 (July): 42-47, 61-63.

Russett, Bruce. 1993. *Grasping the Democratic Peace: Principles for a Post-Cold War World.* Princeton, New Jersey: Princeton University Press.

Ryan, Lyndall. 1981. *The Aboriginal Tasmanians.* London: University of Queensland Press.

Sachar, Howard M. 1969. *The Emergence of the Middle East: 1914-1924.* New York: Alfred A. Knopf.

Sachs, Moshe Y. (Ed.). 1971. *Worldmark Encyclopedia of the Nations: Asia & Australasia.* New York: Harper & Row.

Saeedpour, Vera Beaudin. 1992. "Establishing State Motives for Genocide: Iraq and the Kurds." In *Genocide Watch*, (edited) by Helen Fein. New Haven: Yale University Press, pp. 59-69.

Salisbury, Harrison E. 1985. *The Long March: The Untold Story.* New York: Harper and Row.

Sallagar, Frederick M. 1969. *The Road to Total War.* New York: Van Nostrand Reinhold.

Samuelson, Douglas A. and Herbert F. Spirer. 1992. "Use of Incomplete and Distorted Data in Inference about Human Rights Violations." In *Human Rights and Statistics: Getting the Record Straight*, (edited) by Thomas B. Jabine and Richard P. Claude. Philadelphia: University of Pennsylvania Press, pp. 62-77.

Sandinista Prisons: A Tool of Intimidation. 1986. Washington, D.C.: United States Department of State (Publication no. 9492). August.

Sarkisian, E. K. and R. G. Sahakian. 1965. *Vital Issues in Modern Armenian History: A Documented Exposé of Misrepresentations in Turkish Historiography.* Translated and edited, with an introduction, maps, and postscript by Elisha B. Chrakian. Watertown, Massachusetts: Library of Armenian Studies.

Sathyamurthy, T. V. 1986. *The Political Development of Uganda: 1900-1986.* Brookfield, Vermont: Gower Publishing.

Saunders, J. J. 1971. *The History of the Mongol Conquests*. London: Routledge & Kegan Paul.

Savon, Hervé. 1972. *Du Cannibalisme au Génocide*. Paris: Hachette.

Saxena, N. C. 1984. "The Nature and Origin of Communal Riots in India." In *Communal Riots in Post-Independence India*, (edited) by Asghar Ali Engineer. India: Sangam Books India, pp. 51-67.

Scalapino, Robert A. and Chong-sik Lee. 1972. *Communism in Korea*. Part 1-2. Berkeley: University of California Press.

Schaffer, Ronald. 1985. *Wings of Judgment: American Bombing in World War II*. New York: Oxford University Press.

Schechtman, Joseph B. 1946. *European Population Transfers: 1939-1945*. New York: Oxford University Press.

———. 1953. "Postwar Population Transfers in Europe: A Survey." *The Review of Politics* 15 (4): 151-78.

———. 1963. *The Refugee in the World: Displacement and Integration*. New York: A. S. Barnes and Co.

Schimitzek, Stanislaw. 1966. *Truth or Conjecture? German Civilian War Losses in the East*. Warsaw: Western Press Agency.

Schirmer, Daniel B. 1972. *Republic or Empire: American Resistance to the Philippine War*. Cambridge, Massachusetts: Shenkman Publishing. Distributed by General Learning Press.

Schmid, Alex P. 1985. *Social Defense and Soviet Military Power: An Inquiry into the Relevance of an Alternative Defense Concept*. (Report Prepared for the Project Group Social Defense) Leiden, Holland: Center for the Study of Social conflict (C.O.M.T.), State University of Leiden.

———. 1989. *Research on Gross Human Rights Violations: A Programme*. 2nd enlarged ed. Publication no. 30, Leiden, The Netherlands: The Center for the Study of Social Conflicts.

Schoenberg, Hans W. 1970. *Germans from the East: A Study of Their Migration, Resettlement, and Subsequent Group History Since 1945*. The Hague, Netherlands: Martinus Nijhoff.

Schram, Stuart. 1966. *Mao Tse-tung*. New York: Simon and Schuster.

Seale, Patrick. 1988. *Asad of Syria: The Struggle for the Middle East*. London: I. B. Tauris.

"The Second Coming of Pol Pot." 1988. *World Press Review*, (October): 25f.

Séménoff, E. 1972. *The Russian Government and the Massacres: A Page of the Russian Counter-Revolution.* Westport, Connecticut: Greenwood Press.

Serrill, Michael S. 1987. "Famine." *Time* (21 December): 34-43.

Seshadri, H. V. 1982. *The Tragic Story of Partition.* Bangalore: Jagarana Prakashana.

Sethi, S. S. 1979. *Kampuchean Tragedy: Maoism in Action.* New Delhi, India: Kalamkar Prakashan Pvt. Ltd.

Seton-Watson, Hugh. 1961. *The East European Revolution.* 3rd ed. New York: Praeger.

Severy, Merle. 1987. "The World of Süleyman the Magnificent." *National Geographic* 172 (November): 552-601.

Severy, Merle. 1989. "The Great Revolution." *National Geographic* 176 (July): 18-48.

Shakir, Moin. 1984. "An Analytical View of Communal Violence." In *Communal Riots in Post-Independence India,* (edited) by Asghar Ali Engineer. India: Sangam Books India, pp. 88-103.

Shalom, Stephen Rosskamm. 1984. *Deaths in China Due to Communism: Propaganda Versus Reality.* Occasional Paper no. 15, Center for Asian Studies, Arizona State University.

Sharp, Gene. 1980. *Social Power and Political Freedom.* Boston: Porter Sargent.

Shaw, Stanford J. and Ezel Kural Shaw. 1977. *History of the Ottoman Empire and Modern Turkey.* Vol. 2. New York: Cambridge University Press.

Shawcross, William. 1983. "Cambodia: Some Perceptions of a Disaster." In *Revolution and Its Aftermath in Kampuchea: Eight Essays,* (edited) by David P. Chandler and Ben Kiernan. Monograph Series no. 25. New Haven: Yale University Southeast Asia Studies, pp. 230-58.

———. 1985. *The Quality of Mercy: Cambodia, Holocaust and Modern Conscience, With a Report from Ethiopia.* New York: Simon & Shuster.

———. 1986. *Sideshow: Kissinger, Nixon and the Destruction of Cambodia.* New ed. London: The Hogarth Press.

Shea, Nina H. 1990. "Uncovering the Awful Truth of Nicaragua's Killing Fields." *The Wall Street Journal* August 24, p. A7.

Sheehy, Ann and Bohdan Nahaylo. 1980. *The Crimean Tatars, Volga Germans and Meskhetians: Soviet Treatment of Some National Minorities*. Report no. 6. 3rd ed. New York, New York: Minority Rights Group.

Shelah, Menachem. 1990. "Genocide in Satellite Croatia during the Second World War." In *A Mosaic of Victims: Non-Jews Persecuted and Murdered by the Nazis*, (edited) by Michael Berenbaum. New York: New York University Press, pp. 74-79.

Shepherd, Jack. 1975. *The Politics of Starvation*. New York: Carnegie Endowment for International Peace.

Sheridan, James E. 1975. *China in Disintegration: The Republican Era in Chinese History, 1912-1949*. New York: The Free Press.

Sherman, Richard. 1980. *Eritrea: The Finished Revolution*. New York: Praeger.

Simons, Gerald. 1982. *Victory in Europe*. Alexandria, Virginia: Time-Life Books.

Simpson, Eyler N. 1937. *The Ejido: Mexico's Way Out*. Chapel Hill: The University of North Carolina Press.

Sin Sam-Soon. 1991. "The Repressions of Kim Il-sung." *Korea and World Affairs* (Summer): 279-301.

Singer, Max. 1990. "Militarism and Democracy in El Salvador." *Society* 27 (September/October): 49-56.

Singleton, Fred. 1985. *A Short History of the Yugoslav Peoples*. New York: Cambridge University Press.

SIPRI Yearbook of World Armaments and Disarmament 1968/69. 1970. New York: Humanities Press.

SIPRI Yearbook: World Armaments and Disarmament 1976. 1976. Cambridge, Massachusetts: The MIT Press.

SIPRI Yearbook: World Armaments and Disarmament. 1987. New York: Oxford University Press.

Sisson, Richard and Leo E. Rose. 1990. *War and Secession: Pakistan, India, and the Creation of Bangladesh*. Berkeley: University of California Press.

Sivard, Ruth Leger. 1985. *World Military and Social Expenditures 1985*. Leesburg, Virginia: WMSE Publications.

———. 1989. *World Military and Social Expenditures 1989*. 13th ed. Washington, D.C.: World Priorities.

Sloan, John W. 1983. "Political Terrorism in Latin America." *The Politics of Terrorism*, (edited) by Michael Stohl. 2nd ed., rev. and extended. New York: Marcel Dekker, pp. 377-96.

———. 1984. "State Repression and Enforcement Terrorism in Latin America." In *The State as Terrorist: The Dynamics of Governmental Violence and Repression*, (edited) by Michael Stohl and George A. Lopez. Westport, Connecticut: Greenwood Press, pp. 83-98.

Small, M., and Singer, J. David. 1976. "The War-proneness of Democratic Regimes, 1816-1965." *Jerusalem Journal International Relations* 1 (Summer): 50-69.

———. 1982. *Resort to Arms: International and Civil Wars 1816-1980.* Beverly Hills, California: Sage Publications.

Smith, Frank. 1989. "Interpretative Accounts of the Khmer Rouge Years: Personal Experience in Cambodian Peasant World View." *Occasional Paper No. 18.* Madison, Wisconsin: Wisconsin Papers on Southeast Asia, Center for Southeast Asian Studies, University of Wisconsin-Madison.

Smith, George Ivan. 1980. *Ghosts of Kampala.* New York: St. Martin's Press.

Smith, Martin. 1991. *Burma: Insurgency and the Politics of Ethnicity.* London: Zed Books.

Smith, Roger W. 1987. "Human Destructiveness and Politics: The Twentieth Century as an Age of Genocide." In *Genocide and the Modern Age: Etiology and Case Studies of Mass Death*, (edited) by Isidor Wallimann and Michael N. Dobkowski. New York: Greenwood Press, pp. 21-39.

———. 1991. "Denial of the Armenian Genocide." In *Genocide: A Critical Bibliographic Review: Vol. 2*, (edited) by Israel W. Charny. London: Mansell, pp. 63-85.

Smolowe, Jill. 1992. "Peru: His Turn to Lose." *Time* (September 28): 47-48.

Snow, Clyde Collins and Maria Julia Bihurriet. 1992. "An Epidemiology of Homicide: *Ningún Nombre* Burials in the Province of Buenos Aires from 1970 to 1984." In *Human Rights and Statistics: Getting the Record Straight*, (edited) by Thomas B. Jabine and Richard P. Claude. Philadelphia: University of Pennsylvania Press, pp. 328-63.

Snow, Edgar. 1937. *Red Star over China.* n.p.

Sobel, Lester A. 1979. *Refugees: A World Report.* New York: Facts on File.

Solzhenitsyn, Alexander I. 1963. *One Day in the Life of Ivan Denisovich.* New York: Bantam Books.

———. 1973. *The Gulag Archipelago 1918-1956: An Experiment in Literary Investigation I-II.* Translated by Thomas P. Whitney. New York: Harper & Row.

———. 1975. "Repentance and Self-limitation in the Life of Nations." In *From Under the Rubble,* by Aleksandr I. Solzhenitsyn, et al. Translated by A. M. Brock, et al. London: Collins & Harvill Press, pp. 105-43.

———. 1975a. *The Gulag Archipelago 1918-1956: An Experiment in Literary Investigation III-IV.* Translated by Thomas P. Whitney. New York: Harper & Row.

Soman, Alfred (Ed.). 1974. *The Massacre of St. Bartholomew: Reappraisals and Documents.* The Hague: Martinus Nijhoff.

Song, Chhang. 1977. "Cambodia, in Retrospect." *Honolulu Star-Bulletin* 8 January, p. A-8

Sorokin, Pitirim A. 1937. *Social and Cultural Dynamics: Volume 2: Fluctuation of Systems of Truth, Ethics, and Law.* New York: American Book Co.

———. 1967. *The Sociology of Revolution.* New York: Howard Fertig.

Southwood, Julie and Patrick Flanagan. 1983. *Indonesia: Law, Propaganda and Terror.* London: Zed Press.

Speed, Richard B. III. 1990. *Prisoners, Diplomats, and the Great War.* New York: Greenwood Press.

Spies, S. B. 1980. "Women and the War." In *The South African War: The Anglo-Boer War 1899-1902,* (edited) by Peter Warwick. Burnt Mill, Harlow, Essex, Great Britain: Longman, pp. 161-85.

Sri Lanka: "Disappearances." 1986. New York: Amnesty International. September.

Stannard, David E. 1992. *American Holocaust: Columbus and the Conquest of the New World.* New York: Oxford University Press.

———. 1992a. "Genocide in the Americas." *The Nation* 255 (October 19): 430-34.

Stein, Louis. 1979. *Beyond Death and Exile: The Spanish Republicans in France, 1939-1955.* Cambridge, Massachusetts: Harvard University Press.

Steinberg, Rafael. 1979. *Return to the Philippines.* Morristown, New Jersey: Time-Life Books.

Stepan, Alfred. 1985. "Introduction." In *With Friends Like These: The Americas Watch Report on Human Rights and U.S. Policy in Latin America,* (edited) by Cynthia Brown. New York: Pantheon Books, pp. xv-xxii.

Stewart, George. 1933. *The White Armies of Russia: A Chronicle of Counter-Revolution and Allied Intervention.* New York: Macmillan.

Stewart-Smith, D. G. 1964. *The Defeat of Communism.* London: Ludgate Press.

Stockwell, F. Olin. *With God in Red China: The Story of Two Years in Chinese Communist Prisons.* New York: Harper and Brothers, 1953.

Stohl, Michael. 1987. "Outside of a Small Circle of Friends: States, Genocide, Mass Killing and the Role of Bystanders." *Journal of Peace Research* 24: 151-66.

Stohl, Michael and George A. Lopez (Eds.). 1984. *The State as Terrorist: The Dynamics of Governmental Violence and Repression.* Westport, Connecticut: Greenwood Press.

Storey, Moorfield and Marcial P. Lichauco. 1926. *The Conquest of the Philippines by the United States 1898-1925.* New York: G. P. Putnam's Sons.

Stowe, Leland. *Conquest by Terror: The Story of Satellite Europe.* 1951. New York: Random House.

Stuart-Fox, Martin with Bunheang Ung. 1985. *The Murderous Revolution: Life and Death in Pol Pot's Kampuchea.* Chippendale, N. S. W. Australia: Alternative Publishing Cooperative Ltd.

A Study: Viet Cong Use of Terror. 1966. Saigon, Vietnam: United States Mission. May.

Sturdza, Michel. 1968. *The Suicide of Europe: Memoirs of Prince Michel Sturdza.* Boston: Western Islands Publishers.

Sulc, Lawrence. 1990. "Communists Coming Clean about Their Past Atrocities." *Human Events* (October 13): 12.

Summers, Harry G., Jr. 1990. *Korean War Almanac.* New York: Facts on File.

468 Death by Government

Suny, Ronald Grigor. 1983. *Armenia in the Twentieth Century*. Chico, California: Scholars Press.

Sutherland, N. M. 1973. *The Massacre of St. Bartholomew and the European Conflict 1559-1572*. London: Macmillan.

Sydenham, M. J. 1965. *The French Revolution*. New York: Putnam.

Syria Unmasked: The Suppression of Human Rights by the Asad Regime. 1991. (Middle East Watch) New Haven: Yale University Press.

Szaz, Zoltan Michael. 1960. *Germany's Eastern Frontiers: The Problem of the Oder-Neisse Line*. Chicago: Henry Regnery Co.

Szulc, Tad. 1971. *Czechoslovakia Since World War II*. New York: The Viking Press.

T'ien Ju-k'ang. 1981. *Moslem Rebellion in China: A Yunnan Controversy*. The 42nd George Ernest Morrison Lecture in Ethnology 1981. Canberra: The Australian National University.

Taagepera, Rein. 1980. "Soviet Collectivization of Estonian Agriculture: The Deportation Phase." *Soviet Studies* 32 (July): 379-97.

Taft, Philip and Philip Ross. 1979. "American Labor Violence: Its Causes, Character, and Outcome." In *Violence in America: Historical & Comparative Perspectives*. Rev. ed. Edited by Hugh Davis Graham and Ted Robert Gurr. Beverly Hills: Sage Publications, pp. 187-241.

Talbott, John. 1980. *The War Without a Name: France in Algeria, 1954-1962*. New York: Alfred A. Knopf.

Tambiah, S. J. 1986. *Sri Lanka: Ethnic Fratricide and the Dismantling of Democracy*. Chicago: The University of Chicago Press.

Tang, Truong Nhu. 1985. *A Vietcong Memoir,* with David Chanoff and Doan Van Toai. New York: Harcourt Brace Jovanovich, Publishers.

Tannenbaum, Frank. 1947. *Slave and Citizen*. New York: Alfred A. Knopf.

Tashjian, James H. 1982. "Genocide, the United Nations and the Armenians." In *Genocide and Human Rights: A Global Anthology*, (edited) by Jack Nusan Porter. Washington, D.C.: University Press of America, pp. 129-47.

"Task Force Report." 1972. In *The Wasted Nations: Report of the International Commission of Enquiry into United States Crimes in*

Indochina, June 20-25, 1971, (edited) by Frank Browning and Dorothy Forman. New York: Harper & Row, pp. 104-37.

Taylor, Charles Lewis and Michael C. Hudson. 1972. *World Handbook of Political and Social Indicators.* New Haven: Yale University Press.

Taylor, John G. 1991. *Indonesia's Forgotten War: The Hidden History of East Timor.* London: Zed Books.

"Tears, Blood and Cries:" Human Rights in Afghanistan Since the Invasion 1979-1984. 1984. New York: A Helsinki Watch Report. December.

Teixeira, Bernardo. 1965. *The Fabric of Terror: Three Days in Angola.* New York: The Devin-Adair Co.

Tennien, Father Mark A. 1952. *No Secret is Safe: Behind the Bamboo Curtain.* New York: Farrar, Straus and Young.

Terror in East Pakistan: Foreign Press Reports on Atrocities Committed by Awami League and its Collaborators. n.d. East Pakistan Documentation Series, Karachi: Pakistan Publications.

Thayer, Carlyle A. 1981. "New Evidence on Kampuchea." *Problems of Communism,* (May-June): 91-96.

———. 1989. *War by Other Means: National Liberation and Revolution in Viet-Nam 1954-60.* Boston: Allen & Unwin.

Thayer, Thomas C. 1985. *War Without Fronts: The American Experience in Vietnam.* Boulder, Colorado: Westview Press.

Thomas, Hugh. 1961. *The Spanish Civil War.* New York: Harper & Row.

———. 1971. *The Cuban Revolution.* New York: Harper & Row.

———. 1977. *The Spanish Civil War.* Rev. and enlarged ed. New York: Harper & Row.

Thompson, Sir Robert (Ed.). 1981. *War in Peace: Conventional and Guerrilla Warfare Since 1945.* New York: Harmony Books.

Thompson, Virginia and Richard Adloff. 1981. *Conflict in Chad.* (Research Series no. 45) Berkeley: Institute of International Studies, University of California.

Thurston, Anne F. 1987. *Enemies of the People.* New York: Alfred A. Knopf.

Tilly, Charles. 1979. "Collective Violence in European Perspective." In *Violence in America: Historical & Comparative Perspectives.*

Rev. ed. Edited by Hugh Davis Grahams and Ted Robert Gurr. Beverly Hills: Sage Publications, pp. 83-118.

Time Capsule: History of the War Years 1939-1945. 1972. New York: Bonanza Books.

Timperley, H. J. 1938. *Japanese Terror in China.* New York: Modern Age Books.

Toai, Doan Van. 1990. "Moral and Psychological Lessons of Vietnam." In *The Vietnam Debate: A Fresh Look at the Arguments,* (edited) by John Norton Moore. New York: University Press of America, pp. 31-36.

Todd, Helen. 1991. "A Son's Death in East Timor." *The Wall Street Journal* 3 December, p. A-14.

Tolstoy, Nikolai. 1977. *Victims of Yalta.* London: Transworld Publishers.

——. 1979. *Victims of Yalta.* Corgi edition, London: Transworld Publishers.

——. 1981. *Stalin's Secret War.* New York: Holt, Rinehart and Winston.

——. 1986. *The Minister and the Massacres.* London: Century Hutchinson Ltd.

Tomasevich, Jozo. 1975. *The Chetniks: War and Revolution in Yugoslavia, 1941-1945.* Stanford, California: Stanford University Press.

Tombs, Robert. *The War Against Paris, 1871.* New York: Cambridge University Press.

Totten, Samuel. 1991. "First-person Accounts of Genocidal Acts." In *Genocide: A Critical Bibliographic Review: Vol. 2,* (edited) by Israel W. Charny. London: Mansell, pp. 321-62.

—— and William S. Parsons (Eds.). 1991. "Special Section: Teaching about Genocide." *Social Education* 55 (February): 84-133.

Toynbee, Arnold Joseph (Ed.). 1916. *The Treatment of Armenians in the Ottoman Empire: Documents Presented to Viscount Grey of Fallodon, Secretary of State for Foreign Affairs.* London: Hodder and Stoughton.

——. 1922. *The Western Question in Greece and Turkey: A Study in the Contact of Civilizations.* London: Constable and Co.

——. 1947. *A Study of History.* Abridgment of vols. 1-6 by D. C. Somervell. New York: Oxford University Press.

Trejo, Bernardo. 1964. "Once Again … a Pirate on the Spanish Main." Translated by Gérard de Berly. In *Cuba: Terror and Death. Once Again a Pirate on the Spanish Main*. Miami, Florida: Agencia de Informaciones Periodísticas, pp. 32-82.

Turner, John Kenneth. 1969. *Barbarous Mexico*. Austin: University of Texas Press.

Turner, Robert F. 1972. "Expert Puncture 'No Bloodbath' Myth." *Human Events* (11 November).

——. 1975. *Vietnamese Communism: Its Origins and Development*. Stanford, California: Standford University Hoover Institution Press.

——. 1990. "Myths and Realities in the Vietnam Debate." In *The Vietnam Debate: A Fresh Look at the Arguments*, (edited) by John Norton Moore. New York: University Press of America, pp. 37-59.

Turnwald, Wilhelm K. 1953. "Introduction." In *Documents on the Expulsion of the Sudenten Germans*. Translated by Gerda Johannsen. Munich, Germany: University Press, Dr. C. Wolf & Sohn, pp. vii-xxix.

Tutino, John. 1986. *From Insurrection to Revolution in Mexico: Social Bases of Agrarian Violence 1750-1940*. Princeton, New Jersey: Princeton University Press.

U.S. 1991. "U.S. Aided Indonesian Massacre in 1965." *Internet on the Holocaust and Genocide* (February): 17.

U.S. Imperialists' "Burn All, Destroy All, Kill All" Policy in South Vietnam. 1967. South Vietnam: Committee for Denunciation of the Crimes of the U.S. Imperialists and Their Henchmen.

U.S. War Crimes in Vietnam. 1968. Hanoi: Juridical Sciences Institute under the Viet Nam State Commission of Social Sciences.

Ubelaker, Douglas H. 1992. "North American Indian Population Size: Changing Perspectives." In *Disease and Demography in the Americas*, (edited) by John W. Verano and Douglas H. Ubelaker. Washington, D.C.: Smithsonian Institution Press, pp. 169-76.

Uganda and Sudan, Report No. 66. 1984. London: The Minority Rights Group. December.

Uppal, J. N. *Bengal Famine of 1943: A Man-Made Tragedy*. 1984. Delhi, India: Atma Ram & Sons.

U.S. Congressional Hearing and Visit to East Timor. 1977. Jakarta, Indonesia: Department of Foreign Affairs. July.

Utrecht, Ernst. 1975. "The Military Elite." In *Ten Years' Military Terror in Indonesia*, (edited) by Malcolm Caldwell. Nottingham, Great Britain: Spokesman Books, 41-58.

V.F. 1970. "Document XVIII." In *Operation Slaughterhouse: Eyewitness Accounts of Postwar Massacres in Yugoslavia*, (edited) by John Prcela and Stanko Guldescu. Philadelphia: Dorrance & Co., pp. 232-40.

Váli, Ferenc A. 1961. *Rift and Revolt in Hungary: Nationalism Versus Communism*. Cambridge, Massachusetts: Harvard University Press.

van den Berghe, Pierre L. 1990. "Introduction." In *State Violence and Ethnicity*, (edited) by Pierre L. van den Berghe. Niwot, Colorado: University Press of Colorado, pp. 1-18.

Vash, Edgar. 1980. "The Turmoil of Nicaragua: from Somoza to Sandinistas." In *Issues in Brief*. Washington, D.C.: ACU Education and Research Institute. September.

Veale, F. J. P. 1968. *Advance to Barbarism: The Development of Total Warfare from Serajevo to Hiroshima*. New York: The Devin-Adair Company.

Veenhoven, William A. (Ed.). 1975. *Case Studies on Human Rights and Fundamental Freedom: A World Survey*. 5 vols. The Hague: Martinus Nijhoff.

Verrier, Anthony. 1969. *The Bomber Offensive*. New York: Macmillan.

Vickery, Michael. 1982. "Democratic Kampuchea—CIA to the Rescue." *Bulletin of Concerned Asian Scholars* 14 (October-December): 45-54.

———. 1982a. "Looking Back at Cambodia, 1942-76." In *Peasants and Politics in Kampuchea, 1942-1981*, (edited) by Ben Kiernan and Chanthou Boua. London: Zed Press, pp. 89-113.

———. 1983. "Democratic Kampuchea—themes and Variations." In *Revolution and Its Aftermath in Kampuchea: Eight Essays*, (edited) by David P. Chandler and Ben Kiernan. Monograph Series no. 25. New Haven: Yale University Southeast Asia Studies, pp. 99-135.

———. 1984. *Cambodia: 1975-1982*. Boston, Massachusetts: South End Press.

———. 1988. "Correspondence." *Bulletin of Concerned Asian Scholars* 20 (January-March): 70-73.

———. 1989. "Cambodia (Kampuchea): History, Tragedy, and Uncertain Future." *Bulletin of Concerned Asian Scholars* 21 (April-December): 35-58.

Viet Cong Atrocities and Sabotage in South Vietnam. 1967. Rev. ed. Saigon: Ministry of Information and Directorate of Psy-War Planning.

Vietnam: Under Two Regimes. 1985. Washington, D.C.: U.S. State Department Bureau of Public Affairs Special Report no. 127. April.

Vincent, C. Paul. 1985. *The Politics of Hunger: The Allied Blockade of Germany, 1915-1919.* Athens, Ohio: Ohio University Press.

von Wilpert, Friedrich. 1964. *The Oder-Neisse Problem: Towards Fair Play in Central Europe.* New York: Edition Atlantic-Forum.

Wain, Barry. 1981. "Cambodia: What Remains of the Killing Grounds." *The Wall Street Journal* 29 January.

Walker, Christopher J. 1980. *Armenia: The Survival of a Nation.* London: Croom Helm.

Walker, Christopher. 1988. "Armenian Refugees: Accidents of Diplomacy or Victims of Ideology?" In *Refugees in the Age of Total War,* (edited) by Anna C. Bramwell. London: Unwin Hyman, pp. 38-50.

Walker, Richard L.1971. *The Human Cost of Communism in China. A Study of the Committee on the Judiciary.* United States Senate, Washington, D.C., Government Printing Office.

Wallimann, Isidor and Michael N. Dobkowski (Eds.). 1987. *Genocide and the Modern Age: Etiology and Case Studies of Mass Death.* New York: Greenwood Press.

Walsh, Mary Williams. 1987. "In Colombia, Killings Just Go On and On." *The Wall Street Journal* 17 November, p. 30.

Walter, Eugene Victor. 1969. *Terror and Resistance: A Study of Political Violence with Case Studies of Some Primitive African Communities.* New York: Oxford University Press.

Wangyal, Phuntsog. 1984. "Tibet: A Case of Eradication of Religion Leading to Genocide." In *Toward the Understanding and Prevention of Genocide: Proceedings of the International Conference on the Holocaust and Genocide,* (edited) by Israel W. Charny. Boulder, Colorado: Westview Press, pp. 119-26.

Warwick, Peter (Ed.). 1980. *The South African War: The Anglo-Boer War 1899-1902.* Burnt Mill, Harlow, Essex, Great Britain: Longman.

Webster, Sir Charles and Noble Frankland (Eds.). 1961. *The Strategic Air Offensive Against Germany 1939-1945*. Vol. 4: *Annexes and Appendices*. London: His Majesty's Stationary Office.

Wedgwood, C. V. 1961. *The Thirty Years War*. (Anchor edition) Garden City, New York: Doubleday.

Weiner, Lauren. 1990. "Coca Link Embroils Antirebel War." *Insight* (February 5): 30-31.

Weiss, Aharon. 1990. "The Holocaust and the Ukrainian Victims." In *A Mosaic of Victims: Non-Jews Persecuted and Murdered by the Nazis*, (edited) by Michael Berenbaum. New York: New York University Press, pp. 109-15.

Wertham, Fredric. 1962. *A Sign for Cain: An Exploration of Human Violence*. New York: Macmillan.

Wheeler, Keith. 1983. *The Fall of Japan*. Alexandria, Virginia: Time-Life Books.

Whetten, Nathan L. 1948. *Rural Mexico*. Chicago: The University of Chicago Press.

White Paper on the Crises in East Pakistan. 1971. Islamabad, Pakistan: Ministry of Information and National Affairs.

White, Richard. 1993. "Morality and Mortality." *The New Republic* (18 January): 33-36 (review of David E. Stannard's *American Holocaust*).

White, Theodore H. and Annalee Jacoby. 1946. *Thunder out of China*. New York: William Sloane Associates.

Whiting, Charles. 1982. *The Home Front: Germany*. Alexandria, Virginia: Time-Life Books.

Whitmore, Thomas M. 1992. *Disease and Death in Early Colonial Mexico*. Boulder, Colorado: Westview Press.

"Wholesale Massacre in South Vietnam since the Son My Case." 1972. In *The Wasted Nations: Report of the International Commission of Enquiry into United States Crimes in Indochina, June 20-25, 1971*, (edited) by Frank Browning and Dorothy Forman. New York: Harper & Row, pp. 260-81.

Wiesner, Louis. 1988. *Victims and Survivors: Displaced Persons and Other War Victims in Viet-Nam, 1954-1975*. New York: Greenwood Press.

Wilkie, James W. 1970. *The Mexican Revolution: Federal Expenditure and Social Change Since 1910.* 2nd ed., rev. and extended. Berkeley: University of California Press.

Wilkinson, Paul. 1974. *Political Terrorism.* New York: John Wiley & Sons.

Williams, Peter and David Wallace. 1989. *Unit 731: The Japanese Army's Secret of Secrets.* London: Hodder & Stoughton.

Willoughby, Charles A. 1970. "Forward." In *Operation Slaughterhouse: Eyewitness Accounts of Postwar Massacres in Yugoslavia,* (edited) by John Prcela and Stanko Guldescu. Philadelphia: Dorrance & Co., pp. ix-xiii.

Wilson, Dick. 1982. *When Tigers Fight: The Story of the Sino-Japanese War, 1937-1945.* New York: The Viking Press.

Wise, William. 1976. *Massacre at Mountain Meadows: An American Legend and a Monumental Crime.* New York: Thomas Y. Crowell.

Wiskemann, Elizabeth. 1956. *Germany's Eastern Neighbours: Problems Relating to the Oder-Neisse Line and the Czech Frontier Regions.* New York: Oxford University Press.

Wolff, Leon. 1961. *Little Brown Brother: America's Forgotten Bid for Empire which Cost 250,000 Lives.* New York: Longmans, Green and Co.

Wood, David. 1968. *Conflict in the Twentieth Century.* Adelphi Papers NO. 48. London: The Institute for Strategic Studies. June.

The World Almanac and Book of Facts. Various years. New York: Newspaper Enterprise Association,.

The World Almanac and Encyclopedia 1916. 1916. New York: Press Publishing.

World Armaments and Disarmament: SIPRI Yearbook. Various years. London: Taylor & Francis Ltd,

World Armaments and Disarmament: SIPRI Yearbook. 1987. New York: Oxford University Press.

World Military Expenditures and Arms Transfers 1972-1982. 1984. Washington, D.C.: U.S. Arms Control and Disarmament Agency. (Also for other years.)

World Military Expenditures and Arms Transfers. Various years. Washington, D.C.: U.S. Arms Control and Disarmament Agency.

World Press Review. 1989. (August).

Wragg, David. 1986. *The Offensive Weapon: The Strategy of Bombing*. London: Robert Hale.

Wright, Quincy. 1965. *A Study of War*. 2nd ed., rev. and extended, with a commentary on war since 1942. Chicago: The University of Chicago Press.

Wyden, Peter. 1983. *The Passionate War: The Narrative History of the Spanish Civil War*, 1936-1939. New York: Simon and Schuster.

Wytwycky, Bohdan. 1987. *The Other Holocaust: Many Circles of Hell*. Washington, D.C.: The Novak Report on the New Ethnicity, 1980.

Yathay, Pin. 1987. *Stay Alive, My Son*. New York: The Free Press.

Yerushalmi, Yosef Hayim. 1976. *The Lisbon Massacre of 1506 and the Royal Image in the Sebet Yehudah*. Hebrew Union College Annual Supplements no. 1. Cincinnati, Ohio: Hebrew Union College.

Yi Zheng. 1989. "Four Decades, 60 Million Perished." *Xinwen Ziyou Daobao* (*Press Freedom Herald*) (September 30). Translated for the author by Hua Shiping.

Young, Kenneth R. 1990. "Local and National Influences in the Violence of 1965." In *The Indonesian Killings of 1965-1966*, (edited) by Robert Cribb. Monash Papers on Southeast Asia—no. 21. Clayton, Victoria, Australia: Center of Southeast Asian Studies, Monash University, pp. 63-99.

Young, Marilyn B. 1991. *The Vietnam Wars 1945-1990*. New York: HarperCollins Publishers.

Zaher, U. 1986. "Political Developments in Iraq 1963-1980." In *Saddam's Iraq: Revolution or Reaction?* (Committee Against Repression and for Democratic Rights in Iraq) London: Zed Books, pp. 30-53.

Zasloff, Joseph J. and MacAlister Brown. 1979. "The Passion of Kampuchea." *Problems of Communism*, (January-February): 28-44.

Zawodny, J. K. 1962. *Death in the Forest: The Story of the Katyn Forest Massacre*. Notre Dame, Indiana: University of Notre Dame Press.

Zeleza, Tiyambe. 1989. "Labour, Coercion and Migration in Early Colonial Kenya." In *Forced Labour and Migration: Patterns of Movement within Africa*, (edited) by Abebe Zegeye and Shubi Ishemo. New York: Hans Zell Publishers, pp. 159-79.

Zich, Arthur. 1977. *The Rising Sun.* Alexandria, Virginia: Time-Life Books.

Zielinski, Ryszard. 1961. "Political Origins of the Transfer of German Population to Germany." In *1939-1950 Population Movements Between the Oder and Bug Rivers.* Warsaw, Poland: Zachodnia Agencja Prasowa, pp. 41-72.

Zinsmeister, Karl. 1988. "All the Hungry People." *Reason* 20 (June): 22-30.

Zuccotti, Susan. 1987. *The Italians and the Holocaust: Persecution, Rescue, and Survival.* New York: Basic Books.

Subject Index

349-350; and Yugoslavian
refugees 351-353
United Nations: in Cambodia 200
United States: atomic bombing 41;
bombing in Cambodia 167,
170-173, 176; Civil War 68; and
Germany 303-304; and German
expulsions 305; Indians of 57-59;
in Korea 365-366; and Mexico
388; and Pakistan democide 330;
in Philippines 271-272; and
Turkey genocide 233, 235-236;
and/in Vietnam 245, 255-256,
267-277, 290-291; Vietnam War
deaths 206; in World War II; and
Yugoslavia 361. *See also*
Andersonville prison, My Lai,
Vietnam War
U.S.S.R. 35, 40, 98,107, 109, 120,
288, 297-298, chapter 4; and
China 98; deportation 88;
genocide 28, 80, collectivization
80, 88, famine 80, deportation
80, Great Terror 80-81, in Korea
365-366; and Korean War
373-374, 378-379; Marxism
84-87; NKVD; in Poland 302;
and Yugoslavia 340, 354-355.
See also Bolsheviks, forced
labor, Great Terror, Marxism,
quota, Power, Ukraine
Ustashi (of Croatia) 314, 340,
342-346, 351, 359

Valle Nacional (Mexico) 381-382,
385-386
Van (Turkey) 216, 237
Viet Cong 254-278, 291; in
Cambodia 170
Viet Minh 242, 245-246, 253-254;
Khmer 173

Vietnam (Hanoi) 35, chapter 11;
and/in Cambodia 161, 167-168,
170, 173, 176-177, 190-192,
199-202; nationalists in 246,
291. *See also* Chinese ethnics,
concentration camps, Dien Bien
Phu, executions, forced labor,
Indo-China War, Japan, Laos,
land reform, Marxism, National
Liberation Front, ostracism,
Paris Peace Agreement, Power,
prisoners of war, Provisional
Revolutionary Government,
purge, quota, rebellion, refugees,
terror, United Kingdom, United
States, Viet Cong, Viet Minh,
Vietnam War
Vietnam War 28, 176, 255-278,
289, 292, Tet offensive 257-258,
263. *See also* South Korea,
United States
Vietnam, South 245, 251; guerrilla
war in 254-255; and/in
Cambodia 170, 173, 198. *See
also* deportation, Diem regime,
land reform, noncombatants,
refugees, terror, Vietnam War
Vietnamese ethnics: in Cambodia
168-169, 188, 191, 195
violence. *See* democracy
Volga famine 87

war 3, 12, 24, 47; and democide 37,
40; deaths in 41, 69-70; nuclear
26. *See also* democracy
warlords in china 93, 94, 106, 137,
in Mexico 391-392
witch hunts 62
World War II 24-25
wrecking 37

Name Index